Skateboarding, Space and the City

Skateboarding, Space and the City

Architecture and the Body

Iain Borden

Oxford • New York

First published in 2001 by
Berg
Editorial offices:
1st Floor, Angel Court, 81 St Clements Street, Oxford OX4 1AW, UK
175 Fifth Avenue, New York, NY 10010, USA

Paperback edition reprinted 2003, 2005, 2006, 2010

Berg is an imprint of Oxford International Publishers Ltd.

Library of Congress Cataloging-in-Publication Data
A catalogue record for this book is available from the Library of Congress.

British Library Cataloguing-in-Publication Data
A catalogue record for this book is available from the British Library.

ISBN 978 1 85973 488 9 (Cloth)
978 1 85973 493 3 (Paper)

Typeset by JS Typesetting, Wellingborough, Northants.
Printed in the United Kingdom by Biddles Ltd, King's Lynn.

To my parents, Shelagh and Tony Borden.

'Transform the world' – all well and good. It is being transformed. But into what? Here, at your feet, is one small but crucial element in that mutation.

Henri Lefebvre

Contents

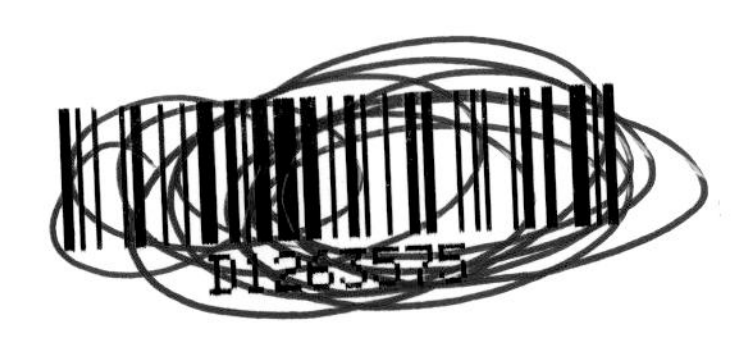

Acknowledgements

This book has taken over a decade in preparation, and many people have helped practically and intellectually over the years. On the history and interpretation of skateboarding, I am particularly grateful to Becky Beal, Michael Blabac, Claire Baker, Neil Bowen, Grant Brittain, Andrew Brooke, Dan Cousins, Jan Doggen, Wayne Fenlon, Nigel Fleet, Chad Ford, Glen E. Friedman, Layla Gibbon, Shaun Gladwell, Paul Haynes, David Hieatt, Kelvin Ho, Andy Holmes, Andy Horsley, David Horwood, Cherstyn Hurley, Steven Hutchins, Katie, Lindsay Knight, Sandra Lenzhölzer, Mike Lorr, Alicia Moore, Alexander Morrison, Kenny Omond, Tom Palmer, Pearl Pelfrey, Stacy Peralta, Ben Powell, Ed Riggins, Charles Room, Ben Sansbury, Jack Smith, David Snow, Bill Stinson, Saul Taylor, Kevin Thatcher, Michelle Tichtin, Arthur Tubb, Daniel Turner, Dirk Vogel, Jon Wood, and Matthew Worland, all of whom variously made comments, shared insights and sent valuable material. Thanks also to David 'Fridge' Belfrage, Sean Goff, James 'Jam' Parry, Peter Staddon, Simon Staddon and others who skated with me in the backwaters of Oxford in the late 1970s; without their co-production of a certain social space, this would not have happened.

I am absolutely indebted to Tim Leighton-Boyce who systematically searched and delivered his large collection of skateboarding magazines and other material – without his help the research would have been impossible. To him I owe very special thanks indeed.

Particular gratitude is also due to the large number of individuals and companies who have graciously granted permission for the reproduction of images, and these are listed in Sources of Illustrations (p. xi). Others who have at various times offered support, information and comments include Jonny Aspen, Larry Barth, Derek Beck, Amanda Birch, Christine Boyer, Catherine Clayton, Nic Clear, Matthew Cornford, Rachel Cottam, David Cross, Marcello Cruz, Allen Cunningham, Paul Davies, James Donald, Gil Doron, Tom Dyckhoff, Michael Edwards, Gavin Elliott, Marcus Field, Paul Finch, Grant Gee, Amelia Gibson, Christine Hawley, Dolores Hayden, Simon Herron, Tom Hines, Kelvin Ho, Paul Hyatt, Susanna Isa, Sarah Jackson, Joel Karamath, Joe Kerr, Nam-Joo Kim, Lesley Latimer, Mark Logue, Sandy McCreery, Glen McDougall, Doreen Massey, Demetrios Matheou, William Menking, Paul Monaghan, Belinda Moore, Morag Myerscough, Ben Nicholson, Alicia Pivaro, Alan Read, Alan Rendell, Beth Rendell, Taina Rikala, Norma Rosso, Katerina Rüedi, Chris Saunders, Joanna Saxon, Irénée Scalbert, Louise Scriven, Sally Shaw, Kath Shonfield, Simparch, Richard Cándida Smith, James Soane, Neil Spiller, Brian Stater, Quentin Stevens, Andy Stone, Elaine Stratford, Paul Sweetman, Philip Tabor, Jeremy Till, Jane Tobin,

David Tong, Christian Unverzagt, Katharina von Ledersteger, Marek Walcek, Kate aan de Wiel, Belinda Wheaton, Caroline Whitehead and Shirley Wong. Particular thanks are due to Barry Curtis, David Frisby, Leonie Sandercock and Ed Soja.

Many of the ideas have benefited from the opportunity to publish and to speak at numerous different institutions and conferences. I am indebted to Ole Bouman, Lucy Bullivant and *Archis*; Sarah Chaplin, *Design History* and the University of Middlesex; *Bauwelt*; Angela Holden, Global Sports, *Board Stupid* and Channel 4 television; Jonathan Charley, Per Kartvedt and the University of Strathclyde; Swati Chattopadhyay and the Society of Architectural Historians; Mike Fordham, *Adrenalin*, *Dazed & Confused* and *Xtreme*; Chelsea College of Art & Design; Marino Folin and Giorgio Piccinato of the Istituto Universitario in Venice; Grant Gibson and *Blueprint*; Niamh Coulter and *Ergo Sum*; Alex Griffin and the other Diploma students of Liverpool John Moores University; Geoff Hanmer, Anna Rubbo and the University of Sydney; Lisa Haskell and the ICA; Curtin University and 'Habitus 2000'; Chu-Joe Hsia, *Intercity Networking* and the National Taiwan University; Jonathan Hill; Ray Hutchison; Katherine McDermott, Sarah Wigglesworth and Kingston University; *The Mag* and Channel 5 television; Trevor Marchand and SOAS; Jeremy Millar, Alec Leggart and the Photographers' Gallery; Anna Notaro, Douglas Tallack and the University of Nottingham; Gordon Reavley and Nottingham Trent University; Kolbjørn Nybø, Halina Dunin-Wuyseth and the Arkitekthøgskolen, Oslo; Tristan Palmer; Richard Patterson and De Montfort University; Steve Pile; David Pinder and Queen Mary Westfield College; SAID at the University of North London; Penny Sparke and the RCA; Nigel Thrift; John Timberlake and *everything*; and Vicky Watson, James Madge, Ed Winters and the University of Westminster.

My thanks also to the copy editor George Pitcher, and to Kathryn Earle and everyone else at Berg.

At The Bartlett, UCL, students in the design studios and, in particular, from the master's programme in architectural history and theory have provided a fruitful arena in which to develop and test ideas. I am particularly indebted to the continued support and friendship of Bartlett colleagues Barbara Penner, Adrian Forty and Graham Ive, who was also the supervisor for this book in its first manifestation as a PhD thesis at UCL. In a special category of her own is Jane Rendell, whose unique brand of fiery, demanding yet generous thinking continues to have a profound influence.

Claire Haywood did Australian research, and more importantly provided constant encouragement and distraction in roughly equal proportions. To her, my thanks and love. Lastly, my parents, Tony and Shelagh Borden, have given unquestioning support over the years. This book is dedicated to them.

Sources of Illustrations

Considerable effort has been made to trace copyright holders of images. The author and publishers apologize for any errors and omissions, and, if notified, will endeavour to correct these at the earliest available opportunity.

1.1 *TransWorld Skateboarding*, vol. 13 no. 5 (May 1995), p. 25. Courtesy of Blind/World Industries.
2.1 *Thrasher*, vol. 9 no. 6 (June 1989), p. 62. Courtesy of High Speed/*Thrasher*.
2.2 *SkateBoarder*, vol. 3 no. 2 (December 1976), p. 89. Courtesy of Emap/*SkateBoarder*.
2.3 *SkateBoarder*, vol. 4 no. 2 (September 1977), p. 7. Courtesy of Tracker/Climax Manufacturing.
2.4 *SkateBoarder*, vol. 4 no. 5 (December 1977), p. 157. Courtesy of Sunset Surf Shop.
2.5 *Thrasher*, vol. 2 no. 5 (May–June 1982), inside front cover. Courtesy of OJ Wheels/Santa Cruz.
2.6 *SkateBoarder's Action Now*, vol. 7 no. 5 (December 1980), p. 81. Courtesy of Kanoa Surf.
2.7 Photograph courtesy of Iain Borden.
3.1 *SkateBoarder*, v.6 n.10 (May 1980), p. 31. Photograph Stoner. Courtesy of Emap/*SkateBoarder*.
3.2 *SkateBoarder*, vol. 6 no. 4 (November 1979), p. 55. Courtesy of Emap/*SkateBoarder*.
3.3 *Thrasher*, vol. 9 no. 6 (June 1989), p. 42. Courtesy of High Speed/*Thrasher*.
3.4 *SkateBoarder*, vol. 4 no. 8 (March 1978), p. 70. Photograph Tom Sims. Courtesy of Emap/*SkateBoarder*.
3.5 *SkateBoarder*, vol. 2 no. 1 (1975), front cover. Courtesy of Emap/*SkateBoarder*.
3.6 *SkateBoarder*, vol. 6 no. 11 (June 1980), p. 47. Courtesy of Emap/*SkateBoarder*.
3.7 *Thrasher*, vol. 9 no. 1 (January 1989), p. 63. Photograph Morizen Föche. Courtesy of High Speed/*Thrasher*.
3.8 *SkateBoarder*, vol. 3 no. 6 (July 1977), p. 80. Photograph Warren Bolster. Courtesy of Emap/*SkateBoarder*.
3.9 *Skateboard!*, no. 5 (January 1978), p. 48. Photograph Boyd Harnell. Courtesy of Felden Productions.

Chapter 1
Introduction

> To discover the uses of things is the work of history.[1]

> Surely it is the supreme illusion to defer to architects, urbanists or planners as being experts or ultimate authorities in matters relation to space.[2]

SKATEBOARDING

Skateboarding is perhaps an unusual object of study for a study in architectural history. But it is precisely its marginal position which enables skateboarding to function historically as a critical exterior to architecture. As such, skateboarding helps to rethink architecture's manifold possibilities.

To give some indication of why this might be the case, consider that skateboarding is local, being fundamentally concerned with the micro-spaces of streets, yet is also a globally dispersed and proliferous practice, with tens of millions of practitioners worldwide. It addresses the physical architecture of the modern city, yet responds not with another object but with a dynamic presence. It says almost nothing as codified statements, yet presents an extraordinary range of implicit enunciations and meanings. It produces space, but also time and the self. Skateboarding is constantly repressed and legislated against, but counters not through negative destruction but through creativity and production of desires. It has a history, but is unconscious of that history, preferring the immediacy of the present and coming future. It requires a tool (the skateboard), but absorbs that tool into the body. It involves great effort, but produces no commodity ready for exchange. It is highly visual, but refutes the reduction of activity solely to the spectacle of the image. It began in the suburbs, but has come downtown to the core of urban conflicts. It is seen as a child's play activity, but for many practitioners involves nothing less than a complete and alternative way of life. It is, therefore, architecture, not as a thing, but as a production of space, time and social being.

1. G.W.F. Hegel, quoted by James Woudhuysen, 'Regeneration Game' conference, Manchester (February 1997).
2. Henri Lefebvre, *The Production of Space* (Oxford: Blackwell, 1991), p. 95.

In order to delineate such concerns, this book proceeds through seven historical chapters which roughly follow the chronological development of skateboarding. For the period of the late 1950s to mid-1970s, Chapter Two *Devices* considers the technical development of the skateboard, before turning in Chapter Three *Found Space* to the spaces of the school yard, bank, ditch, pool and pipe, where skateboarders' spatial tactics of appropriation and colonization are considered. Chapter Four *Constructed Space* focuses on fabricated terrain, principally the purpose-built skatepark, many examples of which were built worldwide in the late 1970s, and the ramp or half-pipe, which took over after the demise of most skateparks in the early 1980s. Chapter Five *Body Space* deals with the 'super-architectural space' by which body, skateboard and architecture are erased and reborn in the encounter between skateboarder and skateboard architecture. The role of the image as an implicated part of skateboarding's space-production is also addressed here. Chapter Six *Subculture* is predominantly social in focus, and provides the necessary consideration of the counter-cultural nature of skateboarding. Attitudes to age, race, gender, class, sexuality, masculinity, the family and general conventions are explored, while specific aspects of skateboard design, music, clothes, language, etc. are also investigated. In Chapter Seven *Urban Compositions* the emergence of streetskating in the 1980s and 1990s is seen to derive from the possibilities of modern architecture, leading to new ways of editing, mapping and recomposing the city. Chapter Eight *Performing the City* concludes by taking a look at the implicit critique made by skateboarding of capitalism and architecture as commodity, and also considers the socio-spatial conflicts and censorship engendered as a consequence of such actions. The last chapter, *Closure and Aperture*, provides some reflections on all of this, both for skateboarding and for the methodology of architectural and urban history as a whole.

In representing this history of skateboarding, certain problematics necessarily remain unresolved. First, despite skateboarding being a global phenomenon, this account is predominantly a history of events in the USA and the UK – other countries are referred to, but only occasionally. Apart from the usual defence of available space, this is perhaps justifiable in that skateboarding, while being highly localized in its specific manifestations, is part of a global network of approximately like-minded practitioners. Nonetheless, certain regionalized differences within skateboarding have no doubt been erased. Similarly, the architecture and the fabric of the city referred to is seen to be more or less generic across cities worldwide.

Second, although concerned with the possibilities for social change, this book cannot, because of its subject matter, consider changes in material conditions but only changes in experience of material conditions. The position taken then is to accept this limitation as a given, and to consider the most positive critical aspects of skateboarding, perhaps to the denigration of a more 'objective' account of its practices.

1.1 Skateboarding and the critique of architecture. Skateboarder: Lavar McBride (1995).

Third, and related to this point, skateboarders' own self-ideology is sometimes taken at face value, used as evidence for a purported meaning or intended effect. At this point the historian's judgement hopefully ensures that no gross instances of false consciousness have been represented as historical fact. At other times, the judgement has been that such a false consciousness is operating, and in such cases the self-ideologies are appropriately critiqued.

Fourth, there is an issue with sources to be noted. Beyond those written by this author,[3] skateboarding has been the subject of comparatively little academic

3. Iain Borden, 'Another Pavement, Another Beach: Skateboarding and the Performative Critique of Architecture', in Iain Borden, Joe Kerr, Jane Rendell with Alicia Pivaro (eds), *The Unknown City: Contesting Architecture and Social Space* (Cambridge, Mass.: MIT, 2001); 'Sprechende Architektur: Skateboarden auf der Stadt', *Bauwelt*, no. 30–1 (18 August 2000), pp. 54–7; 'Beneath the Pavement, the Beach', *Xtreme*, no. 4 (September 1997), pp. 18–19; 'Beneath the Pavement, the Beach: Skateboarding, Architecture and the Urban Realm', in Iain Borden, Joe Kerr, Alicia Pivaro and Jane Rendell (eds), *Strangely Familiar: Narratives of Architecture in the City* (London: Routledge 1996), pp. 82–6; 'Body Architecture: Skateboarding and the Creation of Super-Architectural Space', in Jonathan Hill (ed.), *Occupying Architecture: Between Architecture*

study.[4] A few design-oriented books, notably Patrick Burgoyne and Jeremy Leslie's *Bored*, focus on the surfaces of skateboard clothes, boards and other paraphernalia.[5] Beyond this, the academic and external records of skateboarding are extremely limited. In architecture, this means occasional student architectural projects which address skateboarding from a design perspective,[6] and even more infrequent asides by armchair architectural journalists, with such side-swipes as those at modernist architecture for providing 'high speed race tracks for children on skateboards'.[7] The national press fares a little better, running features on skateboarding every time it has an upturn, usually with the same material about professional skaters, language, music and other subcultural elements.

Within skateboarding itself, beyond a few overviews published in skateboarding magazines over the past twenty years,[8] there have been few historical accounts of its internal practices and development, still less of its wider social meanings.

---

and the User (London: Routledge, 1998), pp. 195–216; 'Chariots of Ire', *Blueprint*, no. 174 (July 2000), pp. 38–42 and front cover; interview conducted by Saul Taylor for *Backside*, no. 9 (Spring 1999), n.p.; 'Laws of Motion', *Adrenalin* (Autumn 1999); 'State of the Art', *Ergo Sum*, no. 2 (Summer 1997), n.p.; 'Taking Over the City', interview with Mike Fordham, *Dazed and Confused*, no. 19 (April 1996), pp. 109–10; 'An Affirmation of Urban Life: Socio-Spatial Censorship in the Late Twentieth Century City', *Archis* (May 1998), pp. 46–51; 'A Performative Critique of the City: the Urban Practice of Skateboarding, 1958–1998', *everything*, vol. 2 no. 4 (March 1999), pp. 38–43, and Taiwanese translation in *Intercity Networking* (National University of Taiwan), no. 7–8 (March 1999), pp. 25–44; 'Skateboarding', in Steve Pile and Nigel Thrift (eds), *City A–Z: Urban Fragments* (Routledge, 2000), pp. 226–8; and 'Speaking the City: Skateboarding Subculture and Recompositions of the Urban Realm', in Ray Hutchison (ed.), *Constructions of Urban Space* (Stamford: JAI Press, 2000), pp. 135–54.

4. Becky Beal, 'Disqualifying the Official: an Exploration of Social Resistance Through the Subculture of Skateboarding', *Sociology of Sport Journal*, vol. 12 no. 3 (1995), pp. 252–67; Becky Beal, 'Alternative Masculinity and Its Effects on Gender Relations in the Subculture of Skateboarding', *Journal of Sport Behaviour*, vol. 19 no. 3 (1996), pp. 204–21; Kelvin Ho, 'Skateboarding: an Interpretation of Space in the Olympic City', *Architectural History and Theory* (1999); David Snow, 'Skateboarders, Streets and Style', in R. White (ed.), *Australian Youth Subcultures: On the Margins and in the Mainstream* (Hobart: Australian Clearinghouse for Youth Studies, 1999), pp. 16–27; and Elaine Stratford, 'Feral Skateboarding and the Field of Transport Planning: Some Observations on the Tasmanian Case', paper presented at 'Habitus 2000' conference, Perth (September 2000).

5. Patrick Burgoyne and Jeremy Leslie, *Bored* (London: Lawrence King and Creative Review, 1997), pp. 11–14 and 47–98; and Cynthia Rose, *Design After Dark* (London: Thames and Hudson, 1991), pp. 56–63.

6. 'Rolling Programme: a Skateboarder's Perspective on Architecture', *The Architects' Journal* (3 October 1996), p. 42; and University of Westminster, BSc Architectural Engineering, *Architectural Engineering Yearbook 5* (London: University of Westminster, 1997), pp. 43–53.

7. Jonathan Glancey, *New British Architecture* (London: Thames and Hudson, 1989), p. 19.

8. See, for example, Lowboy, 'Truth and Screw the Consequences', *Thrasher*, vol. 9 no. 6 (June 1989), pp. 42–3; Don Redondo, 'History of the Skateboard', *Thrasher*, vol. 9 no. 6 (June 1989), pp. 62–7; John Smythe (pseudonym for Craig Stecyk), 'The History of the World and Other Short Subjects, or, From Jan and Dean to Joe Jackson Unabridged', *SkateBoarder*, vol. 6 no. 10 (May 1980), pp. 28–51; and Craig R. Stecyk III, 'Episodic Discontrol or Random Samplings from the Life and Times', in Aaron Rose, *Dysfunctional* (London: Booth-Clibborn, 1999), pp. 6–19.

> There are no official records documenting the progress of skateboarding in the reference sections of your local libraries . . . There's no 'official' version of skateboarding, no one has any claims to ownership.[9]

Books on skateboarding may contain potted histories, but these are typically little more than descriptions of equipment, and generally are aimed at the younger, children's end of the skateboard market. Recently, a few publications have attempted something a little more ambitious: *The Concrete Wave*, by Michael Brooke, gives a general history of skateboarding, while Aaron Rose's *Dysfunctional* captures, mostly through images, the anarchic spirit of skateboarding with considerable verve, as do two photographic collections by Glen E. Friedman.[10] None of these, however, is explicitly concerned with the kinds of cultural, spatial, architectural and urban issues which I address here.

The archive of skateboarding is predominantly the various magazines which have promoted its development. These magazines, including *SkateBoarder*, *Thrasher*, *TransWorld Skateboarding*, *Slap* and *Big Brother* in the US and *Skateboard!*, *R.A.D.* and *Sidewalk Surfer* in the UK, provide the best historical source for skateboarding, and it is these which yield much of the evidence for this book. Their particular value lies in three areas. First, they are an implicated part of the development of skateboarding, and are thus what historians call a primary source – unmediated by the distance of time and backward look of the historian. Second, although often highly intelligent in their articles and reports, particularly through their self-deprecating demeanour, these magazines are not highly theorized. Nor are they the products of professional journalists, but the products of skateboarders themselves who have become journalists through working on such publications. Their agenda is not then the external agenda of the intellectual academic or careerist reporter, but the internal agenda of the intellectually active proponent. For this reason, I have not attempted to undertake a series of interviews or questionnaires with skateboarders, but rather have relied on whatever they saw fit to say and publish at the time. These skateboard magazines speak a certain truth about skateboarding, not just in terms of what they have to say about something, but about the agenda put forward in the first place. They are, then, a more reliable source for, say, a consideration of the body-centric production of space in the skateparks of the 1970s than would be had by asking an older skateboarder to recollect such events some twenty years after the event.

9. 'Moments in Time', *Sidewalk Surfer*, no. 12 (December 1996), n.p.

10. Michael Brooke, *The Concrete Wave: the History of Skateboarding* (Toronto: Warwick, 1999); Rose, *Dysfunctional*; Glen E. Friedman, *Fuck You Heroes: Glen E. Friedman Photographs, 1976–1991* (New York: Burning Flags, 1994) and *Fuck You Too: the Extras + More Scrapbook* (Los Angeles: 2.13.61 Publications and Burning Flags, 1996).

Third, the skateboard magazines are highly illustrated with still and high-speed sequence photography. As such, this imagery as much as the written work provides 'the nearest thing that we have to a historical record of what skateboarding is'.[11] The photograph in fact has a triple value for this history of skateboarding. Most obviously, it provides a window onto the past, showing what went on and where. Second, the photograph is itself an implicated part of skateboarding, a process which is explained in some detail in Chapter Four. Third, the photographs reproduced here perform part of the argument of the book – the images, then, are not so much just representations of what happened but have approximately equal status to the words. Although I have not been able to undertake the use of the image conceptually, as I have argued for in architectural history on other occasions[12] and as was undertaken in the *Strangely Familiar* graphic-text,[13] the performative nature of skateboarding's consciousness (i.e. it ultimately means something when the skateboarder skateboards) means that the image of skateboarding acquires the status of a statement – it is not only a representation of a thing, the meaning of which is clarified through text, but is a representation of an enunciative act and hence carries meaning in a less mediated manner.

ARCHITECTURE AND SPACE

Before entering into the main part of this book and the history of skateboarding, along with its implicit critique of architecture and society, I would like to reflect briefly on some of the methodological implications of this study. In particular, this book is concerned with addressing the question as to how architecture as a set of flows, as a set of experiences and reproductions, can be embedded in the practices of architectural history – for just as architecture is not itself space, but only a way of looking at space,[14] so the history of space is also not the (traditional) history of art and architecture.[15] What are the consequences of this for architectural history?[16]

11. 'Moments in Time', n.p.

12. Iain Borden and Joe Kerr, 'The Importance of Imaging: Reproductions of Architecture and Architectural Reproductions of Concepts', paper delivered at Middlesex University (May 1995).

13. Borden, Kerr, Pivaro and Rendell (eds), *Strangely Familiar.*

14. Lefebvre, *Production of Space*, p. 15.

15. Ibid., p. 127.

16. For other, related discussion of the methodology of architectural history, see also Iain Borden and Jane Rendell, 'From Chamber to Transformer: Epistemological Challenges and Tendencies in the Intersection of Architectural Histories and Critical Theories', in Iain Borden and Jane Rendell (eds), *InterSections: Architectural Histories and Critical Theories* (London: Routledge, 2000); and Iain Borden, Jane Rendell, Joe Kerr and Alicia Pivaro, 'Things, Flows, Filters, Tactics', in Borden, Kerr, Rendell with Pivaro (eds), *Unknown City.*

Traditionally, most architectural historians have concerned themselves with the production of architecture – and at first sight this would seem, given the particular spatial nature of architecture, to be a promising place to look for a history of space and the city. For example, there have been exemplary studies of such things as the labour process of architectural production,[17] the institution of the profession,[18] biographical histories,[19] patrons,[20] education[21] and architectural theory.[22] Such histories, however, replicate exactly that ideological spatial division which occurs between the professions. In short, where for example the space of the body is seen to be the province of medicine, and the space of the landscape as the province of geography, so the space of the built environment is seen to be the province of architecture and, more specifically, of architects and planners. In doing so, architectural historians limit their conception of architectural space to the space of the designed building-object – a fetishism that erases social relations and wider meanings.[23]

To avoid this problem, architectural historians must move away from seeing architecture only as things, imagination as that only of architects, mapping as only by drawing, and space as only interior, façade, composition and garden.

Of course, architectural historians have already tried to do this in a number of different ways, such as reading architecture's iconographic,[24] symbolic[25] and semiological[26] meanings. Recently, a post-structuralist version of such hermeneutical concerns, centred around the US East coast, has followed Jacques Derrida in trying to destabilize architectural semantics.[27] This approach has successfully disrupted commonly-held structures of meaning, showing that such things are always provisional, pregnant with a possibility that lies beyond their apparent closure; yet it remains

17. See for example Richard Goldthwaite, *The Building of Renaissance Florence* (Baltimore: Johns Hopkins University Press, 1980).

18. See for example Andrew Saint, *The Image of the Architect* (New Haven: Yale University Press, 1983).

19. See for example Paul Thompson, *William Butterfield* (London: Routledge & Kegan Paul, 1971).

20. See for example Charles Saumarez Smith, *The Building of Castle Howard* (London: Faber, 1990).

21. See for example Mark Crinson and Jules Lubbock, *Architecture – Art or Profession?* (Manchester: Manchester University Press, 1994).

22. See for example Kenneth Frampton, *Modern Architecture* (London: Thames and Hudson, rev. edn, 1985).

23. Lefebvre, *Production of Space*, pp. 89–91.

24. See for example Rudolf Wittkower, *Architectural Principles in the Age of Humanism* (London: Academy, 4th edn, 1988).

25. See for example Vincent Scully, *The Earth, the Temple and the Gods* (New Haven: Yale University Press, rev. edn, 1979).

26. See for example, Charles Jencks and George Baird (eds), *Meaning in Architecture* (London: Barrie and Rockliff, 1969).

27. See for example Jennifer Bloomer, *Architecture and the Text* (New Haven: Yale University Press, 1993).

within the confines of the framework it is trying to upset: Architecture (capital 'A'). The two-fold result is to rest within a consideration of reading, so reducing architecture to meaning, and, simultaneously, to remain within the architectural canon of such 'great' male architects as Le Corbusier and Loos,[28] consequently leaving the core object of study unchallenged. Architectural history has hence suffered from depoliticization; because of the intense post-structuralist focus on matters of representation in architecture, notions of social change, urban conditions and of social struggles of all kinds have been lost to view. Architecture remains the privileged sphere of professionals and intellectuals, and so outside any revolutionary desire to reformulate its substance and so integrate it with everyday life. Architectural history is in need, therefore, of a reintegration of questions of representation with issues of social and political change.

Architecture does of course have a meaning. But its meaning is neither fixed nor internalized to buildings. Rather,

> [A]rchitecture, like all other cultural objects, is not made just once, but is made and remade over and over again each time it is represented through another medium, each time its surroundings change, each time different people experience it.[29]

Architectural historians have tried to address this issue in different ways. In terms of experience, this has been done through the sensual experience of form,[30] through psychological empathy between form and the subject,[31] or a more bodily enactment of this empathy process.[32] Such histories, however, avoid social or political connotations to experience, and postulate instead the human subject as a universal being, with a constant set of values, senses (primarily sight) and mental faculties. Conversely, those who have emphasized the political, economic and cultural aspects of architecture have tended to see buildings as 'congealed ideology',[33] the products rather than the reproductive agent of social change, and so to ignore the reproduction and experience of architecture.

It might be expected, then, that those who consider the social history of architecture, particularly in relation to everyday or mass cultural processes, would provide a more successful approach to the problem. However, even here, architecture is either reduced to a theatrical backdrop, held apart from the social lives of its inhabitants

28. See for example Beatriz Colomina, *Privacy and Publicity* (Cambridge, Mass.: MIT, 1994).

29. Adrian Forty, 'Foreword', in Borden, Kerr, Pivaro and Rendell (eds), *Strangely Familiar*, p. 5.

30. See for example Paul Frankl, *Principles of Architectural History* (Cambridge, Mass.: MIT, 1968).

31. See for example Heinrich Wölfflin, *Renaissance and Baroque* (Ithaca: Cornell University Press, 1967).

32. See for example August Schmarsow, 'The Essence of Architectural Creation', in Harry Francis Mallgrave and Eleftherios Ikonomou (eds), *Empathy, Form and Space: Problems in German Aesthetics, 1873–1893* (Santa Monica: Getty Center for the History of Art and the Humanities, 1994), pp. 281–97.

33. Forty, 'Foreword', p. 5.

in a kind of formalized ritual of objects and movements,[34] or is used in an explicitly operative manner as a source-book for solutions to present-day problems.[35] These works use an extended temporality to explore post-construction life in the building, but nonetheless treat spatiality or temporality as dimensions separate to the human subject, and not as lived productions. Such works are only a discourse about space, not a discourse on the production of space.[36]

Architectural history has not yet turned from conceptions and meanings of space, or experiences of space, to consider the production of space. To do so requires going beyond objects to processes, where architecture's role in social reproduction is not limited to the spaces it provides or the way it is used, but involves representations embedded in architecture, in codified conceptions of space, in ideological and experiential as well as material aspects of building use. Furthermore, because architecture promotes a knowledge about cities and space, it is also the site of imagination, of experience, of critical re-examination. This phenomenal and intellectual experience of architecture, showing how people encounter architecture in conditions of, for example, danger, exhilaration, anonymity and sexual freedom, has been successfully shown for such cities as Paris, London, Berlin, Los Angeles.[37] Such works, particularly those informed by feminism and Marxism, also help to challenge the universalism of experience and to problematize the identity of the subject, while simultaneously denaturalizing capitalism and its politics of space.

This, then, is the reproduction rather than production of architecture: what are the ways, over time and in space, in which social processes continue to produce, to reproduce the worlds we live in? And how is architecture implicated in this process of reproduction? We might say, following Michel Foucault,[38] that architecture is not an object with a role to play, but is constituted by the discourses and practices of social life. Architecture is not an object but a process, not a thing but a flow, not an abstract idea but a lived thought. Architectural history should follow this course.

A word, also, on epistemology. As already intimated, the role of the 'historian' is not to provide an objective account of the past (such considerations being in any case impossible), but the rethinking of the possibilities of the past, and hence, and most importantly, a rethinking of the possibilities of the present and future.

34. See for example Mark Girouard, *Life in the English Country House* (New Haven: Yale University Press, 1978).

35. See for example Dolores Hayden, *The Grand Domestic Revolution* (Cambridge, Mass.: MIT, 1981).

36. Lefebvre, *Production of Space*, p. 16.

37. Mike Davis, *City of Quartz* (London: Verso, 1991); Elizabeth Wilson, *The Sphinx in the City* (London: Virago, 1991); and Patrick Wright, *A Journey Through Ruins* (London: Flamingo, 1993).

38. Michel Foucault, *The Archaeology of Knowledge* (New York: Pantheon, 1972).

> [L]et us leave a place for events, initiatives, decisions. All the hands have not been played. The sense of history does not suppose any historic determinism, any destiny.[39]

In this light, history-writing becomes a concern with social change, with revolution not as the installation of a definitive programme but as the continual unearthing of human activity. This project means critiquing capitalism through both the negative dialectic which denies and resists capitalism, and through the positive dialectic which restlessly searches for new possibilities of representing, imagining and living our lives. As for Manfredo Tafuri, this architectural history is a form of vigilance,[40] watchful of a revolutionary condition, but is also – and here unlike Tafuri's position of despair – imbued with a more definite political direction, seeking to recognize and celebrate differences, promoting use values over exchange values, and encouraging architectures of pleasure. That is the epistemological ground of this history, and it should be read accordingly.

This does not mean, however, that there is no interest here in the past or 'truth'. Indeed, it is through the investigation of particular architectural space-times that human life can be rethought. Just as theory provides an outside to architecture, so the past provides an outside to the present and hence an opening towards potential futures. This, then, is an architectural history unconcerned with promoting any specific kind of architecture as designed building, but resolutely concerned with a certain kind of life and its reproductive engagement with architecture. This is what Henri Lefebvre calls transduction, that which 'elaborates and constructs a theoretical object, a possible object from information related to reality and a problematic posed by this reality' and which 'assumes an incessant feed back between the conceptual framework used and empirical observations'.[41] The epistemology here is of speculative interpretation and action, at once encouraged and constrained by the empirical ground. Its knowledge is always provisional, formed by the intersection of theory and the architectural object, and awaiting further development in the maelstrom of future histories.

And, indeed, it is Lefebvre's thoughts – not only on politics and disciplinary methodology but also on space and on the everyday – which provide much of the interpretive grounds in this book, either through referral to his ideas or through quotations. In doing so, the purpose is five-fold: to make explicit the methodological procedures that I am following; to help identify new objects of study (in this case, the practice of skateboarding); to provide interpretive tools by which to crack open

39. Henri Lefebvre, *Qu'est-ce que penser?* (Paris: Publisud, 1985), p. 110, quoted in Eleonore Kofman and Elizabeth Lebas, 'Lost in Transposition: Time, Space and the City', in Henri Lefebvre, *Writings on Cities* (Oxford: Blackwell, 1996), p. 53.

40. Manfredo Tafuri, *Architecture and Utopia* (Cambridge, Mass: MIT, 1976).

41. Lefebvre, *Writings on Cities*, p. 151.

this object of study, displacing skateboarding from the 'stuff' of history to the realm of critical thought; to help reinterpret and reconfigure these Lefebvrian theories through their intersection with a particular historical ground; and so ultimately to provide an arena in which to retheorize architecture and architectural history. This book is not, therefore, 'just' a history of skateboarding. It is an intersection of theory and politics with history both as a discipline and as events discernible within a particular practice, that of skateboarding.

Before starting the analysis of skateboarding itself, it is useful to recall briefly some of the main characteristics of Lefevbre's thinking and writing.[42] In particular the work of Henri Lefebvre, and of urban geographers such as David Harvey and Edward Soja who have drawn heavily on Lefebvre, has postulated that space is part of a dialectical process between itself and human agency; rather than an a priori entity space is produced by, and productive of, social being. Time, space and social being are inter-produced. Space-production cannot then be reduced to theories of it, but must be seen as a process involving not only theories but also practices, objects, ideas, imagination and experience.

This has methodological ramifications, not least the need to think about histories of spatiality through different levels of consciousness, temporalities and periodization, social events and actions, and spatial scales. Textual play and the dominance of the scopic regime of epistemology can do no more than allude to such thinking, which must instead rest on the study of particular times, spaces and actions using the full battery of questions and techniques available to the historian. A closer reading of Lefebvre provides further clues as to how the architectural historian of spatiality might approach this task. I can only sketch out these clues here, and there are eight of them.

First, the historian interested in Lefebvre must realize that there is no patented system to be found therein. Instead, Lefebvre delineates a set of theoretical ideas as discursive texts, and which are only ever approximations of a possible subject or method. Lefebvrian thought, as Eleonore Kofman and Elizabeth Lebas note, is more a sensibility than a system.[43] Its ultimate test cannot then rest at the level of theoretical abstraction but must, for the historian, be brought about through an encounter with a specific subject matter.

Second, there are political objectives resonant within such a procedure, keeping an eye on the future as much as on the past or present. The goal is to gradually invoke a total revolution, involving not just the external world of institutions, professions

42. For a longer exposition on these themes, see Iain Borden 'Machines of Possibilities: City Life with Henri Lefebvre', *Archis* (February 2000), pp. 62–8; and Borden, Rendell, Kerr and Pivaro, 'Things, Flows, Filters, Tactics'.

43. Kofman and Lebas, 'Lost in Transposition', p. 8.

and the state but also the internal world of the subjective self, thus leading to a condition of creative production for all peoples in all aspects of their lives.

Third, architecture and the urban realm are identified as the locus of this potential revolution, not as a building programme or drawn projects but as the texture, the 'possibilities machine' appropriated by its residents. Architecture should be at once perceived, conceived and lived.

Fourth, space emerges as an ideological as well as material social production, with late twentieth century space seen to contain within itself a putative successor – differential space – where differences are not only tolerated but also celebrated and emphasized.

Fifth, time also should be considered as a social production in relation to space, and must be rescued from the overbearing quantitative measurement and routinization imposed on it by capitalism, in particular through its consideration in relation to lived experience.

Sixth, everyday life emerges as both the site of increasing domination on the part of capitalism and also one where resistance, recovery and reassertion of other socio-spatial practices may occur. The everyday is not the banal, trivial effect of politics, but the place where politics are ultimately created and resolved.

Seventh, the human subject – and in particular the body – is one of the primary sites of this revolutionary activity, not just in terms of its effect on the external world but as a redefinition and reproduction of the self. Beyond the scopic dependence of the visual on the part of capitalism and many architectural manifestations, the human body bears witness to all senses, emotions, birth and death, and orientations. Different rhythms of space and time are produced by these kinds of fleshy body.

Eighth, and last, these are also bodies which *actively do* something, which have a dynamic operation in the city, and which thereby transform everyday life into a work of art. Actions are important not for their production of things, but for their production of meanings, subjects, relations, uses and desires. To understand human history, in our considerations of the conceived and the lived, representations and experience, we therefore have to be explicit also about what activities are being undertaken – what are the energies deployed, patterns created, objects produced? In short, what productive work is being studied?

This is why the primary object of study for this book – skateboarding, architecture, space and the city – is not so much a specific place (for skateboarding occurs in cities across the world), specific moment (for skateboarding changes over the course of a 40-year history) or specific person or persons (skateboarding is practised predominantly by nameless millions), but is a practice, a particular patterning of space-time produced from a specific body-centred origin. And it is to a consideration of the production of space, time and the subject in this particular urban practice that I now turn.

Chapter 2
Devices

The history of skateboarding is shrouded in mystery.[1]

A typical skateboard, as developed by the mid-1970s, covers three main elements: deck, two trucks and four wheels. The riding surface, or deck, is usually made out of wood, covered with high-friction grip tape similar to sandpaper. Two trucks provide the suspension and turning mechanism, usually by a 'double-action' mechanism consisting of a metal hanger and split axle pivoting around two rubber or urethane bushings on a central king-pin. Turning circle and stability are adjusted by tightening the bushing compression. The truck assembly is cast from an aluminium alloy (originally steel) with steel axles and bolted to the deck via the metal base plate; a 5–15 mm 'riser pad' may be added between base plate and deck to increase wheel clearance and riding height. Wheels, once metal or 'clay', are now exclusively made from moulded polyurethane. Each wheel measures 40–70 mm in diameter and 25–45 mm in width, and contains two sealed bearings held apart by a short metal spacer. This standard skateboard-device specification was not immediately arrived at, however, but developed over twenty or more years, and it is worth recalling this evolution before turning to more overt considerations of space in skateboarding.

SCOOTERS AND SURFING

Despite some curious and idiosyncratic inventions, such as the Chicago-made 'Kne-Koster' (1927)[2] and three-wheeled 'Skooter Skate' (1939),[3] the skateboard seems to have originated in the California of the 1930s–1950s. These scooters were makeshift contraptions, constructed by children from a 2×4-inch (5×10 cm) plank of wood, an apple crate and a single roller skate (2.1).[4] Holding on to the wooden

1. 'Moments in Time', *Sidewalk Surfer*, no. 12 (December 1996), n.p.

2. *Child Life* (November 1927), in 'Trash', *Thrasher*, vol. 12 no. 5 (May 1992), p. 73.

3. John Smythe, 'The History of the World and Other Short Subjects', *SkateBoarder*, vol. 6 no. 10 (May 1980), p. 30.

4. Ben J. Davidson, *The Skateboard Book* (New York: Grosset & Dunlap, 1976), pp. 13–14; Hazel Pennell, *Skateboarding* (London: GLC Intelligence Unit, London Topics no. 24, 1978), p. 1; Don Redondo, 'History of the Skateboard', *Thrasher*, vol. 9 no. 6 (June 1989), p. 62; Smythe, 'History', p. 35; and Michael Brooke, *The Concrete Wave* (Toronto: Warwick, 1999), p. 40.

2.1 Scooter (late 1950s/early 1960s).

handlebars and pushing with one foot, the rider could trundle along the sidewalk, and thus the scooter was essentially a suburban vehicle, confined to the horizontal lines already drawn up by architect and developer.

By the mid- to late 1950s the first skateboards had appeared – at first these were simply short versions of the scooter, with the crate/handlebars left off the 2×4 wood.[5]

> We took an old metal roller skate and strapped it to a short piece of 2×4, hopped on top and took off . . . Wheels? That was whatever came on a roller skate. Strictly metal . . . The roller skate was its own truck. You were stuck with it. They never wore out, but they didn't have any cushioning in them either.[6]

> We were just using 2 by 4's and steel skates, our sister's skates pulled apart and nailed onto a 2 by 4. It was just riding and having fun.[7]

In a significant upgrade, the 2×4 was replaced by short wooden decks measuring about 20 inches (50 cm) long and 6 inches (15 cm) wide, requiring the rider to adopt a free-standing position.[8] Such boards provided, for example, the children of East LA with a form of rattling neighbourhood transport.[9] Smaller than the scooter, the skateboard was easier to manoeuvre and store, but it still stopped and skidded whenever the metal wheels encountered a less than smooth surface; even a pebble

5. Bruce Logan, interview, *SkateBoarder*, vol. 3 no. 4 (April 1977), p. 48; Mary Horowitz, 'Skateboard Decks: Design Symposium', *SkateBoarder*, vol. 4 no. 6 (January 1978), p. 98; Low E. Thompson, letter, *Thrasher*, vol. 12 no. 1 (January 1992), p. 8; Powell-Peralta, advertisement, *Thrasher*, vol. 12 no. 9 (September 1992), p. 24; and Bill Gutman, *Skateboarding to the Extreme* (New York: Tom Doherty Associates, 1997), pp. 5–6.

6. Bob Schmidt, 'The Day They Invented the Skateboard', *DansWORLD* internet site, URL http://web.cps.msu.edu/~dunhamda/dw/invent.html (accessed 17 May 1997). Republished in Brooke, *Concrete Wave*, pp. 18–19.

7. Denis Shufeldt, interview, *SkateBoarder*, vol. 3 no. 2 (December 1976), p. 41.

8. 'Who's Not! Mellow Catnip', *SkateBoarder*, vol. 3 no. 2 (December 1976), p. 88; and Redondo, 'History', p. 64.

9. Marcello Cruz, conversation (26 June 1989).

could prove somewhat difficult. The bearings also could easily seize up. As a result, the typical ride on this rudimentary contraption was 'thirty seconds of gritty trundling'.[10]

> It was wobblier than hell, moved way too fast and vibrated on the asphalt enough to jar every bone in your body and loosen every tooth. It was more like getting electrocuted than anything else . . . Sand and dirt had no problem getting in, and any that did and you were a gonner for sure. You'd lock up and go flying at the worst possible time, usually just when you were trying to avoid the handlebars of a bike or a parked car.[11]

The first commercial skateboards – like the Humco 5-ply deck with 'Sidewalk Swinger' spring-loaded trucks (1956),[12] the Sport Flite and the Roller Derby (late 1950s/early 1960s) – came with steel wheels around 50 mm in diameter and 10 mm wide.[13] The problems these steel wheels posed were partially eased with the adoption of 'composition' or 'clay' wheels, around 50 mm in diameter and 30 mm wide,[14] then being used on commercial rink roller skates. Formed from a composite of clay, plastic, paper, finely ground walnut shells and polymer binding agents, these wheels lasted only a few hours on hard pavement, and were still very vulnerable to surface imperfections, but nevertheless offered a smoother ride.[15]

In these earliest stages, skateboarding remained a predominantly US West Coast phenomenon. While skaters were mostly concerned with simply riding downhill, 'hitting primitive hills at Roger Williams Park and Garden City with rock-hard roller skate garbage wheels',[16] the clay wheels allowed increased control in turning and hence the emulation of a great Californian occupation: the burgeoning surf culture of the late 1950s and 1960s (3.1–3.3).[17] In 1962, Val Surf, a newly founded surf shop in North Hollywood, approached the Chicago Roller Skate company with a

10. Adam, 'A British Skate Story', *Skate Geezer* internet site, URL http://www.interlog.net/~mbrooke/ukstory.htm (accessed 14 October 1997).

11. Schmidt, 'Day They Invented'.

12. 'Trash', *Thrasher*, vol. 12 no. 6 (June 1992), p. 74.

13. Horowitz, 'Skateboard Decks', p. 98; Thompson, letter, p. 8; and Powell-Peralta, advertisement (September 1992), p. 24.

14. Powell-Peralta, advertisement (September 1992), p. 24.

15. Shufeldt, interview, p. 47; La Vada Weir, *Skateboards and Skateboarding* (New York: Julian Messner, 1977), pp. 11–12; National Safety Council, *Skateboarding* (Chicago: Bulletin, The Council, 1978); Rick Blackhart, 'Ask the Doctor', *Thrasher*, vol. 2 no. 1 (January 1982), p. 10; Waldo Autry, interview, *SkateBoarder*, vol. 4 no. 1 (August 1977), p. 108; and Shufeldt, interview, p. 41.

16. Pete Pan, 'The Third Strike', *Thrasher*, vol. 6 no. 6 (June 1986), pp. 50–1.

17. Smythe, 'History', pp. 28–51. On surfing, see Peter L. Dixon, *The Complete Book of Surfing* (1965); Leonard Lueras, *Surfing, the Ultimate Pleasure* (1984); Nat Young with Craig McGregor and Rod Holmes, *The History of Surfing* (Angourie: Palm Beach, rev. edn, 1994); and Craig R. Stecyk III, 'Episodic Discontrol', in Aaron Rose, *Dysfunctional* (London: Booth-Clibborn, 1999), pp. 7–9.

view to obtaining double-action metal trucks and clay wheels ready for assembly.[18] Other trucks available around this time included the Super Surfer, Roller Derby, Roller Sport, x-Caliber and Sure Grip – and these were all devices basically adapted from roller-skate equipment.[19] Surfers wishing to skate bought complete assemblies from Val Surf, or simply fashioned their own decks and bolted on the extra parts (2.2).

> We took chisels and we'd chip the wood and make rockers in our noses and in the tail. They were black and looked like the custom surf designs in either colored marker or airbrush, and we'd lacquer them on.[20]

Systematized production of skateboards began a few years later when Ed Morgan of the Vita-Pact Juice Company of Covina persuaded the firm to diversify into skateboard manufacture. Taking design advice from the professional surfer Hobie Alter, Vita-Pact introduced the 'Hobie' skateboard in 1965 with clay wheels and a

2.2 'Mellow Cat' holding a steel-wheeled skateboard (*c.* 1959).

18. Davidson, *Skateboard Book*, pp. 14–15; and Marilyn Gould, *Skateboarding* (Mankato, Capstone: 1991), pp. 10–11. Val Surf was founded in 1962 by Bill Richards and his three sons Mark, Kurt and Eric. Mark Richards, e-mail (14 April 1999).

19. Redondo, 'History', p. 63; Del *13, 'Talkin' Shop', *Thrasher*, vol. 2 no. 2 (February 1982), p. 13; and Tracker, advertisement, *Thrasher*, vol. 10 no. 2 (February 1990), p. 34.

20. Tony Alva, interview, *Thrasher*, vol. 4 no. 5 (May 1984), p. 28.

fibreglass deck, and went on to make over six million skateboards that year.[21] Other firms also went into production, including Larry Stevenson's Makaha Skateboards (founded 1963), based in the Santa Monica offices of *Surf Guide* magazine.[22] Decks at this time were also a little larger than their 1950s predecessors – averaging around 24x7 inches (60x18.5 cm) in plan form – and overtly shaped like 'miniature surfboards'[23] with curving sides and pointed noses.

By 1962, skateboarding had already reached places like Nevada[24] and the East Coast of the US with a few isolated skateboarders,[25] as well as the various surf towns of south England and Wales.[26] In late 1964 the first issue of *Skate-Boarder* magazine appeared, and by the summer of the following year skateboarding had become a US-wide activity, gaining national television coverage for the International Skateboard Championships at Anaheim,[27] and forming the central motif in the Academy Award-winning film *Skater Dater* (1965).[28] The cover of the 14 May 1965 issue of *Life* magazine featured Pat McGee, the national girl's skateboard champion from San Diego, doing a handstand.[29] Early skateboard teams sprang up, including Hobie, Jacks, Makaha and Bayside.[30] This first phase of skateboarding was, however, short-lived; it peaked in 1965 and by the end of the year *SkateBoarder* magazine had already ceased publication.[31]

Skateboarding continued, with some skaters like Torger Johnson and Davey Hilton becoming well-known for their activities,[32] but the expected demand for skateboards in Christmas 1967 never materialized, leaving Vita-Pact with US$4 million worth of unsold equipment.[33] While skateboarding had reached other

21. Weir, *Skateboards and Skateboarding*, pp. 13–14; 'Trash', *Thrasher*, vol. 12 no. 3 (March 1992), p. 89; and Brooke, *Concrete Wave*, pp. 27–31. Vita-Pact is also variously described as Vita-Pakt or Vita-Pak.

22. Pahl Dixon and Peter Dixon, *Your Complete Guide to Hot Skateboarding* (New York: Warner Books, 1977), pp. 40–2; and *Makaha* internet site, URL http://members.aol.com/makahask8/index.html (accessed 8 November 1997).

23. Bill Bahne, interview, *SkateBoarder*, vol. 5 no. 3 (October 1978), p. 116.

24. Ted Terrebonne, in 'Shooting', *Action Now*, vol. 7 no. 9 (April 1981), p. 41.

25. 'Off the Wall', *SkateBoarder*, vol. 6 no. 5 (December 1979), p. 67.

26. Editor's response to letter, *Skateboard!*, no. 2 (October 1977), p. 20; and Brooke, *Concrete Wave*, p. 27.

27. Smythe, 'History', p. 36.

28. Maggi Russell and Bruce Sawford, *The Complete Skateboard Book* (London: Fontana and Bunch, 1977), p. 10.

29. Jocko Weyland, 'Epiphany at Mecca', *Thrasher*, vol. 17 no. 7 (July 1997), p. 61.

30. Smythe, 'History', pp. 28–51; Don Hoffman, 'Dale 'Sausage Man' Smith', *SkateBoarder*, vol. 6 no. 10 (May 1980), pp. 70–1; and Brooke, *Concrete Wave*, p. 23.

31. Smythe, 'History', p. 36; and Brooke, *Concrete Wave*, p. 24.

32. Gutman, *Skateboarding to the Extreme*, p. 7; Alva, interview, *Thrasher*, pp. 28–30; and Jan Andrejtschitsch, Raimund Kallée and Petra Schmidt, *Action Skateboarding* (New York: Sterling, 1992), p. 11.

33. Dixon and Dixon, *Hot Skateboarding*, p. 42; Weir, *Skateboards and Skateboarding*, pp. 15–16; and Armen Keteyian, 'Chairman of the Board', *Sports Illustrated*, vol. 65 no. 23 (24 November 1986), p. 47.

countries (the UK *Daily Mirror* announced skateboarding as a craze in 1965[34]), it continued mainly as a Californian beach city phenomenon, including places such as Santa Cruz[35] and La Jolla but particularly the Santa Monica and San Fernando areas of LA.[36] Professional skateboard teams also prospered on a small scale, including the Makaha team with skaters such as Ty Page, Bruce Logan and Brad Blank.[37]

THE MODERN SKATEBOARD

Around 1972–3, skateboarding entered its second phase with the introduction of new forms of technology. Most significantly, this involved the replacement of the clay, open-bearing wheels with new wheels such as Roller Sports, Metaflex and Stoker, made from polyurethane hot-poured into moulds, and fitted with loose bearings held together by an adjustable cone system. These first urethane wheels measured around 49 mm in diameter and 30 mm wide, and 90A on the hardness durometer.[38] Although the Vita-Pact/Hobie company had considered using polyurethane for skateboard wheels in 1965, they rejected it for being too expensive; instead, the first successful application of the material was undertaken in 1970–3 by Frank Nasworthy, a former engineering student and surfer living in Encinitas, California. Nasworthy invested US$700 to form Cadillac Wheels and, in conjunction with the roller skate company Creative Urethanes, went into production in 1973 with the first urethane wheel purposely designed for the skateboard.[39] As a slow roller skate wheel, urethane was confined to commercial rink skates,[40] but the softer compositions used for skateboards – developed with help from the Uniroyal chemicals conglomerate[41] – offered the right longevity, speed and traction characteristics.[42] As one skater recalled, 'going from clay to urethane plastic wheels was like moving from a Lada to a Lexus'.[43] Cadillac wheels and various other skateboard components were advertised in US surf magazines[44] and, around 1974–5, fuelled also by the

34. Pennell, *Skateboarding*, p. 1.

35. Tony Roberts, 'Santa Cruz', *Thrasher*, vol. 8 no. 7 (July 1988), p. 79.

36. Smythe, 'History', pp. 28–51.

37. Logan, interview, p. 51; and Ty Page, interview, *SkateBoarder*, vol. 4 no. 2 (September 1977), p. 108.

38. Powell-Peralta, advertisement (September 1992), p. 24.

39. Brooke, *Concrete Wave*, pp. 30–1 and 46–7.

40. Improved urethanes contributed to a resurgence of rollerskating in the late 1970s.

41. Uniroyal, advertisement, *Skateboard!*, no. 14 (October 1978), pp. 82–3.

42. Brian Gillogly, 'Wheels', *SkateBoarder*, vol. 3 no. 4 (April 1977), p. 94; Smythe, 'History', p. 37; Redondo, 'History', p. 62; and David Hunn, *Skateboarding* (London: Duckworth, 1977), p. 4.

43. Michael Brooke, 'Summer 1976. The Bicentennial. Elton John. Chevy Vans. Skateboarding. . .', *DansWORLD* (accessed 11 April 1995).

44. 'Who's Hot! Peter Boronski', *SkateBoarder*, vol. 4 no. 11 (June 1978), p. 108.

re-emergence of *SkateBoarder* in the summer of 1975, skateboarding's second phase began to take off. With the adoption around 1976 of sealed bearings and improved urethanes in such wheels as the Road Rider, Tunnell 'Rocks' and Sims 'Competition' skaters could perform new manoeuvres which, as we shall see, took them away from simple transport or the emulation of surfing.

Skateboard trucks like those made by Sure Grip, X-Caliber, Bahne and Chicago in the early 1970s were still derived from roller skates. Bennett's improved 1974 design was higher and had a wider axle,[45] improving manoeuvrability, stability and rigidity.[46] The Tracker truck (1975) had its king-pin welded directly into the baseplate and tightened by a single lock nut at the hanger-end of the truck (2.3). Although described as a 'revolutionary breakthrough',[47] the aluminium alloy Trackers were simply a refinement of the Bennett type design.[48] Nonetheless, they offered greater strength and ease of use, and by 1978 most trucks were of this arrangement.

By the mid-1970s the modern skateboard had arrived – wooden deck, aluminium alloy trucks with steel axles, and urethane wheels. Specialist models have always been developed for slalom (decks cut away to allow maximum wheel turn, made of fibre-glass or other flexible material), downhill (longer boards, larger wheels, and sometimes ridden as a luge with the skater flat on his or her back, feet first) and freestyle (small boards with parallel sides, narrower trucks and smaller wheels), but generally most skaters have used a standard kind of board. Over the following years, this standard specification was refined but rarely altered in any fundamental way. Decks in the first half of the 1970s were around 24–32 inches (60–80 cm) long and 6.5–7.5 inches (16–19 cm) wide, and by the mid-1970s most boasted a 5–15° rear 'kicktail' (angled rear end, beginning about 0.5 inch (1 cm) behind the

2.3 Tracker truck (1977).

45. 'The Story of Skateboarding', *Skateboard!*, no. 1 (August 1977), p. 20; and Russell and Sawford, *Complete Skateboard*, p. 10.

46. Hunn, *Skateboarding*, p. 4.

47. Bob Biniak, interview, *SkateBoarder*, vol. 4 no. 5 (December 1977), p. 68.

48. Skitch Hitchcock, interview, *SkateBoarder*, vol. 5 no. 7 (February 1979), p. 58.

2.4 Logan, Sims, Sunset, Z-Flex, G&S decks and other skateboard equipment (1977).

rear truck – possibly invented by Larry Stevenson of Makaha skateboards) (2.4).[49] Some were made of plastic polypropylene or aluminium, and others from fibreglass (manufacturers like Bahne and G&S/Gordon & Smith in particular promoted fibreglass 'flex' decks), but most decks were constructed from laminated maple or solid beech, oak or teak.[50]

In the late 1970s, as skaters explored the vertical walls of pools and skateparks, skateboards became much bigger in order to provide extra stability. In the latter half of 1977 the average width of a skateboard deck such as the G&S 'Warptail' was 7.5 inches (19 cm). But from 1973 onward skater Lonnie Toft experimented with 20-inch-wide (50 cm) 8-wheeled and 8–10-inch-wide (20–25 cm) 4-wheeled boards with blunt noses and square tails.[51] In early 1978 the commercial 8-inch-wide

49. 'Off the Wall', *SkateBoarder*, vol. 6 no. 9 (April 1980), p. 72; Redondo, 'History', p. 67; and 'Larry Stevenson: the Father of the Skateboard', in Brooke, *Concrete Wave*, pp. 22–5.

50. Horowitz, 'Skateboard Decks', pp. 94–9; and 'Skata Data', *Skateboard!*, no. 1 (August 1977), p. 39.

51. 'Skate Extra', *SkateBoarder*, vol. 3 no. 2 (December 1976), p. 127; 'Who's Hot! Lonnie Toft', *SkateBoarder*, vol. 4 no. 1 (August 1977), p. 90; Lonnie Toft, interview, *SkateBoarder*, vol. 5 no. 9 (April 1979), p. 35; Lonnie Toft, letter, *SkateBoarder*, vol. 5 no. 6 (January 1979), p. 15; and 'Evolution of the Pig', *SkateBoarder*, vol. 5 no. 4 (November 1978).

(20 cm) Sims 'Toft' model appeared, while LA skaters such as Wes Humpstone and Jim Muir similarly experimented with wider boards.[52]

From this moment things progressed quickly, and, particularly after the adoption of 10-inch-wide (25 cm) decks by Tony Alva and other Santa Monica/Venice Beach skaters in the summer of 1978, many other skaters and manufacturers followed suit.[53] In the UK, skaters such as Marc Sinclair and John Sablosky were riding 9-inch-wide (22.5 cm) Benjyboard decks by June 1978.[54] Before the end of the year most decks measured around 10 inches-wide (25 cm); US firms such as Sims, Alva and Dogtown Skates were quickly followed by Powell-Peralta, Kryptonics and others. Most decks were made of five to nine layers of maple, sometimes with additional fibreglass.[55] Late 1979 onward saw the introduction of concave profiles across the width of decks (Alva, 1979; Santa Cruz, 'Bevel', 1980; Variflex, 'Elguera/El Gato', 1980; Z-Flex 'Z-Winger', 1980) (2.6, 5.1–5.3). Others experimented with longitudinal strengthening beams (Kryptonics 'K-Beam', 1979; Dogtown 'Shogo Kubo Airbeam', 1979), and lightweight foam-cored and graphite construction (Kryptonics, 1978–9; Sims 'George Greenough/Paul Gross' and 'Phase 3 Composite' models, 1979),[56] while many skaters also added various hand-grabbing and board-saving devices to their decks, including side rails and nose- and tail-protectors.[57]

In late 1978–9, truck manufacturers introduced wider models to accommodate the new decks, including the Tracker 'Ex-Track' and 'Six-Track', Lazer 8-inch (20 cm), Megatron 205 mm and Independent 'Superwide' models. The Independent truck, with design input from Rick Blackhart, in particular was a major challenge to Tracker's market domination.[58] Other refinements were also introduced, like ACS and Tracker's lightweight (and very expensive) 90 per cent magnesium models (1978–9), saving 20 per cent of the overall truck weight but with a tendency to brittleness.[59] Trucks could also be modified by adding 'lappers' – devices like the 'Lip Slider' (1978) and 'Clyde Slide' (1979) which prevented the rear truck from being caught on the

52. Andrejtschitsch *et al.*, *Action Skateboarding*, p. 13.

53. Toft, interview, p. 37.

54. John Sablosky, interview, *Skateboard!*, no. 10 (June 1978), p. 52.

55. 'Skata Data: Park Riding Decks', *Skateboard!*, no. 17 (January 1979), pp. 40–1; and 'Skata Data: More Wides, More Bevels', *Skateboard!*, no. 18 (February 1979), pp. 16–17.

56. Dave Goldsmith, 'The Kryptonics Deck: Exclusive Report', *Skateboard!*, no. 14 (October 1978), pp. 60–3; and Sam Fernando, 'Lite Board Symposium: On Weight and Losing Weight', *SkateBoarder*, vol. 6 no. 7 (February 1980), pp. 46–53.

57. Powell-Peralta, advertisement, *SkateBoarder*, vol. 6 no. 8 (March 1980), p. 11; and Del *13, 'Talkin' Shop' (February 1982), p. 13.

58. Rick Blackhart, interview, *SkateBoarder*, vol. 5 no. 3 (October 1978), p. 73; and Rick Blackhart, 'Ask the Doctor', *Thrasher*, vol. 2 no. 5 (May/June 1982), p. 10.

59. Sam Fernando, 'Truck Design Strategies', *SkateBoarder*, vol. 6 no. 9 (April 1980), pp. 66–7.

wall edge – and 'copers' – plastic devices first introduced by Tracker in 1979 that clipped on the truck hanger to decrease wear and increase slide capabilities.[60]

Wheels also improved from better urethane compositions, most famously by Kryptonics who introduced in 1977 soft red (78A durometer) street wheels, hard green (91A durometer) skatepark wheels and an intermediate blue (86A durometer). Powell-Peralta 'Bones' (1978) offered a double radius, and firms such as Road Rider, G&S, Sims and Belair also introduced thicker edge-profile skatepark-oriented wheels.[61] In early 1979 wheels such as the Sims 'Comp II', Alva 'Bevel' and UFO 'Saucer' models gained sophisticated front radius and back 'bevel' or 'conical' profiles intended to widen the wheel track and stop the wheel from getting caught on the wall edge (2.5).[62] Skater Skitch Hitchcock claimed to have originated the conical back edge in late 1977.[63] More idiosyncratic wheels included the rubber and

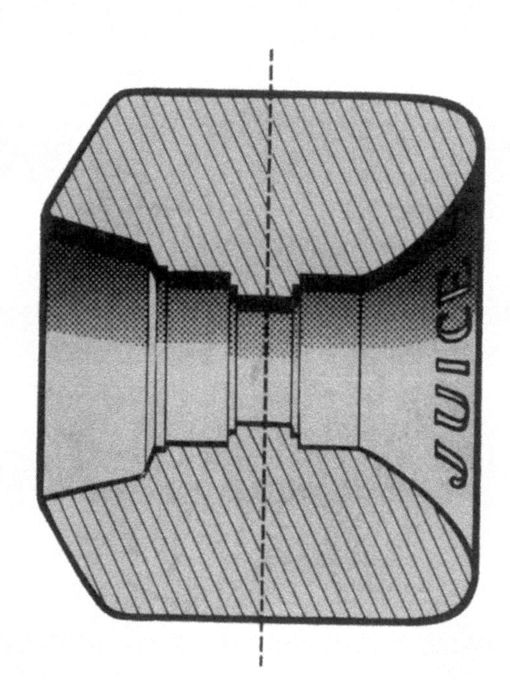

2.5 OJ 'Street Juice' wheel with conical back edge and radial front edge (1982).

60. Curtis Hesselgrave, 'Skate Safe: Maintenance Tips for Boards and Trucks', *SkateBoarder*, vol. 6 no. 2 (September 1979), p. 27.

61. Dave Goldsmith, 'Skata Data: Lime Green and Beyond', *Skateboard!*, no. 11 (July 1978), pp. 44–7.

62. Tim Leighton-Boyce, conversation (7 July 1997); 'Skata Data' (February 1979), pp. 19 and 43; and Redondo, 'History', pp. 63–7.

63. Hitchcock, interview, p. 59.

2.6 Wide skateboards (1980).

urethane Emotion (1977), those with an aluminium ('Gyro', 1979) or plastic (Kryptonics 'C-Series', 1978; Variflex 'X', 1981) hub to reduce weight and increase stiffness, and those with a near-spherical shape (G&S 'Yoyo Roller-balls', 1980).

After a boom period in the late 1970s, in which it enjoyed the dubious publicity in the UK of competitions organized by the BBC 'Nationwide' programme (late 1977)[64] and *The Sun* (1978),[65] skateboarding underwent a serious decline in popularity. However, despite being dismissed as a craze, skateboarding did not disappear entirely, and has since emerged stronger than ever. In the second half of the 1980s skateboarding began its third boom, particularly on the basis of the new interest in street skating.

Skateboard designs also changed in this process. By the end of the 1980s deck designs – such as the G&S 'Danny Webster' (1988) model[66] – included large upturned front ends to help with the new nose-based moves, together with complex

64. 'Lip Torque', *Skateboard!*, no. 6 (February 1978), pp. 32–3.
65. The Sun British Skateboard Championships, advertisement, *Skateboard!*, no. 10 (June 1978), p. 85.
66. 'Product Patrol', *Thrasher*, vol. 8 no. 7 (July 1988), p. 109.

concave lateral profiles and wide flared tails. Others, such as the Christian Hosoi 'Hammerhead' (1985) decks, experimented with modulated plan profiles to provide different hand-holds, while some, such as the Powell-Peralta 'Tommy Guerrero' model (1989), came with a slight 'rocker' shape with up-turned front nose to aid foot placement and turning circle.[67] Most were made of seven-ply maple.[68] Special material decks continued to be made – maple, poplar and vulcanized cellulose laminated 'Boneite' decks (Powell-Peralta, 1987),[69] 'Airtech' foam-cored decks (Santa Cruz, 1986),[70] 'Fiberlite' foam-cores skinned in fibreglass (G&S, 1986–7),[71] and special-order high-tech cores protected by ply and inset bumpers (Schmitt 'X-15', 1990)[72] – but these were exceptional products. Typical deck dimensions in the late 1980s were 31 inches (78 cm) long, 10 inches (25 cm) wide, with 4.5-inch (11 cm) long nose and 6-inch (15 cm) long tail; weight averaged around 1500 gm.[73]

For trucks, in 1982 Tracker experimented with a production 'Ultralite' made of nylon polyamide.[74] By the end of the 1980s, G&S, Tracker and Gullwing were introducing plastic baseplates and hollow steel axles to reduce weight, while most manufacturers offered designs in various enamel colours,[75] but, these minor variations excepted, trucks remained relatively constant in design. Wheels, for their part, became harder at around 97A durometer, optimized for ramp riding.[76] Similarly, toward the end of the decade, tall and narrow wheels around 66–7 mm in diameter and 36 mm wide, such as the Santa Cruz 66 mm 'Bullet' (1988), were developed for vertical riding on large half pipes. At the same time, the first new street-oriented wheels began to appear, and these – such as the G&S 'Bam Bams' (1987), Vision 'Neutrons' (1989), and the Powell-Peralta 'Streetstyle' (1987) – were slightly smaller at 57–61 mm in diameter and 35 mm wide, often with colour graphic designs on their outer sides. Other popular wheel manufacturers included Toxic, Alva and the Australian-made Cockroach.

67. Andrejtschitsch *et al.*, *Action Skateboarding*, pp. 15–16. In the 1970s 'rocker' referred to a single overall concave shape on the deck long axis.

68. 'Skateboard Studies', *Thrasher*, vol. 11 no. 9 (September 1991), p. 37.

69. Powell-Peralta, advertisement, *Thrasher*, vol. 7 no. 2 (February 1987), p. 69.

70. Santa Cruz, advertisement, *Thrasher*, vol. 6 no. 8 (August 1986), p. 32.

71. 'Product Patrol', *Thrasher*, vol. 7 no. 3 (March 1987), p. 109.

72. *R.A.D.*, no. 87 (May 1990), p. 11.

73. 'Product Reaction', *Skateboard!* (second series), no. 39 (January 1990), pp. 10–11.

74. Tracker, advertisement, *Thrasher*, vol. 2 no. 9 (October 1982), p. 3; and 'Showcase', *Thrasher*, vol. 2 no. 11 (December 1982), p. 44.

75. *Intensity Skates* (Maryland), mail order catalogue (1990), p. 6.

76. Powell-Peralta, advertisement (September 1992), p. 24.

NEW SCHOOL

But it was at the beginning of the 1990s that skateboard design experienced the most significant evolution since the wide-boards of the late 1970s. By 1987 US manufacturers were already claiming that over 90 per cent of sales were for street-related equipment,[77] and designs were to respond accordingly. Over 1991–92, during which highly technical, unidirectional streetstyle entrenched its domination over all other forms of skateboarding,[78] skateboards became 'New School'.[79] At the end of the 1980s, the main deck and wheel manufacturers were companies such as G&S, Kryptonics, Vision, Powell-Peralta, Dogtown, Alva, Sims, Schmitt, Walker and Santa Cruz, which had originated in the 1970s. But by 1992, as *Thrasher* skateboard magazine realized, many had been caught out by the new trend.

> The corporate behemoths have gotten fat in their old age and complacency has set in. Just when they've settled into that rocking chair to watch the sun set and pat that mattress full of cash, all hell breaks loose and some kid ollies on their parade. Some big bears in the skateboard business may have disappeared by the time you read this.[80]

In their place, a whole new range of (particularly deck) manufacturers came to the fore including Acme, Alien Workshop, Blind, Chocolate, Foundation, New Deal, Plan B, Real, Think and World Industries. Other companies have included Birdhouse, Blueprint, Consolidated, Element, Firm, Flip, Girl, Invisible, Mad Circle, Neighborhood, Nicotine, Panic, Planet Earth, Shorty's, Spitfire, Stereo, Toy Machine, Toxic, Venture, Zero and Zoo York.

The new decks were slightly longer at 32–33 inches (80 cm) and narrower at 8–9 inches (20 cm) wide, with parallel side rails and near-identical, steeply angled kicktails at front and back – these details accommodated moves done off the board nose and 'switchstance' skating in which skaters rode as much backward as forward (2.7).[81] Some decks in the early 1990s, known as 'slicks', had a layer of slippery thermoplastic bonded to the bottom to facilitate boardslide moves. Skaters using this equipment, in searching for the lightest possible set-up and highest ollie moves, tended to avoid the side rails and nose- and tail-protectors of the 1980s.

Another significant change concerns aesthetics: while older decks often had some kind of design on the underside, with new models brought out annually, by

77. 'Trash', *Thrasher*, vol. 7 no. 7 (July 1987), p. 97.

78. Editorial, *Thrasher*, vol. 12 no. 1 (January 1992), p. 4.

79. 'Skateboarding FAQ', *DansWORLD* (accessed April 1995); and Steve England, 'What Goes Around Comes Around', *Xtreme*, no. 4 (September 1997), p. 27.

80. Editorial, *Thrasher*, vol. 12 no. 3 (March 1992), p. 4.

81. Jake Phelps, 'Switchstance', *Thrasher*, vol. 12 no. 5 (May 1992), pp. 46–9.

2.7 New School deck designs by Ged Wells/Insane (1997). (Photograph Iain Borden)

1995 the turnover rate had become frantic, with new designs frequently produced every few months.[82] Essentially, all skateboard manufacturers now use the same shapes, materials and construction standards, and use graphics to differentiate products and accelerate turnover.[83]

> There are so many companies and so many pros. So many angles have been tried. In the end, all you have to separate you from another company is your graphics.[84]

82. Murray, 'Gentleman's Agreement', *DansWorld* (accessed 20 April 1995). Report of San Diego Trade Show (29 January 1994).

83. Rodney Mullen, interview, *Warp*, vol. 6 no. 3 (August 1997), p. 106; and Murray, 'Gentleman's Agreement'.

84. Moish Brenman, quoted in Patrick Burgoyne and Jeremy Leslie, *Bored* (London: Lawrence King and Creative Review, 1997), p. 49.

Most 'manufacturers' also do not make their decks, but buy unpainted blanks from the three large-scale producers: Taylor-Dykema, Prime and PS Stix.[85] Wheels, similarly, are mostly poured by a few major producers for re-branding,[86] while trucks are predominantly made at two US foundries.[87]

Perhaps because of this, truck design has remained fundamentally unchanged for over two decades, simply widening or narrowing to accommodate changing board widths, although skaters since the early 1990s have particularly favoured low-hanger designs, used without riser pads in order to further reduce ride height.[88] Popular models from the 1980s onward include Thunder, Grind King, Venture and Gullwing, as well as Tracker and Independent. Additions in the 1990s included Destructo, Destroyer, Elevate, Omega and Tensor.

More significant changes occurred in wheel sizes, averaging 45–55 mm in diameter, but occasionally 40 mm or less, such as the Toxic '39er' (1992)[89] and Powell-Peralta 'Mini Balls' 39 mm diameter (1992) models[90] – small size meant lower weight and centre of gravity, so aiding the ollie moves, faster acceleration and slides favoured by street skaters. They also became harder, such as the 101A durometer Toxic 'Meltdown' (1992).[91] Unlike the multi-colour variations of the 1970s–80s, new school wheels tended to be white with applied sidewall graphics. Popular models included those by Big Spin, Birdhouse, Blind, Blueprint, Flip, Foundation, Formula One, Mad Circle, New Deal, Pig, Spitfire, Stereo and STM.

The skateboard-device, then, is a basic piece of equipment, with technology mainly directed at increasing durability and speed while controlling traction and weight. Although some, notably the highly innovative Powell-Peralta, tried to sell skateboards with slogans such as 'avoid obsolete technologies',[92] there have been very few path-breaking designs or production methods. Similarly, while some magazines, particularly the 1970s *SkateBoarder* and *Skateboard!*, undertook serious comparative reviews of components, and ran technical features on, for example, experimental deck construction[93] and wheel characteristics,[94] this was not replicated

85. Editor's response to letter, *Slap*, vol. 6 no. 1 (January 1997), p. 16.

86. Mullen, interview, *Warp*, p. 106.

87. wisentha@netcom.ca (David S. Wisenthal), alt.skateboard, 'Subject. Re. Toy Machine Question (About the trucks)' (posted 1 July 1996).

88. Editorial, *Thrasher* (January 1992).

89. Toxic, advertisement, *Thrasher*, vol. 12 no. 3 (March 1992), p. 67.

90. Powell-Peralta, advertisement (September 1992), p. 24.

91. 'Apocalypse 91', *Thrasher*, vol. 12 no. 1 (January 1992), p. 40; and Toxic, advertisement, *Thrasher*, vol. 12 no. 5 (May 1992), p. 20.

92. Powell, advertisement, *SkateBoarder*, vol. 6 no. 2 (September 1979), p. 23.

93. Horowitz, 'Skateboard Decks', pp. 94–9; and Fernando, 'Lite Board Symposium', pp. 46–53.

94. Goldsmith, 'Skata Data' (July 1978), pp. 44–7; and Mickey Wisternoff, 'Techno Talk: Tread With Care', *Skateboard!*, no. 16 (December 1978), p. 46.

in the later magazines of the 1980s–90s. Skateboards are, then, usually sold on issues of style, general reputation and reliability rather than performance measures.

> A skateboard is a skateboard. They haven't changed. It's the same idea, right? You get on, you go.[95]

For skateboarders, as this suggests, the skateboard-device is similarly easy to understand, requiring almost no maintenance, and no skill to use other than the learned body-skill of balancing and moving on the board. How, then, can this technology be appraised socially and spatially? What can it do, in terms of not technical but political and social performance? What can it offer in the context of the restless search for social change?

When considering skateboarding historically and critically the isolated realms of the hardware – the skateboard and the buildings of the city – are by themselves inappropriate arenas in which to assess skateboarding technologies. In terms of the skateboard itself, *Wall Street Journal* may see vintage skateboards as top collectibles, but the various museums[96] and privateer 'historians' of early skateboards[97] are merely collecting the object-traces of skateboarding, and cannot construct a true history of skateboarding through this activity alone. Similarly, the visual-mental processes of architects, designers and skateboarders – the representational imaginary of urban space, ranging from architectural plans to skateboard magazines and videos – are also by themselves insufficient. Instead, we should consider the integration, to recall Lefebvre, of practices, representations and experiences – the way technologies become lived in social space and time, and so become socially real.[98] The importance of the skateboard as a device is not solely its manufacture or design, but what can be done with it, becoming a lived component of the body, its actions and its self-image in relation to the terrain and architecture beyond. It is with this inter-relation that the rest of this book is largely concerned.

95. Jake Shaft, 'Life, Liberty, and the Pursuit of Longboarding', *Thrasher*, vol. 6 no. 3 (March 1986), p. 59.

96. *SkateLab* internet site (Simi Valley, California), URL http://www.skatelab.com/ (accessed 9 April 1999).

97. 'Trash', *Thrasher*, vol. 17 no. 1 (January 1997), p. 122.

98. Lefebvre, *Production of Space*, pp. 33 and 38–9.

Chapter 3
Found Space

> Just when you get to thinking that you've finally found the limits of what can be done on a skateboard, or of what places are left to be found, something new inevitably turns up again to broaden the imagination and boggle the mind.[1]

INTO THE DEEP END

Skateboarders in Los Angeles first understood space as a pre-existent natural phenomenon, moving through the city's neighbourhood sidewalks just as the freeway system provided an elaborate transport system for its automobile-bound population.

> Seems like you always had your skateboard with you, were always on it. That was your main way of getting around – either the bus or a skateboard.[2]

As with the use of scooters and primitive skateboards in the 1950s and early 1960s, one of the main uses of skateboards continues to be local transportation, particularly for younger practitioners.

Apart from this simple movement, skaters responded to urban space in a more deliberate and substantive manner. Where capitalism sub-divides and controls, measures and turns land into a commodity – in short, produces abstract space[3] – skaters created spatial enclaves within Los Angeles and, subsequently, other cities worldwide. This is one of skateboarding's central features, adopting and exploiting a given physical terrain in order to present skaters with new and distinctive uses other than the original function of that terrain.

Skateboarders in the 1960s–1970s were commonly surfers, and used skateboards when the surf was flat. The suburban modernism of Los Angeles and other Californian oceanside cities allowed frustrated surfers to re-enact the sense of being on the sea, rolling down the tarmac drives and roads of its undulating residential sectors as if they were an ocean wave.

1. Warren Bolster, 'Desert Discovery', *SkateBoarder*, vol. 3 no. 6 (July 1977), p. 73.
2. Jay Adams, interview, *SkateBoarder*, vol. 6 no. 4 (November 1979), p. 52.
3. Henri Lefebvre, *The Production of Space* (Oxford: Blackwell, 1991), *passim*.

> We used to skate a lot when the surf was no good; imitate a surf style or perfect a move.[4]

Or as Jan and Dean sang in 1964, 'you can do the tricks the surfers do . . . grab your board and go sidewalk surfing with me'.[5] This was artificial, second nature[6] architecture, adopted and rethought as natural space (3.1–3.3).

Skateboarding here was about surface horizontality and its gentle curvature. First, skateboarders rode barefoot and upright or, more often, crouched with arms outstretched as a parallel gesture to the flatness of the ground beneath. Second, movement was important, skateboarders seeking to experience through the moving body the expansive stretch of tarmac in all directions; the body and skateboard operated as floating mirror, a few feet or inches above the surface, reflecting its

3.1 Surf-skateboarding on the La Jolla strand (*c.* 1964). (Photograph Stoner)

4. John Milius, in John Smythe, 'The History of the World and Other Short Subjects', *SkateBoarder*, vol. 6 no. 10 (May 1980), p. 33.

5. Jan and Dean, 'Sidewalk Surfin" (1964). Written by Wilson and Christian (London: Rondor Music).

6. Lefebvre, *Production of Space*, p. 109; Lefebvre, *Survival of Capitalism* (New York: St. Martin's, 1976), pp. 14–15.

3.2 The low, pivotal, ground-contact and surf-style skateboarding of Jay Adams. Bay Street, Santa Monica (1975).

planar materiality back onto itself. The skater here was a scanning device, partly like a metal detector, checking for the smallest objects and irregularities, and partly as micro-cartographer, mapping the gently undulating contours (3.2). This 'low center of gravity style' was based on surfing,[7] what *SkateBoarder* called a 'low, pivotal, ground-contact style',[8] replicating on dry land the surfer's traverse across ocean surface and close sensing of changing wave forms.

Early skateboarders also found other terrains, in particular the gently inclined banks of many Los Angeles schoolyards, such as Bellagio, Paul Revere Junior High (Sunset Boulevard and 26th), Brentwood (Montana Avenue and Bundy Drive) and, most famously, the Kenter Elementary School (North Kenter Avenue). Surfer-skaters like Davey Hilton, Steve Hilton, Torger Johnson, Ty Page, Tommy Ryan, John Fries and Danny Bearer used these schoolyard banks around 1968,[9] transcribing surfing

7. Tony Alva, interview, *Heckler* internet site, URL http://heckler.com (accessed 5 May 1996).

8. Stacy Peralta, interview, *SkateBoarder*, vol. 3 no. 1 (October 1976), p. 57.

9. Ty Page, interview, *SkateBoarder*, vol. 4 no. 2 (September 1977), p. 108; Smythe, 'History', pp. 28–51; Alva, interview, *Thrasher*, p. 28.

techniques directly on to the tilted surfaces by riding their clay-wheeled and home-made deck skateboards along the length of the bank, just as a surfer 'carves' across a wave. Other emulations included touching the bank surface as if the surf-skater were trailing the hand in watery spray; or re-enacting surf tricks like the 'hang five' where the rider hangs five toes over the board nose. The nomenclature of these early moves was also borrowed from surfing: a 'frontside' move was where the skater faced the bank/wave, and, conversely, 'backside' referred to a move where the skater's back was turned toward the bank/wave.

> When skating banks, just ride them like a wave . . . Banks are really just cement waves.[10]

> How better to ride a wave of cement than to surf-skate it?[11]

Later in the 1970s, new Los Angeles skaters like Marty Grimes, Tony Alva (5.6), Stacy Peralta and Jay Adams (3.2) further extended the surf-skate bank-riding experiences, incorporating new forms of turns, slides and other manoeuvres, while similar bank moves were undertaken at Hawaii skate spots such as Uluwatu, Wallos and Stoker Hill.[12]

Nor was this kind of activity restricted to those parts of the world with direct access to the sea. In the 1970s, such re-enactments of surfing were also transposed to the unlikely setting of European urbanism, skateboarding bringing the joy of surfing to the humblest municipal housing project.[13]

> I started off by rolling down a hill with a pair of sunglasses on, pretending to be Californian.[14]

In London, the concrete banks below the South Bank's Hayward Gallery proved ideal for early surf-related moves.

> A large paved area sweeps into a three-sided bank and a seemingly endless stream of kids were hurtling up to the bank, riding it, and turning back down and away . . . others were riding along the top edge of the bank, crouched down holding on to their boards ('carving').[15]

10. 'Who's Hot! Paul Constantineau', *SkateBoarder*, vol. 3 no. 2 (December 1976), p. 85.

11. Peralta, interview, *SkateBoarder*, p. 57.

12. Cindy Berryman, 'Skateboarding Hawaii: an Alternative Surf Style', *SkateBoarder*, vol. 3 no. 2 (December 1976), pp. 92–7; 'Who's Hot! Larry Bertleman', *SkateBoarder*, vol. 3 no. 2 (December 1976), p. 80; and 'Who's Hot! Jay Adams', *SkateBoarder*, vol. 3 no. 2 (December 1976), p. 82.

13. Hazel Pennell, *Skateboarding* (London: GLC Intelligence Unit, London Topics no. 24, 1978), p. 1.

14. Ben Powell, in Siân Liz Evans, 'Young, Gifted and Board Stupid', *The Big Issue* (London), no. 126 (17–23 April 1995), p. 18.

15. Stan Hey, 'Wheelers and Dealers', *Time Out*, no. 381 (15–21 July 1977), p. 13.

Cities thus suddenly, it seemed, obtained ocean-like forms – other 'natural' banks in the UK included, for example, Hyson Green in Nottingham.[16]

On one level this activity appears as urban escapism, just as pot-holing and mountaineering make a 'claim to nature' and so 'flee the deteriorated and unrenovated city' in order to 'really' live.[17] However, this early skateboarding was less a form of escape – as surfing might be construed – than it was a repositioning of the urban. Through surf-related moves, skaters recombined body, board and terrain, simultaneously copying one activity (surfing) while initiating a second (skateboarding). The modernist space of suburbia was found, adapted and reconceived as another kind of space, as a concrete wave.

> New hillside housing tracts lost their hideous urban negativity and emerged from the metamorphosis as smooth uncrowded ribbons of winding joy.[18]

This was an attempt to produce from second nature those things which become scarce in capitalism: first nature, air, water, land, light.[19] But, importantly, skaters' 'escape' was ideational rather than physical. This recombination of body, image, thought and action lies at the heart of skateboarding – an integration of abstract and concrete, object and performance, to which I constantly return in this book. It also, therefore, has the potential to avoid the 'enormous disappointment' which arises from trying to relate to 'nature-in-itself'.[20]

The emulation of surfing continued into the 1970s, with skaters finding other, more challenging terrains. Above all, Los Angeles (particularly the Hollywood Hills and moneyed districts of Santa Monica, Malibu and Pacific Palisades) was the 'pool capital'[21] with numerous substantial villas boasting private swimming pools. Somewhere between 1963 and 1965, a doctor called Gary Swanson, a.k.a. 'Swane', drained the water out of his Santa Monica backyard pool, and, realizing that this Californian pool offered a curved transition from base to wall (unlike, for example, the orthogonal section pools typically found in Australia[22]), he rode his skateboard up the rounded sides of the pool's deep end (3.3).[23] Alternatively, it is reported that either the Foxtail pool in Foxtail Park just outside Santa Monica, carved by skaters

16. 'UK News', *Skateboard!*, no. 2 (October 1977), p. 19; and Steve, letter, *Skateboard!*, no. 2 (October 1977), p. 20.

17. Henri Lefebvre, *Introduction to Modernity* (London: Verso, 1995), pp. 72–3; and Lefebvre, *Writings on Cities* (Oxford: Blackwell, 1996), pp. 80 and 158.

18. Stephen Cline, 'Skateboarding in the Dark Ages', *SkateBoarder*, vol. 2 no. 2 (Fall 1975), p. 38.

19. Lefebvre, *Production of Space*, p. 329.

20. Lefebvre, *Introduction to Modernity*, p. 90.

21. 'Pools', *Thrasher*, vol. 4 no. 6 (June 1984), p. 22.

22. Peralta, interview, *SkateBoarder*, p. 56.

23. Lowboy, 'Truth and Screw the Consequences', *Thrasher*, vol. 9 no. 6 (June 1989), pp. 42–3; and Michael Brooke, *The Concrete Wave* (Toronto: Warwick, 1999), p. 38.

3.3 The first pool carve? Gary Swanson in his Santa Monica pool (mid-1960s).

such as Steve Hilton around March 1965, or Roy Diederichsen's pool in Menlo Park and featured in the first issue of *SkateBoarder* in late 1965, was possibly the first to be skated.[24] Whatever the founding event, these kinds of pool were skated regularly after 1965 and became particularly prevalent around 1973–5 and late 1970s.

Others quickly followed the discovery of pools, and sculptural oval and kidney-shaped pools all around Los Angeles were skated. To begin with, the skater's move predominantly meant the surf-derived carve, a fundamental skateboard move where the skater attacks the wall at an slight angle along a single sweeping trajectory, prevented from falling by the centrifugal force generated by their speed (much like the motorcyclists in a fairground 'Wall of Death').

Skateboarding in pools also meant creating an empathy and engagement with the surface of the pool wall. This occurred in two ways, and is particularly connected with the 'kickturn' move – possibly first achieved in a pool by Waldo Autry or Tony Alva in the early 1970s[25] – where the skater rides up the wall in a near vertical trajectory, and then, as the speed drops, lifts the front wheels and pivots 180° around the rear wheels and drops back down the wall. First, through this move, skaters encounter the wallness of the wall, sensing how the pool presents itself as a surface changing from floor to wall under their very feet. The skater's experience is a heightening encounter – the higher up they go, the more vertical, the more wall-like that surface becomes. This involves a quadruple movement of body and architectural surface: initially comes the sudden compression of body hitting the bottom curve of the transition, where terrain is felt to press back on the skater, translating momentum into a forced acceleration of her or his trajectory up the wall;

24. *SkateBoarder*, vol. 1; Smythe, 'History', pp. 28–51; Brooke, *Concrete Wave*, p. 38; Craig R. Stecyk III, 'Episodic Discontrol or Random Samplings from the Life and Times', in Aaron Rose, *Dysfunctional* (London: Booth-Clibborn, 1999), p. 10.

25. Waldo Autry, interview, *SkateBoarder*, vol. 4 no. 1 (August 1977), p. 109.

at this point the second stage arrives, tense compression is released, and the skater feels the enclosed concave curvature of the transition give way to vertical flatness, and to a corresponding sense of speed and expansivity of space. The third stage is that stalling space-time where the skater reaches the top of the trajectory, hangs momentarily, and begins the kickturn – for the skater, this is a highly physical yet simultaneously fantastical and dream-like experience, where space-time are conflated and frozen into a dynamic-yet-stable instance. The fourth moment is the transitional return from pool wall to floor, experiencing in reverse the compression of curvature and body; this last stage is then a recalled rhythm of the first, at once equal and different. This complex procedure is then sequentially replicated, creating a composition of body-time-spaces as the skater combines carves, kickturns and other moves within the same run.

The second engagement with the pool wall is through its pure surface, and particularly its tactility or materiality: smoothness as a texture, like a cloth, and smoothness as a concave plane, like a mathematically complex curve. Here the micro-architecture of surface grain, asperity, cracks and ripple become evident, translated into body space through judder (from wheels, to deck, to feet and upward), slide and grip. Above all, it involves noise, for the skateboarder's traverse on the white wall creates a mono-tonal hum, so near silence yet so clearly audible that it creates a dramatically calm interlude to the high-speed fire rasped out by hard wheels passing over blue ceramic tile and metal truck grinding along concrete coping.

> The way everything sounds is different. Every grind has a strange resonating howl.[26]

> Snarls and growls rise from the deep end as skaters get down and out. Shouts and howls rise from the crowded shallow end full of screaming skaters-in-waiting.[27]

These aural salvos remind us that 'space is listened for, in fact, as much as seen, and heard before it comes into view', that hearing mediates between the spatial body and the world outside it, and that it is therefore not only in a cathedral or cloister that 'space is measured by the ear'.[28] This is a 'sensuous geography'[29] created by a phenomenal experience of architecture, a 'sensory space' constituted by 'an "unconsciously" dramatized interplay of relay points and obstacles, reflections, references, mirrors and echoes'.[30]

26. Rick Blackhart, 'Ask the Doctor', *Thrasher*, vol. 5 no. 1 (January 1985), p. 8.
27. Kevin J. Thatcher and Brian Brannon, *Thrasher* (New York: Random House, 1992), p. 10.
28. Lefebvre, *Production of Space*, pp. 199–200 and 225.
29. Paul Rodaway, *Sensuous Geographies* (London: Routledge, 1994).
30. Lefebvre, *Production of Space*, p. 210.

On one level, these experiences were further extensions of the surf-related nature of skateboarding. As late as 1978 skaters commented that pool skating was 'the closest thing to surfing', and captions in *SkateBoarder* (published by Surfer magazine group) described skaters as 'adapting from waves to walls with stylistic finesse'.[31]

> When skating I try to think of the walls as a wave and try to do those same (surf) moves . . . it's all so inter-related and interchangeable.[32]

> When you're skating a pool, it's almost like surfing. It relates because of the climbing and dropping, and the weightlessness of verticalness.[33]

> Riding the right pool feels just like being weightless in the tube.[34]

Many skaters at this time also preferred to skate barefoot, a body gesture that was in direct emulation of the surfer's 'total "surf" experience', and in particular her or his reading of surface through board and feet up in to the body (3.5).[35]

But pool skateboarding was not just about emulating surfing. Around about 1976–7, skaters' attitude to the pool began to change away from ocean-related movements.

> When you fly up into the air and land on concrete – that's not water.[36]

> Initially surfing was a motivation, but we began to use the terrain as a force, you know to gain speed from the vertical. Most of the older guys just skated over the ground while we worked the surface.[37]

Such 'working the surface' involved thinking less about the pool wall as a concrete wave, and more as an element which, together with the skateboard and skater's own body, could be recombined into an excited body-centric space.

> Round pools with fat coping and wide-open shallow-ends. The faster the better. Go over the light, then the love-seat, through the shallow, carve-grind the deep-end pocket and ride that hip that tips past vert. And what's the matter . . . are you scared to frontside grind over the death-box? Haul ass![38]

31. *SkateBoarder*, vol. 4 no. 6 (January 1978), p. 100.
32. 'Who's Hot! Vince Klyn', *SkateBoarder*, vol. 4 no. 6 (January 1978), p. 101.
33. Bob Biniak, interview, *SkateBoarder*, vol. 4 no. 5 (December 1977), p. 67.
34. Peralta, interview, *SkateBoarder*, p. 58.
35. Del *13, 'Talkin' Shop', *Thrasher*, vol. 2 no. 1 (January 1982), p. 13.
36. Jim Ganzer, in Jay Cocks, 'The Irresistible Air of Grabbing Air: Skateboarding, Once a Fad, is Now a National Turn-on', *Time*, vol. 131 (6 June 1988), p. 91.
37. Stacy Peralta, interview, *Thrasher*, vol. 2 no. 5 (May/June 1982), p. 16.
38. Keith Hamm, 'Coping Conquistadors', *Slap*, vol. 4 no. 9 (September 1995), p. 48.

The first moves in pools done by skaters such as Gary Swanson and Steve Hilton were carves (3.3), but skaters soon found this limiting, realizing that 'carving's cool, but after a while you want to do more than just carve it'.[39] It was therefore during the mid-1970s that Los Angeles 'Z-Boy' (Zephyr skateboard team) skaters such as Jay Adams, Tony Alva, Bob Biniak, Chris Cahill, Paul Constantineau, Shogo Kubo, Jim Muir, Stacy Peralta, Nathan Pratt and Alan Sarlo began to explore both the boundaries of the surface on which they skated and the space beyond, aiming 'to project yourself through the bowl continuously, forever doing off-the-lips, from one wall to another'.[40] To begin with, around 1976, they concentrated on the very top of the pool wall, shuddering over the blue tile to grind the rear truck against the pool coping blocks before dropping back down. Biniak's 'standards for excellence' concerned 'how close you can ride to the top, how long you can ride at the top, how fast you go at the top – frontside off-the-lips at speed, style'.[41]

As the last quotation suggests, this also involved a particular 'style' or attitude to the body-terrain interaction; for many skaters, this was a kind of aggression.

> It was all hardcore aggression. Back then, you knew it was aggression. Alva, J. Adams, Yeron, all those guys. I mean it was 100% aggression.[42]

Skaters adopted a confrontational stance to the pool terrain, seeing it as something dangerous to be conquered. Within this aggression, the edge condition was paramount, the skater addressing the very limits of the wall, and the precise micro-space of the skateboard wheel and truck in relation to that edge.

> It's like you're on about 1/8" edge, just pivoting – because the wheels are just about 1/4" on the edge . . . it's just an edge, just unreal, because you feel everything lifting off, then you feel the edge on the coping while you're turning.[43]

This was a micro-space, measured in fractions of an inch. But it was also more than that.

> Yup edgers. The slim difference between yes and no, between light and dark, genius and insanity – even dawn and dusk. Yeah, it's a fine line, but the results are measured in vertical concrete.[44]

39. Gershon Mosley, interview, *Heckler* (accessed 5 May 1996).
40. Stacy Peralta, in 'Pool Riding Symposium', *SkateBoarder*, vol. 3 no. 1 (October 1976), p. 74.
41. Bob Biniak, in 'Pool Riding Symposium', p. 74.
42. Micke Alba, interview, *Thrasher*, vol. 2 no. 6 (July 1982), p. 32.
43. Rodney Jesse, interview, *SkateBoarder*, vol. 4 no. 10 (May 1978), p. 59.
44. 'Edge!', *Thrasher*, vol. 6 no. 5 (May 1986), p. 35.

The space of the edge was, then, not just a quantitative dimension (as might be the high-jumper's consideration of the bar), nor just an experiential engagement between skateboard and architecture, but simultaneously more meaningful: the symbolic limit of danger and achievement, the boundary and terrain deepest within the skater as well as the furthest limit of her or his externalized activity, representing 'the act of skateboarding as throwing one's self out of control and then attempting to pull it back in'.[45] The edge was the physical and personal edge, the space and moment of confrontation between the self and the external world: 'You can't be on the edge if there is no edge.'[46]

But this, ultimately, was not the final limit. More spectacular than edge-oriented moves, the skateboarder could perform an aerial: pass over the top of the wall, torque around in mid-air while holding onto the skateboard with one hand and return to the side-wall. The first instance of this astonishing spatial invention was either by George Orton (3.4) or, more probably, in 1977 by Tony Alva at the legendary 'Dog Bowl' pool in Santa Monica.[47] As the photographer Glen E. Friedman later recalled,

> Here at the Dog Bowl, T.A. (Tony Alva) perfected the 'frontside air.' I remember seeing him do it the first time above coping. I went back to school the next day and had a tough time just describing it to my friends there, let alone getting them to believe it.[48]

Moves like these initiated a unique airborne spatial experience, wherein space was produced centrifugally, a spiralling field of influence thrown out from the body, and then centripetally, pulling the terrain underfoot back into the realm of body space. The imaginative separation from surfing created by this kind of skateboarding is evidenced in the many new skateboarding moves subsequently exported back to surfing, with surfers attempting boardslides, aerials, ollies and other skate-related moves from the late 1970s onward.[49]

45. Ibid., p. 36.

46. 'How to Build a Skatepark', *Thrasher*, vol. 17 no. 9 (September 1997), p. 74.

47. The event is recorded in Glen E. Friedman, *Fuck You Heroes* (New York: Burning Flags, 1994), n.p. Friedman cites this as the earliest published photograph of a frontside aerial, giving dates of September and October 1977. Friedman's photograph is reproduced in Borden, 'Body Architecture', in Hill (ed.), *Occupying Architecture*, p. 200. *SkateBoarder*, vol. 4 no. 4 (November 1977), pp. 70–1 shows a four-frame sequence by James Cassimus of a frontside aerial by Frank Blood in the Pipeline skatepark. The first frontside aerial was possibly performed by either Alva at the Dog Bowl pool, George Orton at 'Skatopia' skatepark, Buena Park, or Dennis Martinez at 'Skateboard Heaven' skatepark, Spring Valley. 'Air'. *Thrasher*, vol. 4 no. 4 (April 1984), p. 30; and Nicolas Malinowski, 'L'evolution d'une espace', *Noway*, no. 13 (November 1990), p. 10.

48. Friedman, *Fuck You Heroes*, index.

49. Brad Bowman, interview, *SkateBoarder*, vol. 6 no. 6 (January 1980), p. 51; and Craig Fineman, 'Surfer/Skateboarder Steve Olson', *SkateBoarder's Action Now*, vol. 7 no. 2 (September 1980), pp. 35–9.

3.4 Centrifugal and centripetal space production. Frontside aerial by George Orton at Paramount skatepark (1978). (Photograph Tom Sims)

Pool skateboarding opened up a terrain incomparable with any other in the urban landscape.

> Pool skating is it. Sure, I still bomb hills, skate ramps and ditches, and cruise the streets after hours, but pools rule.[50]

Even before the aerial, pool-riding was being seen as the future of skateboarding; significantly, the front cover of the first 1970s re-published *SkateBoarder* showed not the freestylers, high-jumps and gentle riding depicted in the original series a decade earlier, but Gregg Weaver carving barefoot in the 'San Marcos' pool (3.5).[51]

50. Hamm, 'Coping', p. 48.

51. *SkateBoarder*, vol. 1 no. 1 (Summer 1975), front cover; and 'San Diego', *Thrasher*, vol. 9 no. 8 (August 1989), p. 36.

3.5 Gregg Weaver in the San Marcos pool, shown on the front cover of the first re-issued *SkateBoarder* magazine (1975).

> Pool-riding is the state-of-the-art skating style of the 70's. No other type of riding offers such radical departures from the past, and no other form progresses so swiftly towards the future. Pool riding has the juice.[52]

Inspired by these kinds of activity, hundreds of skateboarders took to the pools. In and around Los Angeles, other backyard pools were found and skated, sometimes in the grounds of a burnt-out residence or illegally, without the permission of a temporarily absent owner. A BBC television documentary, 'Skateboard Kings', showed Jay Adams, Tony Alva and other skaters on a search for the perfect Santa Monica backyard pool,[53] while other pools across California were discovered, often only skated for short periods of time and known by descriptive or idiosyncratic labels: 'Alpine', 'Bel Air Pool', 'Canyon Pool', 'Central Pool', 'Dog Bowl', 'Fruit Bowl', 'Grove Bowl', 'Keyhole', 'L-pool', 'Manhole', 'Pearl Pool', 'Sewers', 'Skipper's Pool' and 'Soul Bowl'.[54] They offered an extreme terrain on which skating could take place.

Drainage ditches and other large-scale water-management projects formed another kind of architectural terrain which skaters could utilize. Favoured locations included the 'Toilet Bowl' in the Hollywood Hills – a dry drainage reservoir forming a shallow concrete bowl 75 ft across and 35 ft deep.[55] Other such locations included 'Secret Spot' in the Beverly Hills,[56] the Sepulveda Dam (originally skated in the 1960s), Vermont Avenue funnel and the Escondido reservoir.[57] In northern California, various dams and spillways were supplemented by the 'Arab Pool', 'Dolphin Pool', 'Gilroy Brocerios Bowl' and, in particular, the 'Los Altos' pool.[58] Around Santa Cruz,

52. 'Pool Riding Symposium', p. 62.

53. 'World About Us', BBC2 documentary (Horace Ové, late 1978); Tony Alva, interview, *SkateBoarder*, vol. 4 no. 12 (July 1978), p. 68; and Rad Fox, letter, *Skateboard!*, no. 15 (November 1978), p. 57.

54. *SkateBoarder, passim*. See also Friedman, *Fuck You Heroes*; Glen E. Friedman, *Fuck You Too* (Los Angeles, 2.13.61 Publications and Burning Flags, 1996); and Alba, interview, p. 31.

55. Skip Smith, 'The Toilet Bowl', *SkateBoarder*, vol. 2 no. 2 (Fall 1975), pp. 42–5; 'Who's Hot! Tony Jetton', *SkateBoarder*, vol. 5 no. 6 (January 1979), p. 82; and David Hunn, *Skateboarding* (London: Duckworth, 1977), p. 20.

56. Trip Gabriel, 'Rolling Thunder', *Rolling Stone* (16–30 July 1987), p. 76.

57. Sam Fernando, 'Things are Hot in the Valley', *SkateBoarder*, vol. 4 no. 1 (August 1977), p. 67; Brian Gillogly, 'Skate Parks: Part X', *SkateBoarder*, vol. 4 no. 1 (August 1977), p. 94; and Smythe, 'History', p. 37.

58. Will Edler, 'Radical Northern Realities', *SkateBoarder*, vol. 6 no. 11 (June 1980), pp. 47–51; and 'Who's Hot! Rick Blackhart', *SkateBoarder*, vol. 4 no. 4 (November 1977), pp. 114–15.

3.6 A favoured Northern California skate spot. Rick Blackhart at the Yuvis Spillway (1980).

favoured skate spots included 'The Pit', 'Lipton Bowl', Yvis Spillway (3.6) and Novitiate Winery pool.[59] Ditches and dams were also found in other states across America, such as the Jefferson, Ventura, Commanche and Four-Hills ditches in Albuquerque, New Mexico.[60]

Even more extreme were the large concrete 'full pipes'. At Mount Baldy near Los Angeles (first ridden around 1974–5 or possibly late 1960s), skaters discovered a large circular drainage pipe in which they worked continuously from side to side. Mount Baldy was around 14–15 feet in diameter and 500 feet long (3.7).[61] In Northern California, skaters found the 14-foot diameter Ameron plant pipes near Palo Alto, the 22-foot diameter 250-foot-long Bombora pipeline and the Berryessa/ Bariessa 30-foot run-off pipe.[62]

59. Tony Roberts, 'Santa Cruz', *Thrasher*, vol. 8 no. 7 (July 1988), p. 79.

60. Molly Roache, 'Straight From God's Land of Ditches', *Thrasher*, vol. 7 no. 8 (August 1987), pp. 47–53.

61. Autry, interview, p. 109; Chris Miller, interview, *Thrasher*, vol. 9 no. 10 (May 1989), pp. 62–9 and 102; Eric Dressen, interview, *TransWorld Skateboarding*, vol. 7 no. 3 (June 1989), pp. 97–103 and 160–72; Stacy Peralta, interview, *Skateboard!*, no. 4 (December 1977), p. 38; 'Baldy Pipeline', *Thrasher*, vol. 1 no. 8 (August 1981), pp. 20–1; and Santa Cruz, advertisement, *Thrasher*, vol. 6 no. 9 (September 1986), p. 16.

62. Edler, 'Radical', pp. 47–51; and 'Who's Hot! Rick Blackhart', pp. 114–15.

3.7 Mark Gonzales (left) and Don Pendleton (right) at the Mount Baldy pipe, while being carefully watched by a security guard (*c.* 1987). (Photograph Morizen Föche)

Yet larger 20–22-foot diameter free-standing pipes, part of a US$1.7 billion federal water project, could also be found out near Lake Pleasant and the Biscuit Flats of the Arizona desert; here the extreme flatness and expansivity of the natural terrain contrasted with the pipes, creating a lunarscape dotted with immense concrete forms (3.8).[63] This was 'the dark side of the moon'.[64]

> Taking the main turn-off, and still three miles away, we could just barely see some giant structures across the sandy, flat panorama. 'What are those?' Laura asked. I struggled to drive and look at the same time; everyone started hooting as we moved closer. Pipe sections littered the desert floor everywhere as far as the eye could see.[65]

Within these pipes, skaters instigated a unique spatial exploration. At the long Mount Baldy pipe Chris Miller recalled 'riding all the way through it, doing frontside thrusters as high as you could go, skimming your hand along the wall, going very, very fast'.[66] In the larger-diameter but shorter single-section Arizona pipes, skaters began a more upward and rhythmical spatial experience, moving higher and higher, pushing skateboard and body above the vertical, and up into the zone where the pipe pressed back against the skateboarder; here, not only does gravity pull from below but the pipe pushes from above, the overhang forcing the skater into an ever more compressed board-body-terrain space, desperately re-flowing the push-pull into their own turning manoeuvre, fully exhaling to avoid being pitched out.

> For that one moment, the skater defies the laws of gravity and floats in space.[67]

On completing the turn, the skater falls down the pipe surface, inhaling once again, at first feeling the wall move away from the board until the 9 o'clock position is regained, and then feeling the wall come back to the body on the descent. Furthermore, the skater then immediately begins the encounter with the opposite wall, for, unlike the later skateparks and half-pipe constructions discussed in Chapter Four, the simple circular 'O'-shape section of these full-pipes had no flat-bottom. Consequently skaters undertook a series of immediately-sequential moves on opposite walls – 'forevers' – using the compression-decompression of body and board to gain

63. Bolster, 'Desert Discovery', pp. 72–83; Smythe, 'History', pp. 38 and 44; Bruce Hazelton, 'The Outrageous Pipes of Arizona', *Skateboard!*, no. 6 (February 1978), pp. 46–9; and 'Ride the Wild Tube', *Skateboard Scene*, vol. 1 no. 1 (n.d., c. November/December 1977), pp. 18–19.

64. *SkateBoarder*, vol. 4 no. 1 (August 1977), p. 110.

65. Bolster, 'Desert', p. 80.

66. Miller, interview, *Thrasher*, p. 102.

67. Thatcher and Brannon, *Thrasher* (book), p. 10.

3.8 The 'forever' oscillation within a desert pipe. Gregg Weaver at the 10 o'clock position (1977). (Photograph Warren Bolster)

height, just as a child on a playground swing (3.8).[68] The forever performed a magical rhythm and, emphasized by the strange setting of concrete-meets-lunar-landscape, rapidly attained near mythological status in skateboard culture.

> Even the hardest, the coolest of the cool had to admit – this place was the best![69]

This mystique was further emphasized by the 'unconquered frontier'[70] – the impossible idea that a skater might pass over 12 o'clock and make a full revolution.[71]

68. Waldo Autry and Curtis Hesselgrave, 'How to Get High in the Pipes', *SkateBoarder*, vol. 3 no. 6 (July 1977), p. 79; and Autry, interview, pp. 109–12.

69. Bolster, 'Desert', p. 82.

70. 'Ride the Wild Tube', p. 19.

71. Bolster, 'Desert', p. 82; Peralta, interview, *Skateboard!*, p. 38; and Michael Gumkowski, 'Time Warped', *Thrasher*, vol. 11 no. 9 (September 1991), pp. 62–3, 76 and 80.

(In later years, skateboarders Duane Peters (1970s) and Tony Hawk (1990s) both completed full rotations in pipes, but only did so on specially looped tracks – the move is essentially unachievable on a normal, closed-circle pipe.)[72]

Full-pipes, although largely eclipsed by the many skateparks built in the late 1970s, continued to fascinate skateboarders: for example, in 1979 *SkateBoarder* ran an extended article on the discovery in Mexico of long underground sections of 24-foot diameter cooling pipes, possibly part of the US government's 'Project Atlas' missile complex.[73]

One explanation for the compelling attraction of pools, ditches and full-pipes concerns their appearance as second nature. That these constructions were commonly located in the wastelands, deserts and forgotten spaces of the city was a condition which imbued them with an archaeological character – they appeared to be primeval material elements since forgotten by the inhabitants of the city. They were also all originally to do with the containment and movement of water, the very absence of water heightening the sense of the world having moved from the presence of nature to the domination of nature. As such, they appeared as pure urban and pure second nature, just as pure first nature is at once 'abyss and possible action', yielding a terrifying glimpse of the origins of possibility;[74] in other words, for skaters the ditch, suburban road, pool and schoolyard bank, and particularly the vast sweeps of Californian concrete canalized rivers, causeways, reservoirs and pipes represented the original concrete nature from and against which the possibility of skating was derived. A 'Mellow Cat' cartoon in *SkateBoarder* reflected this meaning, showing a 'dreampipe' in a dinosaur-inhabited hidden valley and reached by way of 'flow portals' and the 'ancient gravitational powers of the Ma-Bu-Hu'.[75]

As a result of the developments in the pipes and pools, publicized in magazines such as *SkateBoarder*, southern Californian skateboarders in places such as Los Angeles and San Diego gained an international reputation.

> Southern California is the Hawaiian Islands of skateboarding. The parks and pools of California are to skating what surf breaks like Sunset Beach, Laniakea or Pipeline are to surfing. It's the proving ground of the best skateboarders of the world.[76]

72. Duane Peters, interview, *Thrasher*, vol. 2 no. 2 (February 1982), p. 26; Don Redondo, 'The Last Ride, or, We've Almost Lost Del Mar', *Thrasher*, vol. 6 no. 2 (February 1986), p. 49; and Tony Hawk, interview, *TransWorld Skateboarding*, vol. 15 no. 10 (October 1997), pp. 112 and 240.

73. Sam Fernando, 'Giant Pipes', *SkateBoarder*, vol. 5 no. 10 (May 1979), pp. 60–8; and Grant C. Reynolds, letter, *SkateBoarder's Action Now*, vol. 7 no. 5 (December 1980), p. 12.

74. Lefebvre, *Introduction to Modernity*, p. 138.

75. Ted Richards, 'Mellow Cat' cartoon, *SkateBoarder*, vol. 4 no. 10 (May 1978), pp. 128–31.

76. Curtis Hesselgrave, 'Krypto Ball', *SkateBoarder*, vol. 4 no. 11 (June 1978), p. 108.

In particular, the skaters of Santa Monica invented a new name for their territory, 'Dogtown'. The name of Dogtown was possibly invented by skater, writer, manufacturer, artist and general skateboard legend Craig Stecyk.[77] But whatever its origins, Dogtown served to set Santa Monica skaters apart from the rest of Los Angeles and California both physically and socially. This was the most intense of skateboarding domains, and became the most famous of skateboard centres, attaining a mythic status and reputation:

> Only God could have created Dogtown.[78]

Indeed, the Dogtown aura had a major influence worldwide, as one skater recalled two decades later.

> It's unbelievable the impact the Dogtown influence had on that teenage boy I was.[79]

SUBURBAN POOL PARTY

Above all, it was the urban spatial tactics of Dogtown's skaters that became most famous, as skaters elsewhere sought not only to emulate the Dogtowners' moves but also the treatment of the city as a whole.

On the one hand, this meant finding locations within the city that could be appropriated for skateboarding. The schoolyard banks, pools, ditches and pipes were all found spaces, already present in the urban realm, which acquired the sense in skateboarding of having been revealed from behind the physical veil of the city. Thus pools were usually on private land, hidden in the back lands of the house lot and obscured by hedges, fences and natural terrain. The drainage ditches were spatially distant from residential areas, found out in the interstitial infrastructural zones, accessible only from unknown (and often protected) entrance points. Pipes, for their part, were mostly in the deserts, away from the city altogether, like forgotten ziggurats within the dense forests of Central America. Even the schoolyard banks, although part of everyday spatial knowledge, were 'discovered' through being rethought as ocean wave. All these terrains were already there, but awaited disclosure.

It also meant inserting a new activity into an area which could accommodate it. Thus while the primary rationale of the villa habitat is that of speculation on plots and property,[80] pool skateboarding was an insertion within suburban residential

77. According to Gabriel, 'Rolling', pp. 73–6, and Brooke, *Concrete Wave*, p. 136.

78. Fido, letter, *SkateBoarder*, vol. 3 no. 6 (July 1977), p. 18.

79. Kent Schiffman, letter, *Thrasher*, vol. 17 no. 9 (September 1997), p. 12.

80. Lefebvre, *Writings on Cities*, pp. 78–9; and Lefebvre, 'Reflections on the Politics of Space', in *Antipode*, vol. 8 no. 2 (May 1976), p. 33.

space – specifically the relatively accessible outdoor space of the pool – and so attacked its property logic, appropriating spaces for use rather than investing for exchange. This process is much more evident in the urban street skating of the 1980s–1990s, to which I return in Chapters Seven and Eight.

The spatial tactics associated with skateboarding were, then, initially those of reconnaissance, roving the city to identify new spaces for skateboarding.

> I guess the most fun was stickin' with all the guys on the team and goin' out and finding pools and stuff.[81]

Journeys by bicycle, car and skateboard were used to survey local neighbourhoods and more distant areas systematically, keeping eyes, ears and nose tuned for such telling signs as 'pump houses, high pool fencing, pool sweeps, slides, the smell of chlorine, inflatable pool toys, solar-power panels, big hoses gushing for days or chlorine deposits (white salt marks) on the gutters of a street',[82] plus pool cleaning trucks and the hum of pump motors.[83] 'It's an art form of sorts, hunting pools.'[84] Very occasionally, a small aeroplane would be deployed to overfly a likely neighbourhood, looking for the tell-tale gleam of a white pool.

Most often, the targets were houses with pools that had been temporarily drained, either for periodic maintenance or for the winter months.[85]

> It's a long alley through a long suburban block, the boundary of a neighborhood of backyards. From the alley we can tell which yards have pools, so we stop at each one and do a pull-up to peek over the wall. Forty-nine times out of 50 the pool is full of crystal clear, refreshing water – inviting but unskateable. But that one smooth-walled, empty bowl is worth every pull-up, every unrewarding alley.[86]

Alternatively, the frequent fires in the Hollywood Hills and Santa Monica mountains often left numerous abandoned homes with ridable pools[87] – for example, on the first day of a major fire in the Santa Barbara area of California some 20 skateable pools were quickly identified.[88] Other favoured targets were homes that were being architecturally remodelled, airport districts with homes that had been abandoned for reasons of health-noise, plus low-rental residential districts and high schools where

81. Adams, interview, p. 53.
82. 'On Being a Pool Mercenary', *Thrasher*, vol. 1 no. 11 (November 1981), p. 21.
83. Bob Denike, 'Skater's Edge', *Thrasher*, vol. 4 no. 5 (May 1984), p. 14.
84. Steve Alba, 'Prime Evil', *Thrasher*, vol. 12 no. 1 (January 1992), p. 49.
85. 'Pool Mercenary', p. 21.
86. Hamm, 'Coping', p. 48.
87. 'Off the Wall', *SkateBoarder's Action Now*, vol. 7 no. 7 (February 1981), p. 16; and 'Pool Mercenary', p. 22.
88. 'Trash', *Thrasher*, vol. 10 no. 10 (October 1990), p. 106.

pools were often drained in order to save costs.[89] Motel pools – such as Pink's Motel in the San Fernando Valley[90] – were a particular favourite as they tended to be slightly larger than the domestic version.[91] Aerial maps were also consulted in the local City Hall, enabling suitable pools to be identified, and the municipal authorities could even be enlisted to drain some pools, as, for safety reasons, Californian codes often required this to be done for pools that had been left unsupervised for longer than two weeks.[92]

These kinds of search were replicated across the USA, where pools were also skated in places such as East Hampton on Long Island,[93] the 'Rathole' in Texas,[94] and even in the UK with the 'Dustbowl' in the grounds of a house under construction in Croydon.[95] Mostly, however, pool-hunting was a Californian activity, as described by Tony Alva.

> The thing we were into most was to find as many skate spots as possible, and making the most of them. We found as many pools as we could and just skated the hell out of them.[96]

Once located, however, a different set of spatial methods set in. Occasionally, the tactic was a one-off hit such as, for example, skateboarding a single session in a backyard pool until the irate owner or police arrived to throw the skaters off the land.

> A common practice in skating pools is the fifteen-minute rule. It usually takes five minutes for the people to realize we're there, five minutes for them to call the cops, and five minutes for the cops to arrive.[97]

Here, the danger of being caught became part of the attraction, heightening the sense of discovery of this otherwise unknown terrain.

89. 'Pool Mercenary', pp. 21–2; and Steve Alba, 'Walk Through the Valley of Death', *Thrasher*, vol. 10 no. 6 (June 1990), p. 50.

90. Boyd Harnell, 'California Pool Project', *Skateboard!*, no. 10 (June 1978), p. 71.

91. Sam P. Jones V, 'The Motel Room', *SkateBoarder*, vol. 3 no. 1 (October 1976), pp. 60–1.

92. 'Pool Mercenary', p. 21.

93. Friedman, *Fuck You Too*, n.p.

94. 'Tres Amigos de Texas', *Thrasher*, vol. 10 no. 3 (March 1990), pp. 60–3.

95. 'Who's Hot: John Sablosky', *Skateboard!*, no. 2 (October 1977), p. 37; 'Star Shots: Jeremy Henderson', *Skateboard!*, no. 5 (January 1978), p. 29; and Tim Lewis, interview, *Skateboard!*, no. 9 (May 1978), p. 62.

96. Alva, interview, *Thrasher*, p. 29.

97. Alba, 'Valley of Death', p. 50.

> If you're going to skate pools and stuff, it's better to be ready for anything . . . ready for police, ready for the owner, for dogs, anything. Part of pool riding is the adventure of being ready for anything that's gonna come down. Same with riding pipes in Arizona, some radical things happen. There's these crazy red-neck sheriffs and you gotta look out for them. You gotta be able to skate good and fast, run good and fast or else be able to fight good . . . It's every man for himself. If the cops come, you're not going to be holding your friend's hand. Everybody's just going to go their separate ways. Just hope you get away with it.[98]

This has been a long tradition in pool hunting, with skaters in the 1980s and 1990s pursuing similar tactics and encountering similar problems.

> One time we went to this one, and we staked it out, it was six in the morning. We got in and bailed it, then kicked it for an hour or so in there, waiting for the right time when no one was around. We started skating and shit, and I had the camera. We rode it for like thirty-forty minutes, then all of a sudden this big fat dude comes running out . . . We just grabbed our shit and hopped like three fences, we had all this shit, this guy was yelling out for blood.[99]

> The riding begins and we trace higher and higher lines through the deep-end, feeling out the transitions. We don't have much time. The house is abandoned and gutted, so there are no residents to oust us. But there are watchful neighbors who'd just as well see a bunch of skaters cuffed and stuffed . . . It's all good fun until Johnny Law arrives.[100]

The emphasis here was on appropriation as spontaneous and the ephemeral – a particularly temporal consideration of the spatial that involves the discontinuous (temporally and spatially) use of particular parts of the city. The social space-time of the pool was thus somewhere between a raid and a party, a short-lived event not to be missed.

> PO-OL PARTY TONIGHT
>
> We're going to have a dry pool party tonight!
> AWRIGHT!
>
> We're going to have a dry pool party awright!
> TONIGHT!

98. Alva, interview, *SkateBoarder*, p. 80.
99. Scott Smiley, interview, *Thrasher*, vol. 16 no. 2 (February 1996), p. 77.
100. Hamm, 'Coping', p. 48.

> We've got nothing better to do
> than skate this pool and pay some heavy dues
>
> Everybody's gonna hang out here tonight!
> AWRIGHT!
>
> We'll pump that water out awright!
> TONIGHT!
>
> We've got nothing better to do
> than pump this pool and have a couple of brews
>
> Don't think about anything else
> we just wanna SKATE
> It'll be dry for only two days
> I don't wanna be LATE.
>
> Harsh vert wall, real blue tiles, death box, coping.[101]

But not all skate tactics were isolated raids. Wherever possible, skaters returned to the same drainage ditch or pool again and again.

> No bust situations are great for morale.[102]

Here naming the space became important, providing a consensus label by which skaters could refer to locations – hence 'Toilet Bowl', 'Dog Bowl', 'Manhole' and so on. In recording these places, photographers such as Friedman sometimes made up the names for ephemeral locations – such as 'BBC Pool', 'Barney Miller's' and 'A-Rab Pool' – when submitting images for publication, but others – such as 'Key-Hole', 'Fruit Bowl', 'Kona Bowl' and 'Soul Bowl' – were frequently used and acquired established reputations.[103] In part this naming process was a matter of communication and orientation, but, contradictorily, it also helped to keep the exact location of the pool hidden from other skaters, and hence to protect the pool from over-use or unwanted attention[104] – this was, once gain, a tactic borrowed from surfers, who had long done this in order to keep certain surf spots from becoming overcrowded. The tactic was also adopted for the desert pipes, whose exact location in Arizona was not disclosed to *SkateBoarder*'s readers.

101. 'Pool Party', *Thrasher*, vol. 2 no. 11 (December 1982), p. 35.
102. Alba, 'Valley of Death', p. 50.
103. Glen E. Friedman, e-mail (29 March 1997).
104. 'Semi Secret Spots', *Thrasher*, vol. 1 no. 1 (January 1981), pp. 22–4.

> Those locations are top secret. You won't find them listed in the Yellow Pages. It's all strictly classified information – unless, of course, you know someone who knows someone who . . .[105]

> You had to hide your pools from people and keep them secret.[106]

> The less people you tell, the longer you will skate . . . The lips of fools lose pools.[107]

For some locations, such as the 'Dog Bowl', skaters negotiated legal access,[108] and here (particularly when published in magazines) the names helped to inculcate the mystique of a remote sun-soaked paradise, clearly real yet excitingly (and frustratingly) known only to a select few.

Protected in this way, some pools and other locations were skated repeatedly, lasting weeks, months or even years; by the end of the 1980s, the 'Buena Vista' pool near Santa Cruz was rumoured to have been empty for over 30 years[109] and skated for over 15 years.[110] In such cases, pools frequently became colonized by skateboarders, who sought to create their own isolated territories, known and accessible to a carefully controlled group. Skateboarders were here acting in a manner akin to anarchist communities, in that they were tending to work with nature (found terrains) and to be spontaneous in their actions. Skaters, again like anarchist communities, also preferred to rapidly replace this spontaneity with the socio-spatial tactic of colonization whenever possible, such that established skateboard locations like the 'Key-Hole', 'Canyon Pool', and 'Soul Bowl' generated their own names, boundaries, access conditions and internal culture. This was particularly evident in the use of graffiti on many colonized pools, where skaters frequently sprayed the terrain surface not only to mark it for themselves, celebrating its transfer to the domain of skateboarding, but also against others, marking off the terrain (3.9). As one skater's poem, 'The Killer Pool', explained:

> The location of this radical spot
> Is kept a secret, believe it or not
> This keeps out the wimps and others who don't skate a lot[111]

105. Mick Angiulo, 'Rampage', *SkateBoarder*, vol. 4 no. 3 (October 1977), p. 61.
106. Gary Cross, in N-Men, interview, *Heckler* (accessed 5 May 1996).
107. Brian Brannon, 'Pool Jones', *Thrasher*, vol. 7 no. 11 (November 1987), p. 87.
108. 'Off the Wall', *SkateBoarder*, vol. 4 no. 5 (December 1977), p. 150; and Tony Alva, interview, *Skateboard!*, no. 5 (January 1978), p. 66.
109. Roberts, 'Santa Cruz', p. 80.
110. 'Somethin' Else', *Thrasher*, vol. 6 no. 3 (March 1986), p. 95.
111. Joe Hartline, 'The Killer Pool', *Thrasher*, vol. 6 no. 3 (March 1986), p. 50.

3.9 Colonized terrain. Steve Ruffing in the graffiti-covered Scron pool, San Fernando Valley (1977). (Photograph Boyd Harnell)

Pools thus became socio-spatial boundaries, those important social spaces forbidding access to anyone outside the sanctioned group.[112]

But above all, it was the presence of skaters, and not just the pool itself, which helped to define the social space of the pool. As Stacy Peralta described it:

> If the boys are there, the competitive thing is really intense. I've seen outsiders who are pretty good skaters just walk away from a heavy session without riding; I guess they thought it was too insane.[113]

It was, therefore, the skaters and their actions which were important – not just the physical architecture of the pool. (Interestingly, skater Alex Moul later had the same to say about urban street skating: 'everywhere is the best: wherever there's a session going on'.)[114]

Beside aiding in territory- and group-formation, specific pools and pipes also served to control the internal relations of particular groups. As Lefebvre notes, people use space, and particularly boundary spaces of passage and encounter, to create their own social identity, and often do so through spaces of ritual and initiation.[115]

> Man does not live by words alone; all 'subjects' are situated in a space in which they must either recognize themselves or lose themselves, a space which they may both enjoy and modify. In order to accede to this space, individuals (children, adolescents) who are, paradoxically, already within it, must pass tests. This has the effect of setting up reserved spaces, such as places of initiation, within social space.[116]

The pools in particular thus became places of initiation, dangerous (through accident or social confrontation) places where young men might prove themselves to their peers.

112. Lefebvre, *Production of Space*, p. 193.
113. Peralta, interview, *SkateBoarder*, p. 58.
114. Alex Moul, in 'Think of Oxford', *R.A.D.*, no. 86 (April 1990), p. 43.
115. Lefebvre, *Production of Space*, p. 193.
116. Ibid., p. 35.

> There was a round pool with thirty foot walls
> To ride this pool you had to have big balls
> Three skaters were dead, two had broken legs
> One had a broken arm and there were four empty kegs[117]

> People who sat around didn't say shit, because it was sweat and you knew there could be a brawl. But the brawl was in the pool. You'd go in the pool and you'd tell the guy to fuck off by doing a better run than his last run. You'd stay in longer.[118]

The focus here was on danger, pain and bodily injury, but also on the competitively collective nature of the group, created from a set of extreme individual attitudes and actions.

> If you get the right combination of terrorists, it's going to happen no matter what. You can't prevent it, can't control it, and can't avoid it.[119]

> When the boys are together, you could never find a more aggressive, arrogant, rowdy, perhaps ignorant bunch of people than my friends. That's the way we are; that's the way we skateboard; that's the way we talk.[120]

It was not the skaters' actions or pools alone which created this condition, but both together, changing specific location and configuration over time.

> The site of these high-octane situations continually floats . . . The site might be in the wilds at a spot known only to the inner circle, or it may be in a more public forum.[121]

Rather than a purely physical or purely social condition, this was a socio-spatial co-production where architecture and activity were concrete enactions of each other.

Together, the tactics of appropriation, colonization and identity formation helped skaters to redefine both the city and themselves. By making a different edit of the urban realm from alternative locations and times, skateboarders transformed the sedately suburban character of Los Angeles into dramatic concrete constructions, exploited under an air of espionage. In terms of the normative context in which skateboarders were operating, it is worth recalling that suburbanites see (falsely) the house as representative of Nature, liberty, privacy and escape from everyday life,[122]

117. Hartline, 'Killer Pool', p. 50.

118. Duane Peters, interview, *Thrasher*, vol. 9 no. 6 (June 1989), p. 94.

119. John Smythe (pseudonym for Craig Stecyk), 'Opening Day at the Park', *SkateBoarder*, vol. 4 no. 2 (September 1977), p. 65.

120. Tony Alva, *SkateBoarder*, vol. 3 no. 3, in Friedman, *Fuck You Heroes*, index.

121. Smythe, 'Opening Day', p. 65.

122. Lefebvre, *Everyday Life in the Modern World* (London: Transaction Publishers, 1984), pp. 121–2; Lefebvre, *Writings on Cities*, pp. 75–6.

a 'mirror of their "reality," tranquillizing ideas, and the image of a social world in which they have their own specially labelled, guaranteed place'.[123] Skateboarders, however, made the suburb explicitly urban in character, rendering it more confrontational, hence disclosing the 'schizophrenic' character of urban space – the coexistence of spaces of play, spaces of exchange and circulation, political space and cultural space.[124] In particular, skateboarders resurrected the dead street of the suburb, not in order to reintegrate it with the residential home but with their own social life.

Thus where the decentralized suburb promotes life as divorced from the city, isolating people from participatory creativity,[125] skateboarders related individual life to the form of the city, reintroducing the city as creative and active oeuvre and thus conceptually moving the suburb closer to the complex contradictions of the city core. These are all aspects of skateboarding which are even more explicit in the street skating of the 1980s and 1990s, and which are discussed in more detail in Chapters Seven and Eight.

Before moving on, however, it is important to realize that there is a problem here: while skaters in their finding and colonization of pools and other terrains implicitly treated space as if it were 'natural', as something to be seized and used as a pre-existent thing, it is in fact a social product. What they thought to have 'found' was really not only a production as first created, but also a production of themselves seeking to use it for skateboarding. And in doing so, skateboarders' reproduction of the architecture and urban space of the city conflicted with the reproduction of that same space by others. Thus the pools and pipes used by skaters were commonly reclaimed by these others (police, owners, developers).

That skaters ultimately lost out in this confrontation is because of an inherent time-space contradiction within their tactics at this stage in skateboarding's development. On the one hand, they undertook what Lefebvre calls a 'primitive history', merely marking, naming and traversing natural space.[126] However, treating buildings and spaces as texts, rather than as 'archi-textures' of time, space and rhythms,[127] means that skateboarders mistook marking natural space for the creation of social space. In particular, where they tried to produce social space, by colonizing space for a period of time, it is precisely the condition of temporality over which they ultimately had no control: although a pool or pipe might be appropriated for a short period of time (a few minutes or hours), the longer temporality of colonization (repeated visits over weeks or months), together with the notion of 'ownership' which

123. Lefebvre, *Production of Space*, p. 309.
124. Lefebvre, *Writings on Cities*, pp. 171–2.
125. Ibid., pp. 75–7.
126. Lefebvre, *Production of Space*, p. 142.
127. Ibid., p. 118.

colonization implies, is not something that other, more powerful social groups were willing to accept. Occasional appropriations might be tolerated, but permanence was not.

These early skateboarders were in fact not so much appropriating as co-opting space and time – a practice which lies intermediate to domination and appropriation, and between exchange and use.[128] Co-optation means taking over without mastering, appropriating without ephemerality, and can be a useful strategy where control is guaranteed by other means such as by political rule or law. Except that skateboarders did not own or otherwise control the spaces which they sought to co-opt; and, therefore, this was not a strategy which for them was likely to succeed on any but the rarest of occasions.

If skateboarders were to be able to skate with impunity, different locations and tactics were required to either escape confrontation altogether or to create confrontation under circumstances that might be controllable by skaters themselves. Above all, this means acting in relation to time as well as space, for 'appropriation cannot be understood apart from rhythms of time and life'. Appropriation is not the simple reuse of a building or space, but a creative reworking of its time and its space.[129] As shown in Chapters Seven and Eight, for skaters this eventually meant a return to city streets.

First, however, I turn to look at a different form of spatial control and production: the purpose-built skateparks of the 1970s. As Muir realized:

> If pool riding is going to survive, you're gonna have to build your own pool to do it.[130]

The next two chapters, therefore, focus on two kinds of constructed terrain. The first is that of the purpose-built skatepark, and Chapter Four investigates the many examples of skateparks that were built worldwide in the late 1970s, as well as looking at the ramp or half-pipe which took over after the demise of most skateparks in the early 1980s. The second constructed terrain is that of the body, and Chapter Five considers the 'super-architectural space' by which body, skateboard and architecture are erased and reborn in the encounter between skateboarder and skateboard architecture.

128. Ibid., pp. 368–9.
129. Ibid., pp. 166–8.
130. Jim Muir, in 'Pool Riding Symposium', p. 75.

Chapter 4

Constructed Space

It's time to build.[1]

CONCRETE UTOPIA

In 1975, southern California had some two million skateboarders.[2] Fuelled by national media coverage in magazines such as *People*, *Sports Illustrated* and *Newsweek*, and by specialist publications such as the re-launched *SkateBoarder* and *Skateboard World* in the US and *Skateboard!*, *Skateboard Scene* and *Skateboard Special* in the UK, skateboarding quickly became a global phenomenon: the US alone had twenty to forty million skateboarders by 1978–9.[3] By 1978, *SkateBoarder* had one million readers and had become extraordinarily influential for manufacturers, photographers, professional and ordinary skateboarders alike.[4]

The other group who read *SkateBoarder* magazine were skatepark designers and investors. Early, unchallenging skateparks had been built in Kelso, Washington, and in Orange County, California, in 1966,[5] together with a community facility with gently rolling paths in the Ventura County area of Los Angeles in the 1970s,[6] but it was predominantly the commercial sector which responded to the skateboarding explosion, creating purpose-built skateparks which exaggerated fragments of the

1. Editor's response to letter, *Action Now*, vol. 7 no. 10 (May 1981), p. 14.

2. La Vada Weir, *Skateboards and Skateboarding: the Complete Beginner's Guide* (New York: Julian Messner, 1977), pp. 14–15; and Hazel Pennell, *Skateboarding* (London: GLC Intelligence Unit, London Topics no. 24, 1978), p. 1.

3. 'Off the Wall', *SkateBoarder*, vol. 4 no. 7 (February 1978), p. 140; Armen Keteyian, 'Chairman of the Board,' *Sports Illustrated*, vol. 65 no. 23 (24 November 1986), p. 47; 'World News', *Skateboard!*, no. 1 (August 1977), p. 17; National Safety Council, *Skateboarding*, (Chicago: Bulletin, The Council, 1978); Hazel Pennell, *Skateboarding*, p. 1; and Phillip M. Wishon and Marcia L. Oreskovich, 'Bicycles, Roller Skates and Skateboards: Safety Promotion and Accident Prevention', *Children Today*, vol. 15 no. 3 (May/June 1986), pp. 11–15, based on American Academy of Pediatricians, *Skateboard Policy Statement* (1979).

4. Glen E. Friedman, e-mail (16 February 1997); and Jay Adams, interview, *SkateBoarder*, vol. 6 no. 4 (November 1979), p. 52.

5. *Popular Science* (April 1966), p. 127, in Brian Gillogly, 'Skate Parks: Part X', *SkateBoarder*, vol. 4 no. 1 (August 1977), p. 95; and Michael Brooke, *The Concrete Wave: the History of Skateboarding* (Toronto: Warwick, 1999), p. 32.

6. Ben J. Davidson, *The Skateboard Book* (New York: Grosset & Dunlap, 1976), p. 46.

4.1 Modulated open spaces used at the first commercial skatepark in California. Carlsbad, (1976). Design by John O'Malley and construction by Jack Graham of Skatepark Constructors. (Photograph Craig Hancock)

city in order to create intentional skateboarding architecture. Such skateparks were promoted as 'one of the 70's most profitable business opportunities',[7] and one national conference for skatepark developers attracted 370 delegates from 35 US states and 8 other countries.[8]

The first commercial Californian skatepark was the concrete 'Carlsbad', opened in the summer of 1975 (4.1). Developed by John O'Malley (design) and Jack Graham (construction) of Skatepark Constructors, the gently-modulated spaces were quite limited in design complexity, and Carlsbad was quickly extended with some more advanced elements. Nor was this activity limited to California, even at this early stage, and by December of 1976 three new parks had been built in Florida –

7. Skatepark Publications, advertisement, *SkateBoarder*, vol. 4 no. 11 (June 1978), p. 28.

8. Mary Horowitz, 'Radical Energy Infiltrates Big Business', *SkateBoarder*, vol. 4 no. 8 (March 1978), p. 120.

'Skatboard (sic) City' (Port Orange/Daytona), 'Paved Wave' (Cocoa) and one other at Pensacola – which continued the tradition of surfing already established in pool skating by mimicking Florida's surfing waves in its architecture, varying the steepness of sections within one run. Skatboard City opened one week before Carlsbad, and so lays claim to being the first proper skatepark.[9] Other skateparks built in 1976 included the 'Yagoo Valley' (Slocum, Rhode Island) and 'Fun Land' (Myrtle Beach, South Carolina) skateparks, this latter facility sporting a bizarre Stars and Stripes colour scheme replete with blue-painted runs decorated with red and white linear stripes.

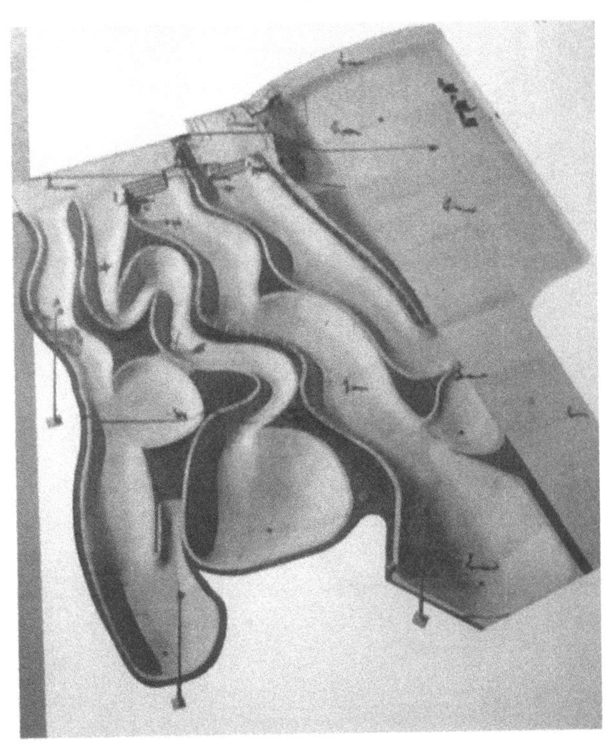

4.2 Individual, linear runs at Concrete Wave, Anaheim, (1977). Developed by C & K Skateparks.

Many new parks were also being planned, and fifteen to twenty skateparks were open by July 1977.[10] Some disclosed the rapid evolution of skatepark design that was by now under way. For example, 'SkaterCross' in Resada, California, offered a variety of elements set within one continuous run.[11] The intention here seems to have been derived both from surfing and from motocross, whereby the skatepark sought to give the skater a long, linear route along which to encounter a number of different spatial situations. Other parks which followed this linear approach to skatepark design included 'Concrete Wave' (Anaheim, California) (4.2) and 'Solid Surf' (Fort Lauderdale, Florida).

9. Bruce Walker, letter, *SkateBoarder's Action Now*, vol. 7 no. 1 (August 1980), p. 15.

10. *SkateBoarder*, vol. 3 no. 6 (July 1977), p. 105.

11. John O'Malley, interview, *SkateBoarder*, vol. 3 no. 6 (July 1977), pp. 105–10; 'Skate Parks: Part IV In Search of Skatopia', *SkateBoarder*, vol. 3 no. 1 (October 1976), pp. 46–53; Brian Gillogly, 'Skate Parks: Part V', *SkateBoarder*, vol. 3 no. 2 (December 1976), pp. 48–55; Brian Gillogly, 'Skate Parks: Part IX', *SkateBoarder*, vol. 3 no. 6 (July 1977), pp. 84–9; Gillogly, 'Skate Parks: Part X', pp. 94–9; 'SkaterCross', Resada, advertisement, *SkateBoarder*, vol. 3 no. 1 (October 1976), p. 30; Bruce Walker, interview, *SkateBoarder*, vol. 3 no. 1 (October 1976), pp. 40–5; and 'The Megalithic Moguls of Carlsbad', *Skateboard!*, no. 7 (March 1978), pp. 56–7.

Whatever their inventiveness, these early skateparks did not, however, offer the challenges of the pipes and backyard pools[12] – many early skatepark developers had never even seen skateboarders in action, and simply fabricated whatever was in their own minds[13] – and many of these early constructions were quickly superseded. One of the premier 'second wave' or 'second generation' skateparks was 'Pipeline' in Upland, in the San Bernadino Valley east of LA, built for around US$125,000. When it opened in May 1977, this skatepark – commonly referred to simply as 'Pipeline' or as 'Upland' – boasted the first circular pipe and fully vertical walls in California intended for skateboarding. The full-pipe (20-foot diameter and 40-foot-long) fed into a 30-foot diameter, 12-foot-deep bowl (4.3). Another bowl measured

4.3 Exaggerated pool and pipe at the Pipeline skatepark, (1977), owned by Jeanne and Stan Hoffman, and managed by their son Don Hoffman. Skateboarder: Gregg Ayres. (Photograph James Cassimus)

12. John Smythe (pseudonym for Craig Stecyk), 'Frontier Tales', *SkateBoarder*, vol. 3 no. 2 (December 1976), pp. 109–11.

13. Horowitz, 'Radical', pp. 120–1; and Wally Inouye, interview, *SkateBoarder*, vol. 4 no. 3 (October 1977), pp. 52–3.

40 feet across and 15 feet deep, with one side overhanging slightly over vertical. Emulating in exaggerated form the pipes, ditches and pools found in the Los Angeles area (especially the nearby Mount Baldy full-pipe) Pipeline was generally considered to be the best skatepark so far[14] – as one skater responded, 'No way, a full-pipe!'[15]

Construction methods as well as the design of skatepark elements were also being developed at this stage, and it is worth noting here that Pipeline and many other skateparks constructed at this time used the gunite process favoured by swimming pool constructors, whereby concrete is sprayed onto a framework – and thus is quite distinct from the *in situ* formwork or prefabricated modules often used in building construction. In the gunite process, cement and sand are mixed without water, forced along a pipe with compressed air, with water introduced at the nozzle end. The amount of water added is controlled by a valve operated by the nozzleman. Gunite is one of the strongest methods of applying concrete, and can be readily applied to vertical or over-vertical walls – but it requires an experienced operator.[16] The other main system used by skatepark constructors was the similar shotcrete or 'wet process', whereby sand, cement and water are pre-mixed before being forced along a pipeline by a pump, with compressed air being added at the nozzle to allow spraying out. This process requires more water than gunite, and so tends to produce a slightly inferior concrete, but has the advantage of requiring less skill on the part of its operator to obtain satisfactory results. The lower pressure of application also means it is less easy to apply to vertical surfaces.[17] In another variant of these methods, an extra smooth finish was also sometimes achieved by covering the concrete with water just before the concrete went off, a technique reportedly used by Wally Hollyday for various Californian skatepark pools.[18]

As design sophistication, construction prowess and market opportunities all increased, and with *SkateBoarder* changing from bi-monthly to monthly publication in the middle of 1977, numerous other US parks opened that year. These included 'Skateboard World' (Torrance, California) designed by Randall Duell and owned by Warwick and Belinda Charlton; 'Skate City' (Whittier, California), incorporating an

14. Brian Gillogly, 'Skate Parks: Part XI', *SkateBoarder*, vol. 4 no. 2 (September 1977), pp. 90–8; Brian Gillogly, 'Skate Parks: Part XIII Breaking New Ground', *SkateBoarder*, vol. 4 no. 4 (November 1977), pp. 92–107; Dudley Counts, 'Upland Gold Cup Finale', *Thrasher*, vol. 1 no. 1 (January 1981), p. 11; 'Upland Pipeline: Closing Comments', *TransWorld Skateboarding*, vol. 7 no. 2 (April 1989), pp. 64–72; Dudley Counts, 'L.A. Skatepark Paradise: Part II', *Thrasher*, vol. 1 no. 4 (April 1981), pp. 9–15; 'Baldy Pipeline', pp. 20–1; and Gerry Hurtado, 'A Radical Decade at the Upland Pipeline', *Thrasher*, vol. 7 no. 6 (June 1987), pp. 77–9.

15. Duane Peters, interview, *Thrasher*, vol. 9 no. 6 (June 1989), p. 34.

16. Gregg Haythorpe, 'Gunite vs. Shotcrete', *Skateboard Scene*, vol. 1 no. 4 (n.d., *c*. February 1978), pp. 46–7.

17. Haythorpe, 'Gunite vs. Shotcrete', pp. 46–7.

18. 'Ears', *R.A.D.*, no. 80 (October 1989), p. 11.

interlocking three-bowl cloverleaf element, full-pipe, capsule pool and small half-pipe; 'Skatopia' (Buena Park, California), opened 1 June, designed and developed by Victor Peloquin, and featuring the 'Escondido Bowl' based in part on the found-space Escondido Reservoir, a 15-foot diameter 175-foot-long half-pipe, and interlocking four-bowl 'Whirlpool' element; 'Skateboard Safari' (West Palm Beach, Florida), owned by Jeff Spencer, featuring the 'Vermont Drop' based on the Californian found-space Vermont Avenue funnel; 'Runway' (Carson, California), also featuring an element based on Vermont Avenue; 'Kona' (Jacksonville, Florida); and 'Longwood Skateboard Track' (Florida), featuring the first full-pipe (12-foot diameter) in a skatepark.[19] Many of these took the same kind of approach as Pipeline, moving away from gentle banks and linear runs of the earlier skateparks to a more dispersed arrangement, in which particular elements are disposed around a field of such elements.

From around 1978, a few months after the first invention of the frontside aerial move (see previous chapter), skatepark design and construction techniques were further refined still further and more precisely for skateboarding, this time avoiding some of the crude elements, transitions and shapes of earlier skateparks. Skaters complained that the existing parks had imperfect surfaces and unfunctional designs and, in particular, that the concrete bowls of even these second-generation skateparks lacked the tiles, coping blocks and smooth white finish of the backyard pools. 'Upland needs coping really bad.'[20] In response to such criticisms, and as competition from other skateparks increased and as skateboard moves became increasingly demanding, many skateparks incorporated pool-style elements. For example, the centrepiece pool at 'Skateboard Heaven', Spring Valley, was a more extreme version of the local backyard 'Soul Bowl' pool much favoured by San Diego skaters, and also included gunite construction, shallow end coves and love seats that had been derived directly from real swimming pools. (In a similar process of replication and transplantation, the main element at the later 'Charleston Hangar Bowl' indoor skatepark (4.15) in Charleston, South Carolina, was based on the architecture of the old backyard San Juan pool in California.[21]) The new pool at Spring Valley was not, however, an exact copy, and where backyard pools were often too small with overly tight transitions and too much vertical wall,[22] the skatepark version offered

19. Gillogly, 'Skate Parks: Part IX', pp. 84–9; Gillogly, 'Skate Parks: Part X', pp. 94–9; Gillogly, 'Skate Parks: Part XI', pp. 90–8; Gillogly, 'Skate Parks: Part XIII', pp. 92–107; 'Off the Wall', *SkateBoarder*, vol. 3 no. 6 (July 1977), p. 128; 'World News', *Skateboard!*, no. 2 (October 1977), p. 22; and Dudley Counts, 'L.A. Skatepark Paradise: Part I', *Thrasher*, vol. 1 no. 3 (March 1981), pp. 10–15.

20. Steve Evans, interview, *SkateBoarder*, vol. 5 no. 6 (January 1979), p. 52.

21. Kevin Wilkins, 'Charleston Hangar Bowl Contest', *TransWorld Skateboarding*, vol. 9 no. 10 (October 1991), p. 71.

22. Chris Miller, interview, *Thrasher*, vol. 9 no. 10 (May 1989), p. 67.

4.4 The lunar-landscape of the mogul field at Carlsbad/Sparks (1977). Skateboarder: Dean Skipper. (Photograph Warren Bolster)

carefully tuned transitions and special slightly over-hanging coping that had been precisely designed for skateboarding; according to Peralta, it was the 'first real pool for skateboarding'.[23] Other parks, such as Carlsbad (renamed Sparks in 1977), added features like large mogul bowl fields, resembling a lunar landscape, in which the flow and transfer of the skater and skateboard from one element to another was encouraged (4.4).[24]

The new parks opened in 1978 further emphasized pool tiles and coping. These facilities included the 'Skate Ranch' (Del Mar, San Diego, California), designed by Curtis Hesselgrave and Tom Inouye, with four pools (one a replica of the local 'Kona' backyard pool),[25] 'Oasis' (San Diego, California), 'Skate in the Shade' (Tempe, Arizona) with pool constructed by Bigelow Enterprises of Mesa, Arizona (run by

4.5 High quality design and construction for a kidney-shaped pool at a third-generation, indoor skatepark, Cherry Hill (1979), owned by Steve Durst.

23. Stacy Peralta, quoted in Brian Gillogly, 'Skate Parks: Part XIV', *SkateBoarder*, vol. 4 no. 5 (December 1977), pp. 82–3.

24. Ibid., pp. 78–81.

25. Garry Davis, 'Del Mar Was . . . ', *TransWorld Skateboarding*, vol. 6 no. 1 (February 1988), pp. 106–11.

former swimming pool builder Duane Bigelow),[26] 'Skatepark Victoria' (Milpitas, California), and 'Winchester' (Campbell, San Jose, California) (5.6). These third-generation skateparks also included the indoor Cherry Hill facility in New Jersey; opened in 1978 and owned by Steve Durst, Cherry Hill had four pools of various configurations, together with a half-pipe leading to a three-quarter pipe, and two reservoir areas (4.5).[27] Dogtown finally acquired its own skatepark with a new facility at Marina del Rey, just south of Venice Beach and Santa Monica; owned and designed by Ray Allen, the Marina del Rey skatepark incorporated features such as the 'Keyhole' and 'Dogbowl' pools (the latter named after the famous local pool), speakers positioned in the vertical pool walls, and shadow-free lighting over all the skating areas (4.6, 5.1, 5.3).[28] Together with Cherry Hill, Marina del Rey rapidly acquired a reputation as one of the most advanced new pool-oriented skateparks. As Jay Adams put it,

> These are the only 2 parks that I enjoy skating at.[29]

As Cherry Hill showed, it was not just California that was responding to the ever-developing skateboard scene. Other advanced parks included 'Get Away' (Huntsville, Alabama), designed by Wally Hollyday and Peter Drotlef, and 'Apple' (Columbus, Ohio), the latter being owned by Gene Goldburg and designed by Hollyday and Drotlef with construction by Bigelow. Apple was a 40,000-square-foot indoor facility boasting no fewer than eight pool-bowls, including an egg-shaped pool, large kidney pool and small keyhole pool. As with many of these new parks, construction techniques were now being seen to be as important as design, and extreme attention was consequently paid to the piano-wire shaping templates, to the application of the concrete and to the gray-coat cement finishing work.[30]

In response to these all-new skateparks, the slightly older parks such as Skatopia, Skate City and Pipeline added their own pools, this element often being constructed with much more care and understanding as to what constituted a skateable terrain.[31] For Skate City, this was a simple keyhole pool,[32] but for Pipeline, this meant replacing the former flat, freestyle area of the skatepark with the famous 'Combi-Pool', constructed in the summer of 1979 – effectively a 32-foot-wide and 12-foot-deep square

26. Duane Bigelow and Wally Hollyday, interview, *SkateBoarder*, vol. 6 no. 8 (March 1980), p. 61.

27. Shogo Kubo, interview, *SkateBoarder*, vol. 5 no. 10 (May 1979), p. 36.

28. Gregg Ayres, 'Ramps 79: a Discussion with Ramp Pioneer Ray Allen', *SkateBoarder*, vol. 5 no. 9 (April 1979), p. 54; and Counts, 'Paradise: Part I', p. 10.

29. Adams, interview, p. 52.

30. Wally Hollyday, letter, *SkateBoarder*, vol. 6 no. 5 (December 1979), p. 17; Michael Musgrave, letter, *SkateBoarder*, vol. 6 no. 7 (February 1980), p. 17; and Bigelow and Hollyday, interview, pp. 64–6.

31. Dee Urquhart and Iain Urquhart, 'A Look at America', *Skateline*, no. 8 (Spring 1982), p. 18.

32. Curtis Hesselgrave, 'Whittier Knights: Skate City – Hester Pro Bowl #4', *SkateBoarder*, vol. 6 no. 5 (December 1979), p. 25.

4.6 Pool at Marina del Rey skatepark, incorpating wall-positioned sound system and shadow-free lighting (1978). Owned and designed by Ray Allen. Skateboarder: David Andrecht. (Photograph Craig Fineman)

4.7 The notorious Combi-Pool, Pipeline, Upland. View over entrance point and shallow end (foreground) towards square (left) and round (right) pools, with intermediary hips (middle). Note the large areas of flat bottom and vertical wall, mediated by fast transitions. Design by Don Hoffman and others, construction by Bigelow Enterprises (1979).

pool with rounded corners and a 30-foot diameter 11-foot-deep circular pool joined together at a common shallow end and entrance point (4.7, 5.10). Designed by Don Hoffman over the course of six months in collaboration with professional skateboarders, and constructed by Bigelow for around US$30,000, the Combi-Pool offered the same white walls, blue tiles and concrete coping as a typical backyard pool, but offered increased depth (and hence more danger), greater areas of wall (3 feet of pure vertical), faster transitions from base to wall, a flat bottom between walls and a smoother surface optimized for skateboard wheels.[33] The shallow end, tight corners of the square pool and the hip where the two pools joined together offered further variations of terrain, and the overall result was 'unquestionably the finest, most demanding terrain ever developed for skating',[34] the 'ultimate

33. Curtis Hesselgrave, 'Hester Finale: Battling in the Badlands, Again', *SkateBoarder*, vol. 6 no. 6 (January 1980), p. 23; Bigelow and Hollyday, interview, p. 61; 'Upland Pipeline', pp. 64–72; Urquhart and Urquhart, 'America', p. 18; Hurtado, 'Decade', p. 78; and *Thrasher*, vol. 9 no. 6 (June 1989), pp. 53–8 and 127.

34. Hesselgrave, 'Hester', p. 23.

playground'.[35] Other skateparks also continued to add similar new centrepiece elements; the 'Ranch' (Colton, California) constructed the rose-tinted 'Hollyday Bowl' to host its Gold Cup event in 1980,[36] and Skateboard World (Lakewood, California) opened a clam-shaped pool in July 1981.[37]

By the end of the 1970s, the Los Angeles region had gained many skateparks of a similar standard to that of Pipeline, including 'Endless Wave' (Bakersfield) and 'Big "O"' (Orange).[38] This was big business; construction costs for a large skatepark averaged around US$200,000–250,000 in the 1975–80 period (although some were built for around US$60,000),[39] while Get Away and Skateboard World may have cost as much as US$1 million.[40] By 1982 over 190 skateparks had been built in the US across at least 35 states, of which over a quarter (48) were in California, 22 in Florida and 16 in Texas.[41] Many boasted large membership figures – 2,000 skateboarders joined the 'Olympic' skatepark at Olympia, Washington.[42]

This specialized architectural activity was repeated throughout America, Europe, South America and Asia. Furthermore, many if not all of these skateparks chose to mimic backyard Californian swimming pools, Arizona pipeline projects and other features of American architecture and civil engineering.

In the UK, skateboarding started to take off in the summer of 1976,[43] with *Skateboard!* magazine (which covered US as well as local skateboarding developments) arguing for new skateparks to be built to accommodate it. This demand was met by over eighty purpose-built skateparks of varying sizes, sophistication and financial basis.[44] By the end of the summer of 1977, these already included 'Skate-Escape' (Portland Bill), built by Lorne Edwards after a visit to the Concrete Wave skatepark in the US,[45] 'Stalybridge Bowl' (near Manchester),[46] 'Watergate Bowl' (near Newquay),[47] and the community 'Meanwhile Gardens' designed by skater

35. Miller, interview, *Thrasher*, p. 102.

36. Curtis Hesselgrave, 'The Ranch/Variflex Cup', *SkateBoarder's Action Now*, vol. 7 no. 4 (November 1980), pp. 19–20; and Counts, 'Paradise: Part II', pp. 12–13.

37. Urquhart and Urquhart, 'America', p. 16.

38. Counts, 'Paradise: Part I', pp. 10–15; and Counts, 'Paradise: Part II', pp. 9–15.

39. 'Skate Parks: Part IV', p. 48; and Hollyday, letter.

40. 'World News', (October 1977), p. 22; and Bigelow and Hollyday, interview, p. 65.

41. Analysis based on Iain Borden, 'Appendix A: Skateparks', in 'A Theorised History of Skateboarding, with Particular Reference to the Ideas of Henri Lefebvre', (University of London/University College London, PhD thesis, 1998). A copy of this listing of skateparks worldwide is available from the author on request.

42. D. David Morin, 'Survival Revival', *SkateBoarder's Action Now*, vol. 7 no. 8 (March 1981), pp. 70–1.

43. Tim Lewis, interview, *Skateboard!*, no. 9 (May 1978), p. 61.

44. *Skateboard!*, *passim*; and Borden, 'Appendix A: Skateparks'.

45. 'Welcome to Skateboard Escape! UK's First Skate Park Opens at Portland', *Skateboard!*, no. 1 (August 1977), pp. 48–51.

46. 'UK News' (October 1977), p. 17; and 'UK News', *Skateboard!*, no. 4 (December 1977), p. 19.

47. 'Wheels Roll Out West', *Skateboard!*, no. 2 (October 1977), pp. 31–5.

Marc Sinclair[48] (Notting Hill, London),[49] but these were as unchallenging as the very first US skateparks, and British skaters were in desperate need of more advanced facilities.[50]

The first commercial skatepark in the UK with vertical bowls for skateboarding was the shotcrete 'Skate City', built by Skate Park Construction[51] and opened in London in the summer of 1977. Although a far cry from the more elaborate contemporary US skateparks, Skate City offered the UK its first real skatepark, with three bowls of varying difficulty, including an 'advanced pipeline' quickly dubbed the Black Bowl, and some indoor wooden ramps.[52]

Apart from innumerable small facilities around the UK, such as the Thruxton bowl,[53] more complex skateparks began to appear in 1978. These included the 'Malibu Dog Bowl' (Nottingham),[54] and 'Skateboard City' (Bolton).[55] With many different investment (Tate & Lyle[56]), swimming pool (Skate Park Construction, an off-shoot of Rainbow Pools[57]), tennis court (En-tout-cas[58]) and construction (Bovis[59]) companies exploiting the new market, but with little expertise, the standards of these facilities were, unsurprisingly, extremely variable; respectable bodies such as the GLC, the National Playing Fields Association and the Sports Council struggled to give out advice on skatepark design and provision.[60] The Malibu Dog Bowl, for example, and despite offering a number of different elements, suffered from severe transitions, inadequate elevation drops into the main bowl, and obstructions. The managers also decided to fit out this indoor skatepark with distracting spotlights, and the overall effect was to render this particular skatepark nearly unridable for any but the most determined and experienced of skaters.[61]

48. Rodga Harvey, in 'The Power of London', *Thrasher*, vol. 6 no. 12 (December 1989), p. 60.

49. 'Skate News', *Skateboard!*, no. 1 (August 1977), p. 13; and Meany, 'Concrete', *Skateboard!* (second series), no. 43 (June 1990), pp. 44–6.

50. Stan Hey, 'Wheeler and Dealers,' *Time Out*, no. 381 (15–21 July 1977), pp. 12–13.

51. Skate Park Construction, advertisement, *Skateboard!*, no. 4 (December 1977), p. 51.

52. 'The Sun Rises on Skate City', *Skateboard!*, no. 2 (October 1977), pp. 28–30; 'UK News', *Skateboard!*, no. 3 (November 1977), p. 8; and François Brown de Colstoun, 'Skate City, London', *Skate* (France), no. 2 (Mars/Avril 1978), pp. 23–5.

53. 'New Parks and Bowls: Thruxton', *Skateboard!*, no. 6 (February 1978), p. 53; and 'Parking It! Thruxton Explored', *Skateboard Scene*, vol. 1 no. 3 (n.d., *c.* January 1978), pp. 42–3.

54. 'Lip Torque', *Skateboard!*, no. 8 (April 1978), p. 50.

55. 'New Parks and Bowls', *Skateboard!*, no. 8 (April 1978), p. 65; and 'Nationwide', *Skateboard Scene*, vol. 1 no. 4 (n.d., *c.* February 1978), p. 39.

56. New owners of Skate City, London. 'Lip Torque', *Skateboard!*, no. 10 (June 1978), p. 37.

57. Tim Leighton-Boyce, letter (5 June 1997).

58. En-tout-cas, advertisement, *Skateboard!*, no. 8 (April 1978), p. 3.

59. Skate City Bovis, advertisement, *Skateboard!*, no. 6 (February 1978), p. 79.

60. Neil Heayes, 'All Aboard for the Skateboard Take-Off', *Contract Journal* (19 January 1978), pp. 22–3.

61. 'New Parks and Bowls', *Skateboard!*, no. 9 (May 1978), p. 48.

By mid-1978, the first 'second-generation' UK skateparks appeared, including the UK£50,000 En-tout-cas-designed park at Southsea, with mogul field and numerous bowls.[62] 'Skateopia' (Knebworth House, Hertfordshire), designed by High-Point Developments of Birmingham and constructed in gunite by Trant Ltd, offered various snake runs, bowls and a half-pipe,[63] while the indoor 'Rolling Thunder' (Brentford, London), named after a Bob Dylan tour, contained numerous bowls and a long half-pipe, and was designed by Richard Wrigley[64] who had previously been responsible for London's 'Skate City'.[65] Other large skateparks included 'Skateworld' (Wokingham),[66] 'Earth and Ocean' (Barnstaple), 'Kelvingrove Wheelies' (Kelvingrove, Scotland),[67] 'Plymouth Skatepark' (Plymouth), 'Skateopia' (Wolverhampton),[68] 'Skatestar' (Guildford),[69] 'Stevenage Skatepark' (Stevenage), 'Southport Skatepark' (Southport), 'Spandrel Skate-Dome' (Uxbridge), 'Arrow' (Wolverhampton) and 'Roxyskate' (Swinton, Doncaster).

Other UK skateparks – principally the shotcrete projects designed by G-Force/Adrian Rolt and built by Skate Park Construction – used standardized elements drawn directly from America (4.8, 4.9, 5.5).[70] This series included the 'Rom' (Romford)

4.8 Standardized skatepark elements at Black Lion, Gillingham (1978). From left to right: keyhole pool, halfpipe, snake run, reservoir. Design by G-Force/Adrian Rolt, construction by Skate Park Construction. (Photograph Ian Dobbie)

62. 'Lip Torque', *Skateboard!*, no. 12 (August 1978), p. 30.
63. 'New Parks and Bowls', *Skateboard!*, no. 12 (August 1978), p. 41.
64. 'Lip Torque' (June 1978), p. 38.
65. 'Skatepark Supertest: Rolling Thunder, Brentford', *Skateboard!*, no. 16 (December 1978), pp. 50–2; and Benito Schwartz, 'Travels with the King, Part III', *SkateBoarder*, vol. 6 no. 5 (December 1979), p. 64.
66. 'New Parks and Bowls', *Skateboard!*, no. 13 (September 1978), p. 42.
67. 'New Parks and Bowls', *Skateboard!*, no. 14 (October 1978), p. 35.
68. 'New Parks and Bowls' (October 1978), p. 33.
69. 'New Parks and Bowls' (September 1978), p. 43.
70. 'Lip Torque', *Skateboard!*, no. 9 (May 1978), p. 38; Skatepark Construction Ltd., advertisement, *Skateboard!*, no. 10 (June 1978), p. 92; *Skateboard!*, no. 16 (December 1978), p. 50; Pennell, *Skateboarding*, pp. 3–4.

4.9 The Californian backyard pool transplanted to Essex. Pool element at the Rom skatepark based on the keyhole pool at Skateboard Heaven in Spring Valley, itself based on the San Diego 'Soul Bowl'. Design by G-Force/Adrian Rolt, construction by Skate Park Construction. Skateboarder: James 'Jam' Parry (*c.* 1980). (Photograph Iain Borden)

(4.9, 5.5, 5.11),[71] 'Barn' (Brighton),[72] 'Beachcomber' (Hemsby, Great Yarmouth),[73] 'Locomotion' (Hemel Hempstead),[74] 'Skatecountry' (Bristol),[75] 'Solid Surf' (Harrow),[76] Kidderminster Safari Park,[77] 'Maddog Bowl' (London)[78] and 'Black Lion' (Gillingham) (4.8),[79] all being variations on the same repertoire of half-pipe, snake-run, moguls, large concrete bowl, keyhole pool and reservoir elements. The standardized pool element was based on the keyhole pool at Skateboard Heaven in Spring Valley,[80]

71. 'Skatepark Supertest: the Rom', *Skateboard!*, no. 15 (November 1978), pp. 33–5.
72. 'Lip Torque' (April 1978), p. 49; and 'New Parks and Bowls', *Skateboard!*, no. 10 (June 1978), p. 62.
73. 'Lip Torque' (June 1978), p. 37.
74. 'Lip Torque' (August 1978), p. 30.
75. 'New Parks and Bowls' (September 1978), p. 41.
76. 'Lip Torque', *Skateboard!*, no. 11 (July 1978), p. 38; and 'New Parks and Bowls' (October 1978), p. 34.
77. 'Lip Torque' (May 1978), p. 38; and 'New Parks and Bowls' (June 1978), p. 61.
78. 'New Parks and Bowls', *Skateboard!*, no. 11 (July 1978), pp. 78–80.
79. 'Lip Torque' (July 1978), p. 37; and 'Skatepark Supertest: Black Lion, Gillingham', *Skateboard!*, no. 17 (January 1979), pp. 26–8.
80. 'Lip Torque', *Skateboard!*, no. 7 (March 1978), p. 36.

itself based on the San Diego 'Soul Bowl'; thus a specific backyard Southern California pool had been transplanted, modified and finally cloned on the other side of Atlantic (4.9). The version at Kidderminster – a 'really heavy pool'[81] – measured 10 feet deep and 22 feet across, boasting Californian blue tiles, coping and white 'marbelite' surface finish.[82] The version at the Maddog Bowl was somewhat larger, at 14.5 feet deep and 26 feet in diameter,[83] but otherwise was the same design. The large 14–15-foot deep 'Vertibowl' (also known as the 'Performance Bowl') element of the Solid Surf and Rom skateparks was similarly based on an American prototype, this time the 'Vertibowl' at Skatepark Paramount (California), where the sunken section was heightened by a purely vertical 4.5-foot wall rising above ground (5.5).[84]

Skateboarders in the UK, as in many other countries, also benefited from innumerable municipal and community facilities built in response to demands from local skateboarders. These ranged from single half-pipes, such as the steel and fibreglass version in the Barton area of Oxford, to the larger concrete-construction community-built projects such as Meanwhile Gardens in London or another in Hereford.[85] Such facilities, although rarely given more than an occasional passing mention in the national skateboard magazines, provided an important basis for everyday skateboarding around the country. In addition, as they were not often dependent on commercial finance and entrance charges, they often continued to operate into the 1980s and beyond, when most of the larger skateparks had closed.

With around 100 skateparks in total constructed in the UK, around 20 were still open by the end of the 1970s.[86] A late addition in 1979 was the indoor 'Skate-slalom' skatepark (Colne, Lancashire), which included a 28-foot diameter, 12-foot deep pool with specially cast coping (by Brian Siddley, using fibreglass moulds to create a shiny, highly-durable marble-like stone composite) and described by visiting Californian Shogo Kubo as the best pool in England.[87] Another late skatepark was 'Rock 'n Roll' (Livingston, Edinburgh), built in 1981 by the Livingston Development Corporation to designs by architect Iain Urquhart, who achieved near-perfect transitions and finish by using a medievalesque template 'transition machine' (5.4).[88]

81. Alex Turnbull, in 'New Parks and Bowls' (June 1978), p. 61.

82. 'New Parks and Bowls' (June 1978), p. 61.

83. 'New Parks and Bowls' (July 1978), p. 78.

84. Brian Gillogly, 'Skateparks: Part Sixteen', *SkateBoarder*, vol. 4 no. 7 (February 1978), pp. 56–7; and Harvey, in 'Power of London', p. 61.

85. Pete Christopherson, 'Hereford Helps Itself', *Skateboard!*, no. 16 (December 1978), pp. 25–7.

86. Schwartz, 'Travels', p. 64; and Borden, 'Appendix A: Skateparks'.

87. 'Off the Wall' (December 1979), p. 66; 'Colne', *Alpine Sports Newsletter*, no. 4 (n.d., c. January 1980), p. 8; and Kenny Omond, 'Up North: Colne Classic', *Alpine Sports Newsletter*, no. 4 (n.d., c. January 1980), p. 3.

88. Architect's drawings (February 1980); *Skateline*, no. 8 (Spring 1982), p. 8; 'Global Skate '82', *Thrasher*, vol. 2 no. 10 (November 1982), pp. 24–6; and Louise Fyfe, 'Street Legal?', *Sport and Leisure* (Sports Council) (May/June 1989), p. 33.

Once again, there was an American model being followed: the pool here (still extant) was based on the Marina del Rey skatepark's keyhole pool.[89]

During the late 1970s, other skateparks were built around the world in, among many other places, 'Caracola Bowl' in Argentina;[90] 'Albany Skateboard Park' in Australia; 'Wave Park' in São Paulo and the 'Anchieta Keyhole' in Brazil;[91] 'Ontaria Skateboard Park' in Canada; 'Park de Carolina' in Ecuador;[92] 'Beton Hurlant' and 'Parc de la Villette' in Paris; 'Erromdardi' and 'Skatepark de St-Jean de Luz' in France; 'Torino Roller Disco' in Italy;[93] 'California', 'Yoyogi' and 'Hewajima' in Tokyo, Japan; 'Skatopistas del Sol', 'Skapistas de Mexico' and 'Dogtown' in Mexico;[94] 'Camino Royal' in Lima, Peru;[95] 'Cresta Wave' in Johannesburg, South Africa; 'New Sport House' in Stockholm and 'Skateland' in Gothenburg,[96] Sweden, as well as many others in countries such as Belgium, Germany, Guatemala,[97] Ireland, Netherlands, Puerto Rico, and Switzerland. In New Zealand the original Californian 'Skatopia' skatepark was cloned at Auckland.[98] Besides design features, other aspects of American skateboarding were also disseminated to other countries. In particular, as can be discerned from the names of many of these skateparks – 'Earth'n'Ocean' (UK), 'Skatewave' (UK), 'Surf News' (South Africa), 'Tiquius Skate and Surf' (Mexico) and so on – many drew symbolic strength from the association with surfing and, by extension, with the Californian origins of skateboarding in the 1950s and 1960s.[99]

Nearly all purpose-built concrete skateparks were either begun or amended before 1982. A small number, however, were constructed after this date, including the council-provided snake run and (unusually) prefabricated concrete, steel coping bowl at the 'Berg Fidel' skatepark (Münster, Germany, 1989), designed in conjunction with Claus Grabke and Titus Dittman.[100] Here, however, the US connection is dramatically weakened, if not entirely severed. In a significant move away from the

89. Urquhart and Urquhart, 'America', p. 18.

90. Javier Alejandro Bianco, letter, *Thrasher*, vol. 3 no. 12 (December 1983), p. 26.

91. Dan Bourqui, 'Photograffiti: the Brazilian Skate Scene', *Thrasher*, vol. 3 no. 7 (July 1983), pp. 28–9.

92. Mic-E Reyes, 'Viva Ecuador: Adventure is Where You Find It', *Thrasher*, vol. 17 no. 1 (January 1997), pp. 78–81.

93. 'Photograffiti', *Thrasher*, vol. 4 no. 5 (May 1984), p. 21.

94. 'McRad', *Thrasher*, vol. 4 no. 4 (April 1984), p. 42.

95. 'Somethin' Else', *Thrasher*, vol. 3 no. 5 (May 1983), p. 47.

96. Brooke, *Concrete Wave*, p. 87.

97. Scott Edwards, 'Photograffiti: 3rd Annual AM Contest Guatemala', *Thrasher*, vol. 3 no. 7 (July 1983), p. 35.

98. Kevin Stringer, letter, *SkateBoarder*, vol. 5 no. 9 (April 1979), p. 18; and Geoff Wright, interview, *Thrasher*, vol. 6 no. 10 (October/November 1986), p. 74.

99. 'Skatepark Directory', *Skateboard!*, no. 16 (December 1978), pp. 20–3; and 'Info', *TransWorld Skateboarding*, vol. 9 no. 11 (November 1991), pp. 92–6.

100. Marco Contati, 'Münster Mösh', *Thrasher*, vol. 6 no. 12 (December 1989), p. 46; 'Ears', *R.A.D.* no. 79 (September 1989), p. 4; and 'A Touch of the Hard Stuff', *R.A.D.*, no. 80 (October 1989), pp. 54–5.

Californian origins of skateparks, the bowl at Münster was 'a pool for the nineties, not an attempt to simulate a backyard swimming pool', and boasted a narrow, high and steep channel entry into a pool with 10-foot transitions, 1.5 feet of vertical wall and a 10-foot flat bottom. These, then, were dimensions and transitions somewhat different to those of many Californian pools, and instead much closer to those of a modern wooden half-pipe (see below).[101] In the UK, the Livingston skatepark was substantially extended according to designs by Kenny Omond (1992).[102] In south England in 1990 Southsea skatepark remodelled one of its old concrete bowls into a circular pool with steel coping.[103] In France, the concrete 'Plage du Prado' skatepark (early 1990s) was built in Marseilles to the designs of an architecture student,[104] while a decade earlier Spanish skaters in Madrid had built themselves a multi-bowl and bank facility.[105] Slovenia had a concrete pool at Kranj,[106] and a number of skateparks were constructed in Brazil, including the compactly-arranged 'Dominio' with two large half-pipes and variegated reservoir element.[107] Even small areas such as the Portuguese-governed territory of Macau gained facilities such as its municipal skatepark in the Jardim Comendador Yo Hin, opened in 1993 (4.10).[108]

In the US, projects in the late 1980s and early 1990s included 'Stone Edge', (Daytona, Florida, 1989), a 'concrete paradise' designed by skater Bill Danforth[109] with number-9-shaped bowl, combi-bowl, peanut bowl and egg bowl, plus a metal half-pipe and multi-ramp street arena, reportedly costing US$750,000.[110] At the other end of the spectrum were four small free-access skateparks in Benicia, Palo Alto, Davis and San Francisco in northern California, opened in 1992.[111] Later on in the decade, a resurgence of concrete outdoor skateparks occurred, and by the turn of the millennium many such skateparks of various sizes, complexity and ownership had opened across the US. *TransWorld Skateboarding* listed more than 180 such facilities in 2000.[112] This has been particularly evident in California where changes

101. 'Hard Stuff', p. 55.

102. Kenny Omond, letter (5 September 1996). See also 'Livingston Gnarl Up', *Sidewalk Surfer*, no. 1 (September–October 1995), n.p.; and Pin, 'Pin Goes to Livingston', *Sidewalk Surfer*, no. 9 (August 1996), n.p.

103. 'Thoughts, Happenings', *R.A.D.*, no. 103 (December 1991), pp. 14–15.

104. 'Ears', *R.A.D.*, no. 103 (December 1991), p. 7; 'Trip Tips: Marseilles and Montpellier', *R.A.D.*, no. 118 (March 1993), pp. 23–5; and 'Rolling Programme: a Skateboarder's Perspective on Architecture', *The Architects' Journal* (3 October 1996), p. 42.

105. 'The Story of the Park', *R.A.D.*, no. 63 (May 1988), p. 31.

106. Mitja Borko 'Scene Slovenia', *Thrasher*, vol. 11 no. 12 (December 1991), pp. 32–3.

107. 'Terrain', *Skateboard!* (second series), no. 46 (September 1990), p. 6; and Thomas Campbell, 'Europe Summer Part 2', *TransWorld Skateboarding*, vol. 14 no. 1 (January 1996), pp. 124–9.

108. Observed, September 1998.

109. Lowboy, 'Truth and Screw the Consequences', *Thrasher*, vol. 9 no. 6 (June 1989), p. 42.

110. Paul Duffy, 'Texas: a State of Mind', *Skateboard!* (second series), no. 46 (September 1990), p. 34.

111. Editorial, *Thrasher*, vol. 12 no. 7 (July 1992), p. 4.

112. 'Skatepark List', *TransWorld Skateboarding*, vol. 18 no. 10 (October 2000), pp. 92–100.

4.10 Municipal skatepark at the Jardim Comendador Yo Hin, Macau (1993). (Photograph Iain Borden)

in legislation removed certain insurance and liability problems (see Chapter Seven). Notably, these new skateparks have included a copy of the infamous Combi-Pool, which had been demolished along with the rest of the Pipeline skatepark in 1989; as if to reinforce the reputation of the Combi-Pool as skateboarding's equivalent of architectural modernism's hugely influential yet short-lived Barcelona Pavilion, originally designed by architect Ludwig Mies van der Rohe and then reconstructed in Barcelona during the 1990s, the skate company Vans chose to fabricate an exact copy of the Combi-Pool in its new Orange County facility.[113]

113. Vans internet site, URL http://www.vans.com (accessed 28 May 2000). This skatepark is viewable on the internet via a live webcam link.

In a somewhat different vein, the highly successful community 'Burnside Project' (Portland, Oregon, 1990 onward) was built on the parking lot of an abandoned hotel beneath the Burnside Bridge. Mark Hubbard, Mark 'Redneck' Scott and other skaters, together with some of the local homeless, fabricated concrete banks, spines, bowls and fun box without official permission (4.11). Most of the cement came as surplus-to-requirements material supplied by the local company Ross Island Sand and Gravel. Burnside is an evolving facility, with skaters constantly changing and adding to its elements, and indeed by 1997 most of the earliest features had been completely rebuilt or buried beneath new elements.[114] Interestingly, at Burnside and at an abortive copycat project in Seattle, many of the elements were designed in part during the process of construction itself, skaters responding to the developing shape of their excavations and formwork to adapt the features before finally setting them in steel re-bar and concrete.[115] As one skater explained the process at Seattle,

4.11 The skatepark as continual appropriation of urban space. Mark 'Redneck' Scott smoothing concrete at Burnside, Portland (*c.* 1997). (Photograph Jon Humphries)

> We kept digging until everyone was satisfied with the shape. There were disagreements such as how many cement blocks of vertical we should add, and whether or not to have a 'double pump' into the deep end. The shape we finally came up with was a somewhat elongated kidney with a deep end of about ten feet (including three blocks of vert), a shallow end of about six feet (with a 45° banked section extending five feet higher) and a hip between the deep and shallow ends.[116]

The city authorities of Portland have successively ignored the park, threatened it with closure around 1994–5, and finally sanctioned the Burnside project as an experiment in community policing, successfully creating a new social space – and not just for skaters – from a previously derelict and dangerous site. Burnside is the

114. Roy the Barbecue Man, 'Portland Project', *Thrasher*, vol. 11 no. 11 (November 1991), pp. 34–5 and 80; 'Burnside Project Update', *Thrasher*, vol. 12 no. 7 (July 1992), p. 22; '15 Free Spots', *Thrasher*, vol. 16 no. 2 (February 1996), p. 32; Noah Martineau, 'A Piss Drenched Bert on the First Day of Spring', *Thrasher*, vol. 17 no. 7 (July 1997), pp. 76–83; Stumpy, 'Burnside (USA)', *Ergo Sum*, no. 1 (n.d., *c.* early 1997), n.p.; 'The Great North West Invaded', *Slap*, vol. 4 no. 9 (September 1995), pp. 34–41; and Paul Fujita, 'Burnside', *TransWorld Skateboarding*, vol. 15 no. 11 (November 1997), pp. 140–57.

115. Nels Gravstad, 'Bowl Builders Busted', *Thrasher*, vol. 12 no. 7 (July 1992), pp. 14 and 22.

116. Ibid., p. 14.

skateboard equivalent of a community squat, a collective-labour developing facility without private ownership – effectively creating a skatepark as a continual appropriation of urban space with the semi-condonement of official institutions. As one skater explained, using this model the 'best skatepark a city could give to its skaters would be a piece of land with nothing on it' and let them design and produce it themselves.[117]

MUTANT WOOD

From 1977 onward, skateparks were also increasingly complemented by the provision, often by skaters themselves, of ramps. At first such ramps were seen as a way of providing vertical terrain for those who were without access to skateparks or Californian pools,[118] and by 1980 the Rampage company had already sold 4,000 sets of ramp design blueprints across America as well as to 45 other countries.[119] Following these early ramp constructions, when many skateparks closed in the early 1980s ramps became the staple terrain for skaters, and greatly contributed to skateboarding's resurgence in the mid-1980s.

> The answer to these blues lies close at hand, at the end of a hammer and a saw. The answer is ramps.[120]

In 1981, *Action Now* (formerly *SkateBoarder*) gave information on ramp construction,[121] and the then new magazine *Thrasher* did likewise,[122] with a 1983 issue giving detailed ramp plans quickly becoming sold out.[123] By the 1990s ramp plans were readily available off the internet.[124]

The first ramps of the 1970s were simple, angled straight surfaces; for example, *Skateboard!* published plans for a 40°-angled, 5-foot-high construction.[125] Skaters

117. Ibid., p. 22.

118. Mick Angiulo, Stan Diego and Mel Cajon, 'Building Your Own Skate Ramp', *SkateBoarder*, vol. 4 no. 3 (October 1977), pp. 22–3; Mick Angiulo, 'Rampage', *SkateBoarder*, vol. 4 no.3 (October 1977), p. 60–9; Who's Hot! Rick Blackhart', *SkateBoarder*, vol. 4 no. 4 (November 1977), p. 115; Brian Gillogly, 'The Ramp Rage: a Perspective', *SkateBoarder*, vol. 4 no. 8 (March 1978), pp. 76–93; and Ayres, 'Ramps', pp. 54–63.

119. Rampage, advertisement, *SkateBoarder*, vol. 6 no. 9 (April 1980), p. 16.

120. Morin, 'Survival', p. 71.

121. Curtis Hesselgrave, 'Ramp Ingredients: What You Need to Build a Ramp', *Action Now*, vol. 7 no. 10 (May 1981), pp. 42–5.

122. 'Ramp Raging', *Thrasher*, vol. 1 no. 7 (July 1981), pp. 12–15.

123. *Thrasher*, vol. 9 no. 6 (June 1989), p. 54.

124. Usenet alt.skateboard (accessed 7 January 1997).

125. Pete Kristopherson, 'Build Your Own Ramp', *Skateboard!*, no. 3 (November 1977), pp. 28–31.

4.12 An early US wooden half-pipe, without flat bottom (1977).

in cities around the world assembled still cruder versions by leaning a 8-foot × 4-foot sheet of wood (often purloined from a nearby construction site) against some steps or other suitable support.[126] The first ramp with a *curved* transition was possibly constructed by Adam Ziolowski in Melbourne Beach, Florida, sometime in the early-mid-1970s.[127]

Later, ramps have tended to be independent structures providing an autonomous terrain for skateboarding; typically of free-standing, timber construction, the most common form is the half-pipe, a name which refers to the U-section profile and two parallel side walls of this kind of ramp. The earliest of these half-pipes tended to be a classic half-circle in section (4.12). From around 1979 onward, however, ramps commonly had a flat bottom inserted between the two transitions[128] (4.13, 4.14) – this was an invention possibly pioneered in Sweden and subsequently brought back to the USA by a visiting Powell-Peralta team in 1980,[129] although local skaters in towns such as Oxford in the UK and no doubt elsewhere were already adding such flat bottoms into their ramps prior to this date. Overall height of these later half-pipes varies between six and fifteen feet, the walls being topped off with a narrow platform. The riding surface is either plywood (often two layers of 9 mm birch ply), masonite (oil-tempered hardboard) or steel (typically 2–3 mm sheets). Coping is also often added using 50–60 mm steel tubing, plastic or even concrete pool coping blocks.[130] The transition section is usually a pure quarter-circle with a radius of eight to twelve feet (although elliptical transitions have occasionally been used[131]), probably for reasons of convenience as much as anything else, allowing ramp-builders to draw out the transition template with a simple compass device made from a nail, length of string and a pencil. Other ramp features include wall-top

126. Tony Magnusson, interview, *Thrasher*, vol. 9 no. 8 (August 1989), p. 46.

127. Walker, letter, p. 15.

128. Ayres, 'Ramps', p. 59.

129. Leighton-Boyce, letter; 'Off the Wall', *SkateBoarder*, vol. 6 no. 10 (May 1980), p. 73; and Stacy Peralta, 'Eurocana Summer Camp', *SkateBoarder's Action Now*, vol. 7 no. 8 (March 1981), pp. 52–5.

130. Dan Adams, 'Building a Ramp', *R.A.D.*, no. 79 (September 1989), pp. 60–1.

131. 'Trash', *Thrasher*, vol. 5 no. 3 (March 1985), p. 59; and 'The San José Skateboard Club', *R.A.D.*, no. 74 (April 1989), p. 57.

4.13 Opening event at an extended mini-ramp, Leamington Spa (1989). (Photograph Tim Leighton-Boyce)

modifications such as 'channels' (a notch cut out from the top side of the wall, like a crenellation), 'extensions' (tombstone-like additions on the top side of the wall) 'escalators' (curved drop in points) and different kinds of coping (4.14).

Ramps are commonly single, large half-pipes, such as those built at an annual summer camp in Sweden,[132] the 'Skatemates' ramp (near Liedsplein, Amsterdam), and Bourges (France),[133] Monrea (Italy),[134] and in the UK at Hastings,[135] Swansea,[136] the Empire State Building (Warrington),[137] Farnborough,[138] Latimer Road (London),

132. *Thrasher, passim.*

133. 'Lost in France', *R.A.D.*, no. 137 (February/March 1995), n.p.

134. Bonassi Massimo, letter, *Thrasher*, vol. 6 no. 5 (May 1986), p. 12.

135. 'A Ramp with a View', *R.A.D.*, no. 80 (October 1989), pp. 16–17.

136. 'More Coke and No Stickers: the Hot Tuna Skatemasters at Swansea', *R.A.D.*, no. 79 (September 1989), pp. 29–31.

137. Tim Leighton-Boyce, 'Goodbye to All That: Ten Years of British Skating', *R.A.D.*, no. 83 (January 1990), p. 45.

138. Rodga Harvey, interview, *R.A.D.*, no. 83 (January 1990), p. 50.

4.14 Tony Hawk's private ramp facility at Fallbrook (*c.* 1989). Note bowl (left), spine connection (middle) to the flat bottom on the half-pipe (right), and variations to the top of the half-pipe wall (far right). (Photograph Annibal Neto)

and Crystal Palace (London) during the mid-1980s.[139] In the US some of the most significant examples included Lance Mountain's ramp (Alhambra, California), Joe Lopes's ramp (San Leandro), Jay Moore's ramp (Eagle Rock), Joe Johnson's ramp (Fort Collins, Colorado), the St. Pete ramp (Florida), the Mile High ramp (Lake Tahoe, Nevada), the Mount Trashmore ramp (Virginia Beach, Virginia), the Cambodia III ramp (Miami, Florida), the 'Great Desert Ramp' (Palmdale, California), and the 'Ramp Ranch' (Atlanta, Georgia).[140] Such ramps were roughly commensurate in size with skatepark pools, and offered a ready substitute terrain for vertical skateboarding

139. Hugh 'Bod' Boyle, interview, *Thrasher*, vol. 10 no. 5 (May 1990), p. 42.
140. '10 Killer Ramps', *Thrasher*, vol. 4 no. 11 (November 1984), pp. 32–7; and *Thrasher*, *passim*.

throughout the 1980s and 1990s. In a rather different form of spatial tactic, and somewhat akin to the Burnside project in Portland, in 1986 the co-operative 'Tennessee Half-Pipe Company' built a number of ramps to create the 'World's Unfair' facility on part of the site of the former 1982 World's Fair in Knoxville. A temporary facility lasting only ten months, the Unfair was a perfect example of the adaptability of the ramp terrain, in this case allowing appropriation of land during an interlude within its more usual, legitimized uses.[141]

Complicated multi-unit ramps are also sometimes built for demonstrations and competitions with half-pipes of varying size and shape placed in combination to enable skaters to transfer directly from one to another. For example, the Vision Skate Escape ramp competition was a spectacular event held at the Bren Center, University of California at Irvine in March 1988, and choreographed by Don Hoffman with live music by the Red Hot Chili Peppers; it featured a custom-built, large, wooden half-pipe with roll-out platform, and a smaller half-pipe back-to-back down half of the opposite side, linked by both spine and a roll-in transfer ramp. The combination was first constructed off-site by Chuck Hultz and Tim Payne, then dismantled and reassembled in the indoor arena two days before the event.[142] In another variation, in 1987, a massive 100-foot-long ramp, L-shaped in plan with bowled-out corner, was constructed at the Raging Waters waterslide park in San Jose.[143] Idiosyncratic ramps were also built for touring demonstrations, such as the polycarbonate Pepsi ramp (1977),[144] or the Turning Point ramp, a see-through 'Lexan' 19-foot diameter capsule-shaped device used for a US exhibition tour in 1979.[145]

At the other end of the spectrum, smaller versions of half-pipes known as mini-ramps became increasingly proliferous at the end of the 1980s, and these were frequently made by skaters for cramped sites, being constructed rapidly and at minimal cost (4.13).[146] The minimal height of these smaller ramps also reduced the possibility of serious injury (although small transitions meant that twisted ankles and sprained wrists were common occurrences).[147] Those who rode full-size vertical half-pipes,

141. Brian Beauchene, 'Unfair, Tennessee', *Thrasher*, vol. 7 no. 3 (March 1987), pp. 53–7.

142. Vision Street Wear, advertisement, *Thrasher*, vol. 8 no. 7 (July 1988), p. 23; 'Victory at Irvine', *Thrasher*, vol. 8 no. 7 (July 1988), pp. 54–60; and observed (20 March 1988).

143. Kevin Thatcher, 'The Rise and Fall', *Thrasher*, vol. 7 no. 11 (November 1987), pp. 66–7; and 'Trash', *Thrasher*, vol. 7 no. 11 (November 1987), p. 103.

144. Brian Gillogly, 'The Pepsi Ramp Perspective', *SkateBoarder*, vol. 4 no. 5 (December 1977), pp. 100–9.

145. Rick Blackhart, 'Ask the Doctor', *Thrasher*, vol. 5 no. 3 (March 1985), p. 10; Gregg Ayres, 'Turning Point Ramp', *SkateBoarder*, vol. 5 no. 12 (July 1979), pp. 70–3; and Friedman, *Fuck You Too*, n.p.

146. Steve Caballero, interview, *Thrasher*, vol. 9 no. 6 (June 1989), p. 49; Bryce Kanights, '6 Foot Under', *Thrasher*, vol. 8 no. 2 (February 1988), p. 46–51 and 91; Tim Payne, 'Ramp World', *Thrasher*, vol. 12 no. 1 (January 1992), p. 28; and 'Return of the Killer Mini Sessions', *R.A.D.*, no. 71 (January 1989), pp. 16–23.

147. Natas Kaupas, interview, *Thrasher*, vol. 8 no. 5 (May 1988), p. 123.

such as Australian professional skater Gary Valentine, were often quite condescending about the focus on mini-ramps in the early 1990s.

> Kids just want to ride up them and do an ollie grab fingerflipplekipplething on it. They just don't wanna skate vert.[148]

Nonetheless, mini-ramps have proven to be extremely popular both with skaters intent on developing intricate lip tricks[149] and with municipal authorities keen to provide relatively risk-free facilities. Many mini-ramps in the UK were also manufactured on a commercial basis – such as the Zebra (steel or concrete),[150] Rareunit (steel) and Freestyle (timber or steel) units – and installed for private or public usage at places such as Bath, Bootle, Chelmsford, Doncaster, Ilchester, Chesham and numerous other sites nationwide.[151] Significantly, these are not the major cities which tended to attract the concrete skateparks, but the small towns and local sites comprising the total urban complex.

Even smaller ramps and obstacles have been built as part of streetstyle courses, as well as for everyday use. Such ramps have ranged from simple quarter-pipes to pyramid- and snowplough-shaped forms (often with metal piping on their upper edges), to handrails, ledges and other elements which mimic the 'natural' features of the quotidian urban street.[152] Small flat-angled 1–3-foot-high launch or jump ramps, from which skaters fly over and beyond the lip, were especially popular in the late 1980s.[153]

All these half-pipes disclose a craft tradition in skateboard terrain (as with some of the early skateparks like Skatepark Soquell where surfers traded labour for skating hours[154]), skateboarders as 'enterprising individuals with a few tools and a little wood'[155] being actively involved in the design and construction of their own physical environment,[156] and often acquiring carpentry skills in the process – as happened when six Southern Ute Indian tribe skaters built a 10-foot-high half-pipe

148. Gary Valentine, interview, *Skateboard!* (second series), no. 46 (September 1990), p. 44.

149. Harvey, interview, p. 51.

150. 'Ears' (December 1991), p. 6.

151. 'Ears', *R.A.D.*, no. 88 (June 1990), p. 88; 'Terrain', *Skateboard!* (second series), no. 41 (April 1990), p. 6; Steve Kane, 'Ramp Lust', *Skateboard!* (second series), no. 41 (April 1990), pp. 12–16; and 'Terrain', *Skateboard!* (second series), no. 45 (August 1990), p. 6.

152. Craig Ramsay, 'The Ramp Page: Street Ramps Part 1', *Thrasher*, vol. 5 no. 2 (February 1985), p. 14; Craig Ramsay, 'The Ramp Page: Street Ramps Part 2', *Thrasher*, vol. 5 no. 3 (March 1985), p. 14; and Don Fisher, 'Ramp-Edge: Structures for Street People', *Thrasher*, vol. 9 no. 11 (November 1989), p. 34.

153. 'One Hit', *Thrasher*, vol. 7 no. 2 (January 1987), pp. 55–61.

154. Tony Roberts, 'Santa Cruz', *Thrasher*, vol. 8 no. 7 (July 1988), p. 80.

155. Morin, 'Survival', p. 72.

156. 'In Praise of Ply', *R.A.D.*, no. 86 (April 1990), pp. 16–17.

with US$5,000 of municipal funds in Ignacio, Colorado.[157] They can also form an interesting juxtaposition with more traditional forms of architecture, the numerous half-pipes dotted throughout urban areas creating a noticeable if impermanent addition to the architecture of their housing stock. For example, in the late 1980s in the Los Feliz area of Los Angeles, Lance Mountain built a 5-foot-high half-pipe for Stacy Peralta in the backyard of the Skolnik House, designed by Rudolph Schindler in 1952.[158] Other professional skaters like Steve Caballero, Ken Park,[159] Jeff Kendall and Tony Hawk also built their own ramps; Kendall's had tight transitions to copy those at Apple skatepark,[160] whereas Caballero's mimicked the overall dimensions of the old skatepark pools, but with larger transitions to give more room to kneeslide when bailing out of a move.[161] Hawk moved to Fallbrook in California because the skateparks had closed, and as a professional skater he needed to build his own facility; it was modified several times, centred around a half-pipe with a partial spine connection to a bowl, all surfaced in plywood and masonite (4.14).[162]

Apart from insertions within the open space of the city, ramps can also form skateparks, and these have taken over from outdoor concrete skateparks typical of the 1970s as the predominant form of purpose-designed skateboard terrain in the 1980s and 1990s. Early ramp-based skateparks dating from the mid-1980s onward included 'Bike Haus' (Hot Springs, Arizona), 'Jeff Phillips Skatepark' (Dallas, Texas) constructed by Payne,[163] 'Rotation Station' (Loves Park, Illinois), 'Mike McGill's Skatepark' (Carlsbad, California) and 'Skatepark of Houston' (Houston, Texas).[164]

Many of these new ramp-based skateparks were indoor facilities – by 1997, 56 of the 129 commercial US skateparks listed in *TransWorld Skateboarding* were indoor facilities.[165] These are particularly useful in places with inclement climates, where cold and wet weather both provide their own hazards to skateboarders: damp conditions quickly cause skateboard wheels to lose their grip[166] and low temperatures increase the chance of serious accident whenever a skater bails out or falls from a move. Hot weather also often restricts skating to evening hours. To avoid these problems, late 1980s and 1990s indoor skateparks have provided all-day, all-year-round skateboard facilities. In the US, they have included 'Southside' (Houston),[167]

157. 'Pay Your Dues', *Thrasher*, vol. 10 no. 5 (May 1990), p. 53.
158. Observed, Los Angeles (May 1988); and 'Trash' (November1987), p. 102.
159. Ken Park, interview, *TransWorld Skateboarding*, vol. 7 no. 2 (April 1989), p. 98.
160. Jeff Kendall, interview, *Thrasher*, vol. 6 no. 12 (December 1989), p. 72.
161. Caballero, interview (June 1989), p. 49.
162. Tony Hawk, interview, *R.A.D.*, no. 88 (June 1990), pp. 26–35.
163. Duffy, 'Texas', p. 38; and Jeff Phillips, interview, *Five 40* (February 1990), pp. 29–35.
164. 'Pay Your Dues', pp. 48–54 and 95.
165. 'The Skatepark List', *TransWorld Skateboarding*, vol. 15 no. 10 (October 1997), p. 78, and vol. 15 no. 11 (November 1997), p. 274.
166. See for example Alidad Fard, 'Rain Damage', *Slap*, vol. 6 no. 9 (September 1997), pp. 58–9.
167. Jeff Taylor, 'Houston, Texas', *TransWorld Skateboarding*, vol. 14 no. 1 (January 1996), pp. 80–7.

'Skatehut' (Rhode Island) with wooden ramps and bowl by Custom Skate Ramps,[168] 'Ramp House' (Carolina Beach, North Carolina),[169] 'Ratz' (Biddeford, Maine), also by Custom Skate,[170] 'Middle School' (Wilmington, North Carolina),[171] 'Charleston Hangar Bowl' (Charleston, South Carolina) constructed by Payne (4.15), 'Skate Zone' (Atlanta, Georgia) also constructed by Payne,[172] and 'Mike McGill's Indoor Skatepark' (Tampa Bay area, Florida).[173]

A total of more than 120 skateparks in at least 43 states were in operation in the US in 1991–92, and more than 165 in at least 38 states in 1997, many of which were indoor and/or wooden ramp-based facilities.[174] Unlike the 1970s skateparks,

4.15 Wooden bowls being built at Charleston Hangar Bowl (*c.* 1991), with design and construction by Tim Payne.

168. Kevin Wilkins, 'New England Hot Spots', *TransWorld Skateboarding*, vol. 9 no. 11 (November 1991), pp. 38–9 and 43.
169. 'Lost Coast of the Carolinas', *Thrasher*, vol. 10 no. 10 (October 1990), pp. 51–4.
170. Wilkins, 'New England', p. 43.
171. *TransWorld Skateboarding*, vol. 14 no. 1 (January 1996), p. 113.
172. Don Fisher, 'Pay to Play', *Thrasher*, vol. 11 no. 9 (September 1991), p. 37.
173. 'Info', p. 92; and Don Fisher, 'Rampage', *Thrasher*, vol. 9 no. 8 (August 1989), p. 30.
174. Borden, 'Appendix A: Skateparks'.

many of this new generation of skateparks were owned and managed by skaters, a factor which undoubtedly contributed to their success.[175] Alternatively, some of these skateparks, such as the 'Kennedy' warehouse facility in San Jose, California,[176] the Powell-Peralta warehouse in Amsterdam[177] with ramps constructed by Payne,[178] and another warehouse in Dewsbury, Yorkshire,[179] were constructed as indoor private ramps open only to club members, an arrangement adopted mainly to help with financing and insurance costs.

In other countries, indoor ramp-based skateparks have ranged from the elaborate, such as 'Skate Ranch' (Vancouver, Canada),[180] 'Ultra' (São Paulo, Brazil),[181] 'Thomas I. Punkt' (Hamburg, Germany),[182] and 'Titus Warehouse' (Münster, Germany),[183] to the moderate, such as 'Simon's Skatepark' (Dublin, Ireland),[184] to the very basic, such as 'Hobbies' (Bandung, West Java, Indonesia).[185] In the UK, ramp skateparks have included 'Skate Shack' (Barrow-in-Furness),[186] 'Skate & Ride' (Bristol),[187] 'Pioneer' (St. Albans), 'Rock City' (Hull), 'Fast Eddies' (Whitley Bay), 'Fearless Ramp Base' (Essex), 'Liverpark' (Liverpool),[188] 'Re-Hab' (Wakefield, owned by Donna and Stephen Jagger) (4.16),[189] 'Radlands' (Northampton, owned by Chris Ince),[190] the lottery-funded 'Mount Hawke' (Cornwall),[191] and the Sony-sponsored 'Playstation' (London). Similar ramp-based facilities were also built in countries such as Argentina, Australia, Belgium, Brazil, Canada, Czechoslovakia, Denmark,

175. 'Pay Your Dues', p. 52.

176. Kendall, interview, p. 74.

177. 'Where?', *R.A.D.*, no. 88 (June 1990), p. 40.

178. 'News', *Skateboard!* (second series), no. 41 (April 1990), p. 5.

179. 'Where?, Dewsbury', *R.A.D.*, no. 83 (January 1990), pp. 38–9.

180. Lance Mountain, 'Ramp Locals', *TransWorld Skateboarding*, vol. 6 no. 1 (February 1988), pp. 94–5.

181. Brooke, *Concrete Wave*, p. 166.

182. *Onboard, The Annual*, no. 1 (1997), n.p.

183. Søren Aaby, 'European Meltdown', *Thrasher*, vol. 12 no. 3 (March 1992), pp. 26–7.

184. 'Simply Simon's', *R.A.D.*, no. 117 (February 1993), pp. 16–20.

185. Wez Lundry, 'Jumpin' in Java: a Solo Mission to Indonesia', *Thrasher*, vol. 17 no. 7 (July 1997), pp. 42–3.

186. Meany, 'Barrow Boys', *Skateboard!* (second series), no. 42 (May 1990), pp. 44–5; and 'In and Around Barrow', *Sk8 Action* (May 1990), pp. 40–5.

187. 'Undercover: a Nearly Comprehensive Indoor Skatepark Guide', *Sidewalk Surfer*, no. 14 (March 1997), n.p.

188. Ibid.

189. Ben, 'Sleepless in Wakefield', *R.A.D.*, no. 137 (February/March 1995), n.p.; and 'Undercover', n.p.

190. 'King Rad!', *R.A.D.*, no. 116 (January 1993), pp. 16–20; 'Undercover', n.p.; 'Five Years On', *Sidewalk Surfer*, no. 23 (January/February, 1998), n.p.; and Steve England, 'What Goes Around Comes Around', *Xtreme*, no. 4 (September 1997), pp. 28–9.

191. 'New Wood Mount Hawke', *Sidewalk Surfer*, no. 20 (September 1997), n.p.

4.16 'This place breeds obstacles like the US government breeds genetic mutants.' Spine ramps at Re-Hab, Wakefield (1995). Skateboarder: Benny.

Dominican Republic, Finland, France, Germany, Greece, Israel, Italy, Japan, Mexico, New Zealand, Norway, Peru, Singapore, Slovenia, South Africa, Spain and Sweden.[192]

Ramp skateparks can also be more quickly built (the original Radlands layout, contained in a 9,500-square-foot area, was constructed in just 10 days by Tim Payne using skateboarder-labour[193]) and more easily modified than concrete skateparks, allowing for example Wakefield and Radlands to exploit cheap out-of-town warehouse space to provide a complex arrangement of wooden ramps and other features. In 1997 Radlands included a 32-foot-wide and 10.5-foot-high vertical half-pipe, 12-foot-wide spine ramp and numerous streetstyle skating obstacles; Wakefield offered a vertical ramp, mini-ramp with 'escalator' and 'volcano' features, vertical wall, jump boxes, free-standing spine, driveways, handrails, hips, wallie pole, plus banks and quarter pipes.[194]

> Wakefield's the best skatepark I think I've ever skated in my life, there's shit everywhere. You don't even know where to go, you just get lost.[195]

These new skateparks thus offered not the spectacular and intimidating forms of the older concrete skateparks of the 1970s, but instead a myriad of ramps sizes and combinations; they focused less on the single, high-performance pool element and more on providing a range of skate terrains from streetstyle obstacles to mini-ramps and large vertical half-pipes.

> Skateparks have generally been built with the idea that very radical haphazard structures are somehow challenging to skateboarders. Nothing could be further from the truth . . . Modern skatepark design is then really a mixture of the urban environment and suggestions of skateboarders. It is emphatically not the crazy, mogul-like fantasies of desk-bound architects. Skateparks are not like ballparks or courts that have set rules regarding dimensions and playing surface.[196]

Taking their cue from this kind of thinking, skateparks such as Radlands and Wakefield (4.16) have also concentrated on constantly adding to and modifying the various elements on offer, creating, in contrast to the largely static and monumental concrete forms of the 1970s skateparks, an ever-changing and more low-key skate environment.[197]

192. Borko 'Slovenia', pp. 32–3; and 'Info', pp. 92–6.
193. 'King Rad!', p. 20.
194. 'Undercover', n.p.
195. Arron Bleasdale, interview, *Sidewalk Surfer*, no. 9 (August 1996), n.p.
196. 'How to Build a Skatepark', *Thrasher*, vol. 17 no. 9 (September 1997), p. 71.
197. Dan Joyce, 'Strange Deaths in Wakefield', *Sidewalk Surfer*, no. 15 (April 1997), n.p.; and 'Radiation', *R.A.D.*, no. 118 (March 1993), pp. 8–9.

> This place (Wakefield) breeds obstacles like the US government breeds genetic mutants.[198]

In such a manner, skateparks finally came of age, as low-cost, ever-mutating and occasionally ephemeral constructions specifically adapted to suit the needs of skateboarders. Pro-design but anti-monumental, their forms and surfaces are skater-centred. This, of course, directly raises the question as to exactly how such forms were encountered and reproduced through the skater's own actions. And it is to a consideration of this process that I now turn.

198. 'Highlights', *Sidewalk Surfer*, no. 13 (January/February 1997), n.p.

Chapter 5
Body Space

> Consciousness is being-towards-the-thing through the intermediary of the body.[1]

SUPER-ARCHITECTURAL SPACE

As Lefebvre notes, spatial practices and representations of space are 'in thrall to both knowledge and power', so leaving 'only the narrowest leeway' to spaces of representation. But, as he also notes, it is through revolt against normative spaces of representation that there is the 'prospect of recovering the world of differences – the natural, the sensory/sensual, sexuality and pleasure'.[2] A fortiori, it is not solely the various constructed architectures of skateboarding which, despite their unique contribution to the specialist typologies of the differentiated built environment, form the principal contribution of skateboarding to architectural space. This contribution lies instead in the performative, representational aspects of skateboarding – its spaces of representation – wherein skateboarders re-image architectural space and thereby recreate both it and themselves into super-architectural space. The more poetic attempts by skateboarders to talk about their activity provides glimpses of this process.

> Your body gets weightless as you drift your airs high.
> The blur of the crowd as you grind on by.
> Grasping the rail for the next coming air.
> Your eyes seek reality, the mind is aware.
> Thrust up the wall and click off the tile
> Extend your back leg, throw in some style
> Pulling back in, the coping looks mean.
> Dodging the hang-up, you land real clean.
> The glare off the tile, the grind marks are clear.
> Getting sketch is no sweat, it's slamming you fear.[3]

1. Maurice Merleau-Ponty, *Phenomenology of Perception* (London: Routledge & Kegan Paul, 1962), pp. 138–9.
2. Henri Lefebvre, *The Production of Space*, (Oxford: Blackwell, 1991), p. 50.
3. Kevin Rucks, 'Bail-If', *Thrasher*, vol. 6 no. 3 (March 1986), p. 51.

This quotation, although perhaps not great poetry, contains much of interest and, in the following, I requote lines as appropriate.

The new constructed skateboard terrains from the 1970s onward replicated but also extremitized the terrains found within the modern city, and so enabled a new form of spatial engagement to occur. And these skateparks also offered a controlled social space free of outraged pool owners and patrolling police. Skateparks and ramps thus provided a theatre for the display of skateboarding in which skateboarding and its body moves became partly spectacularized. This is immediately evident from the new moves that skateboarders invented within these terrains.

Early skateparks tended to encourage surf-related skating (4.1). In 1976, when skateboarders were beginning to explore vertical skateboarding, Bruce Walker described Florida's Skateboard City as being akin to an ocean wave.

> When I first went . . . it was just like surfing . . . You just get up on the wall and sock it through the lip a few times.[4]

Pipeline was similarly compared to surfing.

> Checking out the big bowl is like paddling out to Sunset for the first time. And you can get more weightless in a pipe than any other form of skateboarding . . . that's where the surfing feeling really comes in.[5]

But the second generation of skateparks, particularly the new set-piece pools (4.5–4.7, 4.9, 5.2–5.6, 5.10), inspired a whole new form of skateboarding, with backyard pool moves such as the aerial quickly evolving into new manoeuvres such as the roll-out/roll-in and backside aerial;[6] within a couple of years skaters often had little to say about the surf-skateboarding connection.

> They're related in some ways, but not too many. Surfing is like a whole different thing.[7]

This shift from surfing was stimulated by skaters' own spatial inventiveness but also by the new skateparks, for 'extraordinary terrain dictates extraordinary moves'.[8]

By late 1978, moves were developing rapidly, the most significant being the 'ollie' air, perfected by Florida skater Alan Gelfand, a professional with the Powell-

4. Bruce Walker, interview, *SkateBoarder*, vol. 3 no. 1 (October 1976), p. 41.
5. 'Who's Hot! Michael Williams', *SkateBoarder*, vol. 4 no. 3 (October 1977), p. 99.
6. Doug Schneider, 'Skate Tips: Roll Outs', *SkateBoarder*, vol. 4 no. 10 (May 1978), p. 34; and Doug 'Pineapple' Saladino, 'Skate Tips: the Backside Aerial', *SkateBoarder*, vol. 4 no. 11 (June 1978), p. 48.
7. Micke Alba, interview, *SkateBoarder*, vol. 6 no. 9 (April 1980), p. 26.
8. *SkateBoarder*, vol. 5 no. 7 (February 1979), p. 5.

Peralta team, in the latter half of 1978 (5.1). In the ollie, the skater performs an aerial *without* holding onto the board;[9] the manoeuvre is performed by controlled flight and balance, with a delicate relation between body, board, terrain and gravitational force. Although it was nearly a year before any other skater could emulate Gelfand's innovation, the ollie soon became the single most important 'cornerstone of modern skateboarding',[10] adapted into a bewildering range of variants involving differing directions, rotations and combinations.[11]

5.1 The cornerstone of modern skateboarding. The no-hands, 'ollie' aerial performed by its inventor, Alan Gelfand (1978). (Photograph James Cassimus)

Other technical moves were also developed, including the 'invert' aerial (Bobby Valdez, mid-1978), effectively a one-handed handstand (5.2) a 'layback' (late 1978), stretching the body off the rear of the board and across the pool wall (5.5), and a 'rock 'n roll' (mid-1978), where the skateboard rocks across the top of the wall like a see-saw (7.15). Other moves included the 'alley oop' aerial, a backside aerial with backwards trajectory (mid-1978), 'layback air', a frontside aerial with rear hand grasping the coping and front hand holding the board (Kelly Lind, 1979) (4.6), and 'Miller Flip' (Darryl Miller, 1979), a 360° frontside invert aerial where the skater flips over to descend backwards. The 'Elguerial' backwards invert and fakie ollie were inaugurated by Eddie Elguera and Allen Losi respectively.[12]

By mid-1979, skaters were combining these complex moves within a single run, as with Doug 'Pineapple' Saladino's efforts at a professional contest:

9. Jake Phelps, 'Time Warp: Ollie Inventor Alan Gelfand', *Thrasher*, vol. 12 no. 7 (July 1992), p. 15.

10. Kevin Wilkins, in Rodney Mullen, interview, *Warp*, vol. 6 no. 3 (August 1997), p. 48; and 'Major Moves', *Thrasher*, vol. 11 no. 9 (September 1991), p. 50.

11. 'Modern Moves: Ollie Air', *Thrasher*, vol. 1 no. 4 (April 1981), pp. 18–19.

12. Allen Losi, interview, *Thrasher*, vol. 6 no. 2 (February 1986), pp. 39–40.

> He had his rock 'n roll slides fully wired, sliding three and four coping blocks at a whack. Couple this with long grinders, hand plants, inverts, frontside and backside air all at high speed, and you have an incredible run.[13]

And a few months later:

> Gone are the days where a skater could win with just one extraordinary trick. Pro poolriding has finally grown up into a sport that demands versatility, planning and precision execution.[14]

As this suggests, the skateboarder's body-centric space production also involved a sense of time; such skaters as Micke Alba emphasized an attitude of 'total rad and fast and speed',[15] while skaters including Ziggy Siegfried in 1980 and Neil Blender in the mid-1980s consciously added a greater stall time of several seconds when performing moves such as an invert (5.2).[16] This different treatment of time was in part a regional production, and many UK skaters were surprised to discover that, compared to their own calmly unhurried style, their US counterparts skated at a much greater velocity;[17] as *SkateBoarder* commented of American Eric Grisham, it was 'as if he couldn't slow down if he wanted to'.[18]

By the early 1980s, skaters were not only emphasizing the 'ultra modern moves' but also more extreme 'bionic' versions of the older moves, with aerials rising six feet or more out of the top of the pool wall, or contorted, with the skater's body thrust into strange configurations.

> Every year skateboarding skill quite literally keeps on rising: new unreal bio tricks, impossible variations and combinations of moves and perfection in style – all make past efforts look decidedly tame.[19]

As one commentator put it, these were 'moves I wouldn't have thought possible a year ago'.[20] Eddie Elguera in particular was creating new moves on a monthly basis; his new moves at the Powell-Peralta Marina Cup (late 1980) included a fakie

13. Curtis Hesselgrave, '360 – Oasis Easter Classic', *SkateBoarder*, vol. 5 no. 12 (July 1979), p. 45.

14. Curtis Hesselgrave, 'Whittier Knights: Skate City – Hester Pro Bowl #4', *SkateBoarder*, vol. 6 no. 5 (December 1979), p. 25.

15. Alba, interview, *Thrasher*, p. 31.

16. 'Off the Wall', *SkateBoarder's Action Now*, vol. 7 no. 4 (November 1980), p. 15; and Neil Blender, interview, *Thrasher*, vol. 5 no. 2 (February 1985), p. 28.

17. Tim Leighton-Boyce, conversation (8 July 1997).

18. Curtis Hesselgrave, 'Hester Finale: Battling in the Badlands, Again', *SkateBoarder*, vol. 6 no. 6 (January 1980), p. 30.

19. Iain Urquhart, 'Judging: a Special Report', *Skateline*, no. 8 (Spring 1982), p. 10.

20. Jim Ford, 'King of the Mountain Contest', *SkateBoarder's Action Now*, vol. 7 no. 5 (December 1980), p. 74.

5.2 Time and space production in the stalled, invert air. Skateboarder: Mickie Alba (1980). (Photograph James Cassimus)

ollie 180° into a rock 'n roll, a backside layback grinder tailslide, and a varial layback air into a switch-stance fakie footplant.[21] Elguera's moves marked a shift in body-centric space production, away from single element moves to *combinatorial* moves involving more than one body–board–terrain engagement within a single move. They also, consequently, marked a lengthening of the time of the move. Most significantly, Mike McGill learned his 540° 'McTwist' aerial (1984):[22]

> As he flew out 4 or 5 feet, he went upside down and spun. And kept spinning . . . until he had turned 540°, completely inverted at the 360° point with his head 3 feet above the coping . . . In that moment when he was flying with his top and bottom reversed, everyone who was watching the pool saw something so amazing as to be unbelievable . . . Things had changed. In an instant a new dimension had opened up.[23]

This was a move which heralded a new era again in vertical skating.[24]

By the end of the 1980s, Tony Hawk was doing varial, ollie and flip variants of the 540, and skaters generally were performing even more complicated variations of the combinatorial moves. In particular, by 1988 they began to refocus on the top edge of the wall (rather than just the air above it),[25] including the Jetton grind (frontside grind to revert), cess-slide 50–50s and other such lip tricks as the 'due process' fakie ollie to frontside nosepick, with back truck on deck, followed by frontside aerial to re-enter (Joe Johnson, 1988),[26] fakie ollie 180° nose-taps (Tony Hawk, 1989)[27] and the ollie to front truck grind (Bod Boyle, 1989).[28] These were 'balance point' tricks, where the skater controls the lip with both body and board – through this process, the skater could think of their body and the terrain beneath as one entity.[29] Alternatively, skaters were spending a longer time in the air through ever more complex body–board spatial productions; by 1991, skaters such as Danny Way were experimenting with 900° (2.5 full rotations) aerials.[30] By the same date, skaters were also undertaking many moves backward, or switch-stance.

21. Curtis Hesselgrave, 'The Powell-Peralta Marina Cup', *SkateBoarder's Action Now*, vol. 7 no. 6 (January 1981), p. 65.

22. '540° McTwist', *Thrasher*, vol. 4 no. 10 (October 1984), pp. 32–3; Craig Ramsay, 'When the Hawk Flies', *Thrasher*, vol. 4 no. 11 (November 1984), p. 22; 'Talk', *TransWorld Skateboarding*, vol. 9 no. 10 (October 1991), p. 100; and 'Major Moves', p. 58.

23. Jocko Weyland, 'Epiphany at Mecca', *Thrasher*, vol. 17 no. 7 (July 1997), p. 63.

24. Garry Davis, 'Del Mar Was . . .', *TransWorld Skateboarding*, vol. 6 no. 1 (February 1988), p. 109.

25. Wayne Kerr, 'The Oldest Trick in the Book', *Thrasher*, vol. 7 no. 12 (December 1987), pp. 60–5.

26. Tony Hawk, 'Beyond', *TransWorld Skateboarding*, vol. 6 no. 1 (February 1988), p. 104.

27. 'Ears', *R.A.D.*, no. 80 (October 1989), p 8.

28. 'More Coke and No Stickers: the Hot Tuna Skatemasters at Swansea', *R.A.D.*, no. 79 (September 1989), pp. 29–31.

29. Kerr, 'Oldest Trick', p. 64.

30. Danny Way, interview, *TransWorld Skateboarding*, vol. 9 no. 10 (October 1991), p. 109; and 'Major Moves', p. 55.

These extremely technical and dangerous moves (many performed at eight feet or more above the ground) were partly encouraged by the focus of vertical skating in the 1980s on wooden ramps rather than concrete skateparks. Wooden ramps tended to flex and so be easier to fall on,[31] and offered more predictable transitions. Furthermore, while concave pool walls allowed skaters to 'change direction a lot while moving very fast',[32] this was not possible on the parallel flat walls of a conventional half-pipe, making skaters focus predominantly on the edge of the ramp and the air beyond.

Skaters' own experience of these moves is difficult to access, and their occasional accounts provide only descriptive clues. For example, one experienced skater narrated a run on an early 1980s ramp.

> Standing on top a 10′ high halfpipe with your back foot on your board . . . drop in down the first 2 feet of pure flat wall. Then down the curving slope, across the bottom at speed, bending your knees, and pumping up the other wall. Popping off the lip into the air, the board flying out with you on it, catching it, and keeping it to your feet, turning back in and releasing, trying to avoid a disastrous hang-up on the coping. Grinding on the coping, the metal of the trucks scraping the metal at the top of the ramp with a rough, grating noise. Or going upside down, one arm extended to the top, the other holding the board above your head, stalling, inverted, then coming back in . . . Sliding, flying, hurtling through space, an escaped convict from rigid and normally unavoidable physical laws.[33]

But how is this body space constituted? By what compositional procedures is it produced, and how does it integrate with the space of the skateboard and of the terrain beneath?

Len Lye's short film *Particles in Space* (finished 1979) was created without camera or lens but by scratching directly on to the film, and depicts a swarm of dots and lines pulsing on a black ground. The resulting depiction of compression and tension, eruption and repetition, pulse and stillness, humour and gravity has been described by film-maker and architect Patrick Keiller as the most architectural-spatial film ever made.[34] Although devoid of any 'architectural' subject beyond the development of a sense of space, Lye's film indeed conveys a spatiality absent from most other attempts at representing architecture's spatial character.

It is this exploration which lies within the skateboarder's complex spatial actions, using a series of front-back, left-right, up-down reversals and rotations, in combination

31. Chris Miller, interview, *Thrasher*, vol. 9 no. 10 (May 1989), p. 102; and 'On Board', *Thrasher*, vol. 1 no. 12 (December 1981), p. 43.

32. Miller, interview, *Thrasher*, p. 102.

33. Weyland, 'Epiphany', p. 62.

34. RIBA Architecture Centre, London (20 March 1996).

with precise relations of board, hand/body and terrain, to generate an extraordinary movement and production of body-centric space. As Christian Hosoi described a fellow professional:

> Tony Hawk, who I love to watch skate, is so technical, so precise, so balanced and light footed . . . His body twists from one position to the other, then he goes in backwards.[35]

This, then, is a space of the body. And in this context, the prepositional 'in' of Lye's title – *Particles in Space* – is misleading, for the space is produced *by* that series of dots, through movement and collective evolution. Similarly, the skater's spatial production is a space produced by the skater, out of the dynamic intersection of body, board and terrain. This is the kind of space which Lefebvre describes as having 'properties' (dualities, symmetries, etc.) which come not from the mind, spirit or conscious design, but from a particular occupation of space with particular 'genetic' production operations.[36]

> Before producing effects in the material realm (tools and objects), before producing itself by drawing nourishment from that realm, and before reproducing itself by generating other bodies, each living body is space and has its space.[37]

In this spatial production, space is produced first from within the body[38] (the co-ordinates of left-right, front-back, up-down, spinal rotation, etc.), then centrifugally outward as the body undertakes the dynamics of the move ('your body gets weightless'), then centripetally pulled back in ('pulling back in, the coping looks mean').

> You must get the feeling that your mind is located in your center of gravity. You must think and act from your center. The rest of your body moves around this center point as a wheel moves around its hub.[39]

This is a gestural space of flow and action, of direct engagement with the terrain. On the one hand it is a primary space within and around the body ('extend your back leg, throw in some style'), a form of natural space preserved within abstract space and recoverable through what Lefebvre calls 'spatial architectonics'.[40]

35. Christian Hosoi, interview, *Thrasher*, vol. 9 no. 6 (June 1989), p. 102.
36. Lefebvre, *Production of Space*, pp. 171–3.
37. Ibid., p. 170.
38. Ibid., p. 175–6.
39. Curtis Hesselgrave, 'The Dynamics of Skating – Part II', *SkateBoarder*, vol. 6 no. 11 (June 1980), p. 12.
40. Lefebvre, *Production of Space*, pp. 169–228. See also pp. 229–30.

But even here there is an Other to the body, for remembering that skateboarding had its first origins in surf-related, ocean-based moves, its body-centric space can be seen as an attempt to relate the self to nature. It is, perhaps, a spatial equivalent of Lefebvre's conception that aspects of play can sometimes be the remnant of earlier ways of extending a direct relation to the cosmos.[41] Skateboarding's space-production therefore is not – although Scott Lash has erroneously argued this of Lefebvre's spatial architectonics[42] – purely body-centric and immediate. Rather it is that, as Simmel described the spatiality of social beings,

> Man does not end with the limits of his body or the area comprising his immediate activity. Rather is the range of the person constituted by the sum of effects emanating from him temporally and spatially.[43]

Following these leads, we might then consider that the spatiality of the skateboarder goes beyond the proximate body, and instead is conducted in relation to two physical 'Others' to the skater: the skateboard, and the terrain. I shall deal with each in turn.

To someone learning to skateboard, the skateboard appears as an instrument separate to her or his body, a platform on which to balance – and this is how most 'how to' books explain it. Foot position, standing, pushing off, turning and stopping are followed by 'next steps' involving basic manoeuvres such as kickturns. By contrast, the more proficient skateboarder quickly reconceives of the skateboard as at once separate to, and part of her or his body, and so integral to their relation to the external world ('grasping the rail for the next coming air').

> As the rider gets more advanced, he begins to realize that there are times when there is almost no weight on his feet. This is when he begins to discover that the skateboard as a vehicle, operates more as part of himself than as something he rides on. A basic frontside aerial demonstrates this very well: rider and board work as one unit that moves around a common center of gravity.[44]

Alternatively, in a move like a frontside rock 'n roll (7.15), the board is very much separate to the body, yet intricately related to it through precise foot movements; first the board is pushed away from the body and over the top of the wall, and then brought back under the body using the toe of the rear foot.[45] There are two fulcrum

41. Henri Lefebvre, *Critique of Everyday Life. Volume 1: Introduction* (London: Verso, 1991), pp. 117–8.

42. Scott Lash, 'The Machinic Spider', paper given at 'Parallel Space: the Geography of Virtual Worlds' conference, ICA, London (4 July 1997).

43. Georg Simmel, 'The Metropolis and Mental Life', in P.K. Hatt and A.J. Reiss (eds), *Cities and Society* (New York: Free Press, 1951), pp. 642–3.

44. Curtis Hesselgrave, 'Skate Safe: Balance', *SkateBoarder*, vol. 6 no. 6 (January 1980), p. 13.

45. Eddie Elguera, 'Special Tips, Part 1: Frontside Rock 'n Roll', *SkateBoarder*, vol. 6 no. 8 (March 1980), pp. 38–9.

points here – the deck underside resting on the wall, and the deck kicktail beneath the rear toe – each countered against the other to produce a precise body-board combination.

In such phenomenological acts, the skateboard is not so much used as the simple application of a device against a remote object (Heidegger's *Vorhandenheit*, or 'presentness-at-hand' of the object 'out there'), but rather concurs with the notion of the tool-object as *Zuhandenheit*, or 'readiness-to-hand'.[46]

> The less we just stare at the hammer-Thing, and the more we seize hold of it and use it, the more primordial does our relationship to it become, and the more unveiledly is it encountered as that which it is – as tool.[47]

In skateboarding this primordial relationship is rendered spatial and dynamic, involving the phenomenology of space-time movement as much as essences.

> In the old days you moved *on* the board, while now you move *with* the board and the board moves with you.[48]

For the skater, the skateboard is related to the body through differing kinds of co-ordinate; freestyler Rodney Mullen described it as thinking in categories 'like rolling forward, backward rail, stationary, 50/50 or aerial'.[49] These kinds of category range from the most basic, such as whether the skater stands with left foot forward ('regular foot') or right foot forward ('goofy foot'). Other simple descriptors include ways of moving backward ('fakie', 'switch-stance') or transferring to a backward direction ('revert', 'fakie'). More complicated body-board relations refer to how the board is held with which arm-leg contortion ('indy air', backside aerial with rear hand holding inner edge of board through the legs; 'mute air', backside aerial with leading hand holding forward inner edge of board; 'stalefish', frontside aerial with inner edge held by rear hand reaching around back of the legs), how the board is rotated in the hand ('varial', board rotated about its centrepoint (5.7); 'finger flip', board rotated about its long axis), how the board and skater are related to the ground through the body ('frontside', facing the wall; 'backside', back to the wall; 'layback', stretched out across the wall; 'footplant', foot taken off the board and placed on the top of the wall (5.3); 'invert air', body inverted (5.2)), or how the board and body are related to the ground through the board ('Smith grind', overlapping grind with rear-truck and body over the top of the wall (8.1); 'blunt', stationary or sliding block with nose or tail of the board (7.14)) and so on. Some

46. George Steiner, *Heidegger* (London: Fontana, 1992), p. 89.
47. Martin Heidegger, in Steiner, *Heidegger*, p. 89.
48. Stacy Peralta, interview, *SkateBoarder*, vol. 3 no. 1 (October 1976), p. 57.
49. Rodney Mullen, interview, *Thrasher*, vol. 4 no. 3 (March 1984), p. 32.

5.3 A specific body-board relation in the backside footplant move. Skateboarder: Rodd Saunders, Marina Del Rey skatepark (1979). (Photograph James Cassimus)

descriptors also refer to the time of the move ('axle stall', where the skater comes to momentary rest on the top of the wall; 'fast plant', a backside footplant where the foot is taken off and on again quickly).

Within the act of these skateboarding moves, the skateboard is less a piece of equipment and takes on more the character of a prosthetic device, an extension of the body as a kind of fifth limb, absorbed into and diffused inside the body-terrain encounter.

> Making your board an extension of your body is control of your soul.[50]

And as this quotation suggests, such an act is not only physical but also mental, involving a projection of the self out into the board and space beyond it. Skateboarders even sometimes remark on how their skateboard takes on their own personality, and becomes 'almost an actual part' of themselves.[51] Rodney Mullen again gives an insight into this, conceiving of the skateboard as having both an autonomous, organic life and a requirement to be brought within the body, a process for which technical operations are but a secondary consideration.

> I kick my board around sometimes and watch its motions as it twirls around . . . I get an idea of what I want to do, then I think over it a lot, like where my feet have to be to press the board back. I think about the mechanics of it after the fact.[52]

Or as Bobby Piercy put it, 'the footwork is in relationship to you doing your riding'.[53]

In this kind of interaction, appropriate use, performance and manual action 'possess their own kind of sight', or what Heidegger calls *circumspection*, whereby an intimate knowledge of a craft and instrument leads to a faster, more delicate understanding of the relation between self, tool and object.[54] This tripartite formulation suggests that the relation of board and body is a tool-body relation, but not purely so: the skateboard is also a mediation of the body-terrain space ('dodging the hang-up, you land real clean'). The subject and the tool – here the body and the skateboard – are therefore not the sole producers of space in a Leibnizian sense, in which 'absolute relative' space is waiting to be filled, and where a specific body is considered capable of defining space by gesture and movement.[55] Or in Heideggerean terms, the subject or 'I' is never alone in its experience of *Dasein* (Being), such that

50. 'Blast From the Past', *Thrasher*, vol. 17 no. 9 (September 1997), p. 54.
51. Britt Parrott, 'Friendship', *TransWorld Skateboarding*, vol. 6 no. 1 (February 1988), p. 6.
52. Mullen, interview, *Thrasher*, p. 61.
53. Bobby Piercy, interview, *SkateBoarder*, vol. 4 no. 7 (February 1978), p. 101.
54. George Steiner, *Heidegger*, (London: Fontana, 1992), p. 90.
55. Lefebvre, *Production of Space*, pp. 169–70.

encountering other people and things is part of reciprocal realizations of being.[56] Thus sensory-sensual space is, ultimately, simply a component in the construction of social spaces.[57]

> There is an immediate relationship between the body and its space, between the body's deployment in space and its occupation of space . . . This is a truly remarkable relationship: the body with the energies at its disposal, the living body, creates or produces its own space; conversely, the laws of space, which is to say the laws of discrimination in space, also govern the living body and the deployment of its energies.[58]

In terms of skateboarding's relation to architecture, its production of space is not purely bodily or sensorial; instead, the skater's body produces its space dialectically with the production of architectural space.

What then is the nature of this dialectical interaction? Given the body-centric nature of skateboarding space, it makes sense to consider this in relation to the operations of the skater's body, particularly their multi- and inter-sensory nature.

Architecture frequently operates as a kind of social mirror, forming a kind of Sartrean 'Other's look',[59] the user self-checking her or his identity against a building or boundary.[60] Within this mirror process, modern architectural space – 'the space of blank sheets of paper, drawing-boards, plans, sections, elevations, scale models, geometrical projections'[61] – in particular tends to concentrate on the visual, on objects and surfaces, and correspondingly to ignore the space of the body. And some skateparks were undoubtedly designed more as theme-parks than places for skateboarding, and so relied on this kind of visualization of space; for example, 'The Galaxy' skatepark intended for the San Fernando Valley was themed on the then recent *Star Wars* film.[62]

The constructed spaces of the more successful skateparks were, however, very much directed towards the space of the body, particularly its movement as flow, stall and turning. This can be seen in various aspects of skatepark design. First, the *curvature in plan* of many skatepark elements, particularly the typical roundness of

56. Steiner, *Heidegger*, p. 90.

57. Lefebvre, *Production of Space*, p. 212.

58. Ibid., p. 170.

59. Jean-Paul Sartre, *Being and Nothingness* (London: Routledge, 1989), pp. 252–302. See also Martin Jay, *Downcast Eyes* (Berkeley: University of California Press, 1994), pp. 263–328.

60. Marc Augé, *Non-Places* (London: Verso, 1995), pp. 92 and 101–3; and Iain Borden, 'Thick Edge: Architectural Boundaries and Spatial Flows', *Architectural Design*, special issue on 'Architecture and Anthropology' (October 1996), pp. 84–7.

61. Lefebvre, *Production of Space*, p. 200.

62. 'Are Our Skate Parks Tough Enough?', *Skateboard Scene*, vol. 1 no. 1 (n.d., c. November/December 1977), pp. 36–9 and 52.

pools, intentionally provokes the skater's high-speed carve across the face of the element, while throwing the skater back against herself or himself through a centripetal force (4.5).

> You have more speed in a pool, all your force is going with you.[63]

> In pools and on banks, I try to use the inherent power of the forms. No excess movements here, just working with the natural speed.[64]

While such centrifugal gestures were not always successful – for example, the 'snake run' feature akin to a bob-sleigh run and incorporated in many early skateparks (4.8) was frequently designed without due attention to the curves required by a moving skateboarder[65] – the better features of skateparks, in particular those added in 1978 onward, promoted both speed and new moves; for example, the tight corners of the square component of the Upland Combi-Pool enabled skaters to pump through and gain extra speed on the carve (4.7, 5.10),[66] and also encouraged a host of new moves such as the corner boardslide.[67] Unlike the relatively simple form of half-pipes which tend to stimulate a trick-oriented approach to skateboarding focused on the lip of ramp, elements like the Combi-Pool – a 'pool with a million lines'[68] – tend to encourage a sense of new directions and movements across their whole surface.

> Like on a ramp you learn how to manipulate your board, but in a big pool you just ride it.[69]

Second, the specific design of the *transition* – the curvature in section – of an element's floor-wall relationship produces varying skateboarding conditions. In particular, tighter transitions lead to greater speed and availability of flat wall above, propelling a 'fierce upward drive'[70] to heighten the speed and motion of the body. Again, the 1978 and later elements did this best. As one skateboarder who skated a number of early US skateparks described it,

63. Alba, interview, p. 33.
64. Peralta, interview, *SkateBoarder*, p. 58.
65. Hazel Pennell, *Skateboarding* (London: GLC Intelligence Unit, London Topics no. 24, 1978), p. 4; Wally Inouye, interview, *SkateBoarder*, vol. 4 no. 3 (October 1977), p. 53; and Editorial, *Thrasher* (July 1992).
66. Tony Hawk, interview, *Thrasher*, vol. 9 no. 6 (June 1989), p. 72.
67. 'Focus', *SkateBoarder*, vol. 6 no. 6 (January 1980), p. 45.
68. Dudley Counts, 'Upland Gold Cup Finale', *Thrasher*, vol. 1 no. 1 (January 1981), p 11.
69. Chris Miller, interview, *R.A.D.*, no. 77 (July 1989), p. 43.
70. Sally Shaw, 'Plasticity: a Questioning of Representational and Experiential Production of Space' (B.A. thesis, Chelsea College of Art and Design, 1998).

> The design of the Combi pool . . . was perfectly designed to accommodate the flow and motion of the skateboarder producing a sensation of weightlessness that contributed to the ease in which the body would naturally surge.[71]

The Combi-Pool was also thought by *SkateBoarder* to be particularly suited to a 'multiple line approach' to skating.[72] Similarly, the carefully-tuned variable transitions and plan forms of Livingston pool were considered to be 'years in advance of anything else' (5.4).[73]

Third, *flat bottoms* were first added by skater-designers such as Rob Schlaefli to skatepark pools around 1978–9, allowing greater time between moves on opposite walls and also greater pumping up and down the bordering transitions (4.7).[74] Flat bottoms also create a kind of negative space to the explosive moves and high-speed carves undertaken up on the walls, thus forming a counter-rhythm within the skater's run.

Fourth, *drop-in points* forming the entrance to pools and pipes lead to greater initial speed (4.7, 4.9). They also provide a sense of orientation and directionality to otherwise symmetrical designs.

Fifth, the *smoothness* of the element's surface contributes dramatically to the skater's micro-experience, affecting not only speed and comfort but also noise, grip and predictability. Smoothness of surface also encourages through tactility and empathy on the part of the skater a greater speed and smoothness of her or his own style; surface is translated into body gesture and attitude.

Sixth, the *symmetry* of opposing walls allows a rhythm to be set up by the skater, enabling new moves to be tried out (4.7, 4.9).[75] Good symmetry also allows the compositional sequence of the run to be smoothly extended.

Seventh, the *edge of the wall*, particularly where tiles and/or projecting coping are used, imparts a sudden arrest of that surface, throwing the skater simultaneously off the edge of the element and back onto herself or himself (5.3). These events form contrapuntal moments within the continuity of run generated from symmetry and surface.

Eighth, at the other end of the scale, the *variation and combination* of the elements across a skatepark allow skateboarders to link different kinds of spatial experience, sometimes recombining them together into one run (4.4).

But this constructed skateboarding architecture does not wholly *dictate* the performativity of skateboarding; rather the constructed architecture of a skatepark like the Del Mar Skate Ranch was itself a kind of 'drawing board' on which the

71. Bill Stinson, e-mail (13 May 1997).
72. Hesselgrave, 'Hester', p. 24.
73. Alpine Newsletter, in *Skateline*, no. 8 (Spring 1982), p. 13.
74. 'Life and Death: a Step Beyond Pay Skateboarding?', *Thrasher*, vol. 1 no. 9 (September 1981), p. 19.
75. Stacy Peralta, in 'On the Road with Stacy Peralta', *Skateboard!*, no. 8 (April 1978), p. 52.

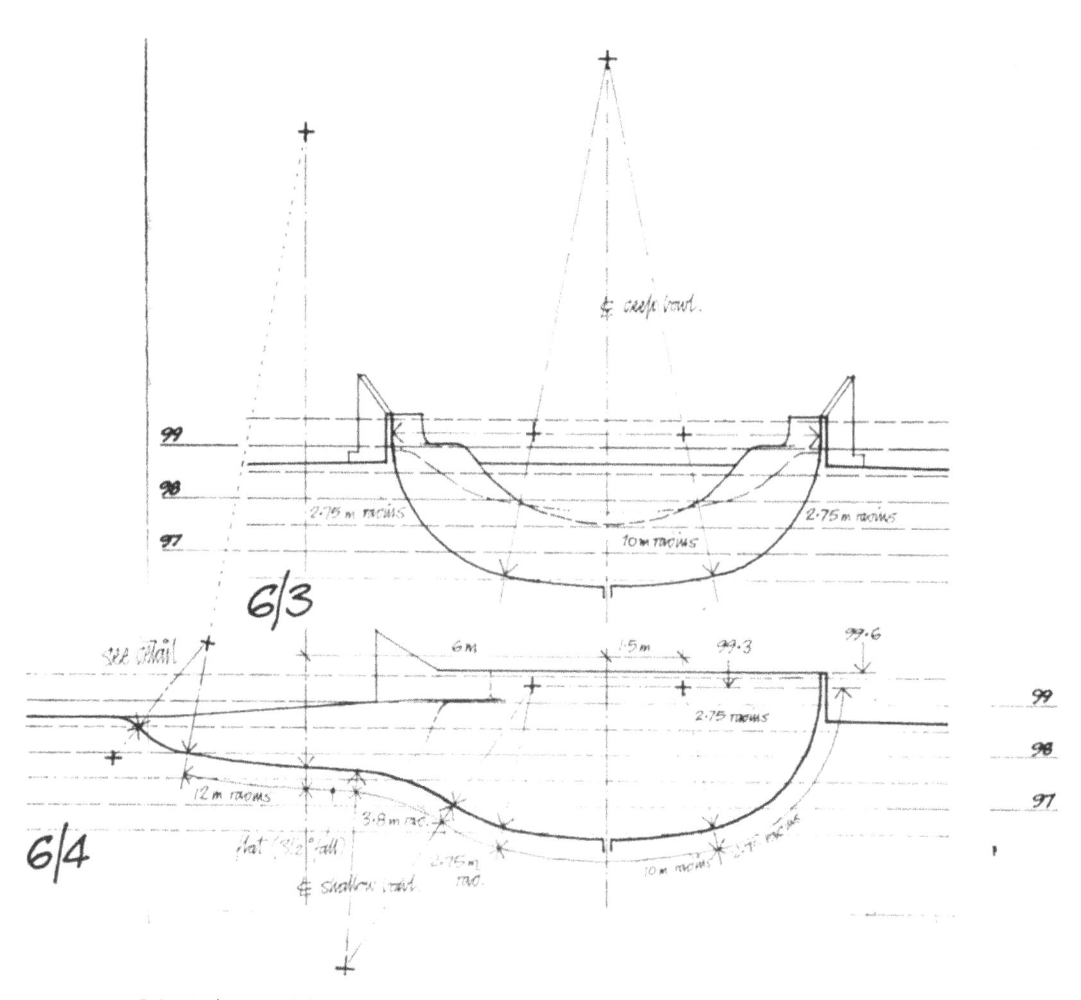

5.4 Architectural design as the projector of bodily flow. Variable transitions of pool section at Livingston skatepark, designed by Iain Urquhart (1980).

production of new moves took place.[76] Insofar as skatepark forms do partially determine skate moves, a process of resistance and re-creation occurs. Not only is the Sartrean look returned, but architecture ceases to be purely the Other, and is instead absorbed into the body–board–terrain relation. The spaces created are thus part of skater as well as of the terrain, and each is a unique, active production.

> The lines a skater takes are like fingerprints.[77]

76. Davis, 'Del Mar', p. 108.
77. Simon Napper, interview, *Skateboard!*, no. 19 (June 1979), p. 30.

This process takes place through a very precise (although undoubtedly limited) *questioning* of architecture put forward by skateboarding. What is this architectural form for? To what purpose can it be put? What is the relation of ground, verticals, textures, surfaces?

> Ask the coping. It quivers at the sight of a pool rider's bare trucks . . . But that's what it's for; its round edge protrudes to be pulverized, its cement cries to be ground to the bone, its fat lip exists as an earthly exit for sky-bound wheels.[78]

The skater's body here interrogates architecture as another body in relation to its own actions, a process described by one skater as the 'instinct to direct a body mass through the "unseen corridors" called lines'.[79]

> Objects touch one another, feel, smell and hear one another. Then they contemplate one another with eye and gaze. One truly gets the impression that every shape in space, every spatial plane, constitutes a mirror and produces a mirage effect; that within each body the rest of the world is reflected, and referred back to, in an ever-renewed to-and-fro of reciprocal reflection, an interplay of shifting colours, lights and forms.[80]

> And in the (deep) end
> The line that you give
> Is equal to the grind
> That you get[81]

Where the architectural space of modernity tends to homogeneity, fusing geometry and the visual, inspiring physical discomfort and erasing localization, the body (such as that of the skateboarder) can project its symmetries and actions onto that architecture, refusing to accept it as a pre-existent world and instead (re)producing architecture on its own terms. These questions are unconcerned with architecture's historical purpose, but are nonetheless demanding in their line of attack, resisting the intellectualization, 'logic of visualization' and 'optical formant' which modern architectural space imposes over other senses.[82]

> A narrow and desiccated rationality of this kind overlooks the core and foundation of space, the total body, the brain, gestures and so forth. It forgets that space does not consist in the projection of an intellectual representation, does not arise

78. Brian Brannon, 'Viva Las Pools', *Thrasher*, vol. 8 no. 7 (July 1988), p. 72.
79. Morizen Föche, 'New Blood', *Thrasher*, vol. 6 no. 3 (March 1986), p. 45.
80. Lefebvre, *Production of Space*, p. 183.
81. Billy Runaway, 'Return to the Beatle Bowl', *Thrasher*, vol. 6 no. 10 (October/November 1986), p. 55.
82. Lefebvre, *Production of Space*, pp. 98, 199–200 and 286.

> from the visible-readable realm, but that it is first of all *heard* (listened to) and *enacted* (through physical gestures and movements).[83]

Skateboarding uses, besides intense vision, a responsivity of touch, sense, balance, hearing, posture, muscular control, strength, agility and fluidity by which to perform. 'You use your whole body and your whole mind, you can't help but flow.'[84] *Skate-Boarder* referred to 'incredible space-orientation (i.e. balance, timing, reflexes)',[85] and to the conception that skateboard moves are 'felt rather than seen'.[86] There is, then, an intense bodily and mental focus within the move, such that the two processes become one.

Much of this stems from the dynamic nature of skateboarding; 'I've gotta be moving fast.'[87] As both Merleau-Ponty and August Schmarsow noted, we tend to relate space to ourselves by envisaging that we are in motion, using terms such as 'extension', 'expanse' and 'direction', and measuring size by the movement of the body and the eye.

> Because movement is not limited to submitting passively to space and time, it actively assumes them.[88]

Or as Schmarsow explains space:

> We cannot express its relation to ourselves in any other way than by imagining that we are in motion, measuring the length, width and depth, or by attributing to the static lines, surfaces, and volumes the movement that our eyes and our kinesthetic sensations suggest to us, even though we survey the dimensions while standing still. The spatial construct is a human creation and cannot confront the creative or appreciative subject as if it were a cold, crystallized form.[89]

Because skateboarding is both body-centric and motile, space is projected from the whole body, and not just the eye or the intellect alone, (or as the skateboarder's poem quoted above puts it, 'your eyes seek reality, the mind is aware/thrust up the wall and click off the tile').

83. Ibid., p. 200.
84. Peralta, interview, *SkateBoarder*, p. 58.
85. 'Who's Hot! Ellen Berryman', *SkateBoarder*, vol. 3 no. 2 (December 1976), p. 90.
86. *SkateBoarder*, vol. 3 no. 5, in Glen E. Friedman, *Fuck You Heroes* (New York: Burning Flags, 1994), index.
87. Napper, interview, p. 54.
88. Merleau-Ponty, *Phenomenology*, p. 102.
89. August Schmarsow, 'The Essence of Architectural Creation', in Harry Francis Mallgrave and Eleftherios Ikonomou (eds), *Empathy, Form and Space: Problems in German Aesthetics, 1873–1893*, (Santa Monica: Getty Center for the History of Art and the Humanities, 1994), p. 291.

> Skateboarding is a sport that requires whole body commitment; in other words, the body must work as a single unit to achieve the maximum potential available . . . put your mind and your body in tune.[90]

Above all, it is the engagement with architecture that is important ('thrust up the wall'), such that the moving body treats architecture as but one projector of space to be interpolated with the projection of space from itself. For example, Lefebvre notes that when one is crossing the street, a conscious calculation must be made of the steps and distance involved.[91] The same thing happens whenever a skater performs a move in relation to a specific piece of terrain, and is particularly explicit in a move such as a 'canyon jump' aerial where the skater crosses the pool's entrance point in an extended lateral pass. Here the skater's questions concern the distance across the gap and the orientation of the bordering walls, and are answered by a move involving speed and a bodily-throw. Thus both the *presence* (the walls) and the *absence* (the gap) of architecture are engaged with, the skater's flight bringing the walls together where otherwise they are not; the gap is at once stressed and removed. In this context, it is significant that for a 1980 competition event at Oasis skatepark the judges considered the 'entire surface of the pool' to include the air above it; the pool's architecture was thus defined not by its own physicality but by the skaters' engagement with it, and their production of a space all over and beyond it.[92]

> Architecture produces living bodies, each with its own distinctive traits. The animating principle of such a body, its presence, is neither visible nor legible as such, nor is it the object of any discourse, for it reproduces itself within those who *use* the space in question, within their lived experience. Of that experience the tourist, the passive spectator, can grasp but a pale shadow.[93]

> Speed will set you free. Speed is the crack between sketch and style. Catch it and then hang on for the glide. With speed, nothing is impossible.[94]

It is then the intersection of the moving body and the physicality of architecture which are important in skateboarding; unlike the scopic-dependence of the tourist gaze,[95] user and architecture come together to create a new spatial event, an

90. Hesselgrave, 'Dynamics', p. 12.
91. Henri Lefebvre, *Writings on Cities*, (Oxford: Blackwell, 1996), p. 220.
92. Curtis Hesselgrave, 'Oasis/G&S Cup', *SkateBoarder's Action Now*, vol. 7 no. 1 (August 1980), p. 24.
93. Lefebvre, *Production of Space*, p. 137.
94. Brannon, 'Viva', p. 75.
95. Dean MacCannell, *The Tourist* (New York, Schocken, 1976/89); John Urry, *The Tourist Gaze* (London: Sage, 1990); and John Urry, *Consuming Places* (London: Routledge, 1995).

occupied territory. Architecture is at once erased and reborn in the phenomenal act of the skater's move.

Space, then, is produced dialectically – both outward from the body, and in relation to skateboard and skateboard terrain, each of the last two being erased within the process. But of course this is not a simple additive procedure, in which the body is preserved in its original state – it too is reformulated. To give a very obvious example of this, my body as I sit and write this sentence on my Apple Mac, involving only the smallest movements of hands, fingers, neck and eyes, is very different to my body as it was constituted in the layback move shown here, some two decades ago (5.5).

That architecture in some way forms its human subjects has often been commented upon. As Beatriz Colomina notes,

> Architecture is not simply a platform that accommodates the viewing subject. It is a viewing mechanism that produces the subject.[96]

5.5 The erasure and reproduction of the body. Iain Borden, layback at the modified Performance Bowl, Rom (1980). (The Performance Bowl is depicted here after the removal of the top-most wall section.)

96. Beatriz Colomina, 'The Split Wall: Domestic Voyeurism', in Beatriz Colomina (ed.), *Sexuality and Space* (New York: Princeton Architectural Press, 1992), p. 83.

But in the architectural formation of skateboarding, this involves more than just vision, for here the space of the body is equally reconstructed as what Lefebvre calls a 'spatial body', subject to the various symmetries, interactions, planes, centres, peripheries and other determinants of space.[97] He also asserts that human beings should not limit their activities to the mastery or appropriation of space but also 'take control of their own nature'.[98] This process comes to the fore in the context of space, the rhythms of time[99] and, in particular, the spatial body. Any study of social being must consequently proceed along these lines.

> Dominated by overpowering forces, including a variety of brutal techniques and an extreme emphasis on visualization, the body fragments, abdicates responsibility for itself – in a word, disappropriates itself . . . Any revolutionary 'project' today, whether utopian or realistic, must, if it is to avoid hopeless banality, make the reappropriation of the body, in association with the reappropriation of space, into a non-negotiable part of its agenda.[100]

Such a project – 'rhythmanalysis' – would also refer to the rhythms of the body, not only as internal rhythms such as breathing, hunger and sleep, but also as relations with the external through sexuality, social life and thought. It might even eventually replace psychoanalysis as 'more concrete, more effective, and closer to a pedagogy of appropriation (the appropriation of the body, as of spatial practice)'.[101] We must then consider skateboarding in this context, as a partial glimpse in the society of the spectacle of a recovery of the body.

Of course other social activities have emphasized the body, but this has variously involved such things as: the world-stage commercialism of professional sport, perhaps most extremely typified by the intense commercialism of the 1996 Atlanta Olympics,[102] including British athlete Lynford Christie wearing contact lenses to transform his eyes into the logo of his sponsors, Puma; the conscious artistic intellectualism of performance art;[103] and the narcissistic 'mirroring body'[104] of such

97. Lefebvre, *Production of Space*, p. 195.

98. Henri Lefebvre, *Introduction to Modernity: Twelve Preludes September 1959 – May 1961*, (London: Verso, 1995), p. 113.

99. Lefebvre, *Production of Space*, pp. 165–6.

100. Ibid, pp. 166–7.

101. Ibid., p. 205.

102. 'Atlanta Chief Sees End of Free Enterprise Games Era', *Oman Daily Observer* (3 August 1996), p. 11; Ian Katz, 'NBC's Schlock Tactics', *The Guardian*, 'Media' section (5 August 1996), p. 13; and Paul Rodgers, 'Winner Takes All', *The Independent on Sunday*, 'Business' section (4 August 1996).

103. Marvin Carlson, *Performance* (London: Routledge, 1996), pp. 101–3.

104. Arthur Frank, 'For a Sociology of the Body: an Analytical Review', in Mike Featherstone, Mike Hepworth and Bryan S. Turner (eds), *The Body* (London: Sage, 1991), pp. 53–4 and 61–8. See also Chris Shilling, *The Body and Social Theory* (London: Sage, 1993), pp. 95–7.

practices as body-building and consumer-shopping, obsessed with their surface and monadic, internalized world. Skateboarding has undoubtedly relied on specific professionals to popularize the activity and, above all, to sell equipment, and has also had sponsorship from major international companies, as with the Pepsi team (1977) and Swatch events (late 1980s and 1990s).[105] And in the 1970s most professional skaters were keen to see skateboarding developed as a professional sport,[106] while occasional events such as the globally-televised Xtreme Games held annually since the mid-1990s thrust skateboarding into a highly spectacularized format.[107] Nonetheless, skateboarding has generally resisted not only outright commercialism and institutional control (with skateboarders in the 1980s actively campaigning for skateboarding *not* to be included in the Olympics[108]), but also the commodification of the body. *Thrasher*, for example, ran a spoof advertisement that 'we're not sure we'd like to see', showing a spectacularized skater promoting a '$100,000 Professional Skate Jam' at the 'All New Skatorium' with a 20,000-seat arena.[109] Or as another skater put it a decade later, 'the only sport that can't be watched is skateboarding. Watching skateboarding is like peanut butter, no jelly.'[110]

Resisting this kind of overt commodification, in skateboarding the skater's body is born from the poetry of its intricate spatial distortions and the rehearsal of its conflictual body–board–terrain events ('the glare off the tile, the grind marks are clear/getting sketch is no sweat, it's slamming you fear'). When a skater such as Tony Hawk performs a 540° aerial variation, his body becomes a 'twisted mass' unrecognizable because of its speed and strange contortion.[111]

> I am not in space and time, nor do I conceive space and time; I belong to them, my body combines with them and includes them.[112]

105. 'Swatch Impact Tour Information Update', *Thrasher*, vol. 9 no. 1 (January 1989), pp. 56–7 and 102.

106. Ellen Oneal, interview, *SkateBoarder*, vol. 4 no. 6 (January 1978), pp. 70–2; Biniak, interview, p. 70; Brian Gillogly, 'The Pepsi Team', *SkateBoarder*, vol. 4 no. 3 (October 1977), pp. 84–93; and Marc Sinclair and Jeremy Henderson, interview, *SkateBoarder*, vol. 6 no. 2 (September 1979), p. 35.

107. Ivory Serra, 'Corporate Death Burger: Xtreme Games, Providence, Rhode Island, 1996', *Thrasher*, vol. 16 no. 11 (November 1996), pp. 52–7; and Airwalk, advertisement, *TransWorld Skateboarding*, vol. 15 no. 11 (November 1997), p. 49.

108. Kevin Thatcher, in Armen Keteyian, 'Chairman of the Board', *Sports Illustrated*, vol. 65 no. 23 (24 November 1986), p. 48.

109. 'Ads (We're Not Sure) We'd Like to See', *Thrasher*, vol. 6 no. 3 (March 1986), p. 27.

110. Meg, 'Get Off the Air!!', *Slap*, vol. 6 no. 9 (September 1997), p. 50.

111. Kevin Wilkins, 'NSA Spring Nationals: Kona USA Skatepark', *TransWorld Skateboarding*, vol. 9 no. 10 (October 1991), p. 43.

112. Merleau-Ponty, *Phenomenology*, p. 140.

The various names given to moves (see earlier in this chapter) are then merely an attempt to understand and classify an otherwise incomprehensible entity. The skater's body itself is an assertive act, constructed out of the activity of skateboarding performed in relation to architecture; as Merleau-Ponty describes it, the spatiality of the body is not an assemblage of points of stimuli, located in relation to other objects, a *spatiality of position*, but is presented to the self as an attitude directed towards a certain task, a *spatiality of situation*.[113]

A production of time is also enacted in this situational space, evident in skateboarding through the skater's run across the architecture of the skatepark element or ramp. Whereas time in capitalism is increasingly dominated by the measured time of clocks and economic rationales,[114] time in skateboarding ranges from the duration of the session, the limit of the run dictated by the skater's own abilities and stamina, and the rhythmic pattern of move–transfer–move–transfer as the skater oscillates between walls. In particular, the run is often performed in a fluid manner where the bewitching pendulum rhythm of the skater moving between one wall and another is interspersed with sudden eruptions of aggressive energy; temporally, a series of calm periods, lasting a few seconds, are punctuated by extreme body-contortions and board–terrain engagement much shorter in duration. In terms of energy, periods of calm efficiency are counterpoised against massive releases and concentrations of effort and physicality.

Within each move this temporality and use of energy is further differentiated; in moves such as aerials the moment at which the skater leaves the wall is perceived as a sudden departure, followed by a suspended section where board and body hang in space, waiting for gravity to pull the combination back down, and then, once again, the sudden re-engagement through reconnection with terra firma. The most explosive part of the move in terms of space and physical complexity then is often, contradictorily, also where temporality seemingly stands still momentarily. The effect is like that of a slow-motion explosion in a movie (5.1, 5.7). And this expenditure of energy and production of time is also enacted in relation to something: the architecture of the skateboard terrain.

> Surplus energy *qua* 'normal' energy relates on the one hand to itself, i.e. to the body which stores it, and on the other hand to its 'milieu', i.e. to space. In the life of every 'being' . . . there are moments when the energy available is so abundant that it tends to be explosively discharged. It may be turned back against itself, or it may spread outwards, in gratuitousness or grace.[115]

113. Ibid., p. 100. See also Lefebvre, *Production of Space*, pp. 42 and 363.
114. Lefebvre, *Production of Space*, pp. 95–6.
115. Ibid., p. 180.

As Lefebvre notes, this is *productive* energy through its producing of some change, no matter how small, in the world.[116]

In summary, skateboarding is a destructive-absorptive-reproductive process of both body and architecture (5.6). Consequently its mode of spatial composition is very different to that of architecture, replacing architecture's 'classicist' mode with one of 'romanticism'.[117]

5.6 Super-architectural space: the deranged destruction and re-birth of body, board and architecture. Skateboarders: Duane Peters and Tony Alva in the Winchester pool (1979). (Photograph Craig Fineman)

> You're dealing with something that's beyond the normal balance of things . . . Redefining the order of things.[118]

In place of the organized cosmos of architecture-classicism's cohesion, internalized hierarchies, imitation and balance, there are the waves, vibrations and oscillations of skateboarding's ludic procedures, suggesting conflict and contradiction, chaos and confusion, internalization of the external world, emotion and spontaneity.

In particular, like Lefebvre's conceptual space-time of rhythmanalysis, this means not so much analysing rhythms as to 'give and abandon oneself to its duration'; to fully engage with architecture as a reproduction of the rhythm of urban life one must not, for example, stand outside a building and stare at its façade, but should be inside and outside of it as when stood at a window or balcony.[119] As an extreme version of this kind of engagement, the skateboarding–architecture encounter involves all manner of physical interrogations, and as such is closer to the rhythms of music or the imagined spaces of poetry and literature than to the sights of the visual arts, linking inner and outer life, body and architecture, action and meaning.[120]

116. Ibid., p. 179.
117. Lefebvre, *Introduction to Modernity*, pp. 322–4.
118. Jerry Casale, interview, *SkateBoarder*, vol. 6 no. 5 (December 1979), p. 35.
119. Lefebvre, *Writings on Cities*, p. 219. See also p. 229.
120. Henri Lefebvre, *Everyday Life in the Modern World* (London: Transaction Publishers, 1984), p. 20; and Lefebvre, *Introduction to Modernity*, pp. 263–4.

> Music – it does something to make you go faster, make your adrenalin pump . . . your feet are set perfect, then you just hear a certain part of a song, say, you're flying down, and you set in your mind that you're going to jam an aerial or something, do something really radical.[121]

Like music and dance, skateboarding creates 'repetitions and redundancies of rhythms' and 'symmetries and asymmetries' irreducible to analytic thought.[122]

> What really makes a trick insane has nothing to do with the trick itself. It's a combination of terrain, the individual, the madness of the moment and the situation at hand.[123]

Skateboarding is like Joyce's 'festival of language, a delirium of words'[124] transposed into a festival of movement, a series of precise spatial-temporal actions rendered demented and deranged, and which ultimately destroys and recreates body, board and architecture together. Through skateboarding, the architecture of the pool and the skatepark 'stands battered and abused'.[125] This is space which is above, beyond, in addition to, and in excess of, the space of objects or the space of the static body. This is super-architectural space.

So far consideration of skateboard performance has been mainly as a pure activity, restricted to the skater's body and immediate terrain. However, it is important to avoid the reductivity Lefebvre notes in Merleau-Ponty, where subject and object are unconsidered in relation to social practice;[126] the space of the body is also the space of others.

> Space – *my* space – is not the context of which I constitute the 'textuality': instead, it is first of all *my body*, and then it is my body's counterpart or 'other', its mirror-image or shadow.[127]

To consider this textual space of many bodies, I focus here on the integrated nature of representations in skateboarding; through this process, the social performativity of the body, skateboard and architecture is partly played out.

121. Rodney Jesse, interview, *SkateBoarder*, vol. 4 no. 10 (May 1978), p. 60.
122. Lefebvre, *Production of Space*, pp. 205–6.
123. 'Major Moves', p. 51.
124. Lefebvre, *Everyday Life*, p. 4.
125. Brannon, 'Viva', p. 72.
126. Lefebvre, *Production of Space*, p. 183 n16.
127. Ibid., p. 184.

SLICES OF TIME

Considering a skateboarder as representation can be undertaken in two ways. I shall deal later with the way in which representations can form a lived component of skaterboarding, but first, and perhaps most obviously, there is the technical image as published medium. Originally, this occurred in skateboard magazines as photographs, and among the most prolific of the US skateboard photographers in the 1970s were *SkateBoarder*'s Warren Bolster (3.8, 4.4), Jim Goodrich, Craig Fineman (4.6, 5.6),[128] James Cassimus (4.3, 5.1–5.3),[129] Ted Terrebonne[130] and freelancer Glen E. Friedman.[131] In the 1980s and 1990s, US photographers included *TransWorld Skateboarding*'s J. Grant Brittain (5.7, 9.1), Geoff Kula and Spike Jonze, and *Thrasher*'s Morizen Föche ('Mo-Fo') (3.7), Jeff Newton, Bryce Kanights and Chris Ortiz.[132] In the UK, 1970s photographers included *Skateboard!*'s Robert Vente, Jerry Young and Ian Dobbie (4.8), and *Skateboard Scene*'s Gregg Haythorpe. In the late 1980s and early 1990s in the UK they included *R.A.D.*'s Jay Podesta (a pseudonym for Vernon Adams) (5.9), Tim Leighton-Boyce (4.13, 5.11, 7.16) and Paul Sunman, and *Skateboard!*'s (second series) Steve Kane and Paul Duffy. In the 1990s they included *Sidewalk Surfer*'s Andy Horsley (7.6, 7.12, 7.14, 8.2), Andy Shaw and Matthew 'Wig' Worland (7.7, 7.13, 8.1, 8.4).

These photographers began with conventional still imagery. After the advent of the first skateparks, they used new high-speed motor-drive technology to capture innovative moves[133] and, in particular, the sequential detail of high-speed skateboard moves (5.1, 5.7). This concern with disclosing the movement of the human body reaches back to the 1870s photography of Eadweard Muybridge,[134] while also intimating the rapid innovation of new skateboard moves.

128. 'Focus: Craig Fineman, Portfolio', *SkateBoarder's Action Now*, vol. 7 no. 4 (November 1980), pp. 38–45; and 'Shooting Gallery', *Thrasher*, vol. 12 no. 10 (October 1992), pp. 40–1.

129. 'Portfolio: Jim Cassimus', *SkateBoarder*, vol. 4 no. 5 (December 1977), pp. 126–30. See also *SkateBoarder* Photo Annual, no. 1 (Summer 1979).

130. 'Shooting', pp. 40–1.

131. Friedman, *Fuck You Heroes*; Friedman, *Fuck You Too: the Extras + More Scrapbook*, (Los Angeles: 2.13.61 Publications and Burning Flags, 1996), especially Sam Sifton 'Afterword'; 'Shooting', pp. 40–1; Friedman, 'Taking and Talking the Killer Photos: a Look Back Over the Years', *Thrasher*, vol. 3 no. 3 (March 1983), pp. 22–7; Ian Christe, 'Setting Fire to the Slackers', *Warp*, vol. 3 no. 1 (February 1995), pp. 36–9; and Heidi Bivens, 'Glen E. Friedman: Fucking Hero – Keeping It Real', *Strength*, vol. 2 no. 8 (n.d., c. November 1997), n.p.

132. 'Shooting Gallery', pp. 44–7; and Bryce Kanights, interview, Heckler (accessed 5 May 1996).

133. Joel Patterson, 'Evidence', *TransWorld Skateboarding*, vol. 14 no. 11 (November 1996), pp. 118–37; and Grant Brittain, 'Everything You Ever Wanted to Know About Skateboard Photography (But Didn't Want to Ask)', *TransWorld Skateboarding*, vol. 14 no. 1 (January 1996), p. 52.

134. Allen Titensor, 'Skate Tips: Don't Let Photos Cramp Your Style', *SkateBoarder*, vol. 4 no. 1 (August 1977), p. 23.

5.7 Motor-drive and wide-angle photographic sequence by Grant Brittain, deployed to capture the fast intricacies of a varial invert (1989). Skateboarder: Ken Park. (Photograph Grant Brittain)

> The boys were dealing with things too rapid to be observed, the kind that are so quick that they are felt rather than seen. The documentation must be done in sequential overdrive . . . 'You should have been here yesterday' has become 'You ought to be here tomorrow.'[135]

> These pictures are already outdated. What you see here is nothing compared to what is going on *now*. These are just slices of time, thousandths of a second from the past.[136]

Skateboard photographers used 15–18 mm wide-angle lenses to get close to the action, emphasizing locational context, at once celebrating and analysing the

135. Adams, *SkateBoarder*, vol. 3 no. 5.
136. 'Pool Riding Symposium', p. 77.

event.[137] Some photographers also use wide-angles to exaggerate the height and posture of moves ('those 15 mm fisheyes distort everything just about right'[138]) and, as such lenses are expensive, to make photographs noticeably 'professional'.[139]

Bolster and *SkateBoarder* experimented in 1978 with 'stroboscopic' images, alongside blurred images, thus 'freezing the feeling by blurring the motion'.[140] Later photographers like Worland have also used stroboscopes.[141] Other techniques have included multi-image frames, or the combination of flash with slower shutter speeds to portray a sharp skater overlaid onto their blurred movement across surrounding terrain (5.6, 8.2, 8.8, 9.1). Although undoubtedly successful as dramatic composites, such images also expose the partial limitation of still photography with respect to time, both eradicating the immediate time of the event, and dehistoricizing the time of its location.[142] Although readily available in the specialist magazines, such images are thus restricted by the limitations of the medium.

In response, the moving image has been exploited. Films of the 1970s such as *Magic Rolling Board* (1977), *Skateboard* (Universal, 1978), *Freewheelin'* (Dir. Scott Dittrich, 1976), *Super Session* (Dir. Hal Jepsen, 1976), *Go For It* (Dir. Hal Jepsen), *Skateboard Madness* (Dir. Hal Jepsen, 1977–82), *Hot Wheels* (James Street, Dir. Richard Gayer, 1978) and *London Skateboards* (Dir. Ian MacMillan, 1978) were supplemented in the 1970s and 1980s with sporadic television coverage on the main US and UK network channels.[143] By mid-1980 Allen, owner of Marina del Rey skatepark, was hosting a weekly cable television programme devoted to skateboarding;[144] *Action Now* similarly launched a television version of itself in mid-1981.[145] Pipeline skatepark had installed a video system for instant feedback by 1980,[146] while skaters in the 1970s often made 8 mm movies.[147]

But the 1980s saw this kind of representation become most important, when skateboarders exploited new camcorder and video technology to capture and distribute skate moves. A large number of skate videos are now available, some as video magazines with skaters from different locations, such as the American *411* or the English *Video-Log*, and others as elaborate manufacturer videos showcasing

137. Friedman, 'Killer Photos', p. 26.

138. Morizen Föche, 'Pipes', *Thrasher*, vol. 4 no. 6 (June 1984), p. 26.

139. Steve Kane, 'ZonaSkane', *Skateboard!* (second series), no. 42 (May 1990), p. 64.

140. 'Focus', *SkateBoarder*, vol. 4 no. 10 (May 1978), pp. 86–97; and Warren Bolster, 'Strobal Highlights', *SkateBoarder*, vol. 4 no. 11 (June 1978), pp. 70–82.

141. Ben Bodilly, interview, *Sidewalk Surfer*, no. 3 (January/February 1996), n.p.

142. 'Strangely Familiar', special issue of *Scan* (Photographers' Gallery, London), vol. 1 no. 1 (1996).

143. 'On Board', *Thrasher*, vol. 1 no. 9 (September 1981), p. 26; and 'Wheels Roll Out West', *Skateboard!*, no. 2 (October 1977), p. 35.

144. 'The Ray Allen Show', advertisement, *SkateBoarder's Action Now*, vol. 7 no. 1 (August 1980), p. 10.

145. 'A.N on T.V.?', *Action Now*, vol. 8 no. 1 (August 1981), pp. 32–40.

146. 'Off the Wall', *SkateBoarder*, vol. 6 no. 6 (January 1980), p. 74.

147. 'Who's Hot! Curt Lindgren', *SkateBoarder*, vol. 3 no. 2 (December 1976), p. 87.

professional team skaters. The latter can be very sophisticated, beginning with the first Powell-Peralta videos of the mid-1980s[148] which 'blew open' the skateboard world.[149] For example, the *Ban This* video (Powell-Peralta, Dir. Peralta and C.R. Stecyk, 1989) manipulated tracked shots, skateboard-mounted cameras, special lighting, overlays, montage, film stock and high-design graphics. Videos such as *Bones Brigade* (Powell-Peralta, 1984), *Future Primitive* (Powell-Peralta, 1986), *Wheels on Fire* (Santa Cruz, 1988), *Streets on Fire* (Santa Cruz, 1989), *Useless Toys* (New Deal, 1991), *Las Nueve Vidas de Paco* (Chocolate/Girl, Dir. Spike Jonze, 1995) and *A Mixed Media* (Panic/Blueprint, 1996) were intended to promote these manufacturers, but also satisfied skaters' demand to see professionals in action. Some were quick to produce, using television rather than film production values; the H-Street company with Mike Ternasky pioneered the exploitation of low-cost camcorders, producing *Shackle Me Not* (1989), *Hocus Pocus* (1990) and other videos by giving camcorders to team riders to shoot their best tricks, then hacking together a quick rough-edit for release.[150] Small companies and new skaters were thus able to record and distribute their moves within weeks, and also, given the rapid development of skate moves, to suggest they were ahead of other, larger companies.

In another variation, since the early 1990s local skaters have also increasingly produced their own videos, using domestic formats for production and dubbing onto standard VCR equipment. The results are sold for minimal cost through local skate shops and mail order; UK examples include *The Hoods* (Big Films, 1997) from Margate, *Raging Hull* (Hull Skaters, 1997) from Hull, *Renaissance* (Wayne Fenlon, 1996–7) from Edinburgh,[151] *Network Neighbourhood* (1997) from Chelmsford,[152] and *A Product of Our Surroundings* (Martin Meegan, 1997).[153] These low-budget videos are filmic equivalents of 1980s and 1990s skate 'zines (see Chapter Six), showing local skaters doing moves in a variety of quotidian skate spots.[154]

> News of modern moves, the tricky tricks and the flippity kicks, spread like wildfire via phone, fax, Xerox and mini-cams.[155]

148. Lowboy, 'The Making of a Skate Video', *Thrasher*, vol. 5 no. 1 (January 1985), pp. 17–21.

149. Brer Mortimer, 'Stacy Peralta', *TransWorld Skateboarding*, vol. 15 no. 11 (November 1997), p. 90; and 'The Day Powell Set London on Fire', *R.A.D.*, no. 71 (January 1989), pp. 26–35.

150. Leighton-Boyce, letter; Leighton-Boyce, 'Goodbye', internet version, *DansWORLD* (accessed 17 March 1995); and wisentha@netcom.ca (David S. Wisenthal), alt.skateboard, 'Subject. Wanted: H-Street Video' (posted 26 June 1996).

151. 'Our Video Review', *Sidewalk Surfer*, no. 14 (March 1997), n.p.

152. 'Our Video Review', *Sidewalk Surfer*, no. 15 (April 1997), n.p.

153. 'Our Video Review', *Sidewalk Surfer*, no. 19 (August 1997), n.p.

154. 'Oscar's for Oxted? It's a Krhyme', *R.A.D.*, no. 103 (December 1991), pp. 24–7.

155. 'Major Moves', p. 48.

These are essentially local and informal communications ('we all try to shoot each other'[156]), giving a sense of a particular place – *Renaissance*, for example, focuses mostly on the 'Bristo Square' skate scene in Edinburgh. Other productions are more artistic in nature. For example, Shaun Gladwell's experimental video installation, *Kickflipping Flâneur* (Artspace, Sydney, 5–28 October 2000), incorporated a tripartite projection exploring the poetic and urban content of skateboarding with equal degrees of emphasis (5.8).[157]

The videos are then perhaps the most accurate way of reproducing the sound and movement of skateboarding, portraying skateboarding at its most prosaic, ordinary in its accessibility and location, extraordinary in its appearance and context.

Furthermore, skaters are increasingly using the internet to receive and post images and movie clips; in 1997 the alt.skateboard site was far more active than in the past few years.[158] From fledgling ventures such as *Thrasher*'s bulletin board[159] and *R.A.D.*'s e-mail address in the mid-1980s,[160] skate cyberspace expanded by 1997 to over 130 sites ranging from commercial manufacturers and shops to professional 'digital magazines' such as *Influx*,[161] *Heckler*[162] and the UK-focused 'digital skate resource' *Project* (begun 1996),[163] to good college sites, such as the *DansWORLD* site,[164] to skaters' own sites such as the Dutch *Hupthur*[165] and female-skater *b-grrrl* from Melbourne,[166] or *Skate Geezer*, catering for veteran skaters of the 1970s–1980s,[167] to the Usenet alt.skateboard site, with incessant conversation on a myriad of topics from how to perform tricks, equipment, phrases, ramp design, drugs, the existence of God, general abuse, to (most popular of all) skate shoe design. Country-specific sites also yield information about places from Finland[168] to Canada.[169] From these sites skaters represent skate moves through textual

156. Dave Kirby and Chris Aylen in 'Oscar's for Oxted?', p. 27.

157. 'Video Review' (March 1997), n.p.; and Shaun Gladwell, *Kickflipping Flâneur* (Artspace, Woolloomooloo, Sydney, 5–28 October 2000): artist's video and accompanying essay by Kit Messham-Muir, 'Practices of the City and the Kickflipping Flâneur' (materials supplied by the artist).

158. Leighton-Boyce, letter.

159. 'On Board', *Thrasher*, vol. 5 no. 8 (August 1985), p. 65; 'Hackin' Off', *Thrasher*, vol. 6 no. 3 (March 1986), p. 79.

160. Tim Leighton-Boyce, interview, *Project* internet site, URL http://www.skateboard.co.uk/project/features/tlboyce/ (accessed 3 August 1997).

161. URL http://www.enternet.com/influx/ (accessed 7 February 1997).

162. URL http://heckler.com/HomePage.html (accessed 7 February 1997).

163. URL http://www.skateboard.com (accessed 27 July 1997).

164. URL http://web.cps.msu.edu/~dunhamda/dw/dansworld.html (accessed 7 February 1997).

165. URL http://www.huphtur.nl (accessed 20 April 1995).

166. URL http://netspace.net.au/~butta/butta1.htm (accessed 7 February 1997).

167. URL http://www.terraport.net/abrook/skategeezer.htm (accessed 7 February 1997).

168. URL http://www.jypoly.fi/~harpuupp/skate.htm

169. URL http://www.geopages.com/Colosseum/2108

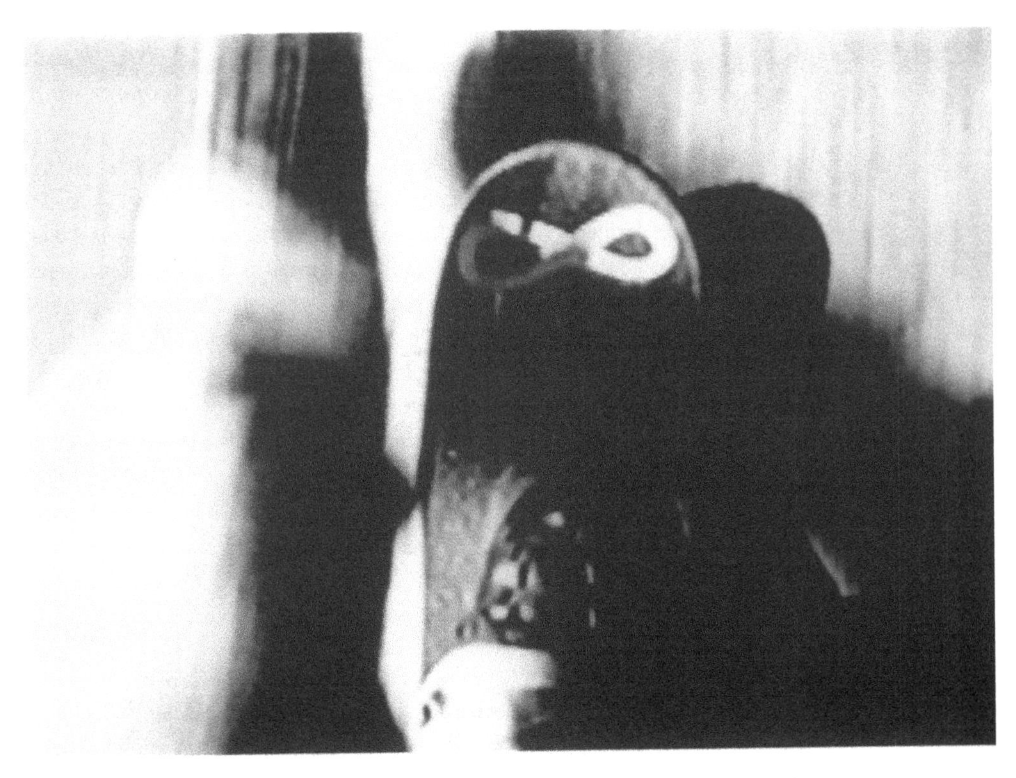

5.8 Still from Shaun Gladwell's video installation, *Kickflipping Flâneur* (Artspace, Sydney, 5–28 October 2000).

descriptions, choreographic codes using the ASCII character set, still photographs and movie clips – all viewable on the screen or down-loaded. The overall effect is to make it easier for skaters to disseminate material globally, certainly compared to their access to commercial magazines or videos.

PROJECTING THE SELF

All these kinds of imagery are central to skateboarding's development. The video has thus been seen as 'a good recording and learning tool',[170] while photographs have been particularly influential.

170. Stacy Peralta, in John Smythe (pseudonym for Craig Stecyk), 'Profile: Stacy Peralta', *SkateBoarder's Action Now*, vol. 7 no. 1 (August 1980), p. 27.

> Without photographs there wouldn't be a global skate scene, there wouldn't be magazines to allow people to ascend into the public consciousness, in short skateboarding wouldn't exist in the same way as it does now.[171]

Clearly magazines and videos have been extraordinarily influential in encouraging new skaters to skate – ('the first thing that inspired me to skate'[172]) and established skaters to develop further. 'We see a hot shot in the magazine, and we have to figure what went on before that.'[173] But what is the process by which this occurs?

To address this question, we must consider that skateboard imagery is significant not only for its instructional properties, for images per se are only an *apparent* stage of the representation process within the skateboarding production of space. Instead, skateboarders use imagery less as pure image, and more as an integration and re-presentation of that imagery through skateboarding practice. The lived representation of skateboard images occurs when skaters undertake the moves themselves, reliving and re-producing photographs, video footage and the internet movie clips through the agency of their body. I now turn to investigate this condition at some length.

The way skaters skate – the elegance, fluidity, speed and, above all, *style* with which they perform – is undoubtedly an important aspect of skateboarding.

> If a rider looks good, if he's got style, his tricks are going to look all the more healthy for it. And he'll feel a lot better . . . a far more complete skater.[174]

> It's not how many hard tricks you can do, it's the way you perform the trick. That's where style comes in.[175]

Style is notoriously difficult to define, and while some see it as an 'economy of motion',[176] ultimately for many skaters it was 'more an attitude than a technique . . . something more akin to a dance'[177] and embedded within the smallest of actions.

> Style isn't the full action-wear wardrobe and the upper lip curled sneer. Style is the backspin on the quarters as you put them in the candy machine.[178]

The visit by Tony Alva (5.6) to Britain in the summer of 1978 produced considerable debate on this matter, for, as a letter to *Skateboard!* made clear, his reputation was founded as much on his skating style as on his technical capabilities.

171. 'Moments in Time', *Sidewalk Surfer*, no. 12 (December 1996), n.p.
172. Hosoi, interview, *Thrasher* (June 1989), p. 62.
173. Henderson (and Sinclair), interview, *SkateBoarder*, p. 30.
174. Danny Acton-Bond, interview, *Skateboard!*, no. 16 (December 1978), p. 31.
175. Steve Caballero, interview, *Thrasher*, vol. 9 no. 6 (June 1989), p. 49.
176. Miller, interview, *Thrasher*, p. 102.
177. Steve Kane, 'Putting the Style into Freestyle', *Skateboard!*, no. 11 (July 1978), p. 83.
178. 'A Matter of Style', *Thrasher*, vol. 7 no. 8 (August 1987), p. 48.

> He managed to express so much of what skating is all about . . . force, grace and sheer fluidity; qualities . . . which take skating beyond the limits of mere accomplishment of 'tricks'. The fact that Alva did not attempt the aerials that Mark Baker achieved could not have mattered less. It was how he skated that made his performances so unforgettable . . . There is too much of this business in skating as to what you can do. The question should be, how do you do it, and with what attitude of mind.[179]

But as must be inferred from this, it is less the style than the moves performed that is most important to many skateboarders. The skateboarder's self-identity is then predominantly based on the number and difficulty of the moves he or she performs. This is seen most explicitly in skateboard magazines, where the highly photographic-based content is complemented by captions which typically identify the name of the skater and the move being performed. The two come together explicitly whenever a new move is named after its inventor, such as 'Bert' (Larry Bertleman), 'Elgarrio/Elguerial' (Eddie Elguera) 'Caballerial (Steve Caballero), 'McTwist' (Mike McGill), 'Miller Flip' (Darryl Miller) or 'Christ air' (Christian Hosoi).

The importance of the move is also evident in that skateboarders spend perhaps more time than any other sports practitioners actually *failing* to do what they attempt. Furthermore, having spent hours or even days trying a move, once it is successfully completed they will often progress immediately to an even more difficult manoeuvre. This was especially true of a highly technical phase in street skating in the 1990s, when skaters, encouraged by camcorder technology, attempted ever more intricate moves until they had just one 'make' recorded.[180] Here, we might even note that skaters share with architects the tendency to treat invention as a highly prized characteristic.

> From the very beginning, skateboarders have been obsessed with forging new directions, inventing new tricks, claiming new obstacles and generally ensuring that the available means of skateboard exploration stay as varied as possible.[181]

> Originality is most important to me . . . skaters that copy a lot aren't skating for themselves.[182]

> Everytime I get on the board, I'm trying to figure out something new.[183]

179. James Fraser, letter, *Skateboard!*, no. 16 (December 1978), p. 60.

180. Leighton-Boyce, letter; Alex Moul, interview, *Sidewalk Surfer*, no. 9 (August 1996), n.p.; and Rune Glifberg, interview, *Sidewalk Surfer*, no. 14 (March 1997), n.p.

181. 'Any Variations?', *Sidewalk Surfer*, no. 14 (March 1997), n.p.

182. Rodney Mullen, in 'Freestyle Fanatics', *Thrasher*, vol. 6 no. 3 (March 1986), p. 35.

183. Oneal, interview, *SkateBoarder*, p. 68.

Many moves are more complex evolutions or variants of old ones, such as the 'fakie rock 'n roll board slide', in which the skater undertakes a combination of the rock 'n roll, sliding the board along the wall ('board slide') as it rocks, and then returns without turning around ('fakie'). The communicative dissemination of such new moves through internet, video and magazine also takes place through language, with a welter of different terms constantly being invented to describe skate moves. To name every skate move would be nearly impossible task,[184] but to give but a few of these, *DansWORLD* listed, among others, 'backside', 'boardslide', 'fakie', 'hard flip', 'heelflip', 'kickflip', 'nollie kickflip', '360 flip', 'varial', 'frontside', 'grind', 'crooked', 'feeble', 'grapefruit', '50–50', '5-O', 'nosegrind', 'Smith', 'lipslide', 'mongo-foot', 'noseslide', 'switch-stance' and 'tailslide'.[185]

'Maximal differences' such as these, based on change, are also complemented by 'minimal differences' based on repetition.[186] Skaters are often obsessed here with that kind of novelty which, rather than being based on creative struggle, aims at simply being seen to be the first to do something.[187] Again, magazines, camcorders and the internet play an important role in this process, disseminating new moves around the world quickly, leading to a series of globally dispersed competitions among local skaters to see who can become the first in her or his own area to recreate the move.[188] Despite the copying involved, skaters see each repetition of a move as a new creation, not so much an emulation as a producing of something forever anew.

> No matter how many times you do something on your board, you never truly repeat yourself, every single trick is absolutely unique.[189]

In either case – the entirely inventive, or the newly produced – the move, then, is that complicated unity of time, desire, space, gesture and tool-manipulation which not only repeats but preserves difference through innovation.[190]

If the move is the measure of status and achievement, then it is also, consequently, the unit of exchange between skaters, and skaters spend much time poring over photographs in order to understand and acquire them. 'First time I saw Caballero doing a frontside slide-and-roll in a magazine I studied that thing for weeks.'[191] This process is analogous to the way consumers accumulate commodities

184. 'Any Variations?', n.p.
185. 'Skateboarding FAQ', *DansWORLD* (accessed April 1995).
186. Lefebvre, *Production of Space*, p. 372.
187. Lefebvre, *Introduction to Modernity*, pp. 185–6 and 196.
188. 'Major Moves', p. 48.
189. 'Moments in Time', n.p.
190. Lefebvre, *Production of Space*, p. 203.
191. Lucien Hendricks, interview, *Skateboard!* (second series), no. 43 (June 1990), p. 27.

and capitalists money, except that of course skateboard moves cannot be hoarded or invested – there is no bank for real moves, only the image bank of the photograph or video – and to maintain ownership skaters must continually re-perform the move. 'Every new transition in your pocket makes you a better skater.'[192] Consequently, when skaters undertake a run, they are not so much performing an act of pure physical spontaneity as reproducing through body-actions the activity of skateboarding as codified in moves and communicated as a set of *produced* images. The skater's move is image and action at once, representation of space and space of representation brought together in a simultaneous production and release of time, energy and space – and is thus in keeping with Lefebvre's call for a production and understanding of the 'interconnections, distortions, displacements, mutual interactions' of these different spaces.[193]

In social terms, the skateboarder's undertaking of a move is a complex intersection of lived experience and mechanically reproduced imagery, in which the latter acts as a kind of mirror, not only reflecting the subject's image back to herself or himself but also extending a repetition/symmetry immanent to the body into space;[194] the mechanical image projects the skater back to both herself or himself and to others. As one skater explained the sense of being a skater:

> To me an image is like when you're standing in a room with two mirrors opposite each other. The first image is you and all the rest are those people who reflect parts of you they choose to carry with them.[195]

That both the image/reflection (as pure image) and the skater's own move (as the momentary equilibrium of gravity and trajectory) are 'weightless' emphasizes the fantastical nature of this projection in which the skater forever dreams – alongside the immediate phenomenal engagement with the terrain – her or his display to the eyes of other skaters.

This is further complicated by the collective nature of skateboarding as a practice in which many skaters perform the same moves, and so act as mirrors for both themselves and others. In terms of specific meetings of skateboarders, this takes the form of the session, when skaters skate together and sometimes in socially aggressive circumstances.

> Sessioneering . . . is that unpredictable aspect of the skateboard experience that occurs whenever the varied personages that comprise the contemporary vanguard assemble together. The action is always faster, always more furious, and limits are always pushed harder than ever before.[196]

192. Jake, quoted by Bob Burnquist, *Thrasher*, vol. 17 no. 9 (September 1997), p. 66.
193. Lefebvre, *Production of Space*, p. 42.
194. Ibid., p. 182 n14.
195. Ryn Reid, interview, *Heckler* (accessed 5 May 1996).
196. John Smythe, 'Opening Day at the Park', *SkateBoarder*, vol. 4 no. 2 (September 1977), p. 65.

As Duane Peters recalled the first years at Pipeline skatepark:

> Sessions got that heavy. It was like a gang fight, but we were skating.[197]

The same condition applied at Solid Surf skatepark in the UK, where the best-known London skaters and 'H-Boyz' (Harrow regulars) took over.[198]

> We would terrorize everybody and take over the best runs. Nobody would skate with us, they would just watch . . . the sessions were heavy and most were intimidated.[199]

The session format involves a group of skaters standing at the pool entrance or half-pipe platform, waiting for their run (5.9). As an informal queuing system (skaters do not stand in line), there is a rough understanding that each skater gets one run in turn; jumping this sequence is sometimes referred to as 'snaking'.[200] Further, it is the ground on which the waiting skaters stand that constitutes the primary social space of the audience; although other non-skaters may look on, it is skaters-only who tend to occupy the entrance point/platform, and it is they who shout encouragement, astonishment and abuse at the skater performing. A skater exiting from a run then forms part of the audience for the next skater and so on. The system thus produces a kind of collective attack on the element being skated, each skater making her or his own contribution to the achievements of the session as a whole.

> I wanna rip! I wanna rip against everybody. I like to skate with a lot of people.[201]

The session is thus a kind of informal competition among individuals, but is also a collective activity.

In this context, every time skaters perform moves, they are both reproducing themselves as themselves (seeing themselves do a move), themselves as other than themselves (seeing themselves in the role of others), and other skaters as themselves (being the reflection of other skaters). Such considerations lie behind Rick Blackhart's (3.6) question as to whether 'if you're skating a ramp and nobody's watching you, are you still skating?'[202] The desire to enact the move is then the desire to be, at the same time, oneself, oneself as someone else, and all other skaters in oneself. And

197. Duane Peters, interview, *Thrasher*, vol. 2 no. 2 (February 1982), p. 34.

198. Rodga Harvey, interview, *R.A.D.*, no. 83 (January 1990), p. 50.

199. Rodga Harvey, in 'The Power of London', *Thrasher*, vol. 6 no. 12 (December 1989), p. 61.

200. Brian Brannon, 'Snakes and Other Reptiles', *Thrasher*, vol. 6 no. 12 (December 1989), pp. 66–9; and 'Skater's Edge: Snaking', *Thrasher*, vol. 7 no. 8 (August 1987), pp. 38–9.

201. Hosoi, interview, *Thrasher* (June 1989), p. 62.

202. Rick Blackhart, in 'Trash', *Thrasher*, vol. 10 no. 5 (May 1990), p. 121.

5.9 The collective space of a mini-ramp platform. (Photograph Jay Podesta/Vernon Adams)

the process by which this occurs is the skate move as something simultaneously performed, mechanically-produced and imagined.

The skate move, like the mirror, does not then *constitute* the unity of the subject,[203] but discloses the consciousness of the skater and her or his body, a bodily version of Lefebvre's reminder that 'there is no form without content, no content without form'.[204] The skateboard move is the projection of the self through the imaginary-and-real medium of the photograph; it is neither pure activity nor image, but a lived image. The skateboard run is at once a communication, development and lived enactment of things such as the *Influx* digital journal or *SkateBoarder* photographs. Every time skaters make moves they are at once replaying photographs and video clips through their own bodies, reliving and reinventing them, and – ultimately – rendering images, moves and themselves into social, fleshy, living entities.

203. Lefebvre, *Production of Space*, p. 185.
204. Lefebvre, *Critique of Everyday Life*, pp. 80–1.

Skateboarding, it is thus revealed, accords with the notion that there is nothing inherently regressive about spectatorship and images, and that readers and communities can be related together through these processes.[205] This has some interesting spatial and temporal effects. Spatially, skaters continually oscillate between the immediate physicality of their bodies and a globally dispersed skate community. There are currently skateboarders in most cities around the world, such that a skater from, say, London's Notting Hill will frequently feel more in common, and have more communication, with other skaters in Mexico City, Prague or Philadelphia than with non-skaters in Notting Hill. As Hugh 'Bod' Boyle saw it:

> I could go to Czechoslovakia and meet someone, couldn't even speak to the guy, but because we skate, have something between us and we can get on.[206]

This community is knitted though a continual exchange and re-experiencing of a lexicon of skate moves. The image becomes not only a locally lived but, simultaneously, a globally reproduced and exchanged phenomenon, part of modernity's intensification of global communication and simultaneity;[207] unlike the purely localized system of gazes in the space of, for example, a theatre,[208] for skateboarders the stage is the skatepark, the street, the magazine and the internet taken together as one worldwide network.

The skateboarder's locality is then not just a 'production of stability' that such localities often invoke, but a response to the emerging meta-space of global mobility;[209] the space is at once stable and unstable, local and global, fixed and dispersed. In this context, the image-move addresses Fredric Jameson's search for a spatialized cognitive mapping to locate the body and self locally and globally;[210] the skater understands both the space of her or his own body and locality, and the space of the world, as a set of globally dispersed intimate localities, and as a series of continually repeated and evolving lexicons of image-moves. And in this they seem to be responding to Lefebvre's 'implosion-explosion' process – that process where an extension of urban phenomena internationally is accompanied by a simultaneous intensifying of the actual urban fabric at the local scale.[211]

205. Ella Shohat and Robert Stam, 'The Politics of Multiculturalism in the Postmodern Age', *Art and Design*, no. 43 (1995), special issue on 'Art and Culture Difference: Hybrids and Clusters', p. 12.

206. Hugh 'Bod' Boyle, interview, *Thrasher*, vol. 10 no. 5 (May 1990), p. 94.

207. Lefebvre, *Writings on Cities*, p. 138.

208. Lefebvre, *Production of Space*, p. 188.

209. Inke Arns, 'Flux Diagrams and Maps of the Trajective', paper given at 'Parallel Space: the Geography of Virtual Worlds' conference, ICA, London (4 July 1997).

210. Fredric Jameson, *Postmodernism, Or, the Cultural Logic of Late Capitalism* (London: Verso, 1991), pp. 38–45. See also Fredric Jameson, 'Cognitive Mapping', in Cary Nelson and Lawrence Grossberg (eds), *Marxism and the Interpretation of Culture* (London: Macmillan, 1988), pp. 347–60.

211. Lefebvre, *Writings on Cities*, p. 71.

Temporally, skate moves are rarely taught or disseminated through codified means; few skaters use books or such things as the *How to Skateboard* video produced by *Thrasher*, relying instead on constant learning from other skateboarders, either directly by copying or by communication over internet and magazine pages. In many cases this occurs locally, as at Sacramento where the older 'N-Men' skaters passed on their knowledge and attitude to the next generation.

> The Sacto tradition is passed along by word of mouth and manifests itself in the style of its younger skaters – who approach modern technique with a tempered, do-or-die philosophy.[212]

Without this constant oral and lived communication, skateboarding moves would cease to be active historical moments, and indeed this has happened to many older skateboard moves – such as the 'tail-block' or 'layback air' – which were once fashionable among skaters but which are now rarely performed.[213] 'What is hip today will soon be passé.'[214]

The 'archive' or bank of moves thus must be constantly re-enacted at a highly localized level in order to survive, both in terms of an individual's own performance and the collective performance of skateboarders as a whole. It is the skaters' continual learning and repeating of moves and tricks which forms 'the basis of skating'.[215]

> Jerry . . . put everyone else to shame: 4 foot backside airs, 3 footish frontside airs & lightning quick & long rock'n'roll slides. Podge skated pretty good but the inverted lay back airs I saw him doing last summer never materialised . . . Paul Price soon had the pipe sussed out with 4 out fakey ollies, frontside airs and rock'n'rolls.[216]

The reporting of a particular skate event such as this one thus focuses not just on what moves each skater did, but on how he or she is managing to repeat and to develop moves; repetition and recurrence become essential components both for the *langue* of skateboard moves and the *parole* of skaters' individual enactions of these moves. It is then in the continual reperformance of the skate move that it is recorded. 'History is something you live, not something you read.'[217]

Returning to the consideration of the image, there are two other roles of the image that should be considered. The first concerns the role of the photographer,

212. Jerry Mander, 'Sacto Locals', *TransWorld Skateboarding*, vol. 9 no. 10 (October 1991), p. 84.

213. Moul, interview, n.p.

214. Tower of Power, 'What is Hip?', in 'Major Moves', p. 49.

215. Hendricks, interview, p. 27.

216. C.K., 'Barnstaple Competition', *Skateboard News*, English Skateboard Association Members Magazine, no. 18 (June 1982), n.p.

217. Stacy Peralta, in 'Trash', *Thrasher*, vol. 9 no. 8 (August 1989), p. 124.

for, as former skateboard editor and photographer Tim Leighton-Boyce points out, skateboard photography goes far beyond the technical exaggeration of space and temporality.[218] Skateboard photographers' deployment of wide-angle lenses is extremely unusual (having initially borrowed the technique from water-bound surf-photographers[219]), for in most other sports photography the main lens is the telephoto. In part skateboard photographers use wide-angles to emphasize location, but also to show other skaters waiting to drop in, thus invoking a sense of collective space around the skater pictured while also suggesting that the viewer too could be part of the session.[220] The optical characteristics of the wide-angle also forces photographer and subject into a proximate spatial relationship, such that the photographer often holds the camera underneath or even within the orbit of the skater's body. At times this immediacy is directly evidenced in the photograph itself: one of Friedman's earliest images of skateboarding – of Jay Adams in the 'Teardrop' pool – shows his own foot at the base of the images, caught in the same frame as the explosive skater.[221] Friedman is not a distant observer, recording the action with an external gaze, but a participant, someone intimately – socially and spatially – connected to the activity in front of the camera.

The second role concerns the image of the terrain in the particular context of the purpose-built skatepark. While everyday architecture is encountered as a natural given, the more spectacular forms of architecture, often those designed by named architects, are revered as much for their aura as for any particular encounter that we have with them. The same may be applied to particular skatepark features, which as given rather than found terrains are always invested with a conscious, representational quality; this is particularly the case with those special attraction features – often the centre-piece pool (Pipeline, Winchester, Marina del Rey, etc.) or long half-pipe (Lakewood) – with a reputation for difficulty and danger.

Particular elements of skateparks become invested with a spectacular life – the Combi-Pool at Pipeline in Upland, for example, 'designed to test and push the limits of skateboarding',[222] generated an aura beyond the basic ground on which skaters skated (4.7). Indeed, this was precisely the intention, for such centrepiece pools were often provided in part to attract publicity to the skatepark.[223] As a result, in undertaking a move in a place such as the Combi-Pool, skaters perceived themselves as much for their positioning within the image of the element as for the simple

218. Tim Leighton-Boyce, conversation (9 August 1996).

219. Friedman, e-mail (16 February 1997).

220. Leighton-Boyce, letter.

221. 'Jay Adams, "Teardrop"', West Los Angeles, California, October 1976', Friedman, *Fuck You Heroes*, first plate, n.p.

222. Don Hoffman, in Hesselgrave, 'Hester', p. 23.

223. Duane Bigelow and Wally Hollyday, interview, *SkateBoarder*, vol. 6 no. 8 (March 1980), p. 65.

phenomenal interaction with a physical terrain. The move became perceived as not just, say, a lien-to-tail, but as a lien-to-tail in the Combi-Pool (5.10).

This may partly explain the frequent territorialization of skateparks, in which 'locals' claimed a skatepark, and specific elements within it, as their own, and consequently met any outsiders with an attitude ranging from disdain to outright aggression.

> The local kids won't even speak to us. They really resent us coming up to 'their' park – they just stand in corners and stare.[224]

In such a process, locals saw the skatepark and its element less as pure image, their intimate and repeated use of it having stripped it of its external aura, and more as a known entity, re-invested with a character of their own construction.

> It was good because it was OUR park and it was us.[225]

This is akin to the way sports fans frequently feel a strong emotional attachment to their team's stadium, or to a particular stand within it.[226] Except that while sports fans' emotional experiences are through witnessing matches, for skateboarders the process is more participatory; through a drawn-out and painful intimacy built up over months and years, skateboarders have an invested physical and emotional relationship with the skateparks' elements.

> I've been skating here (Pipeline) for seven years and I've slammed a lot here. I've been kicked out a lot and let back in. When this place is torn down, I'll probably quit skating. It's the only place I have.[227]

Skaters give to the element, and the element returns to them, a knowledge of each other. The incoming outsider, conversely, threatens to obstruct the intensive local use of the skatepark, getting in the way, and possibly even skating better. Consequently, the dangerous nature and associated aura of some skatepark architecture helped local skaters not only to distinguish themselves from others, but also to create a certain kind of masculinity. This, for example, was one of the characteristics of the Combi-Pool at Upland's Pipeline skatepark, where local pro skaters such as Steve Alba and Jim Gray were able to build up over many years a painful intimacy with the element inaccessible to others.

224. Gilbert Angol, interview, *Skateboard Scene*, vol. 1 no. 5 (n.d., c. March 1978), p. 58.

225. Harvey, interview, p. 50.

226. John Bale, *Sport, Space and the City* (London: Routledge, 1993).

227. Dan Cavaliero, in 'Upland Pipeline: Closing Comments', *TransWorld Skateboarding*, vol. 7 no. 2 (April 1989), p. 70.

> This place separates the men from the boys and a lot of the pros are afraid to come here because they're afraid of getting hurt. The people here know how to deal with the pain.[228]

> Come to Upland and ride the pool and show me you're a man.[229]

However, the spectacular nature of skateparks also created the possibility for skaters to become dissatisfied, becoming bored with skateparks as a whole, perhaps because they no longer provided the right kind of terrain. Alternatively, skateparks and their elements – such as the intimidatingly deep Comb-Pool at Pipeline or the Performance Bowl at London's Solid Surf – were often seen as the 'proving ground'[230] where skaters pitted themselves against particular elements, creating a situation whereby the element may 'win' and thus become a terrain skaters cannot master or relate adequately to. This was certainly the case with Pipeline and the Combi-Pool, a 'concrete nightmare and a concrete wonderland':

> It's bumpy and smooth and unpredictable. It's the only place where you can ride a fifteen-foot-deep bowl, a twenty-two-foot pipe, and do corner airs in a square pool . . . About eighty percent of the pros are afraid to skate here, that tells you how burly it is.[231]

The owners of the Pipeline skatepark, Stan and Jeanne Hoffman, subsequently found that the Combi-Pool was not suited to the more complex (and hence more risky) moves developed in the 1980s.

> The combi-pool doesn't really lend itself to that; it's steep and has a lot of vertical . . . kids found it was hard for them and they didn't look that good here.[232]

In particular, the depth of the Combi-Pool, its large areas of vertical walls and the high-speed required to reach all areas created an overtly challenging architecture that made even professional skaters wary of it.

> The only really good square pool I've seen is Upland and that was so radical that's its not all that rippable. Not right now. It's so steep, it's a rush. When you are up there you're just looking down, going, 'Whoa . . .'.[233]

> It was scary and I usually got hurt there.[234]

228. Steve Alba, in 'Upland Pipeline: Closing Comments', p. 69.
229. Jeff Grosso, interview, *R.A.D.*, no. 64 (June 1988), p. 25.
230. Grosso, interview, p. 25; and *R.A.D.*, no. 83 (January 1990), p. 49.
231. Jim Gray, in 'Upland Pipeline: Closing Comments', p. 70.
232. Jeanne Hoffman, in 'Upland Pipeline: Closing Comments', p. 66.
233. Brad Bowman, interview, *SkateBoarder*, vol. 6 no. 6 (January 1980), p. 53.
234. Ken Park, interview, *TransWorld Skateboarding*, vol. 7 no. 2 (April 1989), p. 98.

At one Hester competition, for example, 'this full on quality took its toll', with many of the professional skaters, including locals such as Steve Alba, suffering heavy falls.[235] The Marina del Rey skatepark suffered similar problems with its original 'Dog Bowl' pool, with four feet of pure vertical at the top of its wall,[236] and a smaller keyhole pool was therefore soon added.[237] The concrete pool at Münster had an equal effect on professional skaters such as Way, who found its size and hard surface somewhat daunting.[238]

Whatever the challenge it offered, unlike the urban streets of the city itself, the skatepark was always a consciously *provided* space, a mental projection and representation of skateboarding terrain. As a result, some skateboarders quickly tired of skating on the same ground.

> That's the thing about skate parks. The Dogtown guys have hit every skate park and ripped it; then they've split, cuz they've taken it to the limit and then get burned out on a spot.[239]

This was particularly evident when skateparks imposed some kind of social regulation system; some, like the Del Mar Skate Ranch, tried to impose strict opening hours, safety rules, entrance charges and general behaviour codes.[240] More usually, skatepark regulations focused on either time periods, with stewards removing skaters after their paid-for session, or occasionally performance, where skaters have to pass some kind of proficiency test before being allowed to 'progress' to more difficult elements within the park. London's Skate City, for example, instituted a coloured-badge system, the highest 'Black Badge' allowing skaters access to the 'Black Bowl'. Such insignia ran contrary to skateboarders' anti-institutional sensitivities.

For some skaters, the skatepark thus appeared as a fixed, institutional entity, involving the segregation of skaters behind fences, creating rules and enforcing them rigidly;[241] 'skateparks are so boring, they're always the same and very restrictive'.[242] This may be why some skaters preferred slides and carves on banks and other more gentle skatepark terrains,[243] such as the shallow 'Brown Bowls' in the Marina del Rey skatepark,[244] partly because they did not represent the extreme

235. Hesselgrave, 'Hester', p. 24.
236. Dee Urquhart and Iain Urquhart, 'A Look at America', *Skateline*, no. 8 (Spring 1982), p. 20.
237. 'Off the Wall', *SkateBoarder's Action Now*, vol. 7 no. 8 (March 1981), p. 16.
238. Way, interview, p. 66.
239. Tony Alva, interview, *SkateBoarder*, vol. 4 no. 12 (July 1978), p. 71.
240. Davis, 'Del Mar', pp. 110–11.
241. 'Life and Death', p. 18.
242. Steve Kane, interview, *Skateboard!*, no. 5 (January 1978), p. 56.
243. Acton-Bond, interview, pp. 28–31, 67 and 69.
244. 'Major Moves', p. 55; and Dudley Counts, 'L.A. Skatepark Paradise: Part I', *Thrasher*, vol. 1 no. 3 (March 1981), p. 10.

5.10 'Come to Upland and ride the pool and show me you're a man.' A high risk, lien-to-tail move in a square corner of the Combi-Pool (*c.* 1989). Skateboarder: Eric Jueden.

challenge of the pool or half-pipe, and partly because they consequently appeared to just be there, allowing skaters to reassume the position of creative adaptive user rather than compelled consumer.

> How immense are the riding possibilities offered by well designed and finely tuned banks . . . they're the very fountain of style and creativity.[245]

> Banks are the most fun and challenging terrains to ride 'cause you can approach them from so many directions and draw so many lines.[246]

Thus in the early 1980s skaters began to turn away from the overtly challenging terrains such as the Combi-Pool to the mini-bowls and banks[247] where they could be more creative and relaxed. Skateboarding resists the subject's reduction to alternately mechanistic performer, mental entity or capitalist competitor, and also resists the dissatisfaction deriving from the consumption of things and things-as-signs.[248] Socially, skaters' dislike of skateparks was also a resistance to the charging of entrance fees and, particularly in the US, the requiring of membership,[249] but also to the imposition of certain safety and behavioural standards. Such economic and social values run against the confrontational and anarchist tendency within skateboarding.

In place of such codification and regulation, skaters enact a 'practical and fleshy body conceived of as a totality complete with spatial qualities (symmetries, asymmetries) and energetic properties (discharges, economies, waste)', a 'practico-sensory totality'.[250] Skateboarding as a quantitative set of places (skateparks, elements) and actions (moves, routes, routines) is further invested not only with quantitative measures (size, height, distance, duration, speed) but also with qualitative measures (difficulty, complexity, invention, surprise) and experiential conditions (noise, texture, sound, flow, touch, rhythm, space-time). Placed within the skater's imaginative absorption of the body-subject as an actively-experienced and produced engagement with the terrain underfoot, this creates an interdependent relation of skater and terrain, each internalized within the other.

> The 'other' is present, facing the ego: a body facing another body. The 'other' is impenetrable save through violence, or through love, as the object of expenditures of energy, of aggression or desire. Here external is also internal inasmuch as the 'other' is another body, a vulnerable flesh, an accessible symmetry.[251]

245. Rockly Brann, 'Bank Riding Symposium', *Skateboard!*, no. 16 (December 1978), p. 43.
246. Stacy Peralta, interview, *Thrasher*, vol. 2 no. 5 (May/June 1982), p. 21.
247. Peralta, in Smythe, 'Profile: Stacy Peralta', p. 29.
248. Lefebvre, *Everyday Life in the Modern World*, pp. 90–1.
249. Don Redondo, 'The Last Ride, or, We've Almost Lost Del Mar', *Thrasher*, vol. 6 no. 2 (February 1986), pp. 49–50.
250. Lefebvre, *Production of Space*, pp. 61–2.
251. Ibid., p. 174.

5.11 Creative, adaptive and relaxed play. Rodga Harvey at Rom skatepark in 1989. (Photograph Tim Leighton-Boyce)

Architecture is both external and internal to skateboarding, its concrete presentness being at once the other and the accessible symmetry to the skateboarder's physical activity – separate to, yet brought within, the skateboarding act. Similarly, the architect as designer of built terrain is both the other to the skateboarder, and re-presented within the skateboarder, the creative act being transposed from the 'classicist' realm of balanced order into the 'romanticist' sphere of destabilized movements. Architecture is dissolved, recast, and rematerialized. Skateboarding is nothing less than a sensual, sensory, physical emotion and desire for one's own body in motion and engagement with the architectural and social other; a Ballardesque crash and rebirth of self, body and terrain.[252]

252. J.G. Ballard, *Crash* (London, Jonathan Cape, 1973).

Chapter 6
Subculture

The opposite of skateboarding is golf.[1]

Just owning a skateboard doesn't qualify one as a skater.[2]

LIVING BY THE BOARD

Today, a loss of identity besets all peoples and individuals, faced with a dissolution of points of reference inherited from the past. This is a 'trial by space',[3] which tests the values of social groups.

> *Thrasher*: What is a non-dictionary, unabridged meaning of life?
> Neil Blender: I think it's all a trial.[4]

What is the particular cultural identity of skateboarders? This is an important question, for the identity of skateboarders continually informs, and is informed by, their spatial activities. Before turning – in the concluding pair of chapters – to the specific spatial practices of streetstyle skateboarding, we must therefore first comprehend that skateboarders create their own *subculture*: a social world in which self-identifying values and appearances confront conventional codes of behaviour.[5]

> Skaters are like . . . the culture that doesn't want. It's tired of the same old paralyzing stenchy activities that have been going on the whole time . . . Music, clothes, words, mags, video, skateboarding is a lifestyle.[6]

Skateboarding, like other subcultures, attempts to separate itself from groups such as the family, to be oppositional, appropriative of the city, irrational in organization, ambiguous in constitution, independently creative, and exploitative of its marginal

1. Steve Rocco, interview, *TransWorld Skateboarding*, vol. 6 no. 1 (February 1988), p. 85.
2. Carlos Izan, 'Aspects of the Downhill Slide', *SkateBoarder*, vol. 2 no. 2 (Fall 1975), p. 32.
3. Henri Lefebvre, *The Production of Space*, (Oxford: Blackwell, 1991), p. 416.
4. Neil Blender, interview, *Thrasher*, vol. 5 no. 2 (February 1985), p. 33.
5. Dick Hebdige, *Subculture* (London: Methuen, 1979), especially pp. 1–19.
6. Stacy Peralta, interview, *Thrasher*, vol. 2 no. 5 (May/June 1982), p. 17.

or 'sub-' status.[7] Skateboarding subculture is obstructive, using irony and other devices to create a 'reasonable distance' between skaters and others, breaking up the kind of familiarity which relies upon a transparent identification.[8]

Thus, while skateboarding subculture at once partakes of and criticizes the atomization and socialization of society within modernity,[9] it also makes a special contribution to that process. In particular, the constitution of skateboarders as a small group, and as young of age,[10] allows them to instigate different courses of action to those of dominated, mass groups and activities. Skateboarders may then be compared with Lefebvre's characterization of the nineteenth-century critical lifestyle, romanticism,[11] for like romanticism skateboarding brings together a concern to live out an idealized present, involves coded dress, language and body language, unites individuals of different social construction, and in general tries to live outside society while being simultaneously within its very heart.[12]

This is a production of the self with regard to the rest of society and to the self. Just as individuals 'are not a passive medium on which cultural meanings are merely inscribed', neither are they an outward projection on to society of a pre-existent presence; instead, individuals are 'multiplied, dynamic, participating and determined', continually producing a 'site of constantly changing mutations of difference, at once stable and dislocated, at once fixed and changing'.[13] Skateboarders' subcultural identity is then a way of thinking, constructing and living that identity in an historical situation.

Skate subculture involves everything skateboarders do; skaters skate 'because they want to totally live it'.[14] As a 'total' activity, skateboarding is inwardly as well as outwardly directed, sustained through all aspects of everyday life, a *style* that finds significance in the slightest things.[15] This is a process readily visible in, for example, novels such as Jess Mowry's *Rats in the Trees* (1993)[16] and Larry Clark's

7. Sarah Thornton, 'General Introduction', Ken Gelder and Sarah Thornton, *The Subcultures Reader* (London: Routledge, 1997), pp. 1–7.

8. Henri Lefebvre, *Critique of Everyday Life. Volume 1: Introduction*, (London: Verso, 1991), pp. 16 and 20.

9. Henri Lefebvre, *Introduction to Modernity: Twelve Preludes September 1959 – May 1961*, (London: Verso, 1995), pp. 187–90.

10. Henri Lefebvre, *The Explosion: Marxism and the French Revolution*, (New York: Monthly Review, 1969), pp. 107–8.

11. Lefebvre, *Introduction to Modernity*, pp. 239–388.

12. Ibid., pp. 301–2.

13. Steve Pile, *The Body and the City: Psychoanalysis, Space and Subjectivity*, (London: Routledge, 1996), p. 74.

14. Christian Hosoi, interview, *Skateboard!* (second series), no. 39 (January 1990), p. 45.

15. Henri Lefebvre, *Everyday Life in the Modern World*, (London: Transaction Publishers, 1984), pp. 36–7.

16. Jess Mowry, *Rats in the Trees* (London: Vintage, 1993).

film *Kids* (1995), in which skateboarding is absolutely embedded into the characters' everyday lives.[17] As skateboarders put it:

> Skaters have a completely different culture from the norms of the world's society. We dress differently, we have our own language, use our own slang, and live by our own rules.[18]
>
> One way or another skating relates to just about every part of my life.[19]
>
> I live skateboarding, I think skateboarding.[20]
>
> Live by the board, die by the board.[21]

IDENTITIES

How then is the subcultural identity of skateboarding formed? Given the bodily nature of skateboarding discussed in Chapter Five, and that capitalism tends to erase distinctions of time and the body,[22] it makes sense to explore the socially constructional categories of age, race, gender, class and sexuality.

Of these, age is for skateboarding perhaps the most obvious, as skateboarding is traditionally practised by people 8–18 years old. Certainly this is the age group that skateboarding appealed to during the 1970s, when the age of Southern Californian skateboarders averaged fourteen,[23] but, following an upward movement through the 1980s–1990s, many are now in their twenties. Skaters also often reach into their thirties and beyond, as evidenced by the *Skate Geezer* internet site for

17. See also, *Kids* (New York: Grove, 1995); Jeremy Millar, 'Larry Clark: Kids', *Great*, magazine of the Photographers' Gallery, London, no. 7 (July–August 1996), pp. 4–5; Elaine Paterson, 'Teenage Rampage', interview of Larry Clark, *Time Out*, London (24 April–1 May 1996), pp. 18–19; Jonathan Romney, 'Postcards from a Teenage Wasteland', *The Guardian*, 'Friday Review' section (9 August 1996), pp. 4–5; Katharine Viner, 'Which Girl is HIV Positive?', interview of Larry Clark, *The Sunday Times*, magazine supplement (21 April 1996), pp. 24–9; and Larry Clark, interview, *Asylum*, no. 2 (n.d., c. Summer 1996), n.p.

18. K. Maeda, letter, Windsor Beacon, California (October 1991), p. 17, in Becky Beal, 'Disqualifying the Official: an Exploration of Social Resistance Through the Subculture of Skateboarding,' *Sociology of Sport Journal*, vol. 12 no. 3 (1995), p. 256.

19. Skatemaster Tate, in David Grogan, and Carl Arrington 'He's Not Lean But His Rap is Mean, So the Thrashers Relate to Skatemaster Tate', *People Weekly*, vol. 27 (8 June 1987), p. 156.

20. Barry Abrook, interview, *Sk8 Action* (May 1990), p. 25.

21. Editor's response to letter, *Thrasher*, vol. 8 no. 7 (July 1988), p. 16.

22. Lefebvre, *Production of Space*, p. 49.

23. Hazel Pennell, *Skateboarding*, (London: GLC Intelligence Unit, London Topics no. 24, 1978), p. 1.

'veteran' skaters[24] and by *Skateboard!*'s 'Old Gold' skater category,[25] but these older practitioners are often discouraged by the 'scornful stares of the expert young' skaters[26] or by conventionalizing peer pressures.

> People look at me like I'm some kind of freak because I'm 20 years old and riding a skateboard.[27]

> The basic attitude I get is, 'You're a professional skateboarder? How old are you?' People consider it to be some little kid's game.[28]

Besides age-prejudice, other difficulties also stand in the way of older skateboarders – they are also often put off by their decreasing ability to withstand the continual body strains and breakages that skateboarding regularly inflicts.

Skateboarding – like romanticism – has values that can transcend barriers of race, gender and class, and so tends to marginalize their importance and significance socially.[29] For example, skaters tend to come from all kinds of class backgrounds.

> There's no class distinctions . . . you see all different types of economic groups skateboarding.[30]

Trading in second-hand equipment, together with possibility of making decks at home from cheap plywood, means that if necessary costs can be kept low; the current focus on street skating rather than skateparks similarly means reductions in admission charges or safety equipment, although, conversely, the tendency to produce ultra-lightweight street skating decks can create high breakage and replacement costs.[31]

Racial and ethnic groups are also more easily integrated into skateboarding than in many other areas of youth culture: 'it's a racially mixed world'.[32]

> In skating, there is no segregation really. You don't look at other skateboarders and become aware of their skin color or the clothes they wear. It just doesn't

24. URL http://www.terraport.net/abrook/skategeezer.htm (accessed 7 February 1997).

25. Adam Peacock, 'Old Gold', *Skateboard!*, no. 12 (August 1978), pp. 70–1; and *Skateboard!*, no. 16 (December 1978), pp. 52 and 56.

26. L. Ruocco, letter, *Skateboard!*, no. 4 (December 1977), p. 35.

27. Brian Casey, in Paul Mulshine, 'Wild in the Streets', *Philadelphia Magazine*, vol. 78 no. 4 (April 1987), p. 120.

28. Peralta, interview, *Thrasher*, p. 17.

29. Lefebvre, *Introduction to Modernity*, p. 322.

30. Marc Sinclair and Jeremy Henderson, interview, *SkateBoarder*, vol. 6 no. 2 (September 1979), p. 35.

31. 'Hell On Wheels', *Bay Guardian*, San Francisco (May 1994), transcribed by Murray, *DansWORLD* (accessed March 1995).

32. Larry Clark, in Viner, 'Which Girl?', p. 29.

> matter. There aren't the biases that exist in other areas of life. It's like we are our own race.[33]

This is particularly true of skateboarding in the 1990s. While skaters in the 1970s tended to be white, blond-haired and called Chip or Brad, in the 1980s skaters were generally of more varied ethnic origin, and called Caballero or Kasai, or in the 1990s Barajas, Hassan, Lieu or Santos. Consequently, there have been little or no racial tensions in skateboarding. Someone like Brian Casey, editor of 1980s skateboard 'zine *Moral Vengeance*, was then a typical relatively well-off white skater, choosing to live in a rough, predominantly black neighbourhood of Philadelphia.[34]

Racial mixing goes beyond simple integration, however; for example, Chuck Treece, a 1980s professional skater from Philadelphia, was guitarist for the 'McRad' and 'McShred' skate-punk-reggae bands,[35] and also black. As such, he had that 'urban mystique that suburban kids cherish',[36] where black, Latino or Asian skaters can be attractive to white suburban skaters, in the same way as the latter are often heavy purchasers of gangsta rap music, or as Jamaican vocal inflections have become hip among white UK kids in the mid-1990s.[37] Christian Hosoi, a professional skater from East Los Angeles in the 1980s, employed graffiti and gang culture in his product graphics and public image – and it is precisely Hosoi's kinds of motif that were emulated by suburban skaters.[38] One advertisement for 'Team Hosoi', for example, depicted Hosoi and another skater caught in the glare of a flash gun, as if arrested during a police gang bust; the gang-style logos on their boards are turned toward the camera, suggesting that the skateboards constitute offensive weapons (6.1).[39] Even earlier, the graphics on 1970s Dogtown skateboards had been derived from Los Angeles Chicano gang-culture lettering styles,[40] while later companies such as Grind King[41] and Neighborhood[42] also displayed gangster environments through deck graphics and advertisements.

Skateboarding subculture is – with some distinct regional variations – a global practice. Besides the numerous titles of the USA and UK, skateboard-related magazines have been produced in countries as diverse as Australia (*Slam*, *Australian Skateboarding*, *Skatin' Life* (6.2), *Speed Wheels*), Brazil (*Brasil Skate*, *Overall*,

33. Billy Miller, interview, *Heckler* (accessed 5 May 1996).
34. Mulshine, 'Wild', p. 122.
35. 'McRad', *Thrasher*, vol. 4 no. 4 (April 1984), p. 42; and Chuck Treece, interview, *Thrasher*, vol. 6 no. 11 (December 1986), p. 74.
36. Mulshine, 'Wild', p. 122.
37. Henry Louis Gates Jnr, 'Black Flash', *The Guardian*, 'The Week' section (19 July 1997), pp. 1–2.
38. Trip Gabriel, 'Rolling Thunder', *Rolling Stone* (16–30 July 1987), pp. 73–4.
39. *TransWorld Skateboarding*, vol. 6 no. 1 (February 1988), p. 38.
40. Andy Holmes, 'Dysfunctional', lecture, Photographers' Gallery, London (14 August 1996).
41. Grind King, advertisement, *Thrasher*, vol. 11 no. 12 (December 1991), p. 25.
42. Armando Barajas, 'My Pro Spotlight', *TransWorld Skateboarding*, vol. 13 no. 5 (May 1995), p. 83.

6.1 Team Hosoi advertisement (1988), drawing on gang culture and imagery. Skateboarders: Christian Hosoi (right) and Monty Nolder (left).

Skatin'), Canada (*Concrete Powder*), France (*B-Side, Skate, Skateboard, Skate France International, Slalom!, Zoom*) Germany (*Monster*), Italy (*XXX*), Japan (*Lovely*), Mexico (*Skate*), Portugal (*Surf/Skate*), Russia (*Skeit Novosti*), Spain (*Tres 60 Skate*) and Sweden (*Funsport, Daredevil*). These magazines, together with the burgeoning use of the internet, ensure that skateboard subculture is a global as well as local activity, with skateboarders being found today in just about every city around the world. This is a spatial dispersion which transcends geographic, national and, often, racial barriers.

Conversely, at a regional level, skaters have often created socio-spatial competition and tense rivalries. On the one hand, there is the 'modern' contradiction between individual loneliness and the bringing-together of masses in large cities;[43] in this context, skateboarding is an attempt to know others in a city of unknowns, without resorting to the institutions of family, school and team sports. It uses the locality of immediate neighbourhoods and schools, but also brings together groups from different schools and neighbourhoods across the city. On the other hand, skateboarders can be very territorial about their district or skatepark. Skaters in the 1970s and 1980s gave cities obtuse names such as 'Dogtown' (Santa Monica) and, in emulation, 'Fog Town' (London), 'Pig City' (Brighton) and so on. More concretely, skaters often reacted with disdain or outright hostility to skaters who came from elsewhere.[44] As Alva described the attitude of the Los Angeles skaters:

> It was a pretty heavy scene. When we're riding somewhere and someone put our area down, we stood up for it. Whether it meant fighting, talking or skating, all the guys were pretty loyal to their home turf and to the influences.[45]

43. Lefebvre, *Introduction to Modernity*, p. 189.

44. 'Fair Comment', *Skateboard!*, no. 16 (December 1978), p. 62; and 'Madness Dominates', *Skateboard!*, no. 16 (December 1978), p. 64.

45. Tony Alva, interview, *Thrasher*, vol. 4 no. 5 (May 1984), p. 29.

6.2 One of the vast number of skateboard magazines produced world-wide: the first issue of the Australian *Skatin' Life* (*c.* early 1988).

Here the city or skatepark functioned as an enclosed, self-contained community in which a sense of conflict enhanced the sense of belonging,[46] and which also, conversely, enhanced intra-regional rivalries.

> Well it was a Souther's mouth who started it, and it is the Dogtown challenge that is going to prove something.[47]

This was not a ghettoization of different *kinds* of skateboarders, but a purely spatial fragmentation. Ultimately, within skateboarding as a whole one finds that allegiances to other skaters, despite territorial rivalries, far outweigh commonality with non-skaters.

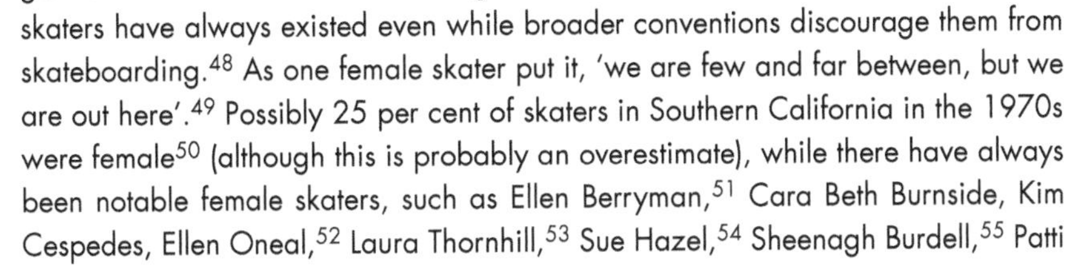

Similar complications exist in terms of the gender relations in skateboarding. Female skaters have always existed even while broader conventions discourage them from skateboarding.[48] As one female skater put it, 'we are few and far between, but we are out here'.[49] Possibly 25 per cent of skaters in Southern California in the 1970s were female[50] (although this is probably an overestimate), while there have always been notable female skaters, such as Ellen Berryman,[51] Cara Beth Burnside, Kim Cespedes, Ellen Oneal,[52] Laura Thornhill,[53] Sue Hazel,[54] Sheenagh Burdell,[55] Patti

46. Henri Lefebvre, *Writings on Cities*, (Oxford: Blackwell, 1996), pp. 66–7.
47. Jim Muir, letter, *SkateBoarder*, vol. 3 no. 6 (July 1977), p. 19.
48. Bonnie Blouin, 'Sugar and Spice . . ?', *Thrasher*, vol. 6 no. 4 (April 1986), pp. 56–61.
49. Blouin, 'Sugar', p. 61.
50. Pennell, *Skateboarding*, p. 1.
51. 'Who's Hot! Ellen Berryman', *SkateBoarder*, vol. 3 no. 2 (December 1976), pp. 90–1.
52. Ellen Oneal, interview, *SkateBoarder*, vol. 4 no. 6 (January 1978), pp. 64–73; and Laura Thornhill and Ellen Oneal, interview, *Skateboard!*, no. 2 (October 1977), pp. 24–7.
53. Thornhill and Oneal, interview, pp. 24–7.
54. Sue Hazel, interview, *Skateboard!* (second series), no. 6 (November 1989), pp. 20–1.
55. 'Starshot: Sheenagh Burdell', *Skateboard!*, no. 16 (December 1978), p. 54.
56. 'Profile: Patti Hoffman', *SkateBoarder*, vol. 6 no. 12 (July 1980), pp. 49–52.

Hoffman,[56] Stephanie Pearson, Michelle Picktin,[57] Elissa Steamer,[58] Vicki Vickers[59] and Gale Webb.[60] In the 1970s *Skateboard Scene* in the UK ran its 'Kate the Skate' column to support young women skaters,[61] and the progessive manufacturer Powell-Peralta similarly encouraged female skaters with advertisements proclaiming that 'Some Girls Play With Dolls. Real Women Skate' (6.3).[62] More recently, in 1996 Thump marketed its 'Tasty' range of decks specifically for female skaters.[63] But these are rare positive promotions of female skaters; while skaters such as Mark Baker acknowledged female skaters' achievements,[64] and conversely others like Christian Hosoi and Craig Johnson stated that women should not skate at all,[65] more usually there is a kind of indifferent acceptance of female skaters by male skaters. Female skaters themselves seem to want more female skaters, but even here some suspicion remains.

> There's a lot of girls that sk8 around here . . . unfortunately, most of them just do it to impress guys and then when they get their man they pretty much quit.[66]

Skateboarding remains a predominantly male activity, and most skate publications usually refer to skaters using the male terms of he, him, his, etc. Notably, another Powell-Peralta advertisement, contemporary with their 'Real Women Skate' advertisement, purported to show 'just some skaters', but close inspection of the scene depicted discloses that all of the skaters just happen to be male.[67] Practices such as these do much to signify the assumption that all skateboarders are male (6.4). While female skaters are not explicitly discouraged, their relative absence is only occasionally noted and implicitly condoned.

External social factors may also lead to young women not taking up skateboarding, as for sport in general.

> Shouldn't a 15-year-old female be more interested in the conquest of young men than handplants and rock 'n rolls? (These are) the traditional implications of being a girl involved in a sport generally regarded as male-oriented.[68]

57. Stephanie Pearson and Michelle Picktin, interview, *Skateboard!* (second series), no. 6 (November 1989), pp. 15–19.

58. *Big Brother*, no. 27 (August 1997), pp. 62–9.

59. Vicki Vickers, interview, *SkateBoarder*, vol. 6 no. 5 (December 1979), pp. 46–51.

60. 'Profile: Gale Webb', *SkateBoarder*, vol. 6 no. 11 (June 1980), pp. 64–5.

61. *Skateboard Scene*, vol. 1 nos. 3–9 (n.d., *c.* January–July 1978).

62. Powell-Peralta, advertisement, *TransWorld Skateboarding*, vol. 6 no. 1 (February 1988), p. 26, and *Thrasher*, vol. 7 no. 12 (December 1987), p. 4.

63. Tasty, advertisement, *Slap*, vol. 5 no. 2 (February 1996), p. 24; and 'Tidbits', ibid., p. 20.

64. Mark Baker, interview, *Skateboard!*, no. 12 (August 1978), p. 54.

65. Meany, 'The XX Factor', *Skateboard!* (second series), no. 6 (November 1989), p. 14.

66. bayern@moran.com (Amanda), alt.skateboard, 'Subject. Re. grrl sk8ers needed!' (5 July 1996).

67. Powell-Peralta, advertisement, *Thrasher*, vol. 8 no. 3 (March 1988), p. 110.

68. 'Profile: Patti Hoffman', p. 49.

6.3 'Some Girls Play With Dolls. Real Women Skate'. Active encouragement of female skaters in a Powell-Peralta advertisement (1988). Skateboarders: Leaf Trienen and Anita Tessensohn.

6.4 'Just Some Skaters'. All male skateboarders in a Powell-Peralta advertisement (1988).

Pressures include those to avoid displaying their bodies in a non-sexualized manner, not to damage or injure their bodies ('I can't blame them for not wanting to get hurt'[69]), to focus on inter-gender social relations rather than self-development or homosocial exclusions of men, and to generally grow up as a (fully sexualized) adult faster than young men. 'The main thing preventing women from participating in this 'sport' of ours is not anything real, just familiar stupid ideologies.'[70] As one female skater recognized,

69. Sean Goff, interview, *Asylum*, no. 2 (n.d., *c.* 1996), n.p.
70. Meany, 'XX', p. 14.

> It's kinda crazy to see a girl out there skating . . . Girls aren't supposed to be tough and if they are they're considered to be butch or tomboy or lesbian maybe.[71]

Furthermore, other aspects of skateboarding enforce male, heterosexual and sexist attitudes to women, and it is here that one of the most common contradictions in skateboard subculture occurs.[72] While advertisers in the 1970s and 1980s were not entirely averse to sexist imagery, in the 1990s this became more commonplace. For example, *Big Brother* magazine explicitly attacked the apparently cosy attitudes of manufacturers, magazines and skateboarders.[73] One of its tactics involved printing explicitly sexist articles, photographs and advertisements. For example, one issue contained readers' letters describing themselves as a 'pussy getting machine', an advertisement for the 'fuct' company with women spanking each other with skateboards, another for 'Hooters' skateboard wheels with breast and nipple graphics and the slogan 'urethane for men', and an article on 'How to Pick Up Girls'.[74] Despite inevitable defences on the grounds of humour and general irreverence, skateboard companies and magazines have increasingly used misogynist treatment of women as a way of selling skateboards. One of the most extreme examples is the World Industries company 'Bitch', which used a traffic-sign style logo depicting a man pointing a gun at a woman's head, with the word 'bitch' above. Although actually an industry in-joke, referring to a disenchanted off-shoot of the 'Girl' company, this was not readily discernible to outsiders – some of the furore surrounding this logo, leading to the removal of product and advertisements from some shops and magazines, was subsequently reported in *Club International*, a UK soft-porn magazine, as an amusing news item.[75]

To raise another form of social difficulty, consider first that much skateboarding takes place collectively, young men watching each other and taking turns to perform. Skaters thus spend much time looking at photographs of other young men, emulating other young men, and displaying themselves to other young men. Skateboarding could thus easily be construed as a homosexual gesture, and perhaps as a result of this possibility many skaters seem to react in a number of different ways.

First, there is homophobia.[76] *Big Brother* itself is not overtly homophobic (despite an obsession with 'circle jerking', masturbation and penis pumps), but this is a constant feature of the alt.skateboard dialogues, in which a rather uninformed debate takes place:

71. Pearson, interview, p. 16.
72. Beal, 'Disqualifying', pp. 264–5.
73. *Big Brother* was sold in 1997 to pornography publisher Larry Flynt.
74. *Big Brother*, no. 19 (n.d., *c.* late 1995), n.p.
75. 'Board Stupid?', *Club International* (February 1995), pp. 10–11.
76. Beal, 'Disqualifying', p. 265.

> Let me tell you a story about gays, ok? Gays wear very tight pants because they like to look at asses, you know to stick their cocks in there and such. Skaters wear very baggy pants, I don't know why we just do. So therefore Skaters cannot be gay.[77]

Similarly, in the film *Kids* two gay men encounter homophobic abuse from skaters hanging out in New York's Washington Park. Such actions are no doubt not unique to skateboarding subculture, but, for some skaters they undoubtedly form part of their everyday language and abuse.

Second, there is an induction to heterosexual and homosocial masculinity implicit in attitudes to gender. As Judith Butler has asserted, gender and sexuality are not fixed and a priori conditions, but social and historical, 'performatively produced and compelled by the regulatory practices of gender coherence'.[78] Again, this is also explicit in *Kids*, and especially evident in the relationship between the two main characters Casper and Telly throughout, and where the youngest boys (who are around 12 years old) are pushed to talk about their sexual proclivities and preferences in a manner that is in fact far in advance of their actual experiences. Through such social activities, skaters, as with other young men, produce themselves as heterosexual males with a particular construction of masculinity. In this light, the exchange of image-moves discussed in the previous chapter may be interpreted as an exchange of (heterosexual) masculinity, with new skaters becoming inducted through their performance of moves into the repertoire of male skate behaviour, ranging from skateboard moves themselves, to forms of dress (such as skaters' display of boxer shorts over the waistband of trousers, a fashion common in the mid-late 1990s), to general codes of behaviour.

This kind of masculinity can also be seen in a particularly physical form in the sticker- and product-tossing that became common to many skate competitions by the mid-1980s. This ritual is often performed within the ramp or skatepark pool, in which professional skaters throw stickers, decks and T-shirts to a 'shark feeding-frenzy'[79] and often violent scrummage of skaters:[80] 'you wrestled control of the first deck from a kid half your size by seizing his hair and punching him out'.[81]

> After they presented the awards, a riot broke out over a sticker toss, and there was biting. One monster broke skin on three victims, while another instigated the crowd with chants of, 'Your mother dances dirty.'[82]

77. blurry999@aol.com, alt.skateboard, 'Subject: Re. Skating is Gay' (accessed 18 June 1996).
78. Judith Butler, *Gender Trouble* (London: Routledge, 1990), p. 24.
79. Brian Brannon, 'Working the Street Beat', *Thrasher*, vol. 6 no. 2 (February 1986), p. 56.
80. 'Midwest Melee #2', *Thrasher*, vol. 4 no. 11 (November 1984), p. 31; and Robert Sullivan, 'Too Much Heat in Vancouver', *Sports Illustrated*, vol. 65 no. 9 (1 September 1986), p. 7.
81. Vernon Wingo, letter, *Thrasher*, vol. 5 no. 8 (August 1985), p. 4.
82. 'Vancouver Contest', *Big Brother*, no. 17 (n.d., c. Summer 1995), n.p.

These events are a form of adolescent male ritual, waging muscular body against muscular body to create pain and so define the skater's own masculinity (and there are similarities here with some of the intensely proximate male bodily homosociality of many music gigs).

> We're all like brothers. We fight like brothers, party like brothers, skate like brothers. We have a good time.[83]

As Ivan Hosoi, father of Christian Hosoi and manager of Marina del Rey skatepark, commented of the skatepark's regular punk rock party events which often cumulated in fights and brawls,[84]

> It was kids letting their aggression out. They wanted to get a little cut and bleed.[85]

This was also the case with skateboarding injuries, where the experience of falling is sometimes seen by skaters as a way of bonding with other male skaters through aggressive masculinity.

> All that gravity sucks you down to the cement and makes you fuckin' slam, it brings your aggression out. You just go 'Fuck!' . . . Blood. Getting hurt. Guys need to do that. Its a way of getting together to get aggro with your friends.[86]

> Give Blood. Skateboard.[87]

In a similar vein are advertisements such as that for the Alva team and its commercial products in 1988. Here twelve men nearly all dressed in black leather stare indifferently and meanly.[88] The general effect is of men relating to men through confrontational aggression and gang-like affiliations, a 'gangster-don't-give-a-shit attitude'.[89] As Tony Alva had previously explained, 'skateboarding is not for sissies'.[90]

The third response is to see skateboarding not as a group practice but as a solitary practice, each person performing as an individual. Here, the sexual politics are about self-satisfaction, where the skater's body-centric space production is self-referential, on the one hand largely absolved of social context and on the other

83. Charlie Ranson, interview, *SkateBoarder*, vol. 5 no. 6 (January 1979), p. 53.
84. Christian Hosoi, interview, *Thrasher* (April 1985), p. 25.
85. Ivan Hosoi, in Gabriel, 'Rolling', p. 76.
86. Christian Hosoi, in Gabriel, 'Rolling', p. 76.
87. *Thrasher*, T-shirt advertisement, *Thrasher*, vol. 12 no. 1 (January 1992), p. 15.
88. Alva, advertisement, Best of *Thrasher*, vol. 1 no. 1 (Winter 1988), p. 11.
89. Brer Mortimer, 'Stacy Peralta', *TransWorld Skateboarding*, vol. 15 no. 11 (November 1997), p. 90.
90. Alva, interview, *Thrasher*, p. 28.

hand imbued with the desire to make the body a realm of highly significant action. Here, that significance is onanistic, an intimate space produced by individuals in search of self-expression, self-fulfilment and self-satisfaction.

Such inward-directed concerns perhaps help explain the connection between skateboarding and the 'Straight Edge' movement of the late 1980s–1990s. Straight Edge young men (and women) – including Danforth and many other skaters – forswore variously unsafe sex (or sex altogether), alcohol, drugs, smoking and meat-eating to focus on the body as a lean, pure development of the self. According to one kind of interpretation, this was a largely middle-class, white rejection of drug-taking, and a self-defence against the challenges of sexuality, without openly embracing Moral Majority 'just say no' values.[91] In skateboarding, Straight Edge became even more explicit through the aggressive use of the body imbued in its spatialized muscularity, appropriative tactics and general subcultural attitudes. Much of this is also latent in skateboarding as a whole, with even non-Straight Edge skaters seeing themselves distinct from the indulgences of non-skaters.[92]

> People that smoke and drink are fake.[93]

The fourth response, as the celibacy of many Straight Edgers suggests, is to deny sexuality altogether, and this can be seen for example in the baggy clothes adopted by many skaters since the late 1980s. Although obviously functional, allowing more freedom to perform moves, such clothes also (even if unintentionally) mask the specific muscularity or shape of the body, and so lessen both the physiological appearance of any skater and the difference between male and female skaters. This may also relate to how skaters are often seen as socially dysfunctional or odd individuals who do not readily fit in with conventional youth cultures. The counter-cultural aspect of skateboarding thus carries within it a social reticence that is not always aggressive or boastful to the rest of society.

> Everywhere I've ever lived and everyone I've ever hung out with has always made me feel out of place. I've never fitted in everywhere . . . That's why I skate.[94]

91. Séan Kirkegaard, 'The XXX Files', *The Guardian*, 'Education' section (24 June 1997), p. iv; and Simon May, 'Straight-Edge and Me', Project (accessed 3 August 1997).

92. Ben Powell, in Siân Liz Evans, 'Young, Gifted and Board Stupid', *The Big Issue* (London), no. 126 (17–23 April 1995), p. 20.

93. Lance Mountain, interview, *Thrasher*, vol. 3 no. 1 (January 1983), p. 28.

94. Dan Cates, 'Comment', *Sidewalk Surfer*, no. 13 (January–February 1997), n.p.

GRAPHIC ATTITUDE

Identity is not who you are, or your ethnic origins, but an individual and collective construction of what you are doing and with what attitude.[95] Or as Paul Gilroy puts it, quoting rap artist Rakim, 'It Ain't Where You're From, It's Where You're At.'[96] What, then, of skateboarding subculture as a general attitude toward other skaters and to non-skaters?

According to Lefebvre, the romantic's 'revolt against society' is also 'a protest against the absence of genuine society', in which individuals express their lack of social base by withdrawing into themselves and into 'isolated groups' and 'deviant milieux'.[97] Or as one skater put it,

> One of the most powerful forces applied to the average teenager is conformity. In school, you are expected to want to join that elite, popular group of people, and use their standards for hairstyle, dress, talk, and spare time. At home, parents want you to join a 'real sport', or get better friends or whatever. Well, remember this, you only live once, so don't live to keep anybody happy but yourself. The genuine people are those who don't choose to follow the lemmings.[98]

Skateboarding subculture sees both a specific lack in society, and itself as somehow more honest, and more directly connected to urban living: 'I'm here to tell the truth, the whole truth, and nothing but the truth.'[99] This is manifested in two distinct yet interrelated aspects of skateboarding subculture: first, the rejection of society as a whole, and second the rejection of the normative patterns of the family and, in particular, the work-leisure, workplace-home socio-spatial routines of the traditional nuclear family.

Rejection of Society

> Choose Life. Choose a job. Choose a career. Choose a family. Choose a f**king big television . . . Choose working in Sandwich jacks 24 hours a day. Choose living with mum and dad 'till death . . . Choose your future. Choose Skateboarding.[100]

95. Ella Shohat and Robert Stam, 'The Politics of Multiculturalism in the Postmodern Age', *Art and Design*, no. 43 (1995), special issue on 'Art and Culture Difference: Hybrids and Clusters', p. 12; and Néstor Garcia Canclini, 'Rethinking Identity in Times of Globalisation', *Art and Design*, no. 43 (1995), special issue on 'Art and Culture Difference: Hybrids and Clusters', p. 37.
96. Paul Gilroy, in Shohat and Stam, 'Multiculturalism', p. 11.
97. Lefebvre, *Introduction to Modernity*, p. 297.
98. Doug, letter, *Thrasher*, vol. 12 no. 6 (June 1992), pp. 7–8.
99. Rocco, interview, p. 85.
100. Harry, 'Comment', *Sidewalk Surfer*, no. 13 (January/February 1997), n.p.

As this quotation (parodied from the film *Trainspotter*) shows, faced with the normative options offered to them by society, skaters are prompted to ask 'am I even existing?',[101] to which their own response is that they exist through electing to skateboard.

In subcultural terms, this is expressed most clearly in the boundaries of the skater's board, body, clothes and actions. While some manufacturers have occasionally tried to create a co-ordinated narrative form – such as the tongue-in-cheek Powell-Peralta 'Bones Brigade' military team imagery of the early 1980s[102] – more usually, subculture is developed through a series of complementary but unconsciously co-ordinated internalized worlds, composed of clothes, music, stickers, board design, language and other forms of communication.

The tensions between skaters and non-skaters are thus reflected in the graphic style which skaters have adopted. Typically, this involves the adoption of certain motifs, foremost of which in the 1980s was the skull (a motif particularly favoured by Vernon Courtland Johnson at Powell-Peralta, influential skater-designer Pushead working for *Thrasher* and Zorlac skateboards, and Rick and Peter Ducommun's Skull Skates company[103]), replacing 1970s surf-related themes of sun and ocean with those of death and primitive survival (6.5, 6.6).[104] If these symbols created a code that was incomprehensible to the outside observer, then it was all to the good; it mattered only that skateboarding as a 'partial group' should be noticed, not be understood.

> These symbols are equivocal and ambiguous. They manifest, yet they translate and express the secret aspirations of each group. They are what unites each group and differentiates it from all the others.[105]

In particular, this imagery involves the bottom of the skateboard deck, where a highly graphic design is usually placed. Invisible while the skateboard is on the ground, the design becomes highly visible when certain above-ground moves are performed (or when the board is being carried). Since the 1980s, starting with companies such as Powell-Peralta and designers such as David Castle at *TransWorld Skateboarding*, skateboard symbolisms have become increasingly pluralistic or 'lateral', including such things in 1997 as light bulbs in a field (Panic 'Light bulbs'

101. Rocco, interview, p. 87.

102. Powell-Peralta, advertisement, *SkateBoarder*, vol. 6 no. 12 (July 1980), p. 7; Powell-Peralta, advertisement, *SkateBoarder's Action Now*, vol. 7 no. 2 (September 1980), p. 11; and Peralta, in John Smythe, 'Profile: Stacy Peralta', *SkateBoarder's Action Now*, vol. 7 no. 1 (August 1980), p. 31.

103. Patrick Burgoyne and Jeremy Leslie, *Bored: Surf/Skate/Snow Graphics*, (London: Lawrence King and Creative Review, 1997), p. 49; 'The Encyclopaedia of Skateboarding', *R.A.D.*, no. 93 (February 1991), p. 38; and Brooke, *Concrete Wave*, pp. 102–5 and 122–3.

104. Mulshine, 'Wild', pp. 119–26.

105. Lefebvre, *Introduction to Modernity*, p. 298.

6.5 1970s surf-related imagery in skateboard T-shirts, for sale at the Val Surf shop in Los Angeles, and advertised on the pages of *SkateBoarder* magazine (1979).

model), semi-naked women (Acme 'Knockers' model), cartoon cows (New Deal 'Happy Cow' model), Escher style geometric patterns (Consolidated 'Pattern' model), aliens (Alien Workshop 'Alien Smacker' model), Oriental figures (World Industries 'Daewon' model), and architects' drawing instruments (Blueprint, 'Grand Architects' model).[106] What they all share is not, then, a common subject matter but a heavily non-realist graphic style, ranging from the airbrushing of heavy metal music album covers to the cartoon style of children's comics, to medieval or oriental illustrative techniques. One particularly prevalent stream within this, especially since the late 1980s, has been an anarcho-punk use of slogans and political imagery, typified by the work of skater-designer Nick Philip, former art editor of the skateboard magazine *R.A.D.*[107] Another stream is a sophisticated typographic and (post)modernist imagery, such as those used in Blueprint skateboard graphics, and which is redolent of such high-profile graphic design groups as Sheffield-based 'The Designers Republic'.[108]

106. *Sidewalk Surfer*, no. 13 (January–February 1997), n.p.

107. Cynthia Rose, *Design After Dark: the Story of Dancefloor Style*, (London: Thames & Hudson, 1991), pp. 57–8 and 60.

108. *Emigre*, no. 29 (Winter 1994), special issue 'The Designers Republic, New and Used'.

6.6 1980s themes of death and primitive survival expressed by the skull motif. Powell-Peralta advertisement (1988).

> Consumer products, advertising, Japanese cartoons, instruction manuals, electronic gadgets, BladeRunner movies, the Macintosh computer – anything relating to current marketing tactics and/or electronics – all find their way into their work, intentionally creating confusion and chaos which . . . appropriately reflects today's society.[109]

Between the two lies the work of those such as skater-designer Ged Wells and his Insane skate clothes company, deploying cartoon imagery of everyday objects and distorted animalistic figures (2.7).[110]

Skateboarding graphics are thus in keeping with the symbolism of Lefebvre's 'partial groups', maintaining a curious mix of the modern, futuristic and old, near and distant, familiar and strange.[111] Like the creation of 'skate rock' music in the 1980s[112] – a mixture of hardcore, rap and other alternative music variants, played by local bands with titles such as Beach Blanket Bongout, McRad, Skatemaster Tate and His Concrete Crew, and Tupelo Chain Sex[113] – the general effect is thoroughly postmodern, an eclectic hybridity of different times, places, cultures and styles. Around 80 per cent of skateboard graphics are done by skaters themselves and, above all, the stylistic and subject hybridity they create suggests an alternative reality, parallel to the everyday world of work, money, leisure time, shopping, routines and realist photography. Skaters such as Mark Gonzales and Neil Blender became as famous for their designs as for their skateboarding prowess,[114] and skate magazines also run occasional features on skater-produced art and design.[115] Exhibitions of skate graphics have been held at such places as the Institute of Contemporary Arts, London ('Uncut', 30–31 August 1997), Thread Waxing Space, New York (Aaron Rose, 'Shred Sled Symposium'),[116] and the Blue Note, London ('Dysfunctional', summer 1995),[117] while other art-events have included Gladwell's video installations discussed in Chapter Five and the transformation of Chicago's Hyde Park Art Center by the artists'

109. Rudy Vanderlans, 'Design Will Eat Itself (Never Mind Paul Rand, Here's The Designers Republic!)', *Emigre*, no. 29 (Winter 1994), special issue 'The Designers Republic, New and Used', p. 2.

110. *Xtreme*, no. 4 (September 1997), pp. 24–6; and Rose, *Design After Dark*, pp. 56–9.

111. Lefebvre, *Introduction to Modernity*, p. 298.

112. *Thrasher*, 1983 onwards, passim.

113. 'Skate Rock Vol. 3 Wild Riders of Boards', *Thrasher*, vol. 6 no. 3 (March 1986), p. 55; 'Skate Rock: Bad Kids Playing Bad Music', *Thrasher*, vol. 9 no. 6 (June 1989), pp. 80–3; Grogan and Arrington 'Not Lean', pp. 155–6; and Mulshine, 'Wild', pp. 121–3.

114. Burgoyne and Leslie, *Bored*, p. 12.

115. See for example 'Expensive Association, or From Hands that Chew', *TransWorld Skateboarding*, vol. 9 no. 10 (October 1991), pp. 46–53; and Robin Davies, 'Canvas', *Thrasher*, vol. 17 no. 7 (July 1997), pp. 22–3.

116. 'Mandatory Information', *TransWorld Skateboarding*, vol. 14 no. 11 (November 1996), p. 50.

117. Thomas Campbell, 'Europe Summer Part 2', *TransWorld Skateboarding*, vol. 14 no. 1 (January 1996), pp. 122–3; and Aaron Rose, 'Dysfunctional: an Exhibition of Skateboard Art and Design', *Big Brother*, no. 19 (n.d., c. late 1995), n.p.

collaborative group SIMPARCH. The latter, *Free Basin* (2000), was an architectural and sculptural project, inserting a pool-shaped wooden bowl into the beaux arts gallery space, and incorporating music, discussions and skate performances.[118]

Thus while attempts are continually made to institutionalize and 'integrate the adolescent in trade and consumption by offering him a parallel everyday life',[119] in skateboarding this process is resisted by young people setting up their own parallel world, distinct from the one organized for them by their parents and by the state. Significantly, it is not so much the product of design that is important in skateboarding, but rather the manner and attitude with which it is deployed; a 'graphic has to have some kind of attitude'.[120] As with Lefebvre, there is 'more importance to style in life than to constructs!'[121]

The resonances of skateboarding postmodern graphic fusions are, then, largely incomprehensible to anyone outside skateboarding's own mind-set and, furthermore, are irrational and incoherent even to skaters themselves. The fast turnover of models and the ephemerality of skateboard decks once in use attenuates this situation still further.[122] In terms of consumer products, for example, skateboard deck designs have often reused such motifs as the Burger King 'Bun Halves' motif (World Industries Jason Lee model, designed by Mark McKee) and Church of Scientology 'Dianetics' logo (World Industries Randy Colvin 'Colvinetics' model) to destabilize their apparent legitimacy.[123] These 'appropriations of mainstream corporate imagery' were meant by skater-designers such as Jeff Klint as a 'post modern commentary;[124] mixed with the other rich graphic and cultural sources open to skaters, such designs are suggestive of the undefined, loose cultural hybridity without strict codes or organization theorized by, among others, Homi Bhabha.[125]

Of course, skateboard culture is commodified in that capitalism markets skateboarding back to its participants, a business variously estimated as being worth between US$300 million[126] and US$500 million[127] per annum in the late 1980s,

118. Anders Smith-Lindall, 'On Exhibit: the Hyde Park Center Picks Up Speed', *Reader*, vol. 29 no. 35 (2 June 2000); and Hyde Park Art Center press releases (2000).

119. Lefebvre, *Everyday Life in the Modern World*, p. 170.

120. Jason Irwin, in Burgoyne and Leslie, *Bored*, p. 49.

121. Lefebvre, *Introduction to Modernity*, p. 357.

122. Burgoyne and Leslie, *Bored*, p. 12.

123. Ed Templeton, 'Programming Injection #2: Skateboard Art and Angry People', *TransWorld Skateboarding*, vol. 14 no. 1 (January 1996), pp. 104–5.

124. 'Trash', *Thrasher*, vol. 17 no. 1 (January 1997), p. 130.

125. Homi Bhabha, *The Location of Culture* (London: Routledge, 1994), p. 4.

126. Gabriel, 'Rolling', p. 76; Armen Keteyian, 'Chairman of the Board', *Sports Illustrated*, vol. 65 no. 23 (24 November 1986), p. 47; and Barbara Manning, 'Teenager Tony Hawk Soars Above Everybody in the Scary Sport of Skateboarding', *People Weekly*, vol. 27 (23 March 1987), p. 49.

127. Jay Cocks, 'The Irresistible Air of Grabbing Air: Skateboarding, Once a Fad, is Now a National Turn-on', *Time*, vol. 131 (6 June 1988), p. 90.

and with around 300–400 professional skaters in the 1990s.[128] But skateboarders try to resist even this process. First, this happens through the generation of non-commodifiable items, which, apart from skate moves themselves, are often forms of language. Some terms relate to moves, as described in Chapter Five, but others are value-laden general descriptions, such as words like cool, gnarly, insane, fat/phat, radical, wicked and sick, all of which signify approval of some kind.

The second resistance to commodification is to gain some control over the manufacturing and retail process itself. Thus while there are few co-operative or co-partnership ventures in skateboarding, shops such as Sumo in Sheffield, Slam City Skates in London and SS-20 in Oxford or manufacturers such as World Industries have played heavily on the fact that they are owned and run by current and/or former skaters. Certainly, skaters such as Tony Alva, Stacy Peralta, Jim Muir and others in the 1970s quickly left the teams of other manufacturers in order to set up their own skater-run companies; Alva Skates began with a series of decks in late 1977.[129] As Alva described the position of professional skaters at this time:

> They were like puppets . . . we finally said, 'we're getting burnt, and we gotta do something about it.' We gotta start our own companies, quit making boards and wheels and money for other people so they can put our names on them and we can promote them with our activity.[130]

Later professional skateboarders such as Steve Rocco (World Industries), Tony Magnusson (H-Street),[131] Mark Gonzales (Blind)[132] and Tony Hawk (Birdhouse)[133] did the same thing. Thus while capitalist economic relations between owners and staff are still largely upheld, there is an attempt made within skateboarding to inaugurate a separate circuit of capital which exists entirely within skaters, skaters buying from other skaters, who in turn reinvest in skateboarding by providing not only better equipment but also sponsorship for skaters, skate events, ramps and so forth.

Ultimately, however, this looks increasingly like being a self-delusional ideology. There are apparently a great number of different skateboard companies, some of them quite small, together with (at the time of writing this) at least three skateboard magazines of distinct voice and worldwide distribution (all three US-based): *Big*

128. Mark O. Waters, 'Speak', *TransWorld Skateboarding*, vol. 9 no. 10 (October 1991), p. 6; 'Hell on Wheels'; and editor's response to letter, *TransWorld Skateboarding*, vol. 15 no. 11 (November 1997), p. 30.

129. Alva Skates, advertisement, *SkateBoarder*, vol. 4 no. 5 (December 1977), p. 169; Tony Alva, interview, *SkateBoarder*, vol. 4 no. 12 (July 1978), p. 68; and Alva, interview, *Thrasher*, p. 33.

130. Alva, interview, *Thrasher*, p. 33.

131. Tony Magnusson, interview, *Thrasher*, vol. 9 no. 8 (August 1989), pp. 49–50.

132. 'Product Patrol', *Thrasher*, vol. 10 no. 7 (July 1990), p. 28.

133. Tony Hawk, interview, *Big Brother*, no. 19 (n.d., c. late 1996), n.p.

Brother, *Thrasher* and *TransWorld Skateboarding*. Together, these suggest an industry made up from a diverse and fragmented set of independent manufacturers.

However, while the numerous retail outlets are indeed commonly independently owned, often acting as much as a kind of hang-out social centre as a shop, the magazines and manufacturers are somewhat different in character. Following the demise of skatepark-based skateboarding, street skating took over, requiring smaller, lighter and more manoeuvrable boards. This equipment also wore out faster as smaller wheels flat-spotted and lighter decks broke more quickly, with skaters needing to buy equipment every few months, or even more frequently.[134] This had clear profit advantages to manufacturers and shops.

> We love it because kids go through the shit even faster.[135]

Furthermore, the profits in the early 1990s increasingly fell to three dominant Californian manufacturers – Fausto Vitello of San Francisco, Steve Rocco of Los Angeles and Lawrence Balma of Torrance – each controlling multitudinous different internationally-distributed companies making skateboard decks, trucks, wheels, clothes, shoes and videos. Complex ownership arrangements masked their direct involvement, but one estimate is that Vitello, Rocco and Balma accounted for 70 per cent of skateboarding sales.[136] This state of affairs was achieved while maintaining the image of an industry constituted by small-scale, independent, skater-run companies. In the 1980s, most skateboard manufacturers tried to promote an industry worth between US$300 and 500 million as a legitimate sport with formalized competition procedures and codes of behaviour;[137] in this they were supported by the magazine *TransWorld Skateboarding* (1983 onward) and by the US National Skateboard Association (NSA), which organized the majority of contests. Against this legitimized corporate image, more recent manufacturers tried to re-emphasize the anarchic tradition within skateboarding. Rocco was particularly adept at this game, setting up World Industries in the late 1980s and *Big Brother* in 1992 to 'turn up the heat on everything'.[138] Rocco positioned himself as a former skateboard professional (7.2) who was personally sympathetic to his team skaters, allowing them to act as they wanted, minimizing rules, and abusing other manufacturers.[139] Similarly, Balma, while less overtly exploitative of a small-scale skater-run company image than Rocco, saw it important – because he was older and a more conventional business-person – to maintain a low-key presence.

134. Goff, interview, n.p.
135. Unnamed skateboard company owner, in 'Hell On Wheels'.
136. 'Hell On Wheels'.
137. Cocks, 'Irresistible', p. 7.
138. Rodney Mullen, interview, *Warp*, vol. 6 no. 3 (August 1997), p. 106.
139. Stacy Peralta, in 'Hell On Wheels'.

> There's a consumer out there who in his early teens really wants to identify with a product. If it's part of one corporation, then maybe it's not so neat.[140]

Balma thus kept hidden from skaters his ownership of skate companies such as Tracker, A-1, Skate Rages, House of Kasai, Limpies and many others.[141] Vitello similarly worked with professional skateboarders to set up seemingly independent small companies, such as Think,[142] while editorials in his *Thrasher* simultaneously affirmed that there were 'so many, small skater-run companies out there'.[143] Rocco also adopted this tactic, using professional skaters to head up seemingly independent brands that were in reality 'new paint on old wood – Rocco will soon have set up every skater in the world with his own company'.[144]

Furthermore, Rocco, Balma and Vitello also each controlled one of the three major magazines which supported their businesses, either through advertisements or stories on skaters sponsored by their companies. For example, in the May 1994 issue of the Vitello-published *Thrasher* 35 per cent of advertising was for Vitello-associated companies, not including the numerous manufacturers to whom Vitello's companies supplied wheels and trucks for rebadging as own-brand equipment. Similarly, Balma's *TransWorld Skateboarding*[145] carried no advertisements from Vitello's competitive High Speed Productions, although it did feature skaters from Balma's competitors.[146]

Perhaps becoming more aware of skateboarding's more profit-oriented side, and like all youth becoming increasingly aware of their own general colonization by business interests,[147] skateboarders have also tried to resist the commodification of skateboarding by, curiously, returning to mainstream products and rejecting skateboarder-targeted products. The logic here is a complex one, and is predicated once again on the need for a subcultural identity to remain apart from more normative lifestyles. Skateboarding has always had its own clothes and safety equipment associated with it, including, in the 1970s and 1980s, specialist shoes from manufacturers such as Vans (founded 1966) and Vision, protective pads from Rector, helmets from Protec and Norton, plus a vast range of proprietary socks, shorts, T-shirts and caps which constituted skateboarding style. In the late 1980s and 1990s, however, skateboarding became a more fashionable activity in general, skateboard

140. Lawrence Balma, in 'Hell On Wheels'.
141. World Industries, advertisement, *Thrasher*, vol. 11 no. 9 (September 1991), p. 16.
142. 'Hell On Wheels'.
143. Editorial, *Thrasher*, vol. 11 no. 9 (September 1991), p. 4.
144. Steve Kane, 'ZonaSkane', *Skateboard!* (second series), no. 45 (August 1990), p. 64.
145. *TransWorld Skateboarding* was sold to the Times-Mirror publishing company in 1997. *Big Brother*, no. 27 (August 1997), p. 27.
146. 'Hell On Wheels'.
147. Lefebvre, *Explosion*, pp. 92–3.

clothing became extremely popular in mainstream culture. For example, in 1997 specialist skateboard shoes by firms such as Vans, Airwalk, Converse and DC could be found in mass-market stores across the UK (Vans and Airwalk reached an annual turnover of US$100 and 200 million respectively by 1996[148]) (6.7). Vans in particular

6.7 Vans and Airwalk skate shoes on sale in a high street shoe shop at The Arndale Centre, Manchester (April 1996). (Photograph Iain Borden)

successfully made the transition into global non-skate markets, becoming by the year 2000 a NASDAQ-traded company, with extensive overseas (non-US) manufacturing operations.[149] Clothes such as those made Stussy, originally marketed to skateboarders in the 1980s, similarly became general high-street fare. As a result, suspicious of the reappropriation of a skate-style by non-skaters, some skateboarders have given up wearing their own subcultural clothing. In doing so, skaters implicitly realize that the right to be different is meaningful only when based on actions to establish differences,[150] and thus that their identity is based on the *activity* of skateboarding, and not purely on the style adopted in clothes, shoes and so forth.

148. 'Mandatory Information', *TransWorld Skateboarding*, vol. 14 no. 5 (May 1996), p. 46.
149. Vans internet site, URL www.vans.com (accessed 1 August 2000).
150. Lefebvre, *Production of Space*, p. 64.

The embeddedness of skateboard subculture with other counter-cultural practices can be seen in the increasing number from the early 1980s onward of 'zines (home-produced magazines, often duplicated on photocopy machines and sold by post at low cost). To begin with, the 'zines focused mainly on skateboarding itself, and in particular the more hardcore elements of its subculture.

> The skate zines speak of alienation, rebelliousness, making your own contests, building your own presence. They're into who's going higher, who's grinding the longest, who's ramp is open, who's building . . . Quotes are frequent such as: 'Everybody was lame at one time', 'Skate or Die', 'Skate Tough or Go Home', 'Don't be a poseur', 'Live to skate and skate to Live', 'Slam the Rules'.[151]

Typical titles here included *Beneath the Grey Dome, Big Beef, Bodyslam, Gut Feel'n, Kona Report, Mutant King Roller, Naughty Nomads, No Pedestrians, Ragged Edge, Skate Fate, Skater of Fortune* and *Tabby News* (US), *Skate On* and *Street Noise* (Australia), *Death Zone* and *Scum* (Germany), *Vertikaal* (Sweden), and *Go For It, Gutterslut, Jammer, Rip'n'Tear, Skate Muties from the 5th Dimension, Skateroo, Sketchy* and *Whiplash* (UK).[152] Later 'zines range from *Duh* (Belgium) and *Backside, Cow Pat, Check My Chops* (6.8), *Spread, New Spurts* and *Chimps* (UK),[153] available for little more than the cost of postage, to nationally distributed, low-budget magazines such as *Ergo Sum* and *Big Cheese*, with articles on skateboarding but also on break dancing, drag racing, clothes, art/graphic design, prostitution, music, snowboarding and bicycle MX.

The most constant form of rejection of society by skateboarding has come not from the 'zines, however, but from *Thrasher* magazine which, despite its Vitello-industry associations has been the most accurate and influential mouth-piece for that young generation identified by Lefebvre as having a 'hatred – blind or conscious – for the pressures exerted by authority, and for the whole range of established "realities"', which is 'no longer seduced, satisfied or overwhelmed by refrigerators and automobiles'; this is a youth who initiates a new way of life via a 'revolutionary romanticism, without theory yet highly effective' and who 'demand while contesting and contest while demanding'.[154]

151. Stacy Peralta 'Skate of the Art, '85', *Thrasher*, vol. 5 no. 8 (August 1985), p. 40.

152. 'Off the Wall', *Action Now*, vol. 7 no. 12 (July 1981), p. 16; Steve Caballero, interview, *Thrasher*, vol. 2 no. 2 (February 1982), p. 37; Tom Hodgkinson, 'Rad, Mad and Dangerous to Know?', *Midweek*, London (18 January 1990), p. 11; Tim Leighton-Boyce, 'Goodbye to All That: Ten Years of British Skating', *R.A.D.*, no. 83 (January 1990), pp. 43–4; Peralta 'Skate', p. 40; 'The Disciples of Skate', *Thrasher*, vol. 4 no. 7 (July 1984), pp. 20–5; and 'Zine Thing', *Thrasher*, vol. 6 no. 5 (May 1986), pp. 50–1.

153. 'Insight', *Sidewalk Surfer*, no. 21 (October–November 1997), n.p.

154. Lefebvre, *Explosion*, pp. 98–9.

6.8 One of the myriad of skate 'zines: *Check My Chops* (1996).

Founded in San Francisco in January 1981 and with a circulation of around 160,000 by 1994,[155] *Thrasher* has offered a complete guide to skateboard subculture including articles on rock music and junk food ('skarfing material – fuelling up for skating', written by Vietnam veteran Chef-Boy-am-I-Hungry[156]) as well as local scene material, reader photographs, competition reports, interviews and manufacturers' advertisements (6.9). Published in the spirit of the 'zines, *Thrasher* has used terse articles and by-lines such as 'Truth and Screw the Consequences' and 'Trash' to present skateboarding as something more than hobby or fashion. Of greater importance is the attitude of skaters: their understanding of what skateboarding is all about.

Thrasher also exemplifies the comic mode within romanticism, which ridicules those in power (both within and outside skateboarding) in order to make them human, but also as a form of vengeance and subversion.[157] Skateboarders find humour in the *values* of the dominant orders and here they directly fulfil one of Lefebvre's political expectations of the youth, ridiculing virtues of decency, respect, ostentatious good health and so on,[158] specifically for skateboarders as represented in such things as signs, private property, function, work, respect for elderly, respect for others, authority against children in general, notions of good behaviour including those to do with movement and noise, the distinction or definition of sports, bodily functions and so on. In turn, skaters' own values become 'acts and decisions, elements in a strategy',[159] forming a subculture that is often based on an anti-order of nihilism, bad taste, scatological humour, swearing, poor diets – anything that might be construed as antagonistic to others.

> Skateboarding is the only thing I have that is worth anything to me. It's the one and only thing that I love. It's the only thing that gives an otherwise empty life some kind of definition.[160]

> In skating, nothing is defined, everything can be new. There are no laws.[161]

The use of ramps in urban areas, for example, almost invariably brings complaints from neighbours about noise, because the repetitive cracks and grinds when the skateboarder engages with the ramp create a sound pattern more akin to

155. 'Hell On Wheels'.
156. *Thrasher*, vol. 5 no. 8 (August 1985), pp. 28–9 and passim.
157. Lefebvre, *Introduction to Modernity*, p. 245.
158. Ibid., pp. 243–4.
159. Ibid., p. 219.
160. Cates, 'Comment', n.p.
161. Dan Adams, in Tom Hodgkinson, 'Rad, Mad and Dangerous to Know?', *Midweek*, London (18 January 1990), p. 11.

6.9 First issue of the counter-cultural and massively influential *Thrasher* magazine (January 1981).

that of a construction site than to that of a residential area: a 'hollow thump upon impact'[162] resounds every time a move is made. Apart from the noise itself, implicit in such complaints is often a dislike of the make-shift appearance of many ramps (which are often made from a patchwork of wood and metal salvaged locally) and of the dishevelled clothing and behaviour of skaters themselves.[163] Where local ordinances allow, neighbours have successfully had ramps removed for creating a 'visible nuisance'.[164] One neighbour complained of a ramp in the beach city of Carmel on similar grounds.

> It's an obscene edifice . . . it's very ugly, it's such a disgrace it should be chopped down this minute.[165]

With objections such as these replicated across the US, it became nearly impossible to build a substantial ramp in, for example, Los Angeles without going to the valleys and outskirts.[166]

Ramps, their users and effects are thus part of the *disorder* that skaters like to create in the city. Above all, what is important is not any specific detail – and indeed there are many skaters who do not drink, take drugs, abuse their own bodies, etc. – but a general manner by which skateboarding subculture replaces conventional city life with a new totalizing self-identity in which partial allegiance is to miss the point. 'Right now, I just care about skating.'[167] This is expressed in skateboarding as a continual undercurrent, but which is also frequently expressed overtly, as in advertisements offering binary opposition choices such as 'Skate or be Stupid'[168] or between skating or a boring job as a wage slave, ending 'Fuck work before it fucks you.'[169]

Rejection of the Family

Another explicit opposition expressed by skateboarding subculture is that against the family, a theme which of course is a general condition of youth cultures which 'revolt against the Fathers'.[170]

162. Rick Blackhart, 'Ask the Doctor', *Thrasher*, vol. 5 no. 1 (January 1985), p. 8.
163. Craig Ramsay, 'The Ramp Page', *Thrasher*, vol. 4 no. 6 (June 1984), p. 46; and 'Mount Frostmore', *Speed Wheels*, no. 2 (n.d., c. August 1988), pp. 22–3.
164. Harry, letter, *Thrasher*, vol. 5 no. 8 (August 1985), p. 4.
165. Mrs Jane Turner, in 'Off the Wall' (May 1980), p. 72.
166. Christian Hosoi, interview, *Thrasher* (June 1989), p. 60.
167. Rocco, interview, p. 87.
168. 'Gotcha' sportswear, advertisement, *Thrasher*, vol. 8 no. 7 (July 1988), pp. 88–9.
169. *Sidewalk Surfer*, no. 13 (January/February 1997), n.p.
170. Lefebvre, *Explosion*, pp. 106–7.

> Skater kids are not kids bred on milk and cookies. They're not kids whose dads gave them batting practice out in the front yard or drove them to the ice-rink. It's not a father-son deal. It's just the opposite.[171]

> *R.A.D.*: What's your relationship like with your parents?
> Simon Evans: It's kinda bad.[172]

With few alternatives outside of the given institutions of school, family and organized recreation, skaters opt instead for a sense of personal freedom that flies in the face of Little League America or normative Britain.[173] One US skater saw skateboarding in the following context.

> Baseball, hotdogs, apple pie, weed, beer, pills, needles, alcohol etc., etc., are all typical hobbies of all the typical people in all the typical states in the typical country of the United States of Amerika . . . Why be a clone? Why be typical?[174]

Similarly, skaters in Oxford were seen to possess 'a vicious disregard for family, society, and the British way of life'.[175] The primary concern of skateboarders is to be not like the conventional family, and, in particular, not to be the conventional son, nor, by extension, to become the conventional father. On a more concrete level, skaters such as Mike Vallely, when they came to be parents themselves, found themselves to be disillusioned with the model of the nuclear family and so often tried to avoid replicating concerns with vaccination, formal schooling and other bugbears of conventional parenting.[176]

Skaters refuse the model of adulthood their parents require them to participate within.[177] In doing so, skateboarders refuse the binary choice of opting between childhood and conventional adulthood, and creating a third condition which is irreducible to the former two. For older skaters, such as Rodga Harvey, Lance Mountain and Steve Rocco, this meant at once being an adult while rejecting some of the normative behaviour patterns that this age conventionally entails.

> I'm 33 now: if I was going to give in to an 'adult' type attitude I'd have given up long ago.[178]

171. Kevin Thatcher, in Gabriel, 'Rolling', pp. 73–6.
172. Simon Evans, interview, *R.A.D.*, no. 114 (November 1992), p. 27.
173. Cocks, 'Irresistible', p. 91.
174. Gary Davis, 'Steep Slopes', *Thrasher*, vol. 3 no. 5 (May 1983), p. 8.
175. 'Oxford Hotters', *R.A.D.*, no. 103 (December 1991), p. 31.
176. Mike Vallely, interview, *TransWorld Skateboarding*, vol. 14 no. 1 (January 1996), p. 97.
177. Lefebvre, *Introduction to Modernity*, pp. 384–5.
178. Rodga Harvey, interview, *R.A.D.*, no. 83 (January 1990), p. 51.

> If it gets too serious, I really don't like it . . . I don't think any skater is into growing up.[179]

> I haven't grown up.[180]

This may also account for some of the adult disdain toward skateboarding, for the skateboarder/child/adult is a continual reminder that the adult did not necessarily have to make the choices he or she did.

This concern with age also, inevitably, has its spatial dimension, for as Lefebvre notes, 'time is distinguishable but not separable from space'.[181] Phenomena such as growth, maturation and ageing are not only temporal but spatial, as with the tree trunk rings which reveal age spatially. In skateboarding, however, this time-age relation is not marked in concrete objects but through the spatial *performances* of skateboarders.

Part of the critique by skaters of public space is then of it as an 'adult' space of serious productivity or consumption, or as a place of 'high cultural' activities. Skateboarding is then a reappropriation of the adult realm, and also, especially as skaters get older, a redefinition of what adult space might be. This is also part of the historical development of skateboarding, for whereas in the 1970s the urban space of the skater was typically that of the suburban drive – a traditional place for children to play, especially in cul-de-sacs – in the 1980s and 1990s this increasingly became the adult space of the city, its streets, squares and roads with all their social complexity and dangers.

'Play' in the street-skating of the 1980s and 1990s (explored in more detail in Chapters Seven and Eight) is then quite different to that of the street skating of 1970s surf-related skateboarding, and has become a rejection not only of the family as a social unit, and of the Father as social role model, but also of the family home as the social space of the young adult. As Piercy put it:

> I'm not interested in staying home and being uncreative.[182]

In turning to urban space, skateboarders in part reject the attempt by capitalism to 'distil its essence into buildings', focusing on the 'genitality' of the family and its biological reproduction.[183] They oppose not just the family per se, but also both its implicated role in capitalist social reproduction and the spatiality implicit in that relation.

179. Lance Mountain, *Thrasher*, in Glen E. Friedman, *Fuck You Heroes: Glen E. Friedman Photographs, 1976–1991*, (New York: Burning Flags, 1994), index.
180. Rocco, interview, p. 86.
181. Lefebvre, *Production of Space*, p. 175.
182. Bobby Piercy, interview, *SkateBoarder*, vol. 4 no. 7 (February 1978), p. 103.
183. Lefebvre, *Production of Space*, p. 232.

This is also how skateboarders ultimately confront the twin problems of alienation and the construction of self-identity. Skaters are alienated by the externally rational world that they are told, as young adults, they must learn about and participate within. Skateboarding, however, encourages them to construct relations with others and the city according to their own values. In isolation from non-skaters but in company with other skaters, skateboarding for them, as does any subculture, produces both new alienations and new groupings; and in terms of social power, skating redefines the site or objective of 'change' such that skaters get power over something, seeking a place over which they have control: a place which is neither school, family home, nor place of work. And it is to this urban realm which we shall turn in the next chapters.

SUBCULTURE AND THE CITY

This is an important part of the argument presented here. If we remain purely within the realm of the social or the symbolic, there are too many delusional ideologies which do not make sense; symbols and social relations in particular provide a veneer concealing underlying contradictions.[184] On the one hand, skaters try to step outside the traditional patterns of normative work patterns, clothes, music and so on, while trying to keep at bay such institutionalizing agencies as the World Skateboard Association (US, 1970s), International Skateboard Association (US, 1970s), Professional Skateboard Association (US, 1970s[185]), National Skateboard Association (US, founded 1981[186]), Pacific Skateboard Association (US, founded 1976[187]) British Skateboarding Association (UK, founded 1977 as an offshoot of the Sports Council)[188] and Scottish Skateboard Association (founded 1977).[189] On the other hand, skaters set up their own semi-conventionalized rules of behaviour, composed of language, clothes, commodity exchanges and so on. In particular, some of the home-produced 'zines such as *Cake-Fat*, *Mad Monks* and *Cow Pat*, through their coverage of issues ranging from video and music reviews, to reports on local skate scenes, to cake recipes, cats, soy milk, manga Japanese graphics, ice cream and

184. Lefebvre, *Introduction to Modernity*, p. 298.

185. 'Association Reports', *SkateBoarder*, vol. 3 no. 6 (July 1977), p. 51.

186. Beal, 'Disqualifying', p. 257; Frank Hawk, interview, *Thrasher*, vol. 6 no. 9 (September 1986), p. 74; and Keteyian, 'Chairman', p. 50.

187. 'Association Reports', *SkateBoarder*, vol. 3 no. 1 (October 1976), p. 40.

188. Barry Walsh, interview, *Skateboard Scene*, vol. 1 no. 1 (n.d., c. November/December 1977), pp. 30 and 35; and Pennell, *Skateboarding*, p. 7.

189. 'Scottish Skateboard Association', *Skateboard!*, no. 16 (December 1978), p. 19.

alien sightings,[190] tend to create a comfortable sense of security in the face of the threatening insecurity of the modern world and city; it is worth noting in this context that the age group of 15–24 year-olds is being increasingly recognized as a stage of vulnerability and high suicide rates, with these young adults threatened by AIDS, unemployment and a general demonization by the rest of society.[191] In this light the search for a kind of counter-cultural stability is more comprehensible; for example, skateboarders' clothes can seem predictably similar, all in the 'rigorously shapeless uniform of baseball caps, T-shirts and shorts'.[192] For example, of fifty or so skaters outside the Rådhus (City Hall) in Oslo on one Spring day in 1997, all but a very few were wearing the same kind of baggy trousers, T-shirt and woolly 'Beanie' hat. Such things are not accidental, and whether overtly counter-cultural or not, they aid in the construction of a particular (genderized) identity.[193] As a result, skaters can replicate within themselves exactly that 'dreary, ludicrous repetition of individuals who are curiously similar in their way of being themselves and of keeping themselves to themselves, in their speech, their gestures, their everyday habits'[194] – a condition parodied in one of Powell-Peralta's advertisements of the early 1990s (6.10).[195]

6.10 '10 top reasons why you should skate. No. 6: It's an expression of your own unique personal style.' Powell-Peralta advertisement, (1992).

Thus while skateboarding is frequently a non-organized or semi-organized activity, skateboarders remain within the realm of their (masculine) private consciousness,

190. *Cow Pat*, Great Missenden, Bucks, no. 3 (1995); *Mad Monks Magazines*, Cardiff, nos. 1–3 (n.d., c. 1995–6); and *Cake Fat*, London, no. 2 (n.d., c. 1996).

191. Janet Watts, 'A Future in the Balance', *The Guardian*, 'Society' section, pp. 2–3 and 9.

192. Romney, 'Postcards', pp. 4–5.

193. Pile, *Body and the City*, p. 75.

194. Lefebvre, *Critique of Everyday Life*, pp. 152 and 237.

195. Powell-Peralta advertisement, *Thrasher*, vol. 12 no. 8 (August 1992), p. 21.

with little sense of communion with their own situation, or with non-skaters; as with any specialism and sub-systems of culture, they often end up communicating only 'their own rules of conduct, their empty shell'.[196]

In particular, as with many young adults, skateboarders have little sense of history, and indeed see ignorance of the past as something to be proud of in their celebration of themselves as a 'pure beginning'.[197]

> Skaters have the memory of a stoner who's spent the last ten years with the shades drawn and his lips glued to the bong.[198]

Young adults' 'arrogant, virtually unmotivated indifference towards the past',[199] is, among skateboarders, even directed at their own history, for skaters sometimes display a general ignorance of the development of skate moves and so on.

> History, by definition, is a dead issue. The past is the past and the future is sometime else. Skateboarding dwells in the present. Yesterday's heroes, the mangled messages left molding by the all-fronts media blitz and tomorrow's tragedies are all meaningless to the contemporary skater. All that matters is the act of skating.[200]

Skateboarding takes place – as far as many skateboarders perceive it – also entirely within the present, such that among skateboarders there is the continual view of themselves as being 'new' pioneers, while in fact previous generations of skaters (3–4 years or more older) have already undertaken similar actions. As such, although history never reproduces itself completely, there is a risk of repeating what has happened before,[201] and it is therefore essential for skateboarders to deny the past.

While skateboarding critiques normative lifestyles, taken as a *purely social* activity it is also exactly this normative lifestyle which it tends to replicate or parallel, creating a 'surrogate social structure, complete with its own rules and rituals'.[202] Or in Antonio Gramsci's terms, skaters actively consent in the transference of ideas from dominant groups to themselves.[203] This is particularly evident in the formation of skateboard companies with professional team skaters, where skateboarding tends to mirror the same business world it purportedly disavows, and where skaters like

196. Lefebvre, *Everyday Life in the Modern World*, p. 70.
197. Lefebvre, *Introduction to Modernity*, p. 161.
198. Mortimer, 'Peralta', p. 90.
199. Lefebvre, *Introduction to Modernity*, p. 161.
200. John Smythe, 'The History of the World and Other Short Subjects, or, From Jan and Dean to Joe Jackson Unabridged', *SkateBoarder*, vol. 6 no. 10 (May 1980), p. 29.
201. Lefebvre, *Introduction to Modernity*, pp. 163–4.
202. Miki Vukovich in Vallely, interview, p. 97.
203. Beal, 'Disqualifying', pp. 252–3.

Hosoi and Hawk earned up to US$200,000 annually, largely from product endorsements.[204] And, increasingly, many professional and semi-professional skaters see their ultimate career not in skateboarding as an activity, but as an industry in which to found a skate-oriented equipment/clothes/shoes enterprise. Notably, the magazine *TransWorld Skateboarding* has always tried to promote this kind of respectable image for skateboarding in contrast to the more counter-cultural stance of *Thrasher*, *R.A.D.*, *Big Brother*, *Sidewalk Surfer* and many other skate publications. Here, then, if we take the oppositional attitude as the core of skateboarding subculture, the danger is that skateboarding merely creates a fiction of itself, disguising the degree to which it is compulsed both by the external world and its own rules.

Yet as Lefebvre notes, the imaginary does not only disguise fictions but also provides the possibility of adaptation;[205] and for skateboarding, it is when placed in relation to spatial concerns, as hinted at in the brief discussion of familial space above, that a more distinct practice is disclosed. If skateboarders, as adolescents, become 'brutally assertive' in the face of their incapacity to impose values, consuming the adult objects that surround them,[206] it is the city that this assertive violence is set against. Indeed, this is a necessary process, for differing social groups can only constitute themselves as subjects through producing a space, lest they stay merely as signs; in order to create, sustain and reproduce an identity for themselves, groups cannot use space as a mirror, but must appropriate space as part of a historical process.[207]

To understand skateboarding we must, then, consider it directly in relation to the spatial. Skateboarding subculture is enacted not as a purely socio-economic enterprise, but as a physical activity, undertaken against the materiality of the modern city, and hence it is when practised as a simultaneously spatial, socially lived and temporal practice that a critique, as we shall now see, does emerge.

> Thrashing is part of a lifestyle, a fast-paced feeling to fit this modern world. Thrashing is finding something and taking it to the ultimate limit – not dwelling on it, but using it to the fullest and moving on. Skateboarding has not yet reached its maximum potential, and who can say what the limits are? To find out – Grab that board! . . . Remember, there are tons of asphalt and concrete being poured every day, so – GRAB THAT BOARD![208]

204. Hawk, interview, *Big Brother*, n.p.; Gabriel, 'Rolling', p. 74; and Keteyian, 'Chairman', p. 48.
205. Lefebvre, *Everyday Life in the Modern World*, p. 90.
206. Lefebvre, *Everyday Life in the Modern World*, p. 91.
207. Lefebvre, *Production of Space*, pp. 416–7.
208. Kevin Thatcher, 'Grab That Board', *Thrasher*, vol. 1 no. 1 (January 1981), p. 6.

Chapter 7
Urban Compositions

> When fun is outlawed, only the outlaws will have fun.[1]

The urban practice of skateboarding implicitly yet continuously critiques contemporary cities. Furthermore, where capitalist abstract space contains within itself the seeds of its successor – Lefebvre's putative *differential space* in which socio-spatial differences are emphasized and celebrated[2] – practices such as skateboarding may thus partially prefigure what this differential space might be.

> Two hundred years of American technology has unwittingly created a massive cement playground of unlimited potential. But it was the minds of 11 year olds that could see that potential.[3]

> Diversity. That's my new word right now.[4]

Through an everyday practice – neither consciously theorized nor programmed – skateboarding suggests that pleasure rather than work, use values rather than exchange values, activity rather than passivity, performing rather than recording, are potential components of the future, as yet unknown city.

To consider this matter, we return to the periodized history of skateboarding, specifically to the late 1970s and 1980s, before moving rapidly to the period from the later 1980s onward.

THE CITY IS THE HARDWARE

> Spring 1981: skating goes underground and back into the streets.[5]

1. Warren Bolster, in John Smythe, 'The History of the World and Other Short Subjects, or, From Jan and Dean to Joe Jackson Unabridged', *SkateBoarder*, vol. 6 no. 10 (May 1980), p. 38.
2. Henri Lefebvre, *The Production of Space*, (Oxford: Blackwell, 1991), pp. 52 and 352–400.
3. C.R. (Craig) Steyck, in Carlos Izan, 'Aspects of the Downhill Slide', *SkateBoarder*, vol. 2 no. 2 (Fall 1975), p. 29.
4. Sasha Steinhorst, interview, *Heckler* (accessed 5 May 1996).
5. Dave Makely, letter, *Action Now*, vol. 7 no. 11 (June 1981), p. 10.

The 1970s skateparks did not usually prove to be good investments, partly due to the general downturn in popularity of skateboarding which occurred in the late 1970s; already in 1978 many US skateparks were insolvent after lavish construction costs had necessitated admission charges of US$3–6 per 2-hour session,[6] and by 1980 many of them had closed.[7] In the UK, peak skateboard sales in Christmas 1977 were followed by decline;[8] some skateparks had already closed by July 1978,[9] and many more by February 1979.[10] By the end of 1981, the remainder were struggling for survival,[11] and by 1982, most UK skateparks had ceased operations. Many met an ignoble fate; for example, Chester's 'Inner City Truckers' concrete forms became derelict and filled with stagnant rain water, with the owner imprisoned for embezzling membership fees (7.1).[12] Even the most successful of the US skateparks faced problems: by 1982, Pipeline's owners felt themselves lucky to attract fifteen skaters per weekend,[13] while Cherry Hill and Apple skateparks were reduced to opening only on weekends.[14]

Other problems faced by skateparks concerned heavy insurance premiums for, despite maintaining 'impressive safety records',[15] skateparks suffered from the US 'liability crisis' where people were always on the look-out to launch a lawsuit for potential financial gain. Such attitudes caused considerable hostility among some skatepark owners and managers.

> Nobody twisted your arm to make you go skateboarding . . . But the American society is so sue conscious that they figure this is the way to riches.[16]

6. Neil Heayes, 'All Aboard for the Skateboard Take-Off', *Contract Journal* (19 January 1978), pp. 22–3; 'The Sun Rises on Skate City', *Skateboard!*, no. 2 (October 1977), p. 29; Armen Keteyian, 'Chairman of the Board', *Sports Illustrated*, vol. 65 no. 23 (24 November 1986), p. 47; and Dee Urquhart and Iain Urquhart, 'A Look at America', *Skateline*, no. 8 (Spring 1982), p. 20.

7. Duane Bigelow and Wally Hollyday, interview, *SkateBoarder*, vol. 6 no. 8 (March 1980), p. 66.

8. Tim Leighton-Boyce, letter (5 June 1997), and phone conversation (1 July 1997).

9. Bruce Sawford, 'Comment', *Skateboard!*, no. 11 (July 1978), p. 35.

10. Bruce Sawford, 'Comment', *Skateboard!*, no. 18 (February 1979), p. 7.

11. Michael Brooman and Colin White, letter, *SkateBoarder's Action Now*, vol. 7 no. 6 (January 1981), p. 12; and 'Concrete: Chester Skatepark – Temple of Doom', *Skateboard!* (second series), no. 41 (April 1990), pp. 32–3, 36–7 and 41.

12. Pete Grant, letter, *Skateboard News*, no. 17 (May 1982), p. 2.

13. 'Upland Pipeline: Closing Comments', *TransWorld Skateboarding*, vol. 7 no. 2 (April 1989), p p. 64–72.

14. 'Off the Wall', *SkateBoarder's Action Now*, vol. 7 no. 8 (March 1981), p. 18.

15. National Safety Council, *Skateboarding*, (Chicago: Bulletin, The Council, 1978), p. 3; 'Skate Parks: Part IV In Search of Skatopia', *SkateBoarder*, vol. 3 no. 1 (October 1976), p. 53; and John O'Malley, interview, *SkateBoarder*, vol. 3 no. 6 (July 1977), p. 109.

16. Jim Levy, 'Skate Park Insurance Discussion', *SkateBoarder*, vol. 4 no. 10 (May 1978), p. 124.

7.1 The majority of 1970s concrete skateparks soon met with an ignoble fate. The derelict Inner City Truckers (1990). (Photograph Meany)

As a result of this situation, by 1978 skatepark owners found good insurance coverage almost impossible to obtain. Pipeline eventually did without insurance altogether, while other skateparks asked for a legally dubious liability release to be signed.[17] In the late 1990s, California would eventually legislate for limited skatepark liability, and designate skateboarding as a 'Hazardous Recreational Activity', both of which would help to prevent participants from suing skatepark managers and owners, but this was over a decade away.[18]

Skatepark owners also faced difficulties from developers seeking more profitable uses for their land as leases ran out.[19] The large size of many US skateparks made

17. Levy, 'Insurance', interview, pp. 120–6; National Safety Council, *Skateboarding*, p. 3; and 'Upland Pipeline', pp. 64–72.

18. California Assembly Bill Number: AB 2487, in Brigette Sheils and Joel Patterson, 'Filling the Void', *TransWorld Skateboarding*, vol. 14 no. 1 (January 1996), p. 164; Simple Skateboards and International Association of Skateboard Companies, advertisement, *Thrasher*, vol. 16 no. 11 (November 1996), p. 35; and 'WE WIN!!! AB 1296 Is Yours!!! Skateboarding Liability Law', *International Association of Skateboard Companies* internet site, URL http://www.skateboard.com/iasc (accessed 7 April 1999)

19. Stacy Peralta, interview, *Thrasher*, vol. 2 no. 5 (May–June 1982), p. 21.

redevelopment particularly attractive[20] – as when Del Mar Skate Ranch was replaced by a hotel complex.[21] Consequently many skateparks ceased operations. The first of the major Californian facilities to go was Big 'O', shortly followed in 1982 by Lakewood which became a McDonald's burger outlet. Runway became an RV showroom, Hi Roller (Boulder, Colorado) was redeveloped as a condominium and rent-a-car development, and Ranch, after some illegal post-closure skateboarding,[22] eventually became a ploughed field.[23] In Florida, only around a quarter of its skateparks remained.[24] Most skateparks were demolished or filled in, but some survived either as ruins or semi-buried, such as the large three-quarter pipe of Big 'O'.[25] Where possible, skaters scavenged coping and other fragments for mementoes or reuse on ramps.[26]

Although some skateparks endured (often through the custom of BMX cyclists[27]), with even a few new facilities built in the 1980s–90s, by the early 1980s the dominance of skateparks over skateboarding was over. In 1980, *SkateBoarder* transmogrified into the 'sports/lifestyle' *SkateBoarder's Action Now* (later *Action Now*),[28] covering the 'new age sports'[29] of snowboarding, windsurfing, body-boarding and BMX. The decline also affected companies, many of which folded, and professional skaters – in 1980 there were 175 pros at the US Gold Cup series, while within a year only 15 were left.[30]

Skateboarding itself, however, did not disappear, but was recharged in response to the changing architectural conditions. 'Take it *where* you want and use it *how* you want'.[31] In the 1980s, skateboarding increasingly focused not on the extreme architecture of the ramp or skatepark terrain (although magazines continued to cover these kinds of skateboarding), but on the quotidian public street.

> Out there in the concrete jungle exist literally thousands of shreddable terrains in the form of banks, ramps, pools, curbs, loading docks, steps, parking garages, your driveway, anything![32]

20. Urquhart and Urquhart, 'America', p. 18.
21. 'Trash', *Thrasher*, vol. 7 no. 11 (November 1987), p. 102.
22. 'Concrete Criminals', *Thrasher*, vol. 3 no. 12 (December 1983), pp. 18–19; and Redondo, 'Last Ride', p. 54.
23. Don Redondo, 'The Last Ride, or, We've Almost Lost Del Mar', *Thrasher*, vol. 6 no. 2 (February 1986), p. 51.
24. Mike Folmer, interview, *SkateBoarder's Action Now*, vol. 7 no. 4 (November 1980), p. 48.
25. *Thrasher*, vol. 9 no. 6 (June 1989), pp. 53–8 and 127.
26. Jocko Weyland, 'Epiphany at Mecca', *Thrasher*, vol. 17 no. 7 (July 1997), p. 62.
27. 'Off the Wall', (March 1981), p. 17.
28. *SkateBoarder's Action Now*, vol. 7 no. 7 (February 1981).
29. *Action Now*, vol. 7 no. 11 (June 1981), p. 5.
30. Murray, 'Gentleman's Agreement', *DansWORLD* (accessed 20 April 1995).
31. Smythe, 'History', p. 31.
32. Craig Ramsay, 'Take, San Jose, For Example', *Thrasher*, vol. 3 no. 5 (May 1983), p. 22.

The use of urban streets was, of course, a long skateboarding tradition, reaching back to the 1960s' use of public roads and the 1970s appropriations of found spaces; even in 1976 as skateparks were being built and pool-riding touted as the ultimate high, *SkateBoarder* magazine continued to publicize street skating.

> Somewhere beyond the formalized spectrum, street skating remains supreme. On the banks, drainage ditches and streets of the land it's coming down hard and heavy . . . working the Amerikan concrete technology for all its worth. While the old flatlanders flounder in their parks, the boys are going upside down in the sewers.[33]

Such skaters were seen as 'urban guerrillas' or anarchists.

> The skating urban anarchist employs the handiwork of the government/urban corporate structure in a thousand ways that the original architects could never even dream of: sidewalks for parking, streets for driving, pipes for liquids, sewers for refuse etc., all have been reworked into a new social order.[34]

Steve Rocco was applying skatepark tricks like aerials, roll-outs and inverts to the streets of Hermosa, California, back in 1978 (7.2),[35] and by 1980 *SkateBoarder* was promoting street skating partly as a return to skateboarding's surf-related roots and partly for the 'new urban terrorist'.[36] Freestyle skating was also invigorated by the street-crossover developments of skaters such as Jim McCall, Bob Schmelzer and Floridans Tim Scroggs and Rodney Mullen.[37] Manufacturers such as Powell-Peralta were anxious to find post-skatepark terrains to stimulate demand,[38] and by 1981 the Santa Cruz company's advertisements focused exclusively on street skating equipment.[39] The Independent truck company was likewise running advertisements

33. John Smythe, 'Frontier Tales', *SkateBoarder*, vol. 3 no. 2 (December 1976), p. 111.
34. Smythe, 'History', p. 29.
35. 'Who's Hot! Steve Rocco', *SkateBoarder*, vol. 6 no. 6 (January 1980), pp. 70–1; Stacy Peralta, 'Skate of the Art, '85', *Thrasher*, vol. 5 no. 8 (August 1985), p. 40; and Steve Rocco, interview, *TransWorld Skateboarding*, vol. 6 no. 1 (February 1988), p. 83.
36. Curtis Hesselgrave, 'Curb Grinding and Other Joys', *SkateBoarder*, vol. 6 no. 6 (January 1980), pp. 34–9; and Steve Rocco, 'Terror in the Streets: Manifesto for the Masses', *SkateBoarder*, vol. 6 no. 11 (June 1980), pp. 33–9.
37. 'Who's Hot! Tim Scroggs', *SkateBoarder*, vol. 5 no. 9 (April 1979), pp. 78–9; D. David Morin, 'Mutt', *Action Now*, vol. 7 no. 11 (June 1981), pp. 28–31; Stacy Peralta, 'Street Performing', *Thrasher*, vol. 2 no. 3 (March 1982), p. 39; 'Freestyle Fanatics', *Thrasher*, vol. 6 no. 3 (March 1986), p. 33; and Lowboy, 'Fear of Freestyle', *Thrasher*, vol. 2 no. 9 (October 1982), pp. 22–33.
38. Rodney Mullen, interview, *Warp*, vol. 6 no. 3 (August 1997), p. 53.
39. Santa Cruz, advertisement, *Action Now*, vol. 7 no. 12 (July 1981), p. 53.

7.2 An early instance of the new street skating. Steve Rocco applying the skatepark-based invert move to a road-side curb (1980).

with lines such as 'Free on the Streets',[40] while Powell-Peralta marketed back-to-basics 'Street Issue' decks.[41]

The first coverage of the new street skateboarding came in *Action Now*,[42] but the April 1982 *Thrasher* was the first 'gnarly street issue' to be largely devoted to streetstyle.[43] *Thrasher* in particular promoted streetstyle as the new force in skateboarding, publicizing California skaters such as John Lucero and Richard Armejo who, deprived of the by now defunct Skate City skatepark in Whittier,[44] began radically extending skateboarding onto the most quotidian of urban elements. Their fundamental move was the 'ollie', the impact-adhesion-ascension procedure by which the skater unweights the front of the skateboard to make it pop up seemingly unaided into the air,[45] Alan Gelfand's skatepark-based invention (see Chapter Five) now being adapted to the street.

Although this new street skating took place right across the US, once more a specific concentration took place in the beach cities of Los Angeles. In particular, 'new blood' Dogtown skaters such as Natas Kaupas, Eric Dressen and Jesse Martinez, along with a plethora of other locals, exploited the ollie in order to ride up onto the walls, steps and street furniture of the Santa Monica strand and Venice Boardwalk.[46] As Natas Kaupas put it,

> I attempt to make everything skateable – walls, curbs, ramps, whatever.[47]

Or in the words of Stacy Peralta,

> Skaters can exist on the essentials of what is out there. Any terrain. For urban skaters the city is the hardware on their trip.[48]

As *Thrasher* inferred through a long list of urban elements, skateboard terrain was no longer restricted to pools, ramps or skateparks, but involved anything encountered in the modern city:

40. Independent, advertisement, *SkateBoarder*, vol. 6 no. 7 (February 1980), p. 3.
41. Powell-Peralta, advertisement (September 1980), p. 11.
42. John Smythe (pseudonym for Craig Stecyk), 'No Parking', *Action Now*, vol. 8 no. 2 (September 1981), pp. 52–7.
43. *Thrasher*, vol. 2 no. 4 (April 1982).
44. Peralta 'Skate', p. 40.
45. Siân Liz Evans, 'Young, Gifted and Board Stupid', *The Big Issue* (London), no. 126 (17–23 April 1995), p. 18.
46. Lowboy, 'Street Sequentials', *Thrasher*, vol. 4 no. 9 (September 1984), pp. 32–9; Morizen Föche, 'New Blood', *Thrasher*, vol. 6 no. 3 (March 1986), pp. 40–7; *Thrasher*, vol. 9 no. 6 (June 1989), p. 53; and Jesse Martinez, 'Venice', *Big Brother*, no. 26 (June 1997), pp. 40–5.
47. Natas Kaupas, interview, *Thrasher*, vol. 8 no. 5 (May 1988), p. 65.
48. Stacy Peralta, interview, *Interview*, no. 17 (July 1987), pp. 102–3.

Alley	Gas pump	Road
Army bunker	Graveyard	Road obstacles
Bank	Gutter	Roller rink
Bedroom	Half-pipe	Run off
Bench	Hand railing	Schoolyard
Bevel	Hill	Seawall
Bike path	Lane divider	Sewer pipe
Brick wall	Launch ramp	Shopping mall
Bridge	Lawn	Sidewalk
Building	Loading dock	Skate park
Bumper	Mailbox	Slide
Car	Meteorite crater	Slope
Casting pond	Mountain	Spillway
Construction site	Parking lot	Stairs
Couches	Picnic table	Statue
Crack	Plank	Street sign
Culvert	Planter box	Street
Curb	Playground	Tennis court
Downtown	Pond	Train track
Drainage ditch	Pool	Tree
Driveway	Public park	Truck
Dumpster	Quarter pipe	Tube
Full pipe	Ramp	Wall
Garage	Reservoir	Wheelchair ramp[49]

Of course this new skating was not just about new terrains, but a mode of engagement. Californian Mark Gonzales ('the Gonz') did more than any other to usher in the new streetstyle skating, with moves such as the first boardslide on a handrail and 180° nosegrinds (7.3).

> With the streets of Southgate as his playground, Mark Gonzales changed the way the world looks at a skateboard. Handrails, stairs, benches and gaps are the canvas of his masterwork.[50]

Visiting UK skaters were amazed in 1984 to see Gonzales do 3-foot-high ollies from the flat onto a wall.[51] Other 1980s streetstylers included Lance Mountain, Matt

49. 'Everything Under the Sun', *Thrasher*, vol. 7 no. 6 (June 1987), pp. 56–9.

50. '*Thrasher* Magazine Skater of the Year: a Twenty Year Retrospective, 1975–1995', *Thrasher*, vol. 17 no. 1 (January 1997), p. 60.

51. Rodga Harvey, interview, *R.A.D.*, no. 83 (January 1990), p. 50.

7.3 One of the most important pioneers of streetstyle skateboarding, Mark Gonzales, grinding a concrete handrail outside a branch of First Interstate bank (*c.* 1987).

Hensely, Tommy Guerrero, Rob Roskopp, Corey O'Brien, Eddie Reategui, Tony Hawk and Jason Jessee, many of whom also skated vertical terrains. Rodney Mullen in particular pursued a highly technical version of streetstyle, with rapid deployment of moves such as 360° ollies and the 'ollie impossible' in which the board is rolled 360° around the rear or front foot.[52]

By the mid-1980s, street skating was fully established as a distinct form of skateboarding.

> It's 1985 and eighty percent of the pros and ams, as well as skaters world wide are doing vertical tricks on the flat ground. The emergence of the new streetstyle is the biggest thing to hit skateboarding since pool riding in the 70's. It's a whole new form, different, yet a combination of all other aspects of skating.[53]

The first streetstyle competition, later recalled as the birthplace of streetstyle skateboarding,[54] took place in April 1983 in Golden Gate Park, San Francisco,[55] and more elaborate such events – with cars, rails, small ramps and other everyday objects, and called things like 'Wake Up and Smell the Pavement', 'Terror in Tahoe', 'Slaughter in the Sierras' and 'Shut Up and Skate' – were soon being organized across the US.[56] But it was predominantly in the city streets themselves that the new skateboarding took place; the Powell-Peralta *Public Domain* (1989) and *Ban This* (1989) videos – among many other such videos – showed skaters in the streets of Los Angeles and Santa Barbara jumping over cars, riding up the walls of buildings, over hydrants and planters, onto benches, flying over steps, and sliding down the free-standing handrails in front of a bank.[57] By 1992, magazines were proclaiming the death of vertical skating; fuelled by the spread of litigation from skateparks to private ramps, by new companies such as World Industries, by the street-level consciousness of magazines such as *Thrasher* and *R.A.D.*, and by its relative immediate accessibility, streetstyle now completely dominated the skate scene.[58]

Television exposure of street skating also became more common in the 1990s, either through cable and satellite (such as the audience of around 45 million for the

52. Mullen, interview, *Warp*, p. 48.

53. Peralta 'Skate', p. 40.

54. 'Who Killed Vert?', *Thrasher*, vol. 12 no. 7 (July 1992), p. 27.

55. 'Trash', *Thrasher*, vol. 3 no. 5 (May 1983), p. 41; Morizen Föche, 'San Franciscan Street Style', *Thrasher*, vol. 3 no. 6 (June 1983), pp. 26–31; and 'Flashbacks', Best of *Thrasher*, vol. 1 no. 1 (Winter 1988), p. 77.

56. *Thrasher*, vol. 5 no. 7 (July 1985), pp. 22–3; and Peralta 'Skate', p. 39.

57. *Public Domain* video (Powell-Peralta, 1988) and *Ban This* video (Powell-Peralta, 1989).

58. 'Who Killed Vert?', pp. 26–33.

ESPN coverage of the multi-sport Xtreme Games[59]) or occasionally on terrestrial channels (often integrated into programmes on snowboarding[60] and general youth culture[61]). Other mass coverage came from films like *Back to the Future* (Dir. Steven Spielberg, mid-1980s), B-movie *Thrashin'* (Fries Entertainment, Dir. David Winters, 1986),[62] *Police Academy 4* (1987) and *Gleaming the Cube* (Twentieth Century Fox/Rank, Dir. Graeme Clifford, 1988). Top streetstyle professionals in the 1990s included, among many others, Salman Agah, Kareem Campbell, John Cardiel, Mike Carroll, Rob Dyrdyk, Reese Forbes, Omar Hassan, Matt Hensely, Frankie Hill, Eric Koston, Jason Lee, John Lucero, Kris Markovitch, Chad Muska, Tom Penny, Andrew Reynolds, Geoff Rowley, Willy Santos, Chris Senn, Daewon Song, Ed Templeton, Chet Thomas, Mike Vallely, Simon Woodstock and Jeremy Wray. Similarly, certain skate spots – such as the Embarcadero ('EMB', the 'Chartres Cathedral of skateboarding'[63]) and Pier 7 in San Francisco[64] – became as well known globally through videos and magazines as had skateparks such as Pipeline, Marina del Rey and Cherry Hill during the late 1970s.

But more than any other phase of skateboarding, streetstyle is based on the everyday activities of its millions of practitioners conducted in cities worldwide ('Everybody, Everywhere!'[65]), rather than on the extreme moves of its most spectacular professionals in extravagant purpose-built facilities or events. As one advertisement put it, every skater is yet 'another nobody'.[66] It is important not to underestimate the sheer quantitative nature of this phenomenon. Already in the early 1980s, Powell-Peralta was receiving letters from countries such as Czechoslovakia, Poland, Sweden, Germany, Thailand, New Zealand, Australia and Canada, plus others in South America and elsewhere,[67] while *Pravda* and regional newspapers were reporting a skateboarding boom in the USSR.[68]

> Feature it: people are building ramps behind the Iron Curtain, they're freestyling in the Arctic, they're concrete carving on the Berlin wall.[69]

59. Ivory Serra, 'Corporate Death Burger: Xtreme Games, Providence, Rhode Island, 1996', *Thrasher*, vol. 16 no. 11 (November 1996), pp. 52–7; and Airwalk, advertisement, *TransWorld Skateboarding*, vol. 15 no. 11 (November 1997), p. 49.

60. 'Board Stupid' (Global Productions/Channel 4, UK, January 1997).

61. 'Passengers' (Channel 4, UK, 8 July 1994); and 'The Mag' (Channel 5, UK, 1 February 1998).

62. Kevin Thatcher, 'Rant and Reel', *Thrasher*, vol. 6 no. 10 (October/November 1986), p. 94.

63. Marc Spiegler, *Metropolis*, in Leah Garchik, 'The Urban Landscape', *San Francisco Chronicle* (late summer 1994), posted on *DansWORLD* (accessed March 1995).

64. Chicken Boy McCoy, 'Pier 7 Locals', *Thrasher*, vol. 17 no. 1 (January 1997), pp. 42–5; and James Kelch, interview, *Thrasher*, vol. 17 no. 7 (July 1997), pp. 57–8.

65. Santa Cruz, advertisement, *Thrasher*, vol. 2 no. 2 (February 1982), inside front cover.

66. Simple, advertisement, *TransWorld Skateboarding*, vol. 15 no. 11 (November 1997), p. 107.

67. Peralta, interview, *Thrasher*, p. 20.

68. 'Off the Wall', *SkateBoarder's Action Now*, vol. 7 no. 6 (January 1981), p. 16.

69. Peralta, interview, *Thrasher*, p. 20.

In 1985–6 skateboarding went through very rapid growth,[70] and reached nearly pre-1980 levels by 1986–88[71] – by 1989, *R.A.D.* sold 60,000 issues every month,[72] while *Thrasher* had a declared global circulation of 245,750 for 1988.[73] In the 1990s, there were healthy skate scenes in places, apart from the established skateboarding countries of Australia, Brazil,[74] Canada, New Zealand, USA, UK and mainland Europe, in others as diverse as Malaysia, Indonesia,[75] Puerto Rico, Costa Rica, Tahiti, Yugoslavia, Slovenia, South Africa, Greenland, Iceland, Japan, China (7.4), Scandinavia (7.5), Saudi Arabia, Turkey, Israel, Iran and Iraq.[76] Absolute numbers of those involved are impossible to fix, but *Time* magazine estimated US skaters in 1988 at 20 million,[77] while another more reliable source estimated around 9.25 million US skaters in 1990, 5.4 million in 1993 and 6.5 million in 1995[78] – 2–8 per cent of the total US population. The total number of skaters in the world is, then, probably *at minimum* 10–20 million or 0.2–0.4 per cent of the total global population of *c.* 5 billion – *TransWorld Skateboarding* estimated the global figure in 1997 at 12 million.[79]

7.4 Street skater in Shanghai (2000). (Photograph Gil Doron)

70. Jeanne Hoffman, in 'Upland Pipeline: Closing Comments', p. 66; and Tim Leighton-Boyce, 'Goodbye to All That: Ten Years of British Skating', internet version, *DansWORLD* (accessed 17 March 1995).

71. Jay Cocks, 'The Irresistible Air of Grabbing Air: Skateboarding, Once a Fad, is Now a National Turn-on', *Time*, vol. 131 (6 June 1988), p. 90; and Phillip M. Wishon and Marcia L. Oreskovich, 'Bicycles, Roller Skates and Skateboards: Safety Promotion and Accident Prevention', *Children Today*, vol. 15 no. 3 (May–June 1986), p. 14, based on American Academy of Pediatricians, 'Skateboard Policy Statement' (1979). One estimate put the 1989 UK skateboarding scene at less than half of the 1970s peak. Editorial, *Skateboard!* (second series), no. 4 (1989), p. 2.

72. Fyfe, 'Street', p. 32.

73. 'Statement of Ownership, Management and Circulation', *Thrasher*, vol. 9 no. 2 (February 1989), p. 108.

74. Luiz Calado, 'Destination: Brazil', *Thrasher*, vol. 11 no. 11 (November 1991), pp. 36–9.

75. Claus Grabke, 'Acht Tage Skating in Indonesien', *Monster*, no. 38 (May/June 1989), pp. 16–17.

76. Editorial, *Thrasher*, vol. 11 no. 11 (November 1991), p. 4.

77. Cocks, 'Irresistible', p. 90.

78. *American Sports Analysis*, in Brigette Sheils and Joel Patterson, 'Filling the Void', *TransWorld Skateboarding*, vol. 14 no. 1 (January 1996), p. 74.

79. Editor's response to letter, *TransWorld Skateboarding*, vol. 15 no. 11 (November 1997), p. 30.

7.5 Street skater outside Oslo's town hall, the Rådhus (2000). (Photograph Iain Borden)

ZERO DEGREE ARCHITECTURE AND URBAN RHYTHM

I have previously argued that purpose-built skatepark architecture can only be comprehended in combination with the skater's body-space, each being reconstructed through encountering its Other. The same is true of streetstyle, where the technical body-space moves such as ollie impossibles, no-complys, shove-its, kickflips, rail-slides, 50–50 grinds, nollies and so on are, by themselves, less than half the story. It is, then, in the engagement with the city that the space of street skating is continually (re)produced.

> *TransWorld Skateboarding*: What inspires you?
> Matt Reason: City skating.[80]

The new street skateboarding was no longer situated in the detached villas and pools of the undulating, semi-suburban Hollywood Hills and Santa Monica canyon and had come downtown.

> I realised that I would have to leave the hills and open countryside to progress in skating. Towards the urban jungle I headed . . . Bigger and more varied types of terrain were my driving force.[81]

> For the type of skating that's going on today, downtown is the place to be.[82]

Where the vertical riders of the 1970s and 1980s were often from the 'suburban recreation grounds',[83] the later streetstyle skaters tended to come from 'the worst parts of towns and know the true meaning of street life'.[84] Thus 1990s skaters have a 'life in the big city'[85] in the streets of not only New York, Washington, San Francisco

80. Matt Reason, interview, *TransWorld Skateboarding*, vol. 14 no. 1 (January 1996), p. 114.
81. Ewan Bowman, 'Comment', *Sidewalk Surfer*, no. 13 (January/February 1997), n.p.
82. Brian Hadaka, in Garchik, 'Urban Landscape'.
83. 'Don't Be a Joey', *Xtreme*, no. 4 (September 1997), p. 20.
84. 'Who Killed Vert?', p. 28.
85. Life Skateboards, advertisement, *Thrasher*, vol. 11 no. 9 (September 1991), p. 21.

and Philadelphia, but also those of London, Reykjavik, Tehran, Vancouver, São Paulo, Prague, Istanbul, Wellington, Beirut, Melbourne, Riyadh, Mexico City, Shanghai and other cities worldwide. The new skateboarding sites are not private houses or suburban roads, hidden from public view, but university campuses, urban squares, public institutions, national theatres, commercial office plazas, as well as the more quotidian spaces of back streets, main roads, alleys, sidewalks, malls and car-parks. All these are appropriations of places, similar to 1970s appropriations of schoolyard banks and pools, but here skateboarders answer Paul Virilio's call for a 'counter-habitation' of habitually uninhabited but nonetheless public 'critical spaces'.[86] But why is this, and what does it mean for the experience of urban architecture?

Compared to the suburbs, city cores offer more opportunities and concentrated heterogeneous social spaces.

> The make-believe existence of the city dweller's environment is less fictitious and unsatisfactory than that of his suburban or new-town counterpart; it is enlivened by monuments, chance encounters and the various occupations and distractions forming part of his everyday experience; city make-believe favours the adaptation of time and space.[87]

The rich architectural and social fabric of the city offers skateboarders a plethora of buildings, social relations, times and spaces, many of which are free to access. And streetstyle skateboarding consequently discloses the 'unlimited possibilities our cities offered'.[88]

> A sea of shapeless angles . . . With an imaginative development corporation and Boro Council with an eye for progressive architecture, but no taste in leisure facility for the plank and four wheeled among us, the option seems to be adaptation.[89]

But making a decision about which spaces and relations to enter into is not easy, since one is conditioned by not only location and economics but time, friendship, gender, race, age, culture and ideology. In particular, it is difficult to make such decisions based on any sense of urban *style*, for while commercialization pervades every aspect of urban life, we have little style of experience beyond the formal 'styles' of architecture and the commodified 'lifestyles' of fashion, food and such like. Analytically, this is in part due to an inheritance from Marx, who tended to

86. Cited in Edward Said, 'Culture and Imperialism', *Design Book Review*, nos. 29–30 (Summer/Fall 1993), pp. 6–13.

87. Henri Lefebvre, *Everyday Life in the Modern World*, (London: Transaction Publishers, 1984), p. 123.

88. Earn Beckinger, 'Baltimore', *TransWorld Skateboarding*, vol. 15 no. 10 (October 1997), pp. 159–64.

89. Wig Worland, 'Milton Keynes', *Skateboard!* (second series), no. 48 (November 1990), p. 18.

reduce urbanization to organization and production, and so ignored the possibilities of adaptation to the city.[90] Instead, Lefebvre argues, productive potential should be oriented to urban society.

> In such a city, creation of creations, everyday life would become a creation of which each citizen and each community would be capable.[91]

For their part in this process, skaters reinterpret the spaces of economic production into areas of broader creativity.

> The corporate types see their structures as powerful and strong. I see them as something I can enjoy, something I can manipulate to my advantage.[92]

How, then, is this adaptation, manipulation and appropriation achieved? It is sometimes argued that the most effectively appropriated spaces are those occupied by symbols,[93] where social relations can be inverted to create heterotopic space[94] – and skaters and other counter-cultural urbanists such as graffiti artists do occasionally work against highly symbolic monuments. For example, favoured skate locations around Europe include town halls (Oslo, 7.5), national theatres (Prague),[95] historical monuments (Christopher Columbus monument, Colón, Madrid),[96] parks (La Villette, Paris) and tourist attractions (Eiffel Tower, Paris).[97]

But, as Lefebvre notes, it is in the open, public space of streets and squares that counter-cultural activities most readily take place, as these spaces are not yet dominated by the state.

> It was in the streets that spontaneity expressed itself – in an area of society not occupied by institutions . . . Social space has assumed new meaning.[98]

Correspondingly, skateboarders implicitly realize the importance of the streets and neglected architecture as a place to act.

90. Lefebvre, *Everyday Life in the Modern World*, pp. 134–5.
91. Ibid., p. 135.
92. Jesse Neuhaus, in Garchik, 'Urban Landscape'.
93. Lefebvre, *Production of Space*, p. 366.
94. Michel Foucault, 'Of Other Spaces: Utopias and Heterotopias', in Joan Ockman (ed.), *Architecture Culture 1943–1968* (New York: Rizzoli, 1993), pp. 422–3.
95. Observed (April 1990).
96. Lance Mountain, 'Spain', *TransWorld Skateboarding*, vol. 15 no. 11 (November 1997), p. 163.
97. Andreas Papadakis, Geoffrey Broadbent and Maggie Toy (eds), *Free Spirit in Architecture* (London: Academy Editions, 1992), pp. 18–19.
98. Henri Lefebvre, *The Explosion: Marxism and the French Revolution*, (New York: Monthly Review, 1969), pp. 71–2.

> In a culture stuck on cruise control, the other skater chooses to operate in a forgotten no-man's land. In fact, the skater thrives on using the discarded, abandoned and generally disregarded portions and structures of the society at large.[99]

> The skaters take the space the others ignore.[100]

In London this has been typified by skaters' adoption of the undercroft of the South Bank, it's angled banks at once on display yet hidden beneath the high art cultural centre, thus turning its discarded forms into a significant social space.

> The heart of London skating is the South Bank. South Bank has always been much more than a collection of shitty little banks. It is the heart and mother of English skating.[101]

Thus rather than the ideologically frontal or monumental, skateboarders usually prefer the lack of meaning and symbolism of everyday spaces – the space of the street, mini-roundabout (7.6), urban plaza, mini-mall – just as graffiti artists tend to tag on out-of-the-way sites.[102]

But what exactly are these spaces without explicit meaning? Most obviously, they are the left-over spaces of modernist planning, or the spaces of decision-making (typically the urban plaza) which symbolize not through overt iconography but through expansivity of space. Lefebvre characterizes these, after Roland Barthes, as a spatial degree zero: zero points of language (everyday speech), objects (functional objects), spaces (traffic circulation, deserted spaces in the heart of the city), needs (predicted, satisfied in advance) and time (programmed, organized according to a pre-existent space).[103] Architecturally, the city is reduced to an instrument, a 'juxtaposition of spaces, of functions, of elements on the ground', where 'homogeneity overwhelms the differences' springing from nature and history, and the city appears simply as the 'likeness of a sum or combination of elements',[104] reduced to the legibility of signs.[105] Socially, this new town constitutes a void, an absence where 'unhappiness

99. Lowboy, 'Skate and Destroy, or Multiple Choices (Something to Offend Everyone)', *Thrasher*, vol. 2 no. 11 (December 1982), p. 25.

100. 'Scary Places', *R.A.D.*, no. 82 (December 1989), p. 23.

101. Mike John, in 'The Power of London', *Thrasher*, vol. 6 no. 12 (December 1989), p. 65.

102. Imogen O'Rorke, 'This is Elk', *The Guardian*, 'Friday Review' section (28 June 1996), pp. 4–5; 'Graffiti: a Brief History of Crime', *Asylum*, no. 4 (n.d., c. February 1996), n.p.; Max Daly, 'Battle of the Art Outlaws', *Big Issue*, no. 247 (25–31 August 1997), pp. 8–9; and 'Just Writin' My Name', *Big Cheese*, no. 5 (July/August 1997), pp. 10–12.

103. Lefebvre, *Everyday Life in the Modern World*, p. 184.

104. Henri Lefebvre, *Writings on Cities*, (Oxford: Blackwell, 1996), p. 127.

105. Henri Lefebvre, *Introduction to Modernity: Twelve Preludes September 1959 – May 1961*, (London: Verso, 1995), pp. 116–26.

7.6 Resistance to zero degree architecture. Harry, ollie over roundabout, Between Towns Road, Cowley, Oxford (1995). (Photograph Andy Horsley)

becomes concrete',[106] or, as skateboard commentators put it, 'urban living is fraught with boredom and frustration – a sea of concrete to roam without purpose'.[107] As one skater recognised:

> There is concrete, asphalt and metal. There is some brick and wood. Every once in a while there is a tree. It is no mystery why the tree is there: someone planned it, just like everything is planned – and then falls apart.[108]

106. Lefebvre, *Explosion*, pp. 104–5.

107. Maggi Russell and Bruce Sawford, *The Complete Skateboard Book*, (London: Fontana and Bunch, 1977), p. 7.

108. Mark Mardon, Frank Magazine, in *Thrasher*, vol. 6 no. 11 (December 1986), p. 73.

Or again:

> We live in a bland culture governed by the sacred principle of CONVENIENCE. Everything around us, right down to the most mundane aspects of our daily lives is pre-planned, pre-arranged and pre-packaged so as to ensure an absolute minimum of time consuming, conscious involvement from us. You don't think so? Look around you.[109]

For the experiencer of such architecture, there is a similarly reductive effect. In Barthes' concept of 'zero point', the neutralization of symbols states coldly what is, as if a simple witness.[110] In terms of architecture, the lack of qualitative differences and corresponding surfeit of instructions is experienced as banal monotony, the urban having lost the characteristics of the creative *oeuvre* and of appropriation; a 'poverty of daily life' derives from the failure to replace the symbolisms, times, rhythms and different spaces of the traditional city with anything other than dwelling units and the constraints of traffic.[111] Thus for skateboarders towns such as Milton Keynes were perceived as having 'no real identity', where culture is alternatively disjointed or non-existent, and where security cameras are 'endlessly re-shooting the most interesting of feature films: everyday life'.[112] In such places, metropolitan dwellers are simply witnesses to the functioning of the city, where the experience of urban space is like that of the museum, with visitors' bodies controlled by an 'organised walking' of contrived route, speed, gestures, speaking and sound[113] – a state referred to by one skater as a 'cotton wool padded, TV programmed world'.[114]

> Our feet wrapped in cotton and leather, we trod upon a concrete and asphalt sheath, the topographical inconsistencies paved over by a more biped-friendly habitat. Mobility is orderly and efficient: sidewalks, stairways and elevators . . . With our eventual adaptation to our contrived civilization, we've adjusted and now take its sheltered nature for granted. *The crosswalk signal turns red too fast. Please pay cashier first. My calling card has too many numbers on it. Don't even think of merging into my lane.*[115]

However, passivity and ennui are not the only possible responses to such reductive architecture. Resistance to the zero degree 'concrete craziness' of places

109. Bowman, 'Comment', n.p.

110. Roland Barthes, *Writing Degree Zero* (London: Cape, 1967); and Lefebvre, *Everyday Life in the Modern World*, pp. 183–4.

111. Lefebvre, *Writings on Cities*, pp. 127–8.

112. Worland, 'Milton Keynes', p. 18.

113. Tony Bennett, *The Birth of the Museum* (London, Routledge, 1995).

114. Phil Chapman, 'Fine Times', *Sidewalk Surfer*, no. 21 (October/November 1997), n.p.

115. Miki Vukovich, 'Please Use the Handrail', *Warp*, vol. 4 no. 1 (April 1995), p. 46.

such as Milton Keynes[116] takes place outside buildings, in the streets, countering the routinized phenomena of privatized urban space and the corresponding pacification of urban experience by enacting a different space and time for the city.

> Projected onto the terrain, it is here that they can transcend themselves – in the streets. It is here that student meets worker, and reason reduced to a function again recovers speech.[117]

> New towns feel like they're waiting. The empty buildings, the deserted walkways heading off to somewhere that hasn't been built yet, the neatly landscaped bits-in-between with benches that have never been sat on . . . desolate wastes, abandoned even by the builders, absolutely dead – until the skaters bring them life.[118]

It is here, then, that skaters consider themselves to be 'one step ahead of the pedestrian or static eye, the architects and the artists',[119] finding at Milton Keynes 'an infinite number of skate spots . . . hundreds of steps, banks, handrails, curbs, carparks, flowerbeds, gaps, benches, blocks, everything'.[120] In such cities worldwide,

> Skaters create their own fun on the periphery of mass culture. Sewers, streets, malls, curbs and a million other concrete constructions have been put to new uses.[121]

Skateboarders target the space-times of the urban degree zero, reinscribing themselves onto functional everyday spaces and objects, seeing skateboarding as 'a challenge to our everyday concepts of the functions of buildings, and to the closed world we create for ourselves out of this massively unlimited city'.[122] For example, a handrail is a highly functional object whose time and use are wholly programmed. It is – like fire hydrants, bus benches, sidewalks and traffic lights – a *signal*, a material element within an urban *semantic field* of precise and imperative utilitarian objects that condition us and with which we cannot converse.[123] Such elements have no *meaning* as such, imparting only a *message*. It is this which skateboarders recognize in statements such as:

116. Matthew Pritchard, interview, *Electronic Bat Eggs/Mad Monks Magazines*, no. 2 (n.d., *c.* 1995), n.p.
117. Lefebvre, *Explosion*, p. 98.
118. 'Scary Places', p. 20.
119. 'Searching, Finding, Living, Sharing', *R.A.D.*, no. 79 (September 1989), p. 15.
120. 'Ears', *R.A.D.*, no. 98 (July 1991), p. 7.
121. Lowboy, 'Skate and Destroy', p. 25.
122. Tom Hodgkinson, 'Rad, Mad and Dangerous to Know?', *Midweek*, London (18 January 1990), p. 10.
123. Lefebvre, *Introduction to Modernity*, pp. 95 and 280.

> Empty of cars, car-parks have only form and no function'.[124]

Or:

> Go on, put something back into the community . . . this, by the way, doesn't mean adding another traffic light.[125]

As a critique of the signal, skateboarders do something. In the case of the handrail, the skateboarder's reuse of the handrail – ollieing onto the rail and, balanced perilously on the skateboard deck, sliding down the fulcrum line of the metal bar – targets something to do with safety and turns it into an object of risk (7.7). The whole logic of the handrail is turned on its head.

> Most people think handrails are for those with mobility problems. Christian Hosoi says they are for ollie nose grinds.[126]

In particular, such streetstyle skateboarding takes its vitality from unexpected eruptions of meaning, actions which retranslate the objects of the city.

> A curb is an obstacle until you grind across it. A wall is but ledge until you drop off it. A cement bank is a useless slab of concrete until you shred it.[127]

Where signals have no expressivity beyond direct signification, skateboarding is a lived utterance, a symbolic *parole* to the univalent *langue* of the city as technical object. Skateboarding is a critique of the emptiness of meaning in zero degree architecture.

How, then, does skateboarding create this critique? What is the precise ground on which it acts? The answer lies less in the realm of semantics, and more in the realm of sensory rhythms and the physical.

While cities are made from social relations as conceived by thought, they are not purely ideational.

> The *urban* is not a soul, a spirit, a philosophical entity.[128]

> Life is but a dream. City streets are a reality.[129]

124. 'Searching, Finding', p. 16.
125. Skin Phillips, 'Gasbag', *TransWorld Skateboarding*, vol. 15 no. 10 (October 1997), p. 12.
126. 'Shudder Speed', *Thrasher*, vol. 11 no. 11 (November 1991), p. 50.
127. 'In the Streets Today', *Thrasher*, vol. 1 no. 1 (January 1981), p. 16.
128. Lefebvre, *Writings on Cities*, p. 103.
129. City Street Wheels, advertisement, *Thrasher*, vol. 5 no. 10 (October 1985), p. 29.

7.7 The sudden eruption of meaning against the utilitarian message of the handrail. Skateboarder: Danny Barley (1997). (Photograph Matthew Worland)

The city, then, is the immediate reality, the practico-materiality with which the urban cannot dispense. And of course this 'architectural fact' necessarily takes on a particular form, creating certain constraints but also openings. The city is presented to the skater as a pre-existent object, who negates it through its opportunities and specifically through exploiting the *texture* of that space.[130] This focus on texture gives skaters a different kind of knowledge about architecture, one derived from an experience of surface and material tactility.

> We grew up skating in New York City. You better believe we know all there is to know about asphalt and concrete.[131]

But what form might this textural exploitation adopt? Here we find some clues in Lefebvre's conception of rhythmanalysis, where he notes, for example, that the remarkable stair architecture of Mediterranean cities provides the space-time rhythm for walking in the city.[132] What then if we applied the same rhythmanalysis to the zero-degree city. What kind of rhythm and experience does it presuppose?

This is exactly the condition for urban skateboarders, being both framed by, and exploitative of, the physical space-times of modernist urban space. As already noted, it is the spaces of the modern metropolis that skateboarders address: squares and streets, campuses and semi-public buildings. Beyond its existence as a functional space, each of these is a raw object, a disposition of three-dimensional form in a universal, abstract space. Space here is simultaneously homogeneous and fragmented into any subdivision wished of it.

> What then is the principal contradiction to be found? Between the capacity to conceive of and treat space on a global (or worldwide) scale on the one hand, and its fragmentation by a multiplicity of procedures or processes, all fragmentary themselves, on the other.[133]

> The truth is to be found in the movement of totalization and fragmentation taken as a whole. This is the truth we read in that obscure and legible text: the new town.[134]

Skateboarders treat space exactly in this way. First, space becomes a uniform entity, in this case a surface on which to skate. All urban elements are thus reduced to the homogeneous level of skateable terrain, for 'anything is part of the run'.[135] Second,

130. Lefebvre, *Production of Space*, p. 57.
131. Empire/Zoo York, advertisement, *Big Brother*, no. 19 (n.d., *c.* late 1995), n.p.
132. Lefebvre, *Writings on Cities*, p. 237.
133. Lefebvre, *Production of Space*, p. 355.
134. Lefebvre, *Introduction to Modernity*, p. 121.
135. Peralta, interview, *Interview*, pp. 102–3.

from this macro conception of space skaters oscillate to the micro conception architectural element; they move from the open canvas of the urban realm to the close focus of a specific wall, bench, hydrant, kerb or rail.

> Bumps, curbs and gaps. The street is really universal.[136]

The spatial rhythm adopted is that of a journey from one element to another, the run across the city space interspersed with momentary settlings on specific sites. This is not an activity which could take place in medieval, renaissance, or early industrial cities – which are consequently considered 'crap to skate'.[137] It requires the smooth surfaces and running spaces of the concrete city and, above all, it requires the object-space-object-space rhythm born from a fragmentation of objects within a homogeneous space (7.8). For example, in one of most extreme modernist architectural environments of the West, skaters found that 'the polished marble planes of (Mies)

7.8 Exploiting the rhythms of modernist urban space and architecture. Phil Chapman, ollie between planters at Milton Keynes (1987).

136. Matt Rodriguez, interview, *Heckler* (accessed 5 May 1996).
137. 'Fire and Friends', *Sidewalk Surfer*, no. 3 (January/February 1996), n.p.

van der Rohe's plazas are Mecca to Chicago's skateboarders'.[138] One commentator noted that such Chicago spaces were the 'natural turf' for skateboarders, whose presence bridges the gap between the public and what critics have called 'relentlessly austere, even inhumane' modern structures by architects such as Mies.[139] Or as *Project* described Chicago:

> The Federal buildings [1959–74, architects Mies van der Rohe and others]: BIG marble benches, nice and long and great for grinds, slides, and tricks off of em.
>
> Amoco Building [1973, architect Edward Durell Stone]: Big marble arrangements, Good stairs and handrails.
>
> Daley Center [1965, architects C.F. Murphy Associates, Loebl, Schlossman & Bennett, and S.O.M.]: 8 step-case, good marble benches.
>
> Prudential Building [1955, architects Naess & Murphy]: Downhill and long marble ledge that is the best for 50–50s.[140]

Rhythmanalysis refers to time as well as space, and thus the temporal rhythms – the various routines, speeds, durations, repetitions – of the city also offer a frame for skateboarders. Here skateboarders respond to the fragmentary temporality of urban space, interweaving their own compositions into regular temporal patterns, such as waging a fast assault on a handrail outside a bank, or adding a speeding skateboard to the slower pattern of pedestrians, 'skating past all the business-suit lames that slog gloomily down the sidewalk, barely lifting their feet, like they're kicking shit with every step' (7.9).[141] As *SkateBoarder* described Rocco's early street-style movements, this was a new time-space inserted among others on the pavement.

> Weaving wildly amidst strand cruisers, roller skaters, skateboarders, and those that still prefer walking, he terrorizes oncoming motion with precision kickflips and slides, always narrowly, but precisely missing, moving on to find vacant areas.[142]

This is a different kind of urban speed, incomprehensible to others.

138. Garchik, 'Urban Landscape'.

139. Spiegler, in Garchik, 'Urban Landscape'.

140. *Project* (accessed 17 August 1997).

141. Brian Casey, in Paul Mulshine, 'Wild in the Streets', *Philadelphia Magazine*, vol. 78 no. 4 (April 1987), p. 120.

142. 'Who's Hot! Steve Rocco', p. 71.

7.9 Avoiding the controlled and commodified times of the city. Scott Johnston in San Franciso (1996). (Photograph Michael Blabac)

> Most of the action seen in skateboarding these days occurs at such a rapid pace that peds [pedestrians] have little chance of understanding what has transformed.[143]

Alternatively, skaters construct a different temporal rhythm by staying longer in an urban plaza as others hurry through, as happens most evenings at London's Euston Station where, while commuters rush to transport connections, a few skaters often spend a few hours riding over its planters, benches and low walls. For the more contested terrains of postmodernity – such as shopping malls or privatized public space – yet another temporal tactic must be deployed. Here, skaters exploit the highly bounded temporality of, for example, London's Broadgate office development – a privatized urban space with precise usage patterns – by skating in weekend and evening hours.[144] As one commentator noted, 'nighttime skateboarders represent a rare example of people using the downtown at night' (7.6, 7.7, 7.13, 8.8, 9.1).[145] Skaters thus use 'the dark urban terrain which would otherwise go unnoticed'[146] – spaces outside their conventional times of use, substituting one temporal rhythm for another. As Arron Bleasdale reflected on a day's life in London:

> Weekends are the best. You can cruise around the City and there's no one there. Meet up at Cantalowes (Camden skate spot) with some people, then head out to the City, skate around, find some new spots then head back to Camden.[147]

This appropriation of the unused time of a particular urban element is also applied to smaller parts of the urban street; the bus bench out of rush hour, or department store car park outside shopping hours, can also be the focus of skateboarders.

Rhythmanalysis is also about the micro experience, the relation of the self to the physical minutiae of the city.

> These are my streets. I know every crack of every sidewalk there is down here.[148]

Beside intense vision, for skaters this involves hearing; the skater responds to the more obvious city sounds, such as a car accelerating or police siren, and also car doors, people talking, footsteps, etc. In particular, the sound of the skateboard over the ground yields much information about surface conditions, such as speed, grip and predictability.

143. Gary Davis, 'Steep Slopes', *Thrasher*, vol. 3 no. 5 (May 1983), p. 8.
144. 'A Day in the City', *Cake Fat*, no. 2 (n.d., *c.* 1996), n.p.
145. Spiegler, in Garchik, 'Urban Landscape'.
146. John Griffin, 'Sub-culture', *Speed Wheels*, no. 4 (n.d., *c.* January 1989), p. 49.
147. Arron Bleasdale, interview, *Sidewalk Surfer*, no. 9 (August 1996), n.p.
148. Tony Alva, interview, *Heckler* internet site, URL http://heckler.com (accessed 5 May 1996).

> Like a blind man, he had to rely on his other senses. He listened to the hum of his wheels, trying to detect if he was in gravel or water or cement or dust.[149]

Here such things as the smoothness of pure tarmac and the 'roaring sound' of wheels[150] combine to create a textual pattern bound into the skateboarder's experience of urban space; 'one thing was music to us all: the sound of urethane rolling along the street or a truck grinding concrete'.[151] Other parts of the skateboard also make distinctive noises important to the skater's performance, such as the grinding of the truck on a curb or the slide of the deck on a ledge or rail. These sounds are part of both the micro-experience of the specific move and an overall sense of what it means to skate:

> I have found my own fulfillment in the rumble clack soar rattle clatter of so many different directions.[152]

> The boys realize the secret thrill of honing out a lapped-over frontside grind at the bricks, hitting a sweeper, smacking the tail and listening to it echo back into the vast, dark parking garage into the night.[153]

Taken together, the various compositional sound rhythms – the monotonal subtle roar of wheels on tarmac, hard rasping of truck on concrete, slippery slide of slick deck on metal rail, rhythmic clicking of paving slabs, combined with intermittent pure silences during ollie flight, and the sudden cracks as the skateboard returns to ground – are a feature of skateboarding's urban space. Skaters thus also add another sound component to the non-skater's experience of the urban realm; the skateboard's distinctive sounds are unlike any others in the city, and overtaking slower pedestrians can cause them consternation: 'When a group of kids skates down a sidewalk you can really hear it'.[154]

Micro rhythmanalysis also involves a sense of touch, generated from direct contact with the terrain – hand on building, foot on wall – or from the smoothness and textual rhythms of the surface underneath, passed up through skateboard into feet and body: 'the actively involved skater relies on his own feedback'.[155]

149. Michael Gumkowski, 'Time Warped', *Thrasher*, vol. 11 no. 9 (September 1991), p. 63.
150. 'Let's Go Skate!', *Slap*, vol. 6 no. 1 (January 1997), p. 39.
151. John, in 'Power of London', p. 65.
152. Hannah Eed, 'Sanctuary', *R.A.D.*, no. 87 (May 1990), p. 70.
153. Davis, 'Slopes' (May 1983), p. 8.
154. Henry Hester, in Bill Gutman, *Skateboarding to the Extreme* (New York: Tom Doherty Associates, 1997), p. 13.
155. Lowboy, 'Skate and Destroy', p. 25.

> I glide over a patch of textured concrete. The little grooves running perpendicular to my flight path pluck a note from my board that I can feel in my body. The noise echoes down the ramp then stops abruptly as I return to porcelain smooth concrete.[156]

As one poetic cartoon said of New York, the 'city rumbles beneath my skate, like the wheels of so many subway trains – with vibrations that carry up through my legs – and remain like magic long after I have gotten off my board'.[157] What matters to skaters sensorially are such things as 'the feeling of a raspy axle grind',[158] or the 'sensation of wheels rolling along the pavement'.[159] In these kinds of urban encounter, small details become highly significant: for example, a curb's precise angle and surface paint determines its slide qualities and so also the moves made against it.[160]

The skateboard run is conducted in relation to zero degree architecture, using its textural and objectival qualities to create a new appropriative rhythm distinct from the routinized, meaningless, passive experiences which it usually enforces; street skateboarding is thus 'a total focus of mind, body and environment to a level way beyond that of the dead consumers'.[161] And the new school skateboard – with its light deck, small wheels, and equal front-back orientation specifically designed for street skating – is a tool absorbed into the new rhythmic production of 'super-architectural space' discussed in Chapter Five.

> Being a skateboarder means that you have some kind of enhanced experience of life. You don't just walk through space, without learning anything about it, or without having a kind of relationship with where you are – through the medium of a skateboard . . . you can actually inter-act with the world around you. This is something rare in this synthetic world of plastic and concrete.[162]

As that suggests, it is not only the city but the body that is changed in the engagement of skater, skateboard and street architecture, for just as we engage with the city more actively when in motion, so we become more bodily aware whenever, for example, we cross the road and necessarily calculate the steps involved.[163] Skateboarders, through their continuous body-centric and motile encounters with different architectural elements, create many such crossings and encounters and so produce

156. El Zopilote, 'Garage Tale', *Thrasher*, vol. 6 no. 5 (May 1986), p. 26.
157. T.J. Richter, 'In the City', *R.A.D.*, no. 83 (January 1990), p. 62.
158. '15 Tricks You Can't Do on a Snowboard', *Thrasher*, vol. 16 no. 3 (March 1996), p. 20.
159. 'Let's Go Skate!', pp. 39–40.
160. Hesselgrave, 'Curb Grinding', pp. 37–9; and Gavin O'Brien, 'Curbs', *Thrasher*, vol. 8 no. 8 (August 1988), pp. 70–4.
161. Ben Powell, 'Not a Toy', *Sidewalk Surfer*, no. 3 (January/February 1996), n.p.
162. 'A Car Full of Monkeys', *Sidewalk Surfer*, no. 20 (September 1997), n.p.
163. Lefebvre, *Writings on Cities*, p. 220.

a greatly intensified version of this process. The outcome is not just a new physiology ('suddenly I had new muscles appearing'[164]), but a newly conscious recognition of the body.

> Ben heard the cries of the other skaters, he felt the cold metal of this truck in his hand, and the rough griptape on his skin. A leaf fire filled his nostrils with the woody smell Ben was fond of, he saw the ramp, he tasted blood.[165]

In terms that recall Simmel's identification of a fundamental reorientation of the physiology and psychology of metropolitan inhabitants,[166] Lefebvre notes that the modern man's physiological functions 'have not yet "adapted" to the conditions of his life, to the speed of its sequences and rhythms', such that 'nerves and senses have not yet been adequately trained by the urban and technical life he leads'.[167] In particular, the modern individual cannot abstract the concept from the thing, creating a confused unity in which relations, order and hierarchy are lost. This is a state of 'deliberate semi-neurosis', partly play-acting and partly 'ambivalent infantilism'.[168]

On the one hand, this is exactly the condition of skateboarders in the modern city, for, in the absence of codified socio-political awareness, many skaters use a 'common sense shut down'[169] to divert attention away from matters of the rational intellect.

> Skateboarding has survived on minimal intellect for years. Yeah![170]

On the other hand, Lefebvre suggests that while such attitudes produce only ambivalent infantilism, the same condition contains seeds of critique and creative production. As he notes, that the modern individual is not yet 'fully adapted' intimates that a process of evolution is under way – an evolution which involves a transformation of senses.

> Practical tools, not simple concepts, are the means by which social man has shaped his perceptible world. As regards the processes of knowledge by means of which we understand this 'world' . . . they are our senses. But our senses have been transformed by action . . . Thus it is that our senses, organs, vital needs, instincts, feelings have been permeated with consciousness, with human reason, since they too have been shaped by social life.[171]

164. Bowman, 'Comment', n.p.
165. Ben Blench, 'Untitled', *R.A.D.*, no. 88 (June 1990), p. 62.
166. Georg Simmel, 'The Metropolis and Mental Life', P.K. Hatt and A.J. Reiss (eds.), *Cities and Society* (New York: Free Press, 1951), p. 635.
167. Henri Lefebvre, *Critique of Everyday Life. Volume 1: Introduction*, (London: Verso, 1991), p. 120.
168. Ibid., p. 120.
169. 'Just Dropping In', *Sidewalk Surfer*, no. 20 (September 1997), n.p.
170. Meg, 'Get Off the Air!!', *Slap*, vol. 6 no. 9 (September 1997), p. 54.
171. Lefebvre, *Critique of Everyday Life*, p. 163.

It is then in lived experience, rather than in abstract theoretical knowledge, that the skateboarder's adaptation can initially be seen. Skateboarding is 'not a theory, it's not a style and it's not a symbol – it's a concrete reality'.[172]

Such concerns directly raise the question of spatiality. The skateboarder's highly integrated sense of balance, speed, hearing, sight, touch and responsivity is a product of the modern metropolis, a newly evolved sensory and cognitive mapping; the aim is not only to receive the city but to return it to itself, to change the nature of the *experience* of the urban realm (7.10). Sound, touch and even smell combine with vision to render architecture into a full body encounter.

> A feel of rhythm and an aroma of sweat overcome my senses on this Wednesday evening as the popping sound of wooden tails and the connection of metal trucks to metal coping takes place.[173]

> After about three hours, I'm good and sweaty . . . The walls have taken on my body's odour.[174]

In this, skateboarding is an untheorized element of praxis, focusing on the sensuous enjoyment of the object (immediate sensing of cities, objects of common use, relationships), on the recognition of particular needs (activity, muscular extension, direct engagement)[175] and on the spatially immediate (the local and nearby).

> Learning the properties of everyday life unwittingly . . . Evolving into a higher state of urban awareness starts with doing and looking. But seeing and feeling begins in this case outside your front door.[176]

Skateboarding is, as *Thrasher*'s first issue described it, 'a fast-paced feeling to fit this modern world',[177] and the skateboarder's own senses are historically produced from the constraints and opportunities of the city.

But unlike the passivity of the body, and the overdependence on the eye within modernity,[178] the skater's body is an active, motile construct, producing all of its senses through the urban practice of skateboarding.

172. 'Sorealism', *Thrasher*, vol. 9 no. 11 (November 1989), p. 73.
173. Chris Carnel, interview of Bryce Kanights, *Heckler* (accessed 5 May 1996).
174. Vaj Potenza, 'Smokestack Lightning', *Thrasher*, vol. 12 no. 3 (March 1992), p. 70.
175. Henri Lefebvre, *The Sociology of Marx*, (New York: Columbia University Press, 1982), p. 38–9.
176. Worland, 'Milton Keynes', p. 18.
177. Kevin Thatcher, 'Grab That Board', *Thrasher*, vol. 1 no. 1 (January 1981), p. 6.
178. Michel Foucault, *Discipline and Punish* (Harmondsworth: Penguin, 1979); Richard Sennett, *Flesh and Stone* (London: Faber and Faber, 1994); and John Urry, *The Tourist Gaze: Leisure and Travel in Contemporary Societies*, (London: Sage, 1990).

7.10 The production of urban bodily senses. Balancing, moving and responding while seeing, hearing and touching architecture in Leicester (1989). (Photograph Captain Wager/ Martin Wager)

> It's better than drugs. You won't believe the adrenalin. The feeling of accomplishment is insane.[179]

> These things have purpose because we have movement as well as vision.[180]

These senses are not then a basic need to be momentarily satisfied,[181] but an enjoyment and reproduction of the city, a sensory-spatial version of the Althusserian concept of ideology as the imaginary representation of the subject's relationship to her or his real conditions of existence.[182] Skaters' actions are how they learn to live with the city, part of the 'enigma of the body' which has the ability to produce differences 'unconsciously' out of linear (in any one run) and cyclical repetitions (repeating moves, repeating the run on different occasions).[183]

Skateboarding also makes skaters active mentally and visually, attentive to the details of urban space (the exact form of a concrete ledge or new hand-rail). 'Streetskating is emptying your mind onto the streets'.[184] Vision, too, is reconfigured from passive reception, dominant sense and detached abstract meditation into an integrated and lived everyday epistemology; for the skater, every aspect of the city street becomes a 'window' from which to contemplate and engage with the unknown city.[185] As with Jean-François Lyotard's conception of the differential spatiality of the visible, vision becomes one among many spatialities produced in the city.[186]

UNKNOWN TERRAINS

What, however, is the meaning that such activities inscribe on zero degree architecture? If skateboarding points towards a different, possible future city, what exactly does it propose, and how are such propositions enunciated?

> The scene is set, the playground open: unknown terrain, unknown features, unknown futures. Maybe. . .[187]

179. Powell, in Evans, 'Young', p. 18.
180. 'Searching, Finding', p. 15.
181. Lefebvre, *Sociology of Marx*, p. 41.
182. Fredric Jameson, "Cognitive Mapping", Cary Nelson and Lawrence Grossberg (eds), *Marxism and the Interpretation of Culture*, (London: Macmillan, 1988), p. 353.
183. Lefebvre, *Production of Space*, pp. 395–6.
184. Bob Denike, in Craig Ramsay, 'Free in the Street', *Thrasher*, vol. 4 no. 7 (July 1984), p. 37.
185. Lefebvre, *Writings on Cities*, p. 224.
186. Larry Barth, 'Immemorial Visibilities: Seeing the City's Difference', *Environment and Planning A*, vol. 28 (1996), pp. 471–93.
187. 'Unknown Feature', *R.A.D.*, no. 97 (June 1991), p. 25.

Lefebvre provides some clues, suggesting for example that state violence (usually latent, occasionally overt) is concerned with accumulation and a political principle of unification.[188] Here we might consider that skateboarding helps declassify space by 'keeping things real',[189] hence disclosing such underlying logics. But what are these declassifications, and what logic is challenged?

Alternatively, we might follow Lefebvre's interest in the festival, the café, the funfair and street, seeing skateboarding as a 'people's event' that escapes industrialization.[190] But what is the skateboarding event, and to where does it escape?

Or we might consider the notion of a new style in urban life, not as formal aesthetics but as an attitude toward work.[191] But how is skateboarding's subculture enacted in urban space, and what is its new productive activity? If everyday life is to be built again, drawing on the opportunities and purposeful attitudes as yet constrained within the new town, what are the new desires, and how are they to be expressed?

For Lefebvre, the answers to such things can only be directions and tendencies. Among these, the simultaneous integration of spontaneity and abstraction is one of the most important.

> The thing is that men have two different ways of creating and producing, and as yet these have not intersected: spontaneous vitality and abstraction. On the one hand, in pleasure and play; on the other, in seriousness, patience and painful consciousness, in toil.[192]

Furthermore, it is in the architecture of the new town, of degree zero, that such integrations will be disclosed, not as an answer but as experiment, a first approximation of differential space and life.

> Our task now is to construct everyday life, to produce it, consciously to create it . . . Here, in the new town, boredom is pregnant with desires, frustrated frenzies, unrealized possibilities. A magnificent life is waiting just around the corner, and far, far away.[193]

We will not, therefore, find a new style of living in the new town, but we will find a way towards it. This means not just the great global cities – London, New York, Paris, Tokyo – but also the 'average, suburban, dysfunctional, adolescent anonymity'[194]

188. Lefebvre, *Production of Space*, pp. 280–1.
189. '86,400 Seconds in the Life of Matthew Pritchard', *Sidewalk Surfer*, no. 15 (April 1997), n.p.
190. Lefebvre, *Critique of Everyday Life*, p. 41.
191. Lefebvre, *Introduction to Modernity*, pp. 92–4.
192. Ibid., p. 125.
193. Ibid., p. 124.
194. Miki Vukovich, introduction to Mike Vallely, interview, *TransWorld Skateboarding*, vol. 14 no. 1 (January 1996), pp. 92–3.

of 'everyday towns'; this, too, concords with the development of skateboarding, for in the UK the foremost centres of skateboarding in the 1990s were no longer (only) London, but smaller towns such as Oxford, Newbury, Wakefield, Northampton, Swindon and Aberdeen. In the US, pre-eminent skate spots of Los Angeles and San Diego were joined by Pittsburgh,[195] Dallas,[196] Edison,[197] Lewisville,[198] Seattle[199] and many others across the country.

> It all started back around 1987 or so in a small boonfuck town called Enterprise, Alabama. In this town I learned tic-tacs, early grabs off launch ramps, rode my first handrail and got laid for the first time. I lived there for five years with roasting rednecks in the unbearable heat . . . There was nothing to do. It was inevitable that I skate.[200]

To begin with it is important to understand the epistemology of this critique. Predominantly, just as skateboarders have little sense of skateboarding's history, so too are they largely unaware of the political nature of their actions – 'I don't read about skating, I just do it'.[201] If all social activities were like this, serious problems would ensue.[202] But it is important not to overreact to this situation. First, skateboarding, as urban practice, renders the subjective into an objective intervention;[203] as Clark explained of *Kids*, skateboarders are 'out there, having confrontations all the time'.[204] Second, the urban activity of skateboarding is *discursively* politicised, and we should therefore appreciate it as a realm where a certain newness is born from knowledge, representation and lived experience enacted together.

There are, in any case, distinct advantages to the sort of lived critique sustained by practices such as skateboarding. While the bourgeoisie discovered history, making it a cornerstone of its own class-consciousness and overloading current culture,[205] skateboarders are not encumbered by the 'tradition of all the dead generations' which 'weighs like a nightmare on the brain of the living',[206] and are free to critique the immediate present. 'The future is now; get on it'.[207]

195. Reason, interview, p. 108.
196. Mike Crum, interview, *Thrasher*, vol. 11 no. 9 (September 1991), p. 40.
197. Vukovich, introduction, p. 92.
198. Neal Hendrix, interview, *Thrasher*, vol. 12 no. 6 (June 1992), p. 28.
199. Scott Smiley, interview, *Thrasher*, vol. 16 no. 2 (February 1996), p. 76.
200. Sean Young, untitled, *Thrasher*, vol. 16 no. 3 (March 1996), p. 55.
201. Jay Adams, in 'Off the Wall', *SkateBoarder's Action Now*, vol. 7 no. 5 (December 1980), p. 18.
202. Lefebvre, *Introduction to Modernity*, pp. 166–7.
203. Lefebvre, *Explosion*, p. 110.
204. Larry Clark, interviewed by Katharine Viner, 'Which Girl is HIV Positive?', *The Sunday Times*, magazine supplement (21 April 1996), p. 29.
205. Lefebvre, *Introduction to Modernity*, pp. 224–5.
206. Karl Marx, 'Eighteenth Brumaire of Louis Napoleon', Karl Marx and Frederick Engels, *Selected Works* (New York: International Publishers, 1986), p. 97.
207. Smythe, 'Frontier', p. 111.

Similarly, the absence of theory or party institutionalism allows for the resurrection of spontaneity as the enemy of power,[208] as skaters realized in the development of street skating in the early 1980s.

> In an American dream turned sour suburban nightmare, the only viable alternative is spontaneous aggression.[209]

Furthermore, such spontaneity undertakes a *generalized* critique against society and the urban,[210] such that skateboarders are largely unconcerned with the function or symbolic presence of any single building or city.

> San Diego indeed does suck, as does LA, San Francisco, San Jo, Phoenix, Cincinnati, Tulsa, Mobile, NY, Stockholm, Berlin, Canberra, Independence, MO, etc. (fill in the name of your town here) – get the picture?[211]

Any architecture will do, for all are implicated in the generic urbanism of what skaters see simply as the 'Skatropolis'.[212]

We might also consider that practices such as skateboarding, while conceptually untheorized, are nonetheless always embedded with ideas.

> Lived experience partakes of the theoretical sphere, and this means that the distinction between conceptualization and life (though not the need to draw distinctions and exercise discernment) is artificial.[213]

Skateboarding should be considered as a *lived* concept, one which both draws occasionally on the conceptual for its rationale and conducts conceptual operations in a non-codified way.

Finally, there is even the possibility that, if representations project themselves in advance of the here-and-now, then being may be ahead of consciousness.[214]

> It's like we're moving on to something else . . . and the thing is, that skateboarding is truly in the forefront.[215]

> Yesterday is history. What will we do tomorrow?[216]

208. Lefebvre, *Explosion*, pp. 52 and 69–70.
209. Smythe, 'No Parking', pp. 53 and 55.
210. Lefebvre, *Explosion*, p. 88.
211. Lowboy, 'Skate and Destroy', p. 24.
212. 'Police Log', *Thrasher*, vol. 7 no. 3 (March 1987), p. 78.
213. Lefebvre, *Production of Space*, p. 316.
214. Lefebvre, *Introduction to Modernity*, p. 133.
215. Peralta, interview, *Thrasher*, p. 18.
216. Editorial, *Thrasher*, vol. 12 no. 5 (May 1992), p. 4.

> Stagnation is death.[217]

Given this self-perception on the part of many skaters, skateboarding just might contain some indication of relations and actions different to the highly codified work-family-leisure routines of late capitalism.

SKATE AND DESTROY

Skateboarding responds meaningfully to the city by making the work of art, saying and living the city on its own terms. Like romanticism, it is not confined to discourse, but works upon a material.[218] What, then, are the marks it makes, and what do they signify? This section deals with the first part of this question, identifying the immediate nature of the physical engagement between skateboard and building.

The streetstyle moves of Los Angeles skaters in the early 1980s did not just transcend the elements of the street but worked against them in a directly physical manner. For skaters such as Dressen and Ron Allen, two of the first of the new street skaters, the marks, scratches, grinds and traces of board paint they left on the walls of Los Angeles buildings were an essential component in their relationship with the physicality of the city.[219]

> This kid simply craved crumbing lips and delighted in the ferocious bit of a bare-axle frontside carve![220]

> Most would call it senseless vandalism, but loafed curbs, dirty buildings, worked planter boxes and broken benches are true things of beauty. Concrete, wood, rock, or anything in the path is worthy of a skater's wrath.[221]

> When the tough get going, the going gets scuffed.[222]

In street skating, the constant planting of hands and feet build gradually to create a grubby reminder of skaters' presence. Urethane wheels and painted deck graphics similarly leave technicolour streaks across walls, ledges and benches. In particular, skateboarders grind their trucks on the edges of walls and street furniture, leaving a series of gouges and striations that ultimately either lead to the rounding-off or break-

217. Jesse Driggs, 'Swamp Trogs from Outer Space', *Thrasher*, vol. 15 no. 9 (September 1995), p. 45.

218. Lefebvre, *Introduction to Modernity*, p. 321.

219. Eric Dressen, interview, *TransWorld Skateboarding*, vol. 7 no. 3 (June 1989), pp. 97–103 and 160–72.

220. Gary Davis, 'Steep Slopes', *Thrasher*, vol. 3 no. 7 (July 1983), p. 6.

221. Jake Phelps, 'Damage Done', *Thrasher*, vol. 12 no. 5 (May 1992), p. 34.

222. Bryce Kanights, 'Scuffs on a Wall', *Thrasher*, vol. 8 no. 5 (May 1988), p. 45.

up of edges, cutting out a ragged silhouette. Skaters also sometimes apply wax to ledges, curbs and other urban elements to improve sliding qualities.

> Visitors? There have always been visitors. I've seen their marks.[223]

In this light, the 'Skate and Destroy' motif introduced by 'Lowboy' in 1982 is understandably one of the most popular and controversial of skateboard symbols and aphorisms (7.11).[224]

But why attack an object in this way? What is there in architecture that might lend itself to such a response on the part of skaters?

If urban space is constituted by violence, either overt or latent, architecture is part of this process, both as immediate compulsion to obey the physical barriers, surfaces, routes and walls it presents to the urban dweller, and also as a continual

7.11 'Skate and Destroy' motif, designed by Lowboy (1982).

223. Photograph caption, Fraser Hamilton, 'All About High Wycombe (and a Jolly Nice Council)', *R.A.D.*, no. 103 (December 1991), p. 19.

224. *Thrasher*, vol. 9 no. 6 (June 1989), p. 53; and Lowboy, 'Skate and Destroy', p. 24.

reminder that transgressions of space and property rights will be met by more active responses. This is architecture's 'phallic formant', symbolizing masculine force as pure image and as the presence of destructive force.[225]

In this context, skateboarders' destructive assault on the micro-boundaries of architecture are a tiny yet significant challenge to the threat of violence, meeting like with like.

> Each notch is evidence of endurance and determination, a message to those who would try and deter us. Each scuff is a marking of territory as surely as dog piss on a fire hydrant.[226]

This is particularly evident if we consider the architecture of the city as a 'writing on the ground',[227] inscribing the legitimacy of owners and managers over others. In this context, urban phenomena such as litter, scuff-marks, smells, noise, pollution, and also deliberate inscriptions of fly-posting, graffiti, skateboard marks, schoolyard scratchings and so on are all versions of a counter-inscription. Youth and children are especially good at this, for while adults disguise marks as the objects they own (porches, home decoration, gardens, cars), young adults make marks on other people's property.

These kinds of urban inscription are then far more than the semantic encounter with the city favoured by architectural and cultural semiologists such as Roland Barthes, Charles Jencks, Umberto Eco and Françoise Choay,[228] who mistake architecture for a text and urban reading as an act of distanced cognition. Instead, as Schmarsow realized long ago, the act of 'reading' a building is a bodily act and an *experienced* cognition.

> As soon as we have learned to experience ourselves and ourselves alone as the center of this space, whose coordinates intersect in us, we have found the precious kernel, the initial capital investment so to speak, on which architectural creation is based.[229]

Furthermore, 'reading' can be entirely different to any intention on the part of the author (architect, planner, urban manager), such that the re-reading is more of a new

225. Lefebvre, *Production of Space*, pp. 286–8.

226. Phelps, 'Damage', p. 34.

227. Lefebvre, *Everyday Life in the Modern World*, pp. 152–4.

228. Charles Jencks, *The Language of Post-modern Language* (New York: Rizzoli, 1977); and Mark Gottdiener and Alexandros Ph. Lagopoulos (eds), *The City and the Sign* (New York: Columbia University Press, 1986).

229. August Schmarsow, 'The Essence of Architectural Creation', in Harry Francis Mallgrave and Eleftherios Ikonomou (eds), *Empathy, Form and Space* (Santa Monica: Getty Center for the History of Art and Humanities, 1994), pp. 286–7.

writing across the face of the page. Thus when a skater such as Gary Chevalier noseslides on the St Cross Library Building in Oxford (1960s, architect Leslie Martin), he is concerned with neither architecture nor architect but with his own spatial production (7.12). Skateboarders and others who inscribe on the city are literally *writing* the city, albeit at the scale of the dispersed, micro-spatial text, creating a series of registers, traces, indexical signs, notches and furrows. Thus skaters talk of 'drawing' lines across pools and banks, 'like Chinese writing'.[230]

Yet contained within this attempt to rewrite city surfaces is a remarkably well-behaved set of objectives. Skateboarding rarely seems to romanticize violence, although some skaters – Duane Peters, for example – certainly make it into a feature of their lives.[231] Furthermore, despite its overt physicality, the 'destroy' in 'Skate and Destroy' is predominantly conceptual, and skateboarding in no way attempts to modify city form in any substantial manner.

> The subject experiences space as an obstacle, as a resistant 'objectality' at times as implacably hard as a concrete wall, being not only extremely difficult to modify in any way but also hedged about by Draconian rules prohibiting any attempt at such modifications.[232]

Instead of counter-domination, skateboarding is an appropriative negation of the space which precedes it. As Lefebvre notes, such negation can exploit the *texture* of space, which offers opportunities to social acts otherwise unconnected with that space.[233] This brings us back to the dependence of skateboarding upon the physicality of zero degree architecture, and forward to the question as to what constitutes skateboarding's negation of space. If skateboarding is an activity external to the function of the spaces on which it acts, but which is also simultaneously rhythmically predicated on the surfaces, formal articulation and frequency of urban architecture, what is the product of this engagement between separate yet connected presences? What supplement is created?

We find the first clues here if we consider skateboarding as at once consumption (skateboarders use buildings) and production (they deploy energies and tools upon a physical resource). And just as manufactured objects often provide traces of the matériel (tools and techniques) used to make them,[234] the marks made by skateboarding are hence a kind of matériel of consumption via the tool of the skateboard and technique of the move. Furthermore, this is a gradual accretion formed by many skaters continually revisiting a particular site.

230. Steve Kane, interview, *Skateboard!*, no. 5 (January 1978), p. 57.
231. Duane Peters, interview, *Thrasher*, vol. 2 no. 2 (February 1982), p. 34.
232. Lefebvre, *Production of Space*, p. 57.
233. Ibid., p. 57.
234. Ibid., pp. 112–13.

7.12 Writing, not reading, the city. Gary Chevalier at the St Cross Library Building, Oxford (1996). (Photograph Andy Horsley)

> A grind mark is trivial when seen as a single scrape but, over time, streams become canyons.[235]

Skateboarding in this sense represents consumption as a collective act of production: that of marks on buildings and urban fabric.

We find here, then, that skateboarding is far more than a simple physical inscription on the city. There are also suggestions that it involves a critique of objects (skateboarding marks urban objects), a reconceptualization of how such objects are mapped and recorded (skaters represent objects through their actions upon them), ownership (skateboarders do not own the things they mark) and consumption–production definitions (skateboarders are 'productive', but not of things). It is to these areas that we now turn.

DECENTRED OBJECTS

Cities are not things, but the apparent form of the urbaniszation process.[236] Cities are filled with ideas, culture and memories, with flows of money, information and ideologies, and are dynamically constitutive of the continual *re*production of the urban. To see the city as a collection of objects is then to fail to see its real character. And this is exactly the failure of skateboarding, which does nothing to analyse the processes which form the urban; instead, the phenomenal procedures of skateboarding rely entirely on the objectival nature of the city, treating its surfaces – horizontal, vertical, diagonal, curved – as the physical ground on which to operate.

Yet within this failure lies a profound critique of the city qua object-thing. Capitalism has replaced the city as oeuvre – the unintentional and collective work of art, richly significant yet embedded in everyday life[237] – with 'repetitive spaces', 'repetitive gestures' and standardized things of all kinds to be exchanged and reproduced, differentiated only by money.[238] Skateboarding, however, at once accepts and denies this presentation of cities as collections of repetitive things. On the one hand, skateboarders accept it, by focusing purely on the phenomenal characteristics of architecture, on its compositions of planes, surfaces and textures as accessible to the skateboarder.

> Look around. Look at a world full of skate shapes . . . shapes left there by architects for you to skate.[239]

235. Phelps, 'Damage', p. 34.
236. David Harvey, *Justice, Nature and the Geography of Difference*, (Oxford: Blackwell, 1996), p. 418.
237. Lefebvre, *Writings on Cities*, p. 101.
238. Lefebvre, *Production of Space*, p. 75.
239. 'Where?', *R.A.D.*, no. 79 (September 1989), p. 18.

Here the city and its architecture is undoubtedly a thing. On the other hand, it is also through this very focus on the phenomenal that a change is made.

> In a world of complex questions, the street strategist must become his own answer. Alleys, curbs, streets, pools, ramps, parking lots, hills, banks, and all other conceivable contours are the arenas of individual advancement. How and what you do with them are your own affair.[240]

When skateboarders ride along a wall, over a fire hydrant or up a building, they are entirely indifferent to its function or ideological content. They are therefore no longer even concerned with its presence as a *building*, as a composition of spaces and materials logically disposed to create a coherent urban entity. By focusing only on certain elements (ledges, walls, banks, rails) of the building, skateboarders deny architecture's existence as a discrete three-dimensional indivisible thing, knowable only as a totality, and treat it instead as a set of floating, detached, physical elements isolated from each other; where architects' considerations of building 'users'[241] imply a quantification of the body subordinate to space and design, the skater's performative body has 'the ability to deal with a given set of pre-determined circumstances and to extract what you want and to discard the rest',[242] and so reproduces architecture in its own measure, re-editing it as series of surfaces, textures and micro-objects.

> Buildings are building blocks for the open minded.[243]

> Skaters are the creators.[244]

Architecture, following Lefebvre's body-centric formulations, 'reproduces itself within those who *use* the space in question, within their lived experience'.[245] This occurs in skateboarding through architecture being encountered in relation to height, tactility, transition, slipperiness, roughness, damage to skin on touching, damage to body from a fall, angle and verticality, sequencing, drops (stairs and ramps), kinks and shape (hand-rails), profiles (edges), materials, lengths and so on. And only a very small part of the architecture is used – the 'building' for a skater is only an extracted edit of its total existence. For example, a particular English school was known by skaters not as a building or for its function, but for its handrails.

240. Smythe, 'No Parking', p. 57.
241. Lefebvre, *Production of Space*, pp. 338–9.
242. Smythe, 'History', p. 29.
243. 'Searching, Finding', p. 15.
244. Editorial, *Thrasher*, vol. 3 no. 2 (February 1983), p. 4.
245. Lefebvre, *Production of Space*, p. 137.

> Travel to Ipswich and ask to check out the school with the handrails, they'll know which one and it's sick.[246]

Also in Ipswich, Suffolk College (7.13) was known primarily for its roof, stairs and ledges, a specific church for the wooden benches outside, another school for some steps, and an entire US air base for a single, yellow fire hydrant.[247] And on the other side of the Atlantic, the Marriott Marquis Hotel in New York (1985, architect John Portman), offering the usual Portman features of vast glass elevations, spectacular atrium, rocket ship elevators and internal glitz,[248] was reconceived by skaters as 'modern day skate architecture' with 'tight transitions', 'black walls', a street-level walkway and planters.[249] Similarly, New York's Museum of Natural History became '100 yards of Italian marble, marble benches curbed for frontside and backside rails, six steps, and statues of famous dudes with marble bases . . . basically an awesome skate arena'.[250]

What ties these elements together is neither compositional, structural, servicing nor functional logic, but the entirely separate logic of 'another art form'[251] composed from the skateboarder's moves. Significantly, 1990s magazines introduced longer-sequence shots, with twenty-eight or more frames in one image, as a way of representing the travelling, sequential nature of street skating.

The extended compositional run of street skaters is, however, ultimately beyond the reach of a single photograph, and is particularly evident when skaters move rapidly from one building or urban element to another. Such 'strategies embracing architecture'[252] select what in design-architectural terms are a discontinuous series of walls, surfaces, steps and boundaries, but which in skateboarding's space-time become a flow of encounters and engagements between board, body and terrain.

> You can throw you board down and skate around for hours hitting anything that crosses your path.[253]

> It's a total attack approach where the skater is not a separate entity from his terrain, slaloming to avoid everything in his way. Now he is the terrain with all its intricate pieces. Everything he approaches is part of his whole ride.[254]

246. 'Fire and Friends', n.p.
247. Ibid.
248. Elliott Willensky and Norval White, *AIA Guide to New York* (New York: Harcourt Brace Jovanovich, 3rd edn, 1988), p. 230.
249. Kevin Wilkins, 'New England Hot Spots', *TransWorld Skateboarding*, vol. 9 no. 11 (November 1991), p. 43.
250. Pete and the Posse, letter, *Thrasher*, vol. 11 no. 9 (September 1991), p. 6.
251. Simon, in Hodgkinson, 'Rad', p. 11.
252. Santa Cruz, advertisement (July 1981), p. 53.
253. Ricky Oyola, 'City Skating', *Sidewalk Surfer*, no. 2 (November/December 1995), n.p.
254. Peralta 'Skate', p. 40.

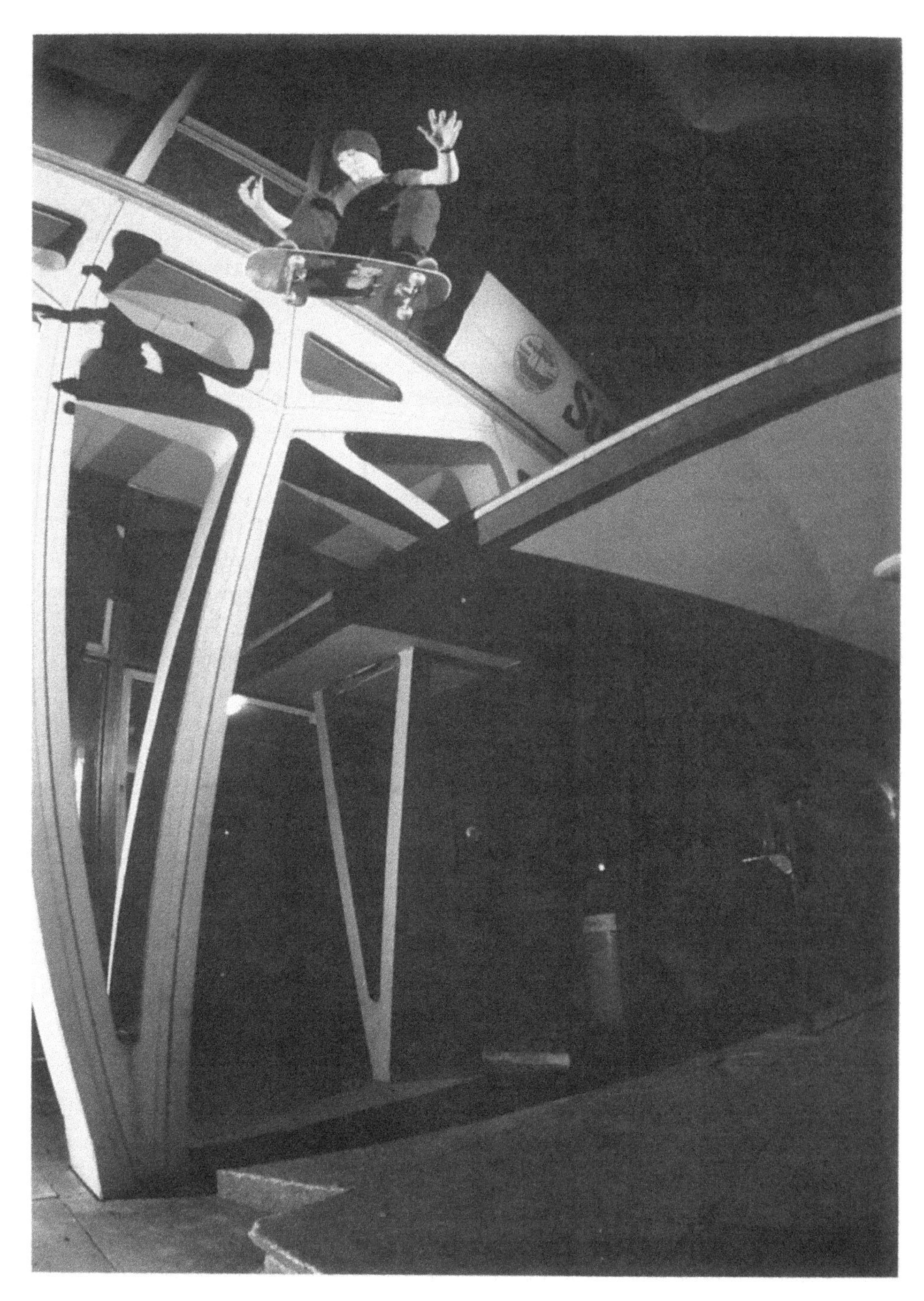

7.13 The reduction of architecture to an element. Frank Stephens, ollie off the roof of Suffolk College, Ipswich (1995). (Photograph Matthew Worland)

> Find it. Grind it. Leave it behind.[255]

Skateboarding here resists the standardization and repetition of the city as a serial production of building types, functions and discrete objects; it decentres building-objects in time and space in order to recompose them as a strung-out yet newly synchronous arrangement. For example, the path from Fifth and Maple Street to downtown in San Diego was composed of a route 'chock full of fun lines: lots of bumps, rails, ledges, banks, *et al* [*sic*], scattered along a downhill cruise'.[256]

Skateboarding also suggests that cities can be thought of as series of micro-spaces, rather than comprehensive urban plans, monuments or *grands projets*. Consequently, architecture is seen to lie beyond the province of the architect and is thrown instead into the turbulent nexus of reproduction.[257]

> On the street the urban blight is being reworked to new specifications. The man on the avenue is the architect of the future. The blind are no longer leading the blind. There are now no formalized plans. Invent your own life.[258]

Through such compositions, skateboarding brings back that which strictly economistic Marxism evacuates – it brings back the dream, imaginary and 'poetic being',[259] what Peralta called the 'skate of the art'.[260] Skateboarding points to the resurrection of the urban not as a product, but as a way of living.

> *The urban* . . . is a mental and social form, that of simultaneity, of gathering, of convergence, of encounter (or rather, encounters). It is a *quality* born from quantities (spaces, objects, products). It is a *difference*, or rather, an ensemble of differences . . . the *urban* could present itself as *signifiers* whose *signifieds* we are presently looking for.[261]

> Movement means vitality in a rotting reality.[262]

And it is specifically the skateboarder's performative body which provokes the revenge on leisure and work spaces.

255. 'Blast From the Past', p. 56.
256. Roman de Salvo, 'In Hot Pursuit of a Dude Called Donger', *Heckler* (accessed 5 May 1996).
257. Iain Borden, Joe Kerr, Alicia Pivaro and Jane Rendell, 'Narratives of Architecture in the City', in Borden, Kerr, Pivaro and Rendell (eds), *Strangely Familiar: Narratives of Architecture in the City* (London: Routledge 1996), p. 9.
258. Smythe, 'No Parking', p. 55.
259. Henri Lefebvre, *Espaces et Sociétés*, vol. 4 (1976–8), p. 270, cited in Kofman and Lebas, 'Lost in Transposition', in Lefebvre, *Writings on Cities*, p. 23.
260. Peralta 'Skate', pp. 38–40.
261. Lefebvre, *Writings on Cities*, p. 131.
262. Smythe, 'No Parking', p. 57.

> Thanks to its sensory organs, from the sense of smell and from sexuality to sight (without any special emphasis being place on the visual sphere), the body tends to behave as a *differential field*. It behaves, in other words, as a *total* body, breaking out of the temporal and spatial shell developed in response to labour, to the division of labour, to the localizing of work and the specialization of places.[263]

Other recompositions of architecture are also suggested in this process. Most obviously, skateboarding displaces the building's function from interior to exterior; when *Skateboard!*, for example, in one pair of illustrations contrasted a skater's action on a building exterior with the lifeless internal escalators, it implied that the building's function was not its commercial work but its relation to the skater's interrogation.[264]

What, however, do such recompositions of architecture suggest? What compositional mode do they deploy? What do they imply for a politics of space in the modern city? What do they mean, what effect do they have, and what do they provoke in response?

SPEAKING THE CITY

Skateboarding is an aesthetic rather than ethical practice, using the 'formants' at its disposal to create an alternative reality.[265] As *Thrasher* referred (semi-seriously) to the artistic practice of skateboarding, this was a 'Sorealist' activity.

> Sorealism tears artistic ideologies out of sterile galleries and incestuously exclusive cliques and slaps them down on the pavement for the whole world to see. It's art on real terms.[266]

Skateboarders, then, analyse architecture not for historical, symbolic or authorial content but for how surfaces present themselves as skateable surfaces. This is what *Thrasher* calls the 'skater's eye':

> People who ride skateboards look at the world in a very different way. Angles, spots, lurkers and cops all dot the landscape that we all travel.[267]

263. Lefebvre, *Production of Space*, p. 384.
264. Worland, 'Milton Keynes', p. 22.
265. Lefebvre, *Introduction to Modernity*, p. 321.
266. 'Sorealism', p. 67
267. 'Skater's Eye', *Thrasher*, vol. 17 no. 1 (January 1997), p. 71.

How then does this aesthetic activity take place? What techniques or modes of representation are involved?

Cities are at once real and coded, imagined and mediated.[268] Skaters enact an extreme version of this process, such that the internalization of imagery identified in Chapter Five also has its urban concomitant wherein physical phenomena, conscious representations and the skateboarder's lived experience of the city are constantly remade. It is to this triadic inter-production which we now turn, showing how skateboarders' particular urban representation is less map or text and more a performance akin to spatialized and temporalized speech.

As shown above, skateboarders undertake a discontinuous edit of architecture and urban space, recomposing their own city from different places, locations, urban elements, routes and times, involving the twin processes of asyndeton (omitting certain elements) and synecdoche (substituting one part for the another, or the whole) (7.14).[269]

> A world that no-one else can see, a world the pedestrians and motorists cannot share. An alternative reality, co-existing on a different plane.[270]

The city for the skateboarder becomes a kind of *capriccio*, the tourist's postcard where various architectural sites are compressed into an irrational (in time and space) view,[271] except the editing tool is here not eye, camera or tourist coach but motile body. Such 'urban transcendentalism' means an appreciation of those everyday architectures generally disregarded by non-skaters.

> Benches, banks and smooth pavement are what skaters really like. Citizens use some of these elements everyday, almost to the point of excess, but still have no appreciation for the structure itself.[272]

It also means a different kind of canon of city architecture is drawn up – substituting everyday architecture for great monuments and buildings by famous architects. The city for skateboarders is not buildings but a set of ledges, window sills, walls, roofs, railings, porches, steps, salt bins, fire hydrants, bus benches, water tanks, newspaper stands, pavements, planters, curbs, handrails, barriers, fences, banks, skips, posts, tables and so on (all elements engaged with by skaters in a single issue of *Sidewalk Surfer*.)[273] 'To us these things are more'.[274] New York, for

268. Victor Burgin, *Some Cities* (London: Reaktion, 1996), p. 175.

269. Michel de Certeau, *The Practice of Everyday Life* (Berkeley, California: University of California Press, 1984), pp. 101–2.

270. 'Where?' (September 1989), p. 18.

271. Barry Curtis, 'Venice Metro', in Borden, Kerr, Pivaro and Rendell (eds), *Strangely Familiar*, p. 45.

272. Ron Allen, 'Urban Transcendentalism, Part 2', *Slap*, vol. 4 no. 9 (September 1995), p. 8.

273. *Sidewalk Surfer*, no. 12 (December 1996).

274. 'Searching, Finding', p. 15.

7.14 Editing and speaking the city. Arron Bleasdale in London (1996). (Photograph Andy Horsley)

example, is for skaters not the New York of the Statue of Liberty, Times Square, 42nd Street, Central Park and the Empire State Building but of the Bear Stearns Building (46th and 47th, Park and Lexington), 'Bubble banks' (south side of 747 3rd Avenue), 'Harlem banks' (Malcolm X Avenue and 139th) (7.15), 'Brooklyn banks' (Manhattan end of Brooklyn Bridge), Washington Square Park, Mullaly Park in Brooklyn, Marriott Marquis Hotel (45th and Broadway), Bell Plaza banks, etc.[275] Washington, by the same process, became known architecturally to skaters as Pulaski Park, National Geographic Building, Federal Welfare Archives, Georgetown School banks, 'Gold Rail' and 'White Steps'.[276] Other cities receive the same treatment:

7.15 Alternative canonic architecture in the city. Harlem Banks, Malcolm X Avenue and 139th St, New York. Skateboarder: Jeremy Henderson, frontside rock 'n roll (1990). (Photograph Marco Contati)

275. Marco Contati, 'New York, New York', *Skateboard!* (second series), no. 43 (June 1990), pp. 32–41; 'Skatetown: New York City', *Thrasher*, vol. 9 no. 10 (October 1989), pp. 58–65 and 106; and Wilkins, 'New England', p. 43.

276. Pete Thompson, 'Washington DC', *TransWorld Skateboarding*, vol. 13 no. 5 (May 1995), pp. 86–9; and Andy Stone, interview, *TransWorld Skateboarding*, vol. 13 no. 5 (May 1995), pp. 90–3.

Rotterdam is perceived as the Weena covered walkway, Beurs stairs, Blaak interchange, Oosterhof mall and Alexanderpolder station;[277] Sydney is Martin Street, the MLC bump and World Trade Centre;[278] Manchester is Albert Square, the Curbs, the Gasworks, the Crown Courts, St Ann's Square and Exchange Square;[279] and Tokyo becomes Akihabara Park, 'jabu jabu' banks in Shinjuku, ledges at Tokyo Station, curbs at Yotsuya Station, banks at Tokyo Taikan and various runs across the Aoyama-Omotesando-Harajuku-Shibuya area.[280]

What is the mode involved in such a recomposition? Occasionally, this takes the form of a map or geographic list, such as alternative routes through Bristol[281] or the *Knowhere* internet site, where nearly every skate location in the UK is identified.[282] Magazines in the 1990s, particularly *R.A.D.* and *Sidewalk Surfer*, have tended to focus less on professional skaters, major cities and well-known skate places and more on local skate scenes – the 'streets and back yards of Anytown'[283] – such as those in Oxted, Ipswich, Oxford, Milton Keynes, High Wycombe, Stroud, Cirencester and Cardiff; in the US, a single issue of *Slap*, for example, covered not San Diego and Los Angeles but Sacramento (California), Fort Lauderdale (Florida) and the urban backwaters of Nevada, Utah, Iowa, Kentucky, Connecticut, and New Jersey.[284] *Thrasher* and *R.A.D.* consistently did the same in the 1980s. In such articles, the reader-skater finds descriptions of local banks, rails, curbs, etc., not just to encourage a visit, but to generally demonstrate that such locations are to be found in all urban centres, and so available to all urban skaters (7.16).

> Here are more pictures of Everyman skating in Everytown. It could be your town. It could be you.[285]

> Think of all the different types of terrain: curbs, hills, ditches, pools, ramps, ledges, bumps . . . Challenge yourself. Skate something different . . . Go skate.[286]

277. Rud-gr, 'Rotterdam', *Duh*, no. 7 (Spring 1995), pp. 21–5.
278. Kelvin Ho, 'Skateboarding: an Interpretation of Space in the Olympic City,' *Architectural History and Theory*; (1999).
279. Chris Blue, 'Board Stupid', *City Life* (c. August 2000), pp. 17–19.
280. journal@maxx.mc.net (Satsuma), alt.skateboard, 'Subject. Re. A Little Japan SK8 Info' (29 June 1996); and Russell Waterman, 'Tokyo Listings', *R.A.D.*, no. 98 (July 1991), pp. 40–1.
281. Steve Kane, 'Street Life: Bristol', *Skateboard!*, no. 15 (November 1978), pp. 36–9.
282. *Knowhere* internet site, URL http://www.state51.co.uk/state51/knowhere/skindex.html (accessed 7 February 1997).
283. 'From Surf to Hellbows: the Styling of Street', *R.A.D.*, no. 75 (May 1989), p. 60.
284. *Slap*, vol. 6 no. 1 (January 1997). See also Jerry Mander, 'Sacto Locals', *TransWorld Skateboarding*, vol. 9 no. 10 (October 1991), pp. 80–5.
285. 'Scary Places', p. 20.
286. 'Let's Go Skate!', pp. 36–40.

This is a communication which engenders empathy and similarity between towns and skaters, not a spectacularized Other of terrain and personalities.

In their own locality, therefore, the skateboarders' cognitive representation is neither map nor directory, for skateboarding is 'hard to put onto paper',[287] nor of a spectacularized centre-point, but a mental knowledge composed of highly detailed local knowledge about dispersed places, micro-architectures and accessible times.

> ALWAYS be on the alert for a possible spot . . . Be alert . . . keep your eyes open and your head oscillating.[288]

> Adventuring around and finding new spots is without a doubt the best aspect of city skating.[289]

Skaters' representations thus have more in common with the Situationist tactics of the *dérive*, *détournement* and psychogeography – 'maps' composed from the opportunities offered by the physical and emotional contours of the city, and, above all, enacted through a run across different spaces and moments.[290]

> I'm directed most to movements, the way I travel, the directions I move in. I follow my feelings.[291]

> When you have no destination, the only reason for movement is the enjoyment of all your movement.[292]

> Skating is a continual search for the unknown.[293]

Skateboarders' representational maps are thus always *situated* through a continual reliving of the city – 'an open mind always seeking out new lines and possibilities'.[294] Skaters attempt neither to 'see' the city nor to comprehend it as a totality, but to live it as simultaneously representation and physicality.

287. Bowman, 'Comment', n.p.

288. Gary Davis, 'Radical Manifesto', *Thrasher*, vol. 2 no. 2 (February 1982), p. 18, reprinted from *Skate Fate* (Cincinnati, Ohio).

289. Oyola, 'City Skating', n.p.

290. Guy Debord, 'Introduction to a Critique of Urban Geography', and 'Theory of the Dérive', in Ken Knabb (ed.), *Situationist International Anthology* (Berkeley: Bureau of Public Secrets, 1981), pp. 5–8 and 50–4.

291. Rodney Mullen, interview, *R.A.D.*, no. 74 (April 1989), p. 28.

292. 'Skating Alone', *R.A.D.*, no. 76 (June 1989), p. 22.

293. Caine Gayle, 'Multiple Choice Through Words and Pictures', *Slap*, vol. 4 no. 9 (September 1995), p. 33.

294. Christopher James Pulman, 'An Environmental Issue', *Sidewalk Surfer*, no. 1 (September/October 1995), n.p.

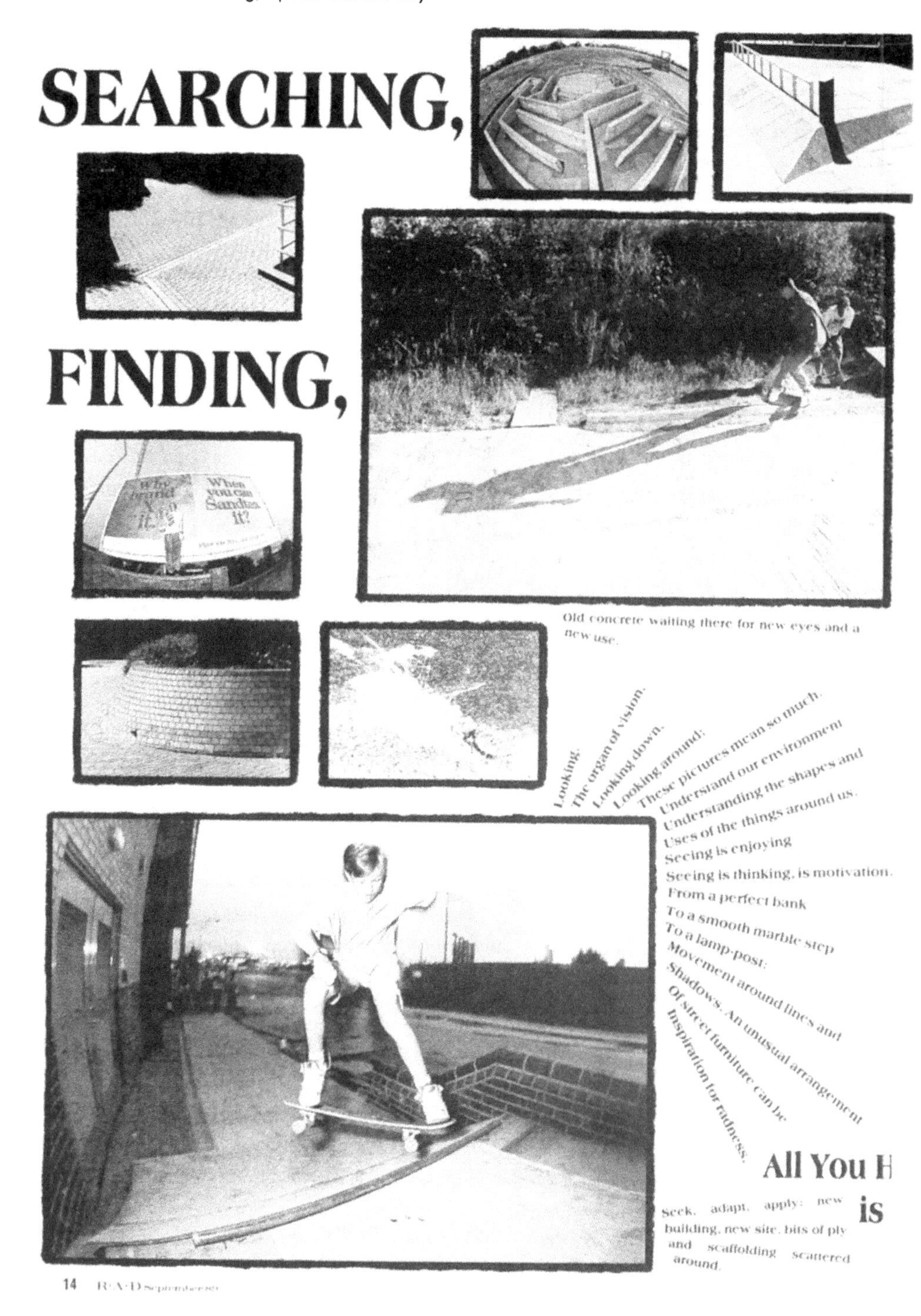

SEARCHING,

FINDING,

Old concrete waiting there for new eyes and a new use.

Looking.
The organ of vision.
Looking down.
Looking around:
These pictures mean so much.
Understand our environment
Understanding the shapes and
Uses of the things around us.
Seeing is enjoying
Seeing is thinking, is motivation.
From a perfect bank
To a smooth marble step
To a lamp-post:
Movement around lines and
Shadows. An unusual arrangement
Of street furniture can be
Inspiration for radness.

All You H

is

Seek, adapt, apply: new building, new site, bits of ply and scaffolding scattered around.

14 R.A.D September 89

7.16 'Searching, Finding, Living, Sharing'. Psychogeographic mapping of everyday urbanism in *R.A.D.* magazine (September 1989).

LIVING,

Buildings are building blocks for the open minded.

SHARING

One step ahead of the pedestrian
Or static eye, the Architects and
Artists, the people who look at
Shapes and patterns around themselves
And see beauty in these things people
Have created from pattern and relationships of shapes to
Shapes and people to shapes.
To us these things are more. These things have
Purpose because we have movement
As well as vision.

Concrete grips — or slides

ıve To Do
'hink Rad

> Walls aren't just walls, banks aren't just banks, curbs aren't just curbs and so on . . . mapping cities out in your head according to the distribution of blocks and stairs, twisting the meaning of your environment around to fit your own needs and imagination. It's brilliant being a skateboarder isn't it?[295]

Another distinction from conventional maps concerns temporality. In the aerial form of map, the entire city is understood simultaneously within a single glance – but in skateboarders' cognitive mapping the time is that of the run, composed of disparate objects in a sequence (linear time), with some objects 'read' once (isolated time), others encountered several times (repeated time) and still others returned to again and again on different occasions (cyclical time). The whole run can also be repeated the same or differently (differential time).

> Ridin' from spot to spot, at high speed, during rush hour is my version of the ultimate test for any urban 'street skater'. On a good day, when all the stop lights are working in my favour, I feel like I've figured out where my place is in this fucked-up world. That lasts for maybe a minute, then the feeling disappears and I'm lost again. So it goes.[296]

Skateboarders are thus more concerned with temporal distance as proximity (temporal closeness of things, temporal locality), and its repetition, than with time as a valuable resource or measure of efficiency; time for skaters is what is lived, experienced and produced, not what is required.

> It's about time, it's about space, it's about time to skate someplace.[297]

Interestingly, 1970s skaters referred to the skating event as a 'session' – a temporal term; 1990s street skaters, however, increasingly refered to the act of repeatedly skating at a particular place as 'localizing'[298] it – a spatial term. While both 'session' and 'localize' are active meanings – processes which skaters *do* to the terrains around them – in the latter's spatialized term, duration is relocated from a regime of routine and sequence into indeterminacy – a notion not of accuracy but of looseness, of time being adapted to the act of skating. The skateboarder's time is a social time.

Another aspect of this sense of adaptive temporality concerns memory and documentation, for the skateboarder's is not a historical but an everyday memory, often surviving only for the period in which a set of places are skated. Skateboarders thus negate the 'historical' time of the city, being wholly unconcerned with the many

295. 'Twisted', *Sidewalk Surfer*, no. 14 (March 1997), n.p.
296. Driggs, 'Swamp Trogs', p. 43.
297. Rick Blackhart, 'Ask the Doctor', *Thrasher*, vol. 11 no. 11 (November 1991), p. 24.
298. 'The *R.A.D.* Encyclopaedia', *R.A.D.*, no. 88 (June 1990), p. 60.

decades and processes of its construction, so that the city appears out-of-the-blue with no temporal past. 'I've always lived for the present. I live for the present'.[299]

Nor is the city *recorded* by skateboarders, but is that of the here-and-now, the immediate object, reborn each day of the skater's run. 'This isn't art, it isn't business, it's life'.[300] Just, then, as skateboarders do not attempt to understand the city, nor do they try to document it. Skateboarding leaves almost no text to be read; its marks and assaults leave virtually no discernible script for others to translate and comprehend. We must then revise our earlier depiction of skateboarding as a mode of writing to that of *speaking* of the city – that 'speech doubling'[301] which at once interrogates and increases the meaning of the city, while leaving its original text intact. Above all, speech requires the actual presence of the subject, the active speaker of the city, and so is not 'cool' but 'hot'.[302] Speaking-skateboarding is not a mimicking of the city, an oration of a pre-given text, but a performative utterance wherein the speakers form anew themselves and the city.

> The new urban strategist realizes that while it may not pay to be different, no one can really afford the price of being the same. In the new master plan, conformation has been replaced by confrontation. Act, don't *re*act, turn off the air conditioner go outside and move.[303]

It is, therefore, in the continual performance of skateboarding that its meaning and actions are manifested; as one skateboard maxim puts it, 'shut up and skate', or:

> Watchin' and Wonderin' won't get you there.
> Grab your board and get outta that chair.[304]

These are not things which can be simply seen or understood through pure abstraction; like rhythms, skateboarding requires a multiplicity of senses, thoughts and activities to be represented and comprehended. Rhythms disclose things, not through explanation or codified interpretation, but through lived experience. Above all, because the experiencers relate the fundamental conditions of their own temporality to that of the world outside, they create a subject–object engagement that is ultimately a lived form of dialectical thought.

299. Rune Glifberg, interview, *Sidewalk Surfer*, no. 14 (March 1997), n.p.
300. Mark Gonzales, in 'Trash', *Thrasher*, vol. 16 no. 2 (February 1996), p. 139.
301. Lefebvre, *Everyday Life in the Modern World*, p. 176.
302. Ibid., p. 177.
303. Smythe, 'No Parking', p. 57.
304. Bonnie Blouin, 'I See You', *Thrasher*, vol. 6 no. 3 (March 1986), p. 51.

> Here is found that old philosophical question (the subject and the object and their relationships) posed in non-speculative terms, close to practice. The observer at the window knows that he takes as first reference *his time*, but that the first impression displaces itself and includes the most diverse rhythms.[305]

> Leaves in the city
> Swirl into dry piles of
> garbage salad and drown in puddles
> of grease. City grime
> fills in cracks and blends,
> I skate to the tune of the crackle.[306]

Skateboarding is then a kind of unconscious dialectical thinking, an engagement with the spatial and temporal rhythms of the city, skateboarders using themselves as reference but then rethinking the city through their actions. The question now begs as to what thoughts are made through such actions. What does skateboarding implicitly say about the city and its architecture?

305. Lefebvre, *Writings on Cities*, p. 227.
306. Chauf Fer, 'Jump in the Leaves', *Thrasher*, vol. 6 no. 3 (March 1986), p. 52.

Chapter 8
Performing the City

You self-righteous, blind, arseholes.
YOU CANNOT CONTROL THE USE OF PUBLIC SPACE.[1]

COMMODITY CRITIQUE

Zero degree architecture is a field of the meaningless, a series of signals, a code reductive in individual signs and complex in its multitudinous instructions. Yet the architecture and spaces of the modern city are not wholly constraining, for there is a contradiction between the homogenizing reduction of space by business, and the open differentiation of urban space in the city as a whole[2] – and it is this contradiction that skateboarding works within. While advertisements and controlled spaces contribute to the 'terrorism' of everyday life,[3] part of the intensification of the everyday as a mode of production and of administering society,[4] skateboarding offers both an apparently non-commercial realm of compensation and a confrontation of the instructive mechanics of signals.

> There are no more white lines to stay within, sidewalks to conform to or bases to tag. It's all an open highway with hydrants, curbs, bumpers, shopping carts, door handles and pedestrians.[5]

Skateboarding counters signal architecture with a body-centric and multi-sensory performative activity, and with an indifference to function, price and regulation, creating new patterns of space and time, and turning the signals of the city into ephemeral symbols of everyday meaning and duration (8.1).

1. 'Insight', *Sidewalk Surfer*, no. 23 (January/February, 1998), n.p.
2. Henri Lefebvre, *The Production of Space*, (Oxford: Blackwell, 1991), pp. 18–19; and Henri Lefebvre, *Writings on Cities*, (Oxford: Blackwell, 1996), pp. 140–1.
3. Henri Lefebvre, *Everyday Life in the Modern World*, (London: Transaction Publishers, 1984), pp. 143–93. See also Philip Wander, 'Introduction', Lefebvre, *Everyday Life in the Modern World*, p. xv.
4. Henri Lefebvre, 'Toward a Leftist Cultural Politics: Remarks Occasioned by the Centenary of Marx's Death', in Cary Nelson and Lawrence Grossberg (eds), *Marxism and the Interpretation of Culture*, (London: Macmillan, 1988), pp. 79–80.
5. Stacy Peralta, 'Skate of the Art, '85', *Thrasher*, vol. 5 no. 8 (August 1985), p. 40.

8.1 Indifference to function, price and regulation. Matt Pritchard, smith grind on the window ledge of a branch of Barclays Bank, Cardiff (1997). (Photograph Matthew Worland)

Consider also that signals are not there for their own sake, so that when skaters confront these signals they are also necessarily critiquing their underlying logic of profit, exchange, efficiency, control, normalcy, predictability, regulated space and time. Skateboarding, therefore, challenges the notion that space is there to be obeyed, and that we exist solely as efficient automata within the processes of exchange and accumulation. Furthermore, if skateboarding suggests the move from things to works, from design to experiential creativity, there should also be a corresponding shift in production and labour and in consumption, exchange and use. It is to these areas which we now turn.

BEYOND THE SHINY PRODUCT

Architecture is intended for the production of things – either products as commodities in factories, knowledge in universities and museums, labour power in housing, information and decisions in offices, and so on. In this sense all buildings are places of the expenditure of energy, engaged in the production and distribution of things. Skateboarding, however, offers no such contribution, consuming the building while not engaging with its productive activity. Consequently, it implicitly denies both that labour should be productive of things and that architecture should be directed toward that purpose.

> They'll never get out of that grind except by dying. I wonder why they ever wanted to get in.[6]

> Life's not a job, it's an adventure.[7]

For example, *Thrasher* ridiculed in a spoof advertisement the labour of a 'pool service technician' attending to the maintenance of empty, skateable swimming pools.[8] The clear implication is that, by contrast, productive labour of skateboarding produces neither things nor services, but is a pleasure-driven activity of its own.

Furthermore, this productive-of-nothing labour is disruptive to the optimal management of urban space. Where business invades not only economics and politics but also social experience, setting itself up as model for social administration in general,[9] skateboarding rejects the 'efficiency' and 'economic' logic of urban space, undertaking an activity which, by business standards, has an entirely different rationale.

6. Brian Casey, in Paul Mulshine, 'Wild in the Streets', *Philadelphia Magazine*, vol. 78 no. 4 (April 1987), p. 120.

7. Chip Morton, in 'Trash', *Thrasher*, vol. 9 no. 1 (January 1989), p. 124.

8. 'Ads (We're Not Sure) We'd Like to See', *Thrasher*, vol. 6 no. 3 (March 1986), p. 28.

9. Lefebvre, *Everyday Life in the Modern World*, p. 66.

> In a culture that measures progress in terms of cost per square foot, the streetstylist takes matters into his own hands. He dictates his own terms and he makes his own fun.[10]

This is particularly evident in the city centre, which is increasingly becoming the centre of *decision-making*, and the new centrality of power.[11] Skateboarding is here irrational, for why would one spend so much time balancing on a piece of wood with four wheels? Why would one confront the logic of walking and looking by going up as well as along, touching as well as seeing, impacting as well as remaining apart?

> The true skater surveys all that is offered, takes all that is given, goes after the rest and leaves nothing to chance. In a society on hold and planet on self-destruct, the only safe recourse is an insane approach.[12]

This irrationality is particularly evident if we consider that the basic spatial plane of street skating is 2–4 feet above the conventional urban ground of the pavement. Furthermore, its architecture is frequently vertical, as in street skating moves such as ollies or wallriding.

> Wallriding is the most nonsensical facet of skateboarding, an art of mind over matter.[13]

This 'irrationality' pervades skateboarding practices. For example, when the Vans Warped competition tour came to London's Canary Wharf in the summer of 1996, skaters spent as much time skating the surrounding banks, steps, blocks, gaps, walls and pathways of this decision-making centre as on the competition site itself.[14] Given that Canary Wharf is one the great centres of the global city,[15] skateboarding in such places also helps deny the logic of the city as pre-eminently existing solely for the benefit of global forces and flows of information and capital. It reminds us that the city is also a series of diverse place-specific phenomena,[16] ignorance of the global serving to heighten awareness of the local.

10. John Smythe, 'No Parking', *Action Now*, vol. 8 no. 2 (September 1981), p. 55.
11. Lefebvre, *Writings on Cities*, p. 73.
12. John Smythe, 'The History of the World and Other Short Subjects, or, From Jan and Dean to Joe Jackson Unabridged', *SkateBoarder*, vol. 6 no. 10 (May 1980), p. 29.
13. 'Shudder Speed', *Thrasher*, vol. 11 no. 11 (November 1991), p. 52.
14. Juliette Elliott, 'Vans Warped Tour', *Big Cheese*, no. 2 (n.d., c. early 1997), pp. 14–15.
15. Susan Fainstein, *The City Builders* (Oxford: Blackwell, 1994), pp. 197–201; Anthony D. King, *Global Cities* (London: Routledge, 1990), pp. 98–9; and Diane Ghirardo, *Architecture After Modernism* (London: Thames and Hudson, 1996), pp. 187–94.
16. Lefebvre, *Writings on Cities*, pp. 111–12.

Episodes like this, enacted in the heart of the business city, show that skateboarding is part of that great dialectic between labour and non-labour. Mike Vallely's attitude to waged labour is typical to that of many skaters: 'I've told myself from the age of twelve, "I'll never work a day in my life."'[17] In reaction to such attitudes, one critic railed that skateboarding 'appears to serve no known purpose in life and does nothing to raise national productivity'.[18] That, however, is exactly the point.

Nonetheless, the triumph of non-labour does not entail so much an absence of effort[19] as a redefinition of what 'production' might mean, and it is here too that skateboarding offers some insights. At first sight, skateboarders' labour produces no 'products' beyond the move, a 'commodity' exchangeable only by means of performative action, so appears to waste effort and time. But that 'principle of economy' which sees a 'waste' of energy as abnormal is itself a reduction of life to mere survival.[20] Skateboarding, in contrast, undertakes a release of energy that either creates or modifies space, espousing play (*ludo*), art and festival – Eros (the pleasure principle) opposed to Thanatos (the reality or productivity principle).[21]

> When they work, we'll skate.[22]

The labour of skateboarding is then not the production of commodities but the effort of play, the ludic.

> Each trick is the result of the dedication that you've put into skateboarding, years and years of concentration and commitment to increasing your abilities and potential for enjoyment, because you genuinely want to, not because you've been brainwashed into wanting.[23]

Or as one skateboarder put it, skaters have 'moved beyond shiny products and consumerism'.[24]

> All of us we're all existing beyond their shit stained grasp. They (the outside world) can't understand us now, they can't even rip us off anymore. Fuck the fashion theft, you know it doesn't matter. Everyone has the ability to use skating to rise above the repressive, hassle filled, cess pit world. We can all become higher types.[25]

17. Mike Vallely, interview, *TransWorld Skateboarding*, vol. 14 no. 1 (January 1996), p. 95.
18. Jane Haas, in 'Off the Wall', *SkateBoarder*, vol. 6 no. 6 (January 1980), pp. 74–5.
19. Henri Lefebvre, *The Survival of Capitalism: Reproduction of the Relations of Production*, (New York: St. Martin's, 1976), p. 16.
20. Lefebvre, *Production of Space*, pp. 176–9.
21. Lefebvre, *Production of Space*, p. 177; and Lefebvre, *Writings on Cities*, p. 171.
22. Gareth Catterick, letter, *Sidewalk Surfer*, no. 15 (April 1997), n.p.
23. Ewan Bowman, 'Comment', *Sidewalk Surfer*, no. 13 (January–February 1997), n.p.
24. Ben Powell, 'Not a Toy', *Sidewalk Surfer*, no. 3 (January–February 1996), n.p.
25. Ibid.

Unlike the machine, aimed at the production of things,[26] the skateboard-tool aims to produce new moves and spaces, creating new *kinds* of labours as uses and pleasures outside of normative work. Production becomes 'liberating actions of pure creativity/ giving',[27] generating qualities, experiences, phenomenal encounters, relations of body and thing, pain and fun.[28]

> You earn quality when you skate.[29]

> Happiness and fun are our staple experiences and, thank christ, they always will be.[30]

Similarly, the reproduction of labour power becomes not reproduction of future workers[31] but of energetic desiring bodies, capable of creative expenditures of effort. Skateboarders, as young adults, see themselves not as the reserve army waiting to serve in industry, but as living according to a different rationale. The totality with which skateboarders conceive of their opposition to work and career patterns is crucial, for, as shown in Chapter Six, skateboarders do not so much temporarily escape from the routinized world of school, family and social conventions as replace it with a whole new way of life.

> Forget about the mainline and the fast line; the edge of the glide is all that is of value.[32]

> I'm not gonna be stuck in an office someday.[33]

Skateboarding, particularly for those in their twenties or older, thus becomes far more than leisure or respite from school or work; it is considered to be a way of life outside of 'labour' altogether (8.2).

One contradiction here is that the extraordinary architectural wealth of the city, from which skateboarding is born, is itself a product of waged labour. It could be argued here that skateboarding is a revival of the 'dead labour' (Marx) contained in the city's means of production.[34] On the one hand, this might relate to the reuse

26. Lefebvre, *Production of Space*, p. 344.
27. Steven Eye, in 'East Coast: Thawing Out', *Thrasher*, vol. 3 no. 6 (June 1983), p. 33.
28. Lefebvre, *Writings on Cities*, p. 171.
29. Neil Blender, interview, *Thrasher*, vol. 5 no. 2 (February 1985), p. 28.
30. 'Any Variations?', *Sidewalk Surfer*, no. 14 (March 1997), n.p.
31. Karl Marx, *Capital: a Critique of Political Economy. Volume 1*, (Harmondsworth: Penguin, 1976), pp. 717–8.
32. Smythe, 'History', p. 29.
33. Mulshine, 'Wild', p. 126.
34. Lefebvre, *Production of Space*, p. 348.

8.2 Alternative forms of labour. Pin, wall ride on the window ledge of a Social Security office (1997). (Photograph Andy Horsley)

of derelict city spaces, as with many UK 1970s skateparks such as Rolling Thunder in the disused Brentford Market, Chiswick,[35] The Cage in a former Brighton fish market,[36] or Mad Dog Bowl (London), Malibu Dog Bowl (Nottingham)[37] and others built in old cinemas. But these are rare instances compared to the globally dispersed and locally focused activity of 1980s–1990s street skating, and so it is, above all, skateboarders' production of space that facilitates this revival of dead labour and so promotes use over exchange:

> Through the production of space . . . living labour can produce something that is no longer a thing, nor simply a set of tools, nor simply a commodity. In space needs and desires can reappear as such . . . spaces for play, spaces for enjoyment, architectures of wisdom or pleasure. In and by means of space, the work may shine through the product, use value may gain the upper hand over exchange value.[38]

Skateboarding is a resurrection of the dead labour of construction, either as a new use for an unused building, as a new use for a building simultaneously being used for something else, or a new use space with an ambiguous purpose. Thus skateboarding's revival of 'dead labour' occurs from the moment the building is constructed, and does not have to await the end of its constructional or functional life-cycle.

There is, then, a temporal production also at work here. Capitalism is a mixture of production and speculation, alternatively sacrificing long-term social benefits to short-term profits or short-term social needs in favour of programmed investment schedules.[39] Skateboarding time, in contrast, is immediate, no more than a second (single move), minute (run), weeks and months (repeated visits), or few years (a skater's individual activity). Skateboarding time is also discontinuous, composed of a few minutes here and there, spread over space, and in between the socially programmed activities of production and exchange. It is an alternating rhythm within the regular cyclical rhythm of the city.[40] For example, the long temporality of property ownership, the medium temporality of lease arrangements or the short temporality of the parking meter are all avoided by skateboarders (7.9). While 'economic space subordinates time to itself', and 'political space expels it as threatening and dangerous',[41] skateboarding promotes an appropriative recovery of time as well as of space. Skateboarding reasserts the here-ness and now-ness of architecture.

35. Trip Gabriel, 'Rolling Thunder', *Rolling Stone* (16–30 July 1987), pp. 50–2.
36. 'Lip Torque', *Skateboard!*, no. 9 (May 1978), p. 37.
37. 'Lip Torque', *Skateboard!*, no. 8 (April 1978), p. 49.
38. Lefebvre, *Production of Space*, p. 348.
39. Lefebvre, *Production of Space*, pp. 335–6.
40. Lefebvre, *Writings on Cities*, p. 221.
41. Lefebvre, *Production of Space*, p. 95.

> Performance transportation is the present and the future. Take it where you want and make it go where you want to take it. Tomorrow is today and you are it.[42]

> Time has come . . .[43]

Skateboarding is 'one rythmical (*sic*) expression in a multitude of rythmical (*sic*) expressions',[44] and thus helps to restore the oeuvre by creating a schizophrenic coexistence of space-times of play, exchange, circulation, politics and culture.[45]

> The citizen resists the State by a particular use of time. A struggle therefore unfolds for appropriation in which rhythms play a major role. Through them social, therefore, civil time, seeks and manages to shield itself from State, linear, unirhythmical measured and measuring time . . . Time is hence linked to space and to the rhythms of the people who occupy this space.[46]

In this coexistence of urban time-spaces we see the dialectic of labour and non-labour at work, wherein skateboarding shows that the production of space is exactly that, and not a production of things in space. And it shows that time as well as space is produced through appropriation, resisting by entangled polyrhythms the domination of space on the part of State power.

GIFTS OF FREEDOM

Skateboarding involves a critique of the processes of exchange and consumption in the modern city, and, above all else, proposes a reassertion of *use* values as opposed to exchange values. Again, this requires elaboration.

Capitalist space, as commodity, can be likened to any goods – simultaneously abstract and concrete, and produced for the purposes of exchange.[47] We have already seen how a different attitude to labour and production leads skaters to negate the productive labour and routinized work that goes on inside buildings. Thus by the simple act of reasserting use values – using space without paying for it – skateboarding is similarly indifferent to the exchangeability of these places through rents, leases and freeholds. As *Sidewalk Surfer* put it, skaters oppose 'the real criminals, who despoil the world in their never ending quest for capital'.[48]

42. Smythe, 'No Parking', p. 55.
43. Black Label, advertisement, *Thrasher*, vol. 16 no. 3 (March 1996), p. 29.
44. Steve Shaw, 'Club Method Air', *Skateboard!* (second series), no. 39 (January 1990), p. 38.
45. Lefebvre, *Writings on Cities*, pp. 170–2.
46. Ibid., p. 237.
47. Lefebvre, *Production of Space*, pp. 306–7.
48. Editor's response to letter, *Sidewalk Surfer*, no. 14 (March 1997), n.p.

> The oeuvre is use value and the product is exchange value. The eminent use of the city, that is, of streets and squares, edifices and monuments, is *la Fête* (a celebration which consumes unproductively, without other advantage but pleasure and prestige and enormous riches in money and objects).[49]

> Any place you have concrete you can excel. You don't need anything else to do it, you don't need teams, you don't need much money, and it's infinitely adaptable to circumstances.[50]

Skateboarding thus works, like the *fête*, through the great wealth of objects at its disposal but, unlike the *fête*, without the squandering of money and without actually owning them.

> The streets are owned by everyone. Streets give the gift of freedom, so enjoy your possession.[51]

Abstract space, beyond a commodity in itself, is also the 'medium of *exchange*',[52] and this is increasingly the model for the city, where all buildings and spaces are considered as opportunities for commodity exchange and purchase,[53] such that 'exchange value is so dominant over use and use value that it more or less suppresses it'.[54] But it is precisely this focus on the medium of exchange which skateboarding rejects. Where the managers and owners of abstract space wish that society was solely directed at commodity production, exchange and consumption, by occupying those spaces immediately external to stores and offices skateboarders refuse to engage in such processes and instead insert use values where there are supposed to be none – in the *places* of exchange. Skateboarders, then, 'represent more than just secondary users; they essentially redefine business and governmental spaces'.[55] This kind of attitude is also evident in skaters' frequent refusal in the 1990s to pay skatepark charges, preferring to skate elsewhere in the city.

> London skaters aren't willing to pay. They'd rather go and skate the streets, there's sick spots everywhere.[56]

49. Lefebvre, *Writings on Cities*, p. 66.
50. Stacy Peralta, interview, *Thrasher*, vol. 2 no. 5 (May–June 1982), p. 21.
51. Brad Erlandson, in 'Sacramento', *Slap*, vol. 6 no. 1 (January 1997), p. 53.
52. Lefebvre, *Production of Space*, p. 307.
53. Michael Sorkin (ed.), *Variations on a Theme Park* (New York: Noonsday, 1992).
54. Lefebvre, *Writings on Cities*, p. 73.
55. Marc Spiegler, *Metropolis*, in Leah Garchik, 'The Urban Landscape', *San Francisco Chronicle* (late summer 1994), posted on *DansWORLD* (accessed March 1995).
56. Arron Bleasdale, interview, *Sidewalk Surfer*, no. 9 (August 1996), n.p.

As such, skateboarding is a small fragment of that utopian conception of the urban as use, not exchange (8.3).

> Urban society, a collection of acts taking place in time, privileging a space (site, place) and privileged by it, in turn signifiers and signified, has a logic different from that of merchandise. It is another world. The *urban* is based on use value.[57]

This is one of the main reasons why urban street skating is more 'political' than 1970s skateboarding's use of found terrains; street skating generates new uses that at once work within (in time and space) and negate the original ones.

The opposition of this city of use to the abstract space of economic rationalism is further emphasized if we consider that society itself is being ever more organized for the purposes of the consumption of goods,[58] and that use values are increasingly denied in the act of consumption – we are encouraged to consume signs and ideologies rather than uses.

In architectural terms, this process of the consumption of signs is to be found in the increasing spectacularization of architectural function into pure form, whereby history, meaning and politics alike are reduced to the thin surface of 'popularist' postmodern imagery, creating an urban realm more akin to the theme park than to a lived city. Such a lack of distinction between things, and images and signs derived from things, leads to a great dissatisfaction in their consumption.[59] Skateboarders, like everyone else, are confronted with the heightening intensification of advertising in new places and lines of vision.[60]

> I grabbed my skateboard and started rolling towards downtown. All around me there were billboards with new cars, cell phones, fast food, giant heads smoking six foot long cigarettes. Posters advertised movies and TV shows, clothes I couldn't afford being worn by people who looked too good to be human. Everyone wanted my attention.[61]

But in the face of such commodification, street skating does not consume architecture as projected image but as a material ground for action and so gives the human body something to do other than passively stare at advertising surfaces; its motility creates an interest in other things, materials, forms and in the skater's own physical presence in the city.

57. Lefebvre, *Writings on Cities*, p. 131.
58. Lefebvre, 'Towards a Leftist Critique of Politics', pp. 79–80.
59. Lefebvre, *Everyday Life in the Modern World*, p. 90.
60. Iain Borden, 'Thick Edge: Architectural Boundaries in the Postmodern Metropolis', in Iain Borden and Jane Rendell (eds), *InterSections: Architectural Histories and Critical Theories* (London: Routledge, 2000), pp. 235–40.
61. CSTR, 'Urban Blight', *Slap*, vol. 4 no. 9 (September 1995), p. 60.

8.3 A gift of freedom: the use value of the city. Skateboarder: John Reeves (1995).

> There was all sorts of craziness going on around me, all over the city, but I skimmed above it on my skateboard. Just gliding along, protected by my board.[62]

Skateboarding in this sense is not only a reassertion of use values, but also of the spatiality and temporality of human needs, desires and actions. As skater Ewan Bowman put it,

> Happiness is a state of mind that takes years to achieve, an equilibrium that comes about after hard work and commitment to following your own directions, and acting on your own personal desires, not those thrust upon you by multi corporate entities. There are only a few routes to authentic happiness left that haven't been turned into theme parks for the brain dead, or criminalised out of existence. Thankfully, skateboarding is one those alternative routes to fulfilment.[63]

The tactics here are both spatial and temporal, seizing specific spaces for small periods of time; skateboarding is thus rhythmically out-of-step with the dominant routines of the city, 'inconsistent with the adapted pace and uses of our molded environment',[64] creating a counter-rhythm of moves and runs. Skateboarding shows that the temporality of appropriation is different to that of ownership, seeking an active, moving time related to the specific needs and actions of urban dwellers.[65]

> Appropriated space must be understand in relation to time, and to rhythms of time and life.[66]

For example, Bowman explained his urban experience of London as a mixture of different speeds, actions and emotions.

> The raddest thing about skating here is skating on the roads in amongst the traffic, the fear and the adrenalin mixing as you skate from spot to spot nearly being hit by cars. That's a mad rush going through your body, over-taking the cars, being overtaken, going through a red light in a junction, dicing with big metal f**kers that would probably kill you.[67]

Or as an American skater reflected:

> If you haven't dodged traffic in the urban jungle, then you haven't lived . . . Whatever gets in my way is skated and vacated as I weave through the throngs of suit-wearing mutards that do their best to get in the way.[68]

62. Ibid.
63. Bowman, 'Comment'.
64. Miki Vukovich, 'Please Use the Handrail', *Warp*, vol. 4 no. 1 (April 1995), p. 46.
65. Lefebvre, *Production of Space*, p. 356.
66. Ibid., p. 166.
67. Bowman, 'Comment'.
68. Jesse Driggs, 'Swamp Trogs from Outer Space', *Thrasher*, vol. 15 no. 9 (September 1995), p. 43.

Significantly, this spatiality and temporality is different to that of 1970s found terrains; whereas the latter colonized a specific place for a weekend or afternoon, and so mimicked the idea of ownership, urban street skating is more ephemeral, taking over a number of sites for shorter periods, often just a few minutes or seconds. 'Always move on.'[69] For example, New York skaters considered 20 minutes to be a lengthy session on a single site.[70]

> Stagnating at the same spot is a step backward to a place where the regular world will always know where to find us.[71]

Urban skateboarding is not so much a colonization as a series of rolling encounters, an eventful journey. It is also, consequently, the reverse of the temporal logic of built-in obsolescence; where capitalism produces objects which wear out faster than necessary (a light-bulb), or which become technically out-of-date (audio formats), skateboarding creates a *use* which is shorter than the life-time of the object.

> Televisions, file cabinets, and cars are the offal of a disposable society. Wasted resources alone are a crime, but not recycling is high treason . . . From now, its search and destroy.[72]

Skateboarding here is a critique of ownership, but not of wealth. If society should involve the rehabilitation of wealth as the socialized sharing of amenity,[73] possession is not private ownership but the ability to 'have the most complex, the "richest" relationships of joy or happiness with the "object"'[74] – we should own not nothing but more of things, without recourse to legal relations.[75] And it is this which street skating addresses, being concerned with those parts of the city 'which people own but no one possesses'.[76]

> The important thing is not that I should become the owner of a little plot of land in the mountains, but that the mountains be open to me.[77]

Or as one skater put it: 'Just because you own it doesn't mean you're in charge of it.'[78]

69. 'Where?', *R.A.D.*, no. 79 (September 1989), p. 18.
70. Kevin Wilkins, 'New England Hot Spots', *TransWorld Skateboarding*, vol. 9 no. 11 (November 1991), p. 43.
71. 'Skate Junkies', *Thrasher*, vol. 12 no. 1 (January 1992), p. 51.
72. Ibid., p. 51.
73. Lefebvre, *Critique of Everyday Life*, p. 154.
74. Ibid., p. 156.
75. Ibid., pp. 157–8.
76. Steve Kane, interview, *Skateboard!*, no. 5 (January 1978), p. 56.
77. Lefebvre, *Critique of Everyday Life*, p. 158.
78. Todd Swank, in 'Trash', *Thrasher*, vol. 11 no. 11 (November 1991), p. 90.

If the relation between the skater and the city is not one of production or exchange, what is it? For the skateboarder, consider that 'primary relationships are not with his fellow man, but with the earth beneath his feet, concrete and all'[79] – the relation is of the self to the city, where human needs are rescued from the blind necessity of staying alive to become the appropriation of the self and the city together. Thus where possession focuses on the sense of having, the rejection of ownership enables the resurrection of all the senses;[80] and where some have seen the modern architecture of the city as alienating of the self,[81] this architecture can also be the means by which social relations are constructed. Practices such as skateboarding therefore suggest not only the re-distribution of urban space according to the maxim 'to each according to his needs',[82] but also the reformulation of the self according to the physical potential of the built environment. The experience of the self in relation to the city is, then, neither production nor consumption, but having that 'mad rush' described by Bowman above. 'It's all amazing, an unexplainable feeling that you have to feel to understand'.[83]

This occurs emotionally as well as physically, so that just as the skater's body is developed perceptually and physiologically, so the relation to the city becomes one of attraction and respect. Our relations with cities are like our relations with people,[84] and as one Brighton skater described this town – known as 'Pig City' – this was a conceptual and not purely geographic relationship.

> Not everyone who lives here and skates, lives in Pig City. It's a place that you live in your head.[85]

In this context, it is unsurprising that the Red Hot Chili Peppers, a band closely associated with skateboarding, often include what amount to love songs to cities in their recordings, including, in 'Under the Bridge', one to Los Angeles and the individual's movement through it.[86] In 'Under the Bridge', the city is a place of love, desire, turmoil and uncertainty. It is not owned, but related to.

In terms of social relations with others, the Self and the Other are not cut off but mediated by the city.[87] Where the city frequently tries to dictate the social identity

79. Mulshine, 'Wild', p. 120.
80. Lefebvre, *Critique of Everyday Life*, pp. 173–4.
81. Richard Sennett, *The Conscience of the Eye* (London: W.W. Norton, 1992).
82. Henri Lefebvre, *The Sociology of Marx*, (New York: Columbia University Press, 1982), p. 115.
83. Bowman, 'Comment'.
84. Victor Burgin, *Some Cities*, (London: Reaktion, 1996), p. 7.
85. Twiggy, in Tim Dunkerley, 'Baker's Back', *Skateboard!*, no. 18 (February 1979), p. 20.
86. Red Hot Chili Peppers, 'Under the Bridge', *Blood, Sugar, Sex, Magik*, audio compact disk (Warner Bros., 1991), especially first two verses.
87. Lefebvre, *Writings on Cities*, p. 236.

of its inhabitants,[88] a spatialized version of the 'marketing orientation' which encourages people to play a role,[89] skateboarders use their particular appropriation of the city to construct themselves and their relations with others; the rhythm of the city as external to the self and the rhythm of the self as intimate forms of consciousness and behaviour are counterposed.[90]

> The skater is not a separate entity from his terrain . . . he is the terrain with all its intricate pieces.[91]

> It's the only thing that I know how to do, and if I ever stopped doing it I would be no one . . . Skateboarding is my only identity for better or worse.[92]

In particular, for the skater it is the outdoor spaces, not interiors, which form the socio-space of self-identity and construction – a theme implicit throughout both Lefebvre's writings[93] and skateboarding subcultural practice.

> Our home life is exposed on the pavement. Everybody joins in with us, let's get rid of the cars and put all the furniture into the street. One big living room, and everyone's welcome.[94]

> Skaters are a different breed. Not a breed apart. A breed that exists within a steel, asphalt and concrete framework.[95]

The meaning of skateboarding, then, comes from its engagement with the spatial nature of production, exchange, consumption and its reassertion of use values, together with the subcultural values of a generalized rejection of society already identified above. Significantly, when *Thrasher* first showed the new street skating, it was not the skaters as individuals but their performance of moves which they promoted as 'studies in non-conformity'.[96] We must therefore consider that the spatial act of skateboarding is meaningless devoid of its subcultural attitudes, while, conversely, its subcultural attitudes have no substance except as produced in space in relation to

88. Borden, 'Thick Edge', pp. 84–7.
89. Wander, 'Introduction', pp. xi–xiv; and Erich Fromm, *Man for Himself* (Greenwich: Fawcett, 1967), pp. 75–89.
90. Lefebvre, *Writings on Cities*, pp. 235–6.
91. Peralta, 'Skate', p. 40.
92. Dan Cates, 'Comment', *Sidewalk Surfer*, no. 13 (January/February 1997), n.p.
93. Eleonore Kofman and Elizabeth Lebas, 'Lost in Transposition', in Lefebvre, *Writings on Cities*, pp. 7–8.
94. Ged Wells, 'World on a Cleaning Rota', *R.A.D.*, no. 100 (September 1991), p. 77.
95. Editorial, *Thrasher* (February 1983).
96. Morizen Föche, 'New Blood', *Thrasher*, vol. 6 no. 3 (March 1986), p. 47.

urban architecture. This is a true dialectic of the social and the spatial, each produced through the other. Rather than allowing architecture and the city to dictate who he or she is, the skateboarder poses in response the question of 'who am I?' (8.4).

In terms of the kind of society this might indicate, clearly skateboarders as a group of young people are not about to take over the revolutionary mission of the proletariat;[97] as 'small bait in a sea of corporate sharks'[98] they in no way seek to fundamentally alter anything. 'We're not out to fight the world'.[99] A *Thrasher* cover proclaiming 'Skaters of the World Unite' over an image of Lenin was simply rhetoric, highlighting a feature on skaters in different countries worldwide.[100]

8.4 A gift of freedom: questioning the self and the city. Skateboarder: Howard Cooke (1996). (Photograph Matthew Worland)

97. Lefebvre, *Introduction to Modernity*, pp. 339–40 and 359.

98. Bonnie Blouin, 'Skater's Edge', *Thrasher*, vol. 8 no. 7 (July 1988), p. 35.

99. Editorial, *Thrasher*, vol. 12 no. 6 (June 1992), p. 4.

100. 'If the Skaters Are United, They Can Never Be Divided', *Thrasher*, vol. 9 no. 2 (February 1989), front cover and pp. 60–7.

Nor do skateboarders undertake in any way a self-critique, relying instead on an adolescent marginal negation of the adult world.[101] They offer only an 'infra-politics' of resistance, a 'hidden transcript' intelligible only to other skaters.[102] On the other hand, young people prefigure the horizon of the future,[103] becoming increasingly dominant in UK inner cities and new towns such as London, Slough and Luton (while retirement towns like Christchurch, Worthing and Eastbourne absorb older populations),[104] so allowing their beliefs and activities to become explicit in these areas. In particular, this prefigurement is enacted through an 'ironic' assault on the rest of the world, exploiting their position of weakness to become 'aggressive whenever the opportunity arises' and so to defiantly 'irritate giants'.[105] Thus through highlighting certain conflicts (especially private property and social use, rational efficiencies and social space), skaters utilize their position of weakness (youth) to irritate authority and convention, thereby making comments regarding the whole nature of the city: 'always question authority'.[106]

As such, although a 'counter-culture' or 'alternative society' is always difficult to define, skateboarding concurs with Lefebvre's idea that a new society might include a primacy of use over exchange, a countering of quantity by quality, and that the centralized rationale of capitalism and state can be challenged through 'local powers', however small.[107] Skateboarding is 'an infinite postmodern mutant',[108] a critical tactic that denaturalizes the city of abstract space and exchange. It suggests that changing the manner of consumption can help identify new, radical requirements that the city must meet; that confronting needs and desires – not products and things – creates change;[109] and it proposes a return to art not as aestheticism but adaptation of time and space, an engagement with objects unrestricted to their use qua commodities but as the common property of social experience.[110]

> Skateboarding is an adaptation to the concrete jungle, a sport for the evolving American landscape . . . streetstyle is about turning the ugly urban shit around you into fodder for fun.[111]

101. Lefebvre, *Everyday Life in the Modern World*, p. 91.

102. J. Scott, *Domination and the Arts of Resistance* (New Haven: Yale University Press, 1990), p. 199, in Becky Beal, 'Disqualifying the Official: an Exploration of Social Resistance Through the Subculture of Skateboarding,' *Sociology of Sport Journal*, vol. 12 no. 3 (1995), p. 261.

103. Lefebvre, *Introduction to Modernity*, p. 359.

104. David Brindle, 'Inner Cities Get Younger as Elderly Turn Wales Grey', *The Guardian* (10 July 1997), p. 10, based on Office for National Statistics, *Regional Trends* (London: Stationery Office, 1997).

105. Lefebvre, *Introduction to Modernity*, pp. 8–9.

106. Joel Patterson, 'Redeye', *TransWorld Skateboarding*, vol. 14 no. 1 (January 1996), p. 104.

107. Lefebvre, *Production of Space*, pp. 381–2.

108. 'Any Variations?', n.p.

109. Judith Williamson, *Consuming Passions* (London: Marion Boyars, 1988), pp. 229–33.

110. Lefebvre, *Everyday Life in the Modern World*, p. 89.

111. Gabriel, 'Rolling', p. 74.

Skateboarding shows that pre-existing uses of space are not the only possible ones, that architecture can instead be productive of things, and consumed by activities, which are not explicitly commodified. Buildings, architecture and urban space, we might propose, should be thought of as places of use, lived experiences, love, objects and concepts all at once. Here, architecture is not a thing, but part of the appropriation of the world, life and desires, space and time.[112] Correspondingly, socio-spatial freedom becomes not the negative, bourgeois right of separation from others, but Marx's 'development of human powers as an end in itself'.[113]

SKATEBOARDING IS NOT A CRIME

Skateboarding is antagonistic towards the urban environment ('a skateboard is the one thing you can use as a weapon in the street that you don't get patted down for'[114]). In redefining space for themselves, skateboarders take over space conceptually as well as physically and so strike at the heart of what everyone else understands by the city; they 'hammer the panic buttons of those uninterested in this pursuit of thrill and achievement'.[115]

> Skating . . . makes you appreciate things on a different level.[116]
>
> Around 37th, there is a quiet garden spot where students can relax in the shade of some flowering trees and enjoy a restful moment. Be sure to do some grinds on the edge of the steps down to this place, or just drop right down them (there are only two). Do a slide or something before you go. They're in a city. Don't let them forget it.[117]

This is the most overt political space produced by skateboarders, a pleasure ground carved out of the city as a kind of continuous reaffirmation of one of the central Lefebvrian slogans of 1968, that beneath the pavement lies the beach.[118]

As Lefebvre notes, hegemony and homogeneity are refused by different groups' rhythms of time and space. Or as one skater saw it, 'some of us, at some point of

112. Henri Lefebvre, *The Explosion: Marxism and the French Revolution*, (New York: Monthly Review, 1969), p. 22.

113. Lefebvre, *Critique of Everyday Life*, pp. 170–1.

114. Craig Stecyk, in Gabriel, 'Rolling', p. 76.

115. Vukovich, 'Handrail', p. 46.

116. Simon, in Tom Hodgkinson, 'Rad, Mad and Dangerous to Know?', *Midweek*, London (18 January 1990), p. 11.

117. Casey, in Mulshine, 'Wild', p. 126.

118. Rob Shields, An English Précis of Henri Lefebvre's 'La Production de l'Espace' (University of Sussex: Urban and Regional Studies Working Paper no. 63, 1988), p. 2.

the song, skip out of our track'.[119] Rhythms are, then, always in negotiation with each other, and polyrhythmy is always a conflict.[120] Yet this is not always a conflict of equal powers. Skateboarders' actions are neither a significant force nor a real threat to established ideologies. Its mode of critique, as noted above, is ironic – weak yet ever defiantly aggressive.

As such, it is important to identify the results of this kind of critical activity. Even in the 1960s skaters met with protests from the California Medical Association and legislative restrictions imposed by city councils.[121] In the 1970s, Los Angeles skaters met with fines of US$250–2,000 for riding in pools and full-pipes,[122] while in Florida and across the US skaters encountered similar reactions.[123]

> Every time someone managed to find a slight slant, the cops would erect a NO SKATEBOARDING SIGN.[124]

City ordinances of the 1970s were mostly intended to reduce collisions between skaters and pedestrians, and were passed in places ranging from Santa Monica and Carmel in California to Zurich and The Hague.[125] Such legal actions, fuelled by innumerable local newspapers articles about the 'hazards of skateboarding',[126] were also common in the UK: Kensington Gardens Broadwalk was resurfaced with gravel to deter skateboarders;[127] 20 Dudley skateboarders faced public prosecution under local by-laws in 1978;[128] and skaters were banned from places as diverse as Blackpool promenade,[129] Cardiff roads,[130] British Rail concourses and (perhaps wisely) platforms,[131] and London's Royal Festival Hall.[132] While *The Times* saw skateboarding as the 'best youthful antidote to urban boredom that has come along

119. Miki Vukovich, introduction to Vallely, interview, p. 92.

120. Lefebvre, *Writings on Cities*, pp. 238–9.

121. Ben J. Davidson, *The Skateboard Book*, (New York: Grosset and Dunlap, 1976), p. 15.

122. Wally Inouye, interview, *SkateBoarder*, vol. 4 no. 3 (October 1977), p. 58; and Jim W., letter, *SkateBoarder*, vol. 4 no. 4 (November 1977), p. 26.

123. 'Who's Hot! Greg Loehr', *SkateBoarder*, vol. 3 no. 1 (October 1976), p. 83.

124. Greg Meisched, *SkateBoarder*, vol. 4 no. 6 (January 1978), p. 105.

125. Peralta, interview, *SkateBoarder*, p. 58; 'An American bro', letter, *SkateBoarder*, vol. 5 no. 12 (July 1979), p. 18; 'Off the Wall', *SkateBoarder*, vol. 6 no. 10 (May 1980), p. 72; and 'World News', *Skateboard!*, no. 2 (October 1977), p. 23.

126. 'UK News', *Skateboard!*, no. 2 (October 1977), p. 14.

127. Editorial, *Skateboard!*, no. 1 (August 1977), p. 11; and 'The Story of Skateboarding', *Skateboard!*, no. 1 (August 1977), p. 20.

128. 'Lip Torque' (March 1978), p. 35.

129. 'UK News' (October 1977), p. 14.

130. 'Lip Torque' (March 1978), p. 35.

131. 'Lip Torque' (June 1978), p. 36.

132. 'Lip Torque' (February 1978), p. 33.

for years',[133] more usually the cry, as in London's *Evening News*,[134] was to ban skateboarding from city streets.[135]

Another area of institutional concern addressed the physical safety of skateboarders themselves.[136] 'Official' advice here addressed a range of issues: equipment standards, 'safe' skateboarding procedures, tuition and first aid. Pseudo-scientific surveys of skateboard equipment were carried out in the UK by the consumer organization Which? and the Royal Society for the Prevention of Accidents (RoSPA).[137] In 1977, the US National Safety Committee and Consumer Product Safety Committee (CPSC) discussed standards for skateboards, skateparks and personal safety equipment.[138] A number of detailed studies of personal safety in skateboarding were carried out in the late 1970s. One such study by the CPSC estimated that 325,000 skateboard-related accidents took place in 1978,[139] while various organizations in the US and the UK, such as RoSPA, tried, without success, first to ban skateboarding altogether[140] and then to institutionalize it through public service announcements, organized training programmes, a national conference and an accident prevention code with the unlikely title of *The Skatcats Quizbook*.[141] Safety films were also produced in the USA for skaters and parents to watch.[142] Even skateboard magazines themselves frequently ran features on these issues, such as the 'Skate Safe' column in *SkateBoarder*, and 'The Skateboarding Safety Code' in

133. Editorial, *The Times* (7 January 1978), p. 13.

134. Editorial, *Evening News* (4 January 1978, closing prices edition), p. 6.

135. Hazel Pennell, *Skateboarding*, (London: GLC Intelligence Unit, London Topics no. 24, 1978), p. 3.

136. S.M. Christian and O. Khan, 'Skateboarding Injuries: a Current Appraisal', *British Journal of Sports Medicine* (August 1980); I.S. Fyfe and A.J. Guion, 'Accident Prevention in Skateboarding', *Journal of Sports Medicine and Physical Fitness* (September 1979); R.W. Hawkins and E.D. Lyne, 'Skateboarding Fractures', *The American Journal of Sports Medicine* (March/April 1981); National Safety Council, *Skateboarding*; Pennell, *Skateboarding*; G.W. Rutherford, J.I. Friedman, S.P. Beale and V.R. Brown, *Hazard Analysis Injuries Associated With Skateboards*, Consumer Product Safety Commission, Directorate for Hazard Identification and Analysis, Division of Program Analysis, Product Code 1333 (Washington: The Directorate, 1978); and Phillip M. Wishon and Marcia L. Oreskovich, 'Bicycles, Roller Skates and Skateboards: Safety Promotion and Accident Prevention,' *Children Today*, vol. 15 no. 3 (May–June 1986), pp. 73–6.

137. 'Skateboards', *Which?* (December 1977), p. 643; and Royal Society for the Prevention of Accidents, 'The Hidden Dangers' (RoSPA/Fulmer Research Institute: December 1977), in Pennell, *Skateboarding*, p. 3.

138. Editorial, *SkateBoarder*, vol. 3 no. 6 (July 1977), p. 20.

139. National Safety Council, *Skateboarding*, p. 2.

140. 'Skateboarding and Safety', *Skateboard!*, no. 1 (August 1977), p. 53; and 'UK News' (October 1977), p. 14.

141. Pennell, *Skateboarding*, pp. 2–3; and Wishon and Oreskovich, 'Bicycles, Roller Skates and Skateboards', p. 15.

142. Pennell, *Skateboarding*, p. 3.

Skateboard!;[143] while professional skateboarders often contributed to safety clinics in the 1970s.[144]

This did not, however, stop groups such as the 'Americans for Democratic Action' calling for a complete skateboarding ban and the CPSC from considering similar legislation.[145] Skateboards were banned entirely in Norway in 1979, and skaters were forced to smuggle boards across the border and to skate in surveillance-free areas.[146] This regulation was relaxed by 1985,[147] but street skating was not made legal until the early 1990s.[148]

Such concerns have now died away, perhaps from the realization that skateboarding although physically robust is not inherently life-threatening;[149] common skatepark injuries typically concerned only minor sprains and breaks to the wrist.[150] Exceptions tended to occur when skaters collided with cars[151] or skated on such inappropriate areas as car park roofs.[152]

Instead, the intensification of skateboarding in public streets has led to a more pervasive form of repression. Some US cities such as San Samon and San Diego in California placed curfews or banned skateboarding in public areas,[153] while Dogtown skaters in Venice Beach had to fight off a ban in 1989.[154] 'Skateboard ticket' fines for US$75 were being handed out by Huntingdon Beach police in 1995.[155]

143. 'The Skateboarding Safety Code', *Skateboard!*, no. 1 (August 1977), p. 53.

144. Peralta, interview, *SkateBoarder*, p. 58; 'Off the Wall', *SkateBoarder*, vol. 3 no. 2 (December 1976), p. 123; Waldo Autry, interview, *SkateBoarder*, vol. 4 no. 1 (August 1977), p. 114; and Brian Gillogly, 'The Pepsi Team', *SkateBoarder*, vol. 4 no. 3 (October 1977), pp. 84–93.

145. Sally Anne Miller, guest editorial, *SkateBoarder*, vol. 5 no. 6 (January 1979), p. 40. See also Susan King (Chairperson, Consumer Product Safety Commission), interview, *US News and World Report* (2 October 1978).

146. Stein Thue, letter, *SkateBoarder*, vol. 6 no. 5 (December 1979), pp. 15–17.

147. 'Off the Wall', *SkateBoarder's Action Now*, vol. 7 no. 6 (January 1981), p. 18; Leroy Noll, 'What am I Doing Here?', *Thrasher*, vol. 5 no. 10 (October 1985), p. 37; and *Forskrift om Rullebrett* (Oslo: Miljøverndepartementet, 3 May 1989).

148. 'Oslo Punk Ramp', *Skateboard!* (second series), no. 39 (January 1990), p. 42. See also Thomas Knudsen/*Strictly Underground Skateboard Magazine* (Norway), letter, *Cake Fat*, no. 2 (n.d., c. 1996), n.p.

149. Wishon and Oreskovich, 'Bicycles, Roller Skates and Skateboards', p. 14.

150. Curtis Hesselgrave, 'Skate Safe: Notes on Protecting Your Wrists', *SkateBoarder*, vol. 5 no. 10 (May 1979), p. 28.

151. Laura Thornhill and Ellen Oneal, interview, *Skateboard!*, no. 2 (October 1977), p. 25; Barry Walsh, interview, *Skateboard Scene*, vol. 1 no. 1 (n.d, c. November/December 1977), p. 30; and 'Mandatory Information', *TransWorld Skateboarding*, vol. 13 no. 5 (May 1995), p. 38.

152. Pennell, *Skateboarding*, p. 2.

153. 'Skater's Edge', *Thrasher*, vol. 7 no. 10 (October 1987), p. 37; and 'On Board', *Thrasher*, vol. 9 no. 5 (May 1989), p. 124.

154. 'Venice Skaters Rolling to a Halt', *Outlook Mail* (Los Angeles), vol. 8 no. 7 (24 May 1989), p. 1.

155. Luke McKirdy, interview, *Sidewalk Surfer*, no. 2 (November/December 1995), n.p.

Other such legislation was passed in Arizona,[156] Chicago[157] Denver,[158] Fort Worth,[159] Philadelphia,[160] Portland,[161] Sacramento,[162] San Francisco,[163] Santa Cruz,[164] Savannah[165] and elsewhere across the US.[166] In the UK, city councils including Chelmsford,[167] Birmingham,[168] Manchester,[169] Leeds[170] and Plymouth[171] banned skateboarding from parks and promenades. In a particularly unenlightened piece of petty-mindedness on the part of its burghers, on 23 December 1996 Derby used by-laws to institute a skateboard no-go area in a whole sector of its city centre.[172] While some parts of the world, notably Tasmania, Brisbane and Melbourne have recently begun to actively encourage skateboarding in certain parts of the city,[173] the more general pattern of anti-skate legislation has been repeated worldwide, whether in Australia,[174] Sweden[175] the Netherlands,[176] Brazil,[177] Canada[178] and so on. The overall effect has been to embed the threat of arrest, fines and even imprisonment within skateboarding's everyday activity (8.5).

Abstract space is more often about prohibitions than stimulation (except concerning consumption),[179] and this often involves issues of time. While the UK Labour

156. Skaters for the American Way, letter, *Thrasher*, vol. 8 no. 7 (July 1988), p. 14.

157. Jesse Neuhaus, 'Chicago', *Big Brother*, no. 28 (September 1997), pp. 49–50.

158. Julian Kates, letter, *Thrasher*, vol. 4 no. 11 (November 1984), p. 4.

159. Kevin Ogloughlin, letter, *Slap*, vol. 6 no. 1 (January 1997), p. 16.

160. Arch and Nick, letter, *TransWorld Skateboarding*, vol. 6 no. 1 (February 1988), p. 12; and 'Mandatory Information' (May 1995), p. 38.

161. Paul Fujita, 'Burnside', *TransWorld Skateboarding*, vol. 15 no. 11 (November 1997), p. 142.

162. Jerry Mander, 'Sacto Locals', *TransWorld Skateboarding*, vol. 9 no. 10 (October 1991), p. 84.

163. Lowboy, 'Skate and Destroy, or Multiple Choices (Something to Offend Everyone)', *Thrasher*, vol. 2 no. 11 (December 1982), p. 27; and 'Trash', *Thrasher*, vol. 6 no. 5 (May 1986), p. 80.

164. Tony Roberts, 'Santa Cruz', *Thrasher*, vol. 8 no. 7 (July 1988), p. 82.

165. Bonnie and Clyde, 'Savannah Slamma II', *Thrasher*, vol. 8 no. 7 (July 1988), p. 46.

166. 'News: Ban on City Skating?', *Skateboard!* (second series), no. 40 (February/March 1990), p. 4.

167. Siân Liz Evans, 'Young, Gifted and Board Stupid', *The Big Issue* (London), no. 126 (17–23 April 1995), p. 20; and Frederick Muir, 'On a Roll', *Los Angeles Times* (31 May 1989), pp. 1 and 8.

168. 'Insight', *Sidewalk Surfer*, no. 13 (January/February 1997), n.p.; Sarah Nelson, 'Skateboarding is Not a Crime', *Asylum*, no. 4 (n.d., *c.* February 1997), n.p.; and David Bell, 'City's War on Skate Menace', *Evening Mail*, Birmingham (Saturday 26 October 1996), p. 1.

169. *Project* (accessed 3 August 1997).

170. Jamie Wilson, 'Skaters Face Ban From City Centres', *The Guardian* (6 December 1997), p. 6.

171. 'Plymouth Double-Take', *Skateboard!*, no. 16 (December 1978), p. 18.

172. *Backside*, no. 4 (n.d.), n.p.

173. Stratford, 'Feral Skateboarding'.

174. 'News', *Skatin' Life* (March/April 1989), pp. 26–7.

175. *Cow Pat*, no. 3 (1995), n.p.

176. John P. Dessing, letter, *Slap*, vol. 6 no. 9 (September 1997), n.p.

177. 'Skate não é Crime', *Overall*, no. 10 (June/July 1989), p. 68.

178. Jane O'Hara, 'Trouble in Paradise', *Maclean's*, vol. 100 no. 14 (6 April 1987), p. 48; and Tom Oho, letter, *TransWorld Skateboarding*, vol. 15 no. 11 (November 1997), p. 25.

179. Lefebvre, *Production of Space*, p. 319.

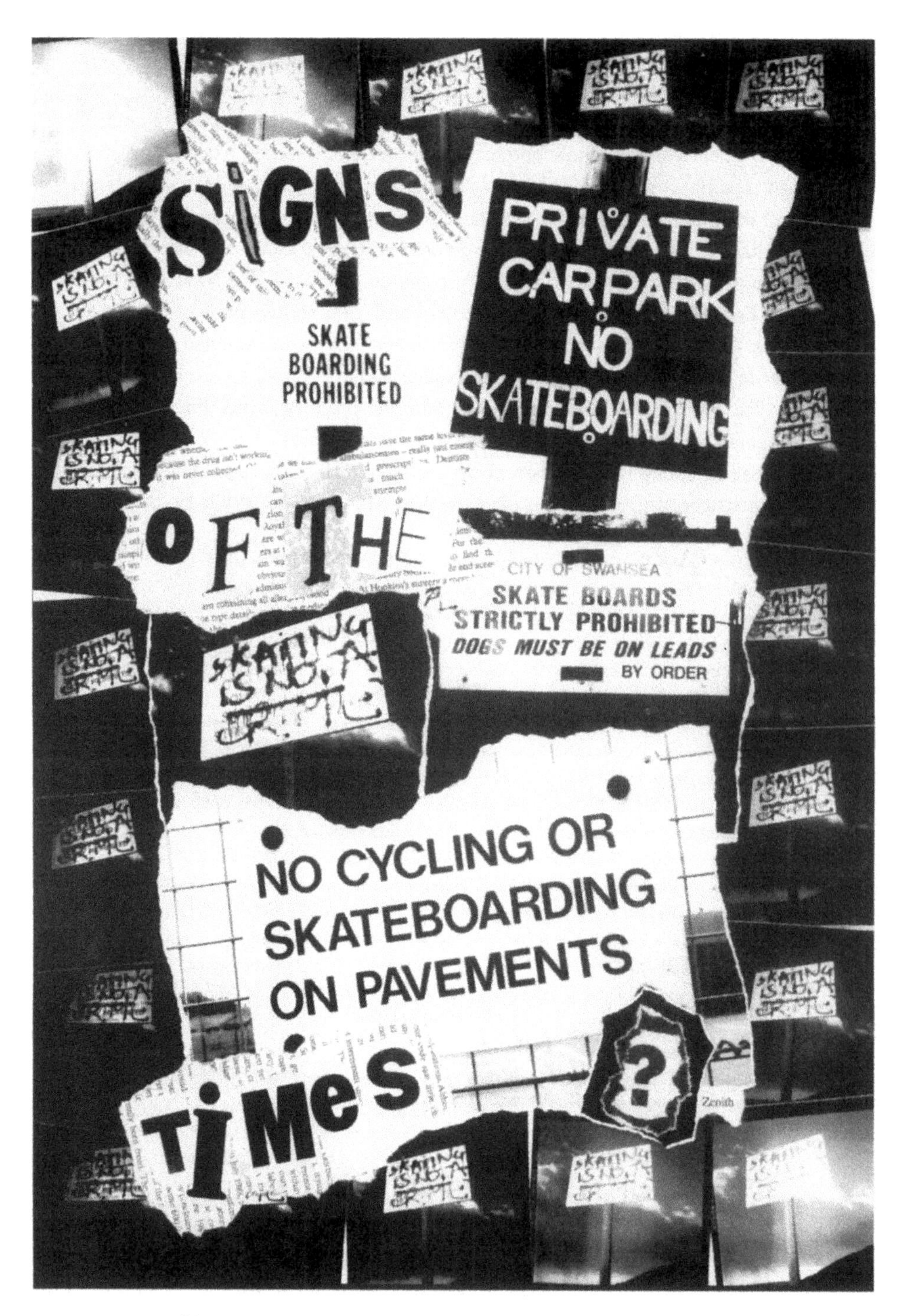

8.5 Signs of the times: no skateboarding (1990).

Party and police forces consider imposing curfews for children,[180] for many skateboarders this has long been a reality; San Francisco City and County, for example, banned skateboarding from all roads and sidewalks during night-time hours.[181] Skateboarding, contradictorily, is at once 'criminalized' as a night-time activity (as US President George Bush remarked of skateboarders, 'just thank God they don't have guns'[182]) and represented as 'child's play' at other times. Even usually thoughtful newspapers such as the *Washington Post* have cited skateboarding as an irresponsible and vandalous activity to be banned from city streets.[183]

In more spatial terms, particularly in those areas hovering between private and public domains, skateboarders have encountered a politics of space similar to the experiences of the homeless. Like the homeless, skateboarders occupy urban space without engaging in economic activity of interiors, to the annoyance of building owners and managers.

> The local business leaders do not want the kids interfering with their customers. Kids are only OK when they are spending money.[184]

As a result, urban managers have declared skaters as trespassers, or cited the marks skateboarding causes as proof of criminal damage: 'they smash up all the new kerbs and scratch all the banisters'.[185] Skaters are also arrested for waxing curbs and other street architecture.[186] Even private citizens seem to delight in 'confiscating' skateboards – an action which legally is theft[187] – while skate magazines have since the late 1980s detailed a litany of aggressive actions by skater-phobic police officers and neighbourhood residents. To give one specific example, at the prestigious Liverpool Street and Broadgate office development in London's City area, skateboarders who frequented the stone benches on Bishopsgate, and more occasionally the street furniture deeper within its pseudo-public spaces, chipped away edges and

180. Alan Travis and Martin Wainwright, 'Labour "Under-10s Curfew" Plan Ignites Row', *The Guardian* (3 June 1996), p. 3; Editorial, 'A Curfew on Commonsense: Jack Straw's Rightward Lurch', *The Guardian* (3 June 1996), p. 10; and John Arlidge, 'Police Propose Curfew on Town's Youngsters', *The Guardian* (4 October 1997), p. 6.

181. 'Trash', *Thrasher*, vol. 6 no. 5 (May 1986), p. 80.

182. 'Trash', *Thrasher*, vol. 12 no. 3 (March 1992), p. 74.

183. Diane de Bernardo, 'Monumental Indifference: No One Is Stopping Skateboarders From Riding Roughshod Over Our Town', *Washington Post* (3 December 1995), in 'Mandatory Information', *TransWorld Skateboarding*, vol. 14 no. 5 (May 1996), p. 44.

184. Frank Hamlin, 'Safety in Downtown Santa Rosa', *Project* (accessed 3 August 1997).

185. Parodied in Fraser Hamilton, 'All About High Wycombe (and a Jolly Nice Council)', *R.A.D.*, no. 103 (December 1991), p. 19.

186. 'Mandatory Information' (May 1995), p. 38.

187. Steve Kane, 'Jersey', *Skateboard!* (second series), no. 39 (January 1990), p. 27; and Phraeza, 'Fiction?', *Sidewalk Surfer*, no. 15 (April 1997), n.p.

left coloured streaks.[188] The City Corporation, its police force and private security forces consequently began systematic video surveillance of skateboarders, and implemented a UK£30 fine. Skaters were removed from the site, or prosecuted using legislation dating from 1839.[189]

> With sparks flying and the grinding sound of truck against marble echoing throughout the night sky, we are inevitably clocked by the notoriously petty Liverpool Street security brigade.[190]

Another, 1990 by-law banned skateboarders from all City walkways, with a UK£20 fine.[191]

A different response by urban managers has been similar to their actions against the homeless. Where the homeless are ejected from business and retail areas by such measures as curved bus benches, window-ledge spikes and doorway sprinkler systems,[192] so skaters encounter rough-textured surfaces,[193] spikes and bumps added to handrails, blocks of concrete placed at the foot of banks, chains across ditches and steps, and new, unridable surfaces such as gravel and sand. Leicester Council spent UK£10,000 making the banks around its Crown Court unskateable,[194] while the Broadgate managers added vertical dividers to the Bishopsgate benches (a favourite place for board-slides) in the summer of 1997 (8.6).[195] In Sydney, Chifely Square was rendered unskateable by urban managers who flattened the various benches and other pieces of street furniture, and added raised anti-skate screws to their upper surfaces.[196] By the year 2000, similar actions and devices had been much copied, and became commonplace in urban squares and building frontages worldwide.

There is an increasing tendency for the state and pseudo-official groups to confront spatialized forms of social protest, ranging from the 'zero tolerance' of the UK Labour Party toward graffiti artists,[197] mass arrests made at 'Reclaim the Streets'

188. Tim Hood, 'Wednesday July 30th 1997', *Sidewalk Surfer*, no. 21 (October/November 1997), n.p.

189. City police officer, conversation, Bishopsgate, London (22 June 1997).

190. Hood, 'Wednesday'.

191. 'News: Ban on City Skating?', p. 4; and 'We Are Illegal', *Sidewalk Surfer*, no. 15 (April 1997), n.p.

192. Mark Cole, 'Making a Point with Spikes and Studs', *The Independent* (12 October 1994), p. 26; Mike Davis, *City of Quartz* (London: Verso: 1990), pp. 223–63; and Borden, 'Thick Edge', pp. 84–7.

193. 'Trash', *Thrasher*, vol. 9 no. 1 (January 1989), p. 123.

194. Louise Fyfe, 'Street Legal?', *Sport and Leisure* (Sports Council) (May–June 1989), p. 33; and 'Lame Leicester', *R.A.D.*, no. 75 (May 1989), p. 5.

195. Observed (September 1997).

196. Kelvin Ho, 'Skateboarding: an Interpretation of Space in the Olympic City', *Architectural History and Theory* (1999).

197. Catherine Bennett, 'Why the Writing's On the Wall for Graf Art', *The Guardian* (3 July 1996), p. 15.

8.6 Benches modified with anti-skateboarder dividers at the Broadgate office development, Bishopsgate frontage, London (1997). (Photograph Iain Borden)

event-parties,[198] 'farm watch' schemes set up in the countryside to prevent raves,[199] and direct action taken against road protesters.[200] In Germany, the annual 'Chaos Days' anarcho-punk festival held in Hanover is now controlled by police out-numbering punks by six to one.[201] Skateboarding does not mount the kind of explicit political critique of many of these groups, nor does it provoke much social disruption. But it threatens nonetheless because it is neither explicit protest nor quiet conformism, game nor sport, public nor private activity, adult nor childish and, above all, precisely because it is a spatially and temporally *diffused* and *dispersed* activity. Depite the pervasiveness of anti-skate measures, the repression of skateboarding is rarely

198. Alex Bellos and Duncan Campbell, 'Violence at Dockers' Demo', *International Guardian* (14 April 1997), p. 4; John Vidal and Alex Bellos, 'Trees Planted in Fast Lane at Road Protestors' Party', *The Guardian* (15 July 1996), p. 7; and John Vidal and Alex Bellos, 'Protest Lobbies Unite to Guard Rights', *The Guardian* (27 August 1996), p. 5.

199. 'Rave Watch', *The Guardian*, 'Society' section (16 October 1996), p. 1.

200. John Vidal, 'Gone to Ground', *The Guardian*, 'Weekend' section (22 February 1997), pp. 30, 31, 33, 35 and 37.

201. Denis Staunton, 'Punks on Parade', *The Guardian* (29 July 1996), p. 16.

systematic, certainly when compared to national laws against serious crimes. But it does point towards a heightening confrontation between counter-culture and hegemonic social practices, whether in London:

> You always get grief from security guards, the police and drunk businessmen.[202]

Or small-town America:

> Much of America is small towns where there is little or no crime . . . Why not go down the street and find some skaters making some noise and drag them downtown . . . Naturally we were the scapegoats of the whole town. Every crime or act of vandalism was blamed on us.[203]

The consequence has been that from the mid-1990s onward skateboarding has been ever-increasingly repressed through a pervasive tightening of geographically-dispersed localized conventions, laws and reactions.

> Hardly a session goes by these days without someone hurling threats of bye-laws, cops and/or fines in our faces. Gone are the days when complaints about skateboarders were met with uncomprehending indifference from the relevant authorities.[204]

Or as one skater commented after having moved to central London:

> I hadn't counted on being moved on by the police every minute; had not expected to encounter so many skater-hating pedestrians and had not even begun to imagine that such ignorant gorillas could be employed as security guards at the new office complexes that served as our work hours playground.[205]

But treating skateboarding as a crime verges on the ludicrous, and such accusations 'are founded on nothing and soon fall apart under cross examination'.[206] Consider the comparison with automobiles.

> Skateboard made of wood, metal and plastic, costs about £100, runs on leg power; causes chips and scratches on bits of stone and metal. Car, costs a fortune, runs on poisonous shit, pollutes the air and water, fills the city with 'smog', causes the death of hundreds of thousands of people every year. Mmmm?

202. Piers Woodford, in Evans, 'Young', p. 19. See also Hoad, 'Wednesday'.
203. 'Gutter Talk', *Thrasher*, vol. 12 no. 3 (March 1992), pp. 89 and 92.
204. 'We Are Illegal'.
205. Phraeza, 'Fiction?'
206. 'We Are Illegal'.

> And yet despite all this cars are o.k. but skateboards are evil, objects of vandalism, a dangerous menace that *must be* stopped.[207]

One US skateboard company made similar comparisons, this time with more serious crimes.

> We live in a society where thieves, rapists and murderers enjoy the luxury of wandering the streets clueless, while skaters are constantly bombarded with signs, harassment and just about every type of brainwashing known to man.[208]

Considered this way, skateboarding can only be rendered criminal through the most petty-minded of laws. This is largely because skateboarding is aimed at the appropriation – and not domination – of time and space, and so cannot be readily represented as a truly illegal activity. Nonetheless, because skaters care little of ownership, they do *implicitly* oppose this capitalist principle. 'All space is public space'.[209] Thus although skateboarding confronts neither the *causes* nor the *conditions* of zero degree architecture, they do simply deny its implicit logic, and hence its *symbolic* repression.[210] Legislature directed at skateboarding is perhaps then not so much concerned with a crime as finding ever new ways for the conventionalized operations of the society to be legitimized.[211] According to Derby's City Centre Manager, the main reasoning for banning skateboards from the town centre, beside restricting (minor) damage to benches, was 'so that councillors wouldn't have to look out of their windows and see . . . untidy people skating'.[212] 'Disorder' in the form of 'untidiness' rather than any real crime is then what is being confronted here; in such circumstances skateboarding is one of those 'false crimes' used to help legitimize conventional orders and power,[213] and is consequently legislated against to help validate the business- and commodity-oriented city. This much is also evident when one considers that the only places in San Francisco where skateboarding was *entirely* banned, notably, were its business districts and roads.[214]

Furthermore, activities such as skateboarding allow the State to divert attention from real problems and to create room for new actions.[215] The rave parties and travellers in 1990s Britain thus resulted in the Conservative government's *Criminal*

207. Ben Powell, 'The Number One Four Wheeler', *Sidewalk Surfer*, no. 9 (August 1996), n.p.
208. Santa Monica Airlines, advertisement, *Thrasher*, vol. 8 no. 3 (March 1988), p. 7.
209. 'We Are Illegal'.
210. Lefebvre, *Explosion*, p. 105.
211. Karl Marx, 'A History of Economic Theories', in Karl Marx, *Selected Writings*, Tom Bottomore and M. Rubel (eds) (Harmondsworth: Penguin, 1956), pp. 167–8, in Lefebvre, *Introduction to Modernity*, p. 23.
212. Reported in Saul Taylor, e-mail (29 March 1999).
213. Lefebvre, *Introduction to Modernity*, p. 23.
214. 'Trash' *Thrasher*, vol. 6 no. 5 (May 1986), p. 80.
215. Lefebvre, *Explosion*, p. 76.

8.7 'Skateboarding is Not a Crime'. Powell-Peralta advertisement in *Thrasher* magazine (1987).

Justice Act, through which it gained a range of powers previously denied to it and entirely out-of-scale with the problem at hand.

On this level, the conflict between skateboarding and hegemonic practices is representational. It is telling here that the most *co-ordinated* resistance on the part of skateboarding to the rest of society has come not from spatial contestations but in such campaigns as those to 'Stop Skate Harassment'[216] or assert that 'Skateboarding Is Not a Crime' (8.7). This latter programme, begun in late 1987, used stickers in particular, plastered over every available public surface. Similar challenges to the rationality of banning skateboarding can be seen in a myriad of other tactics, such as the 'Skateboarding Allowed' stencils applied to the street architecture of Pier 7 in San Francisco.[217]

Ultimately, being banned from the public domain becomes simply another obstacle to be overcome, and so even adds to the anarchist tradition of skateboarding.

> I'm one of the many skaters in the world and I, for one, like skate harassment. Have you ever thought of the rush you get kicking down the street from some raving shop owner, or even better, the police?[218]

> They can kick us out, but we don't care, we'll be back. In the meantime, we'll just go on to the next spot and keep breaking it down.[219]

> For all you hopeful law enforcers out there, YOU'LL NEVER GET US OFF THE STREETS![220]

> The point is f**ck 'em all, they can't touch us now.[221]

216. *Thrasher*, 1982 passim.
217. 'Trash', *Thrasher*, vol. 16 no. 11 (November 1996), p. 131.
218. Homey, letter, *Thrasher*, vol. 9 no. 6 (June 1989), p. 8.
219. Jake Phelps, 'Damage Done', *Thrasher*, vol. 12 no. 5 (May 1992), p. 37.
220. Meg, 'Get Off the Air!!', *Slap*, vol. 6 no. 9 (September 1997), p. 50.
221. Powell, 'Not a Toy'.

8.8 'Movement without words'. Skateboarder: Matt Mumford (1995).

Legislation and authority are there to be resisted, for 'reinterpretation and often downright subversion of such regulation is the skateboarder's creed'.[222] In this respect, skateboarders are part of a long process in the history of cities, a fight by the unempowered and disenfranchised for a distinctive social space of their own. In doing so, they bring time, space and social being together through a performative confrontation of the body and board with the architectural surface; theirs is 'not only the space of "no", it is also the space of the body, and the space of "yes", of the affirmation of life'[223] (8.8).

> This is just a small dream. A dream of endless pure creation. A movement without words.[224]

222. Vukovich, 'Handrail', p. 46.
223. Lefebvre, *Production of Space*, p. 201.
224. 'That Thing', *R.A.D.*, no. 75 (May 1989), p. 45.

Chapter 9
Closure and Aperture

I began this book with the aim of identifying 'a new kind of architectural history, one with new objects, methods and questions'. This concluding section therefore addresses such concerns by way of a summary of what has gone before, giving a sense of closure to the book. I then turn to give a few intimations, identifying new directions and tendencies, for which no specific prescriptions can be given here. Future work, future architectural histories, future time-spaces alone will move things on once again.

SKATEBOARDING, SPACE AND THE CITY

Throughout this book, the theoretical ideas of Henri Lefebvre have been ever-present, pointing the way towards new conceptions of space, representation, experience, epistemology, political objectives, architecture and the urban realm, time, everyday life, the human subject and the body, rhythms and actions.

Chapter Two *Devices* began the extension of this kind of thinking into a study of a specific urban practice: skateboarding. While the skateboard itself is a relatively basic piece of technology, its deployment within the space of the city yields some significant social, spatial and conceptual effects. Chapter Three *Found Space* disclosed how even at its outset skateboarding dissolved the physicality of the modern city into an imaginative re-enaction of another space, the skateboarder's micro-experience of the found terrain causing a new space-production to occur. At a macro scale, the city was surveyed for specific kinds of space – primarily banks, ditches, pools and pipes – in order to locate and appropriate such spaces for as long a time as possible, thus colonizing them as localized territories of competition and rivalry. By implication, the city too was redefined from a place of suburban homogeneity and comfort to that of confrontation and conflict. Yet skateboarders ultimately had little control over such processes, their temporal tactics falling foul of the legalized forms of property ownership.

Chapter Four *Constructed Space* therefore began by showing how skateboarders from the mid-1970s onward enjoyed the benefits of their own legalized spaces. A rapid construction of skateparks took place, with over 190 constructed in the US and about half that figure in the UK, beside numerous other examples worldwide. Such skateparks initially copied surf wave forms and pipes, and then backyard pools, before quickly creating new terrains which while based on pools were designed primarily with skateboarders' movements in mind. During the 1980s, wooden-based ramp and half-pipe constructions came to the fore, either as stand-alone elements or as the basis for new skateparks, many of which were indoor facilities.

The spatial nature of these skateparks is not best understood, however, solely through conventional architectural historical notions of production such as design, construction, authorship, intention and evolution, but also through the skateboarder's engagement with these terrains. Chapter Five *Body Space* shows how in skateparks and on ramps skaters developed an ever more complex series of technical moves, each with a precise consideration of time, space and speed. Space here is a production outward from the skater's body, created in relation to genetic properties of its symmetries and orientation. However, this is not the only space production involved. The skateboard itself is another focus, at once external to and absorbed within the dynamism of the skater's move, a mediation and tool necessary to the skater's relation to the terrain underfoot. And, just as importantly, architecture is questioned by the skater for its ability to project space in relation to the move. Verticals, curves, symmetries, projections, transitions and so forth are brought to life, no longer static objects or formal qualities but now propulsive elements, the skater becoming like the metal ball propelled between the accelerative cushions, roundels and flippers of a pinball machine. All takes this place in the course of an event, the movement of the skater; as a result all three projectors of space – body, tool, architecture – are erased and reproduced. This is what I term 'super-architectural space', space that lies beyond the space of subject, tool or terrain, and which is compositionally quite distinct from the ordered hierarchies of architecture-as-object, architecture-as-drawing or architecture-as-idea; it is a rhythmical procedure, continually repeated yet forever new, like the waves of the sea, the playing of music or declamation of poetry.

The process by which this occurs is not solely phenomenal, however, and the role of the image is also significant. While photography, film and video have always been important to the communication of skateboarding, it is in the lived experience of skateboarding that the full power of these media comes to the fore. The skateboarders' move is a reperformance of the imagery that they see in magazines and videos, and hence is a unit of exchange between each other. In performing the move, skaters are therefore at once undertaking a directly experienced action while also projecting an image of themselves as seen by both themselves and by others. The skater's move is at once action, image and social relation, and is also at once a local and globally dispersed phenomenon. Similarly, particular elements within a skatepark take on a mediated aura, both through imagery of such elements shown in magazines and videos and through reputation born from painful encounters.

Chapter Six *Subculture* pursued a direction intimated at in Chapter Five: skaters' relations with themselves and with others. In particular, skateboarding is seen here to be an oppositional subculture, by which skaters constitute a complete way of life for themselves. Skaters are shown to be predominantly young men in their teens and early twenties, with broadly accommodating dispositions toward skaters of different classes and ethnicity. Gender relations are, however, more problematic, with female skaters usually discouraged by the forces of convention, including within skateboarding those of sexist objectification. Similarly, homophobic attitudes have also been increasingly evident in the 1990s – one way in which skaters try to fabricate a homosocial masculinity between each other. In terms of relations with the external world, skateboard subculture uses a range of differing graphics, words and ideologies to create a generalized rejection of this external world, particularly aspects of paid work and the family.

Ultimately, however, skateboarding takes its meanings not from its equipment or surfaces but from its actions. Chapter Seven *Urban Compositions* therefore turns to consider the emergence of streetstyle skating in the 1980s and 1990s. Responding to the possibilities of everyday architecture, the new street skateboarding appropriates any element in the urban landscape, seeking to use the meaningless, zero degree modernism of the new town and city centre as places to assert new meanings and actions. Skateboarders create new edits of the city, rethinking architecture as a set of discrete features and elements, and recomposing it through new speeds, spaces and times during their run through the city. Furthermore, the body is also recomposed in the process, thus resisting the intense scopic determinations of modernist space through a reassertion of touch, hearing, adrenalin, rhythms, balance, movement and highly detailed focus.

Once again, this also involves a different compositional process to that of architecture as conventionally considered. Here, the composition is not that of writing, drawing or indeed any form of codified theorization, but the performative act of skateboarding itself. The edit and mapping of architecture and the city on the part of the skater produces few visual codifications, but is instead a situated and 'spoken' record, continually relived in time as well as space.

Unlike, however, the super-architectural space of 1970s skateboarding in skateparks, this is an action which takes place in public, in the semi-official, semi-private zone of city streets, and hence has an entirely different social character. Chapter Eight *Performing the City* considers some of the subcultural attitudes identified in the previous chapter in this urban context, thus disclosing that skateboarding's marks, scratches and other material manifestations are only the traces of much deeper critique of contemporary urban life. Embedded in the actions of skateboarders are reconceptualizations of architecture as reproducible micro-spaces rather than produced *grands projets*; production not as the production of things but of play, desires and actions; the purpose of space as use rather than exchange; richness as social wealth rather than ownership; place as composed of time and speed as well as a quantity of space; and the city as interrogator rather than determinant of the self (9.1).

9.1 Skateboarding, space and the city. Skateboarder: Joe Pino, Coronado Island (1996). (Photograph Grant Brittain)

Lastly, Chapter Eight also shows some of the social responses to this kind of skateboarding. Despite its lack of real criminal activity, skateboarding has become increasingly repressed and legislated against, not by national or federal laws but by a series of local reactions aimed at suppressing that which is different (and misunderstood). Skateboarding also becomes a way of increasing local powers, an excuse rather than a cause. Conversely, such laws add to the anarchic character of skateboarding, part of its continual dependence on, as well as struggle against, the modern city.

ARCHITECTURE AND APPROPRIATION

The theorized history of skateboarding undertaken here obviously, as with any historical writing, has its limitations. There has been, for example, comparatively little consideration of the skateboarding industry or of the economics of skatepark construction and demolition. Similarly, there have been few comparisons between skateboarding and other forms of spatial practice, and none between skateparks and other forms of leisure space such as football stadia or swimming pools. Instead, the focus has been on the practice of skateboarding as a form of experience of architecture, and, consequently, on issues pertinent to this intersection of a particular practice and architectural forms.

As such, following a kind of Lefebvrian methodology and history hinted at above, we can begin to delineate a kind of architectural history which does not focus on things, effects, production, authorship or exchange but upon process, possibilities, reproduction, performance and use. Space, time and social being must be considered equally, with particular regard to political goals, everyday life, the human subject, the body and its various actions. The particular study of skateboarding further shows how this might involve the consideration of not only built spaces but also tools, everyday spaces, imaginative experiences, city mapping, body moves, compositional processes, social relations, images both visual and lived, social identities and rejections, graphically presented designs and surfaces, textual discourses, urban terrains, implicit or performative critiques, institutional responses and subcultural re-responses.

To undertake further architectural historical work in this vein could then be a repetition of this kind of study, looking for these kinds of thing in a different yet similar historical arena: the history of urban cycling, running and driving, or of scaffolding, couriering and radio broadcasting, or of countless other urban spatial practices, could all be subjected to such an analysis. However, such a study would, inevitably, not be the same, either in its methodology or in its evidential conclusion. I shall end here by drawing out just a few of the underlying themes in this study which seem to me be already 'not the same', which are already indicative of unresolved problems and hence future directions for historical work. They range from the practical to the thematic to the epistemological.

To begin with the most practical issue, it seems to me that for this kind of history to succeed, it is likely that traditional techniques of observation may not be sufficient, for, like texts, 'no camera, no image or sequence of images can show these rhythms'.[1] This then is partly a matter of analysis and partly a matter of communication, for the study of the performative and everyday may require an integrative consideration of sound, vision, movement and even touch and smell to convey something of the experiential nature of these processes. History as film, history as music, history as media-montage might all be possible responses. On another practical note, this book has relied heavily on magazines for its archive, and thus certain practices would not be as easily researched by this procedure – illegal activities such as drug-smuggling would be particularly resistant to such analysis.

More conceptually, the main ground that this theoretized history of skateboarding opens up seems to me to be the question of how to construct a materialist history of the experience of architecture. In particular, how can one relate the specific phenomenal procedures by which people engage with the built world to the ideological and material processes which condition them? In particular, is there a correlation between walking, talking, breathing, listening and so forth in the same way that has begun to be understood for vision and the gaze? It may well be, then, that further theoretical study of the encounter and debate between existentialism, phenomenology and Marxism in the 1950s would be a fruitful arena of further theoretical study. How might, for example, we relate Merleau-Ponty's assertions that the body 'contributes more than it receives', and that 'movement, touch, vision' are all part of the 'paradox of expression',[2] to the strictures and demands of the modern, capitalist city?

Rather than the repetition of this kind of study onto new activities, I would suggest here that the way to progress such a materialist history of experience of architecture is by looking at the more fundamental processes by which architecture is engaged. This would mean thinking about *elemental modes* rather than activities or functions, and different kinds of *elemental spaces* rather than the bounded spaces of buildings, cities or countries. By elemental spaces I am thinking of things such as the boundaries, doors, windows, bridges, regions and so on – anything that might have a typologiocal or generic form. By elemental modes I am thinking of things such as conditions of the body, direction, or attitude to space.

Such things on their own would, of course, not be enough – the task would be to combine these kinds of phenomenological and social concern with the particular

1. Henri Lefebvre, *Writings on Cities*, (Oxford: Blackwell, 1996), p. 227.

2. Maurice Merleau-Ponty, *The Visible and the Invisible* (Evanston: Northwestern University Press, 1968), p. 144.

economic, material, ideological, cultural and social conditions of specific space-times and peoples. In particular, bearing in mind a Lefebvrian sensibility to always search for differential space, it seems that we are in need of such a consideration in the context of a theory and history of *appropriation*. What does it mean to adopt, take over, colonize, emulate, repeat, work within, work against, reimagine, retemporalize, reject, edit and recompose the spaces of the city and its architecture? How can differential space be sought in the land and epoch of the commodified, the abstract, the homogenized, the reductive and the powerful? Only here, I suggest, will a properly materialist history of the experience of architecture emerge.

Bibliography

GENERAL

John Allen and Michael Pryke, 'The Production of Service Space', *Environment and Planning D: Society and Space*, vol. 12 (1994), pp. 453–75.

Vered Amit-Talai and Helena Wulff (eds), *Youth Cultures: a Cross-Cultural Perspective* (London: Routledge, 1995).

Libero Andreotti and Xavier Costa (eds), *Situacionistas, Arte, Política, Urbanisme/ Situationists, Art, Politics, Urbanism* (Barcelona, Museu d'Art Contemporani de Barcelona, 1996).

Libero Andreotti and Xavier Costa (eds), *Theory of the Dérive and other Situationist Writings on the City* (Barcelona, Museu d'Art Contemporani de Barcelona, 1996).

Marc Augé, *Non-Places: Introduction to an Anthropology of Supermodernity* (London: Verso, 1995).

Ira J. Bach (ed.), *Chicago's Famous Buildings* (Chicago: University of Chicago Press, 3rd edn, 1980).

John Bale, *Sport, Space and the City* (London: Routledge, 1993).

Roland Barthes, *Writing Degree Zero* (London: Cape, 1967).

David Bell and Gill Valentine (eds), *Mapping Desire: Geographies of Sexuality* (London: Routledge, 1995).

Alex Bellos and Duncan Campbell, 'Violence at Dockers' Demo', *International Guardian* (14 April 1997), p. 4.

Walter Benjamin, *Charles Baudelaire: a Lyric Poet in the Era of High Capitalism* (London: Verso, 1985).

Walter Benjamin, *Illuminations* (New York: Schocken Books, 1969).

Walter Benjamin, *One Way Street and Other Writings* (London: Verso, 1979).

Catherine Bennett, 'Why the Writing's On the Wall for Graf Art', *The Guardian* (3 July 1996), p. 15.

Tony Bennett, *The Birth of the Museum* (London, Routledge, 1995).

Marshall Berman, *All That Is Solid Melts Into Air: the Experience of Modernity* (Oxford: Polity, 1982).

Andrew Blake, *The Body of Language: the Meaning of Sport* (London: Lawrence & Wishart, 1996).

Iain Borden, 'Machines of Possibilities: City Life with Henri Lefebvre', *Archis* (February 2000), pp. 62–8.

Iain Borden, 'Space Beyond: Space and the City in the Writings of Georg Simmel', *The Journal of Architecture*, vol. 2 (Winter 1997), pp. 313–35.

Iain Borden, 'Thick Edge: Architectural Boundaries and Spatial Flows', *Architectural Design*, special issue on 'Architecture and Anthropology' (October 1996), pp. 84–7.

Iain Borden and David Dunster (eds), *Architecture and the Sites of History: Interpretations of Buildings and Cities* (Oxford: Butterworth Architecture, 1995).

Iain Borden, Joe Kerr, Alicia Pivaro and Jane Rendell (eds), *Strangely Familiar: Narratives of Architecture in the City* (London: Routledge 1996).

Iain Borden, Joe Kerr, Jane Rendell with Alicia Pivaro (eds), *The Unknown City: Contesting Architecture and Social Space* (Cambridge, Mass.: MIT, 2001).

Iain Borden and Jane Rendell (eds), *InterSections: Architectural Histories and Critical Theories* (London: Routledge, 2000).

Iain Borden, Jane Rendell and Helen Thomas, 'Knowing Different Cities: Reflections on Recent European City History and Planning', Leonie Sandercock (ed.), *Making the Invisible Visible: Insurgent Planning Histories* (Berkeley: University of California Press, 1998).

Donna Braden, *Leisure and Entertainment in America* (Dearborn, Michigan: Henry Ford Museum and Greenfield Village, 1988).

Michael Brake, *Comparative Youth Culture: the Sociology of Youth Culture and Youth Subcultures in America, Britain and Canada* (London: Routledge, 1985).

David Brindle, 'Inner Cities Get Younger as Elderly Turn Wales Grey', *The Guardian* (10 July 1997), p. 10.

Victor Burgin, *Some Cities* (London: Reaktion, 1996).

Marvin Carlson, *Performance: a Critical Introduction* (London: Routledge, 1996).

Ellis Cashmore, *Making Sense of Sport* (London: Routledge, 2nd edn, 1996).

Iain Chambers, *Migrancy, Culture, Identity* (London: Routledge, 1994).

Iain Chambers, *Popular Culture: the Metropolitan Experience* (London: Routledge, 1988).

Beatriz Colomina, *Privacy and Publicity: Modern Architecture as Mass Media* (Cambridge, Mass.: MIT, 1994).

Beatriz Colomina (ed.), *Sexuality and Space* (New York: Princeton Architectural Press, 1992).

Steven Connor, *Postmodernist Culture: an Introduction to Theories of the Contemporary* (Oxford: Blackwell, 1989).

Max Daly, 'Battle of the Art Outlaws', *Big Issue* (London), no. 247 (25–31 August 1997), pp. 8–9.

Mike Davis, *City of Quartz: Excavating the Future in Los Angeles* (London: Verso, 1991).

Guy Debord, *Comments on the Society of the Spectacle* (London: Verso, 1990).
Guy Debord, *Society of the Spectacle* (Detroit: Black and Red, 1983).
Michel de Certeau, *The Practice of Everyday Life* (Berkeley, California: University of California Press, 1984).
Elin Diamond (ed.), *Performance and Cultural Politics* (London: Routledge, 1996).
Susan Fainstein, *The City Builders* (Oxford: Blackwell, 1994).
Pasi Falk, *The Consuming Body* (London: Sage, 1994).
Mike Featherstone, Mike Hepworth and Bryan S. Turner (eds), *The Body: Social Process and Cultural Theory* (London: Sage, 1991).
Johan Fornäs and Göran Bolin (eds), *Youth Culture in Late Modernity* (London: Sage, 1995).
Michel Foucault, *The Archaeology of Knowledge* (New York: Pantheon, 1972).
Michel Foucault, *Discipline and Punish: the Birth of the Prison* (Harmondsworth: Penguin, 1979).
Michel Foucault, 'Of Other Spaces', in Joan Ockman (ed.), *Architecture Culture 1943–1968: a Documentary Anthology* (New York: Rizzoli, 1993), pp. 420–6.
Michel Foucault, *Power/Knowledge. Michel Foucault: Selected Interviews and Other Writings 1972–1977*, ed. Colin Gordon (New York: Harvester Wheatsheaf, 1980).
Michel Foucault, 'Space, Knowledge, and Power', *Skyline* (March 1982). Reprinted in Paul Rabinow (ed.), *The Foucault Reader*, pp. 239–56.
David Frisby, *Fragments of Modernity: Theories of Modernity in the Work of Simmel, Kracauer and Benjamin* (Cambridge, Mass.: MIT, 1986).
David Frisby, *Simmel and Since: Essays on Simmel's Social Theory* (London: Routledge, 1992).
David Frisby and Mike Featherstone (eds), *Simmel on Culture* (London: Sage, 1997).
Simon Frith, *Downtown: Young People in the City Centre* (Leicester: National Youth Bureau, 1981).
Simon Frith, *Music for Pleasure* (Cambridge: Polity, 1988).
Erich Fromm, *Man for Himself: an Enquiry into the Psychology of Ethics* (Greenwich: Fawcett, 1967).
Nick Fyfe, 'Contested Visions of a Modern City: Planning and Poetry in Post-war Glasgow', *Environment and Planning A*, vol. 28 (1996), pp. 387–403.
Ken Gelder and Sarah Thornton, *The Subcultures Reader* (London: Routledge, 1997).
Diane Ghirardo, *Architecture After Modernism* (London: Thames and Hudson, 1996).
John Gillis, *Youth and History: Tradition and Change in European Age Relations, 1700–Present* (New York: Academic Press, 1981).
Paul Gilroy, 'It Ain't Where You're From, It's Where You're At . . . the Dialectics of Diasporic Identification', *Third Text*, no. 13 (Winter 1990/91).
Jonathan Glancey, *New British Architecture* (London: Thames and Hudson, 1989).
Mark Gottdiener, *The Social Production of Urban Space* (Austin: University of Texas, 1985).

Mark Gottdiener and Alexandros Ph. Lagopoulos (eds), *The City and the Sign* (New York: Columbia University Press, 1986).
Christine Griffin, *Representations of Youth: the Study of Youth and Adolescence in Britain and America* (Cambridge: Polity, 1993).
'A Curfew on Commonsense: Jack Straw's Rightward Lurch', *The Guardian* (3 June 1996), p. 10.
'Rave Watch', *The Guardian*, 'Society' section (16 October 1996), p. 1.
Stuart Hall and T. Jefferson (eds), *Resistance Through Rituals: Youth Subcultures in Post-War Britain* (London: Hutchinson, 1976).
David Harvey, *The Condition of Postmodernity: an Enquiry into the Origins of Cultural Change* (Oxford: Basil Blackwell, 1989).
David Harvey, *Justice, Nature and the Geography of Difference* (Oxford: Blackwell, 1996).
David Harvey, *The Urban Experience* (Oxford: Basil Blackwell, 1989).
Jeff Hearn, *Men in the Public Eye: the Construction and Deconstruction of Public Men and Public Patriarchies* (London: Routledge, 1992).
Dick Hebdige, *Hiding in the Light: On Images and Things* (London: Routledge, 1988).
Dick Hebdige, *Subculture: the Meaning of Style* (London: Methuen, 1979).
Martin Heidegger, *Basic Writings* (London: Routledge, rev. edn, 1993).
Martin Heidegger, *Being and Time* (Oxford: Basil Blackwell, 1962).
Leo Hendry, Janet Shucksmith, John Love and Anthony Glendenning, *Young People's Leisure and Lifestyles* (London: Routledge: 1993).
Rémi Hess, *Henri Lefebvre et l'aventure du siècle* (Paris: Editions A.M. Métailié, 1988).
Jonathan Hill (ed.), *Occupying Architecture: Between Architecture and the User* (London: Routledge, 1998).
Arthur Hirsh, *The French Left: a History and Overview* (Montréal: Black Rose, 1982).
Paul Hirst, 'Foucault and Architecture', *AA Files*, no. 26 (1993), pp. 52–60.
bell hooks, *Yearning: Race, Gender, and Cultural Politics* (London: Turnaround, 1989).
Johan Huizinga, *Homo Ludens* (New York: Beacon, 1950).
Peter Jackson, *Maps of Meaning: an Introduction to Cultural Geography* (London: Routledge, 1992).
Fredric Jameson, 'Architecture and the Critique of Ideology', Ockman, Berke and McLeod (eds), *Architecture Criticism Ideology* (Princeton: Princeton University Press, 1985), pp. 51–87.
Fredric Jameson, *Postmodernism, Or, the Cultural Logic of Late Capitalism* (London: Verso, 1991).
Max Jammer, *Concepts of Space: the History of Theories of Space in Physics* (New York: Dover, 3rd edn, 1993).
Martin Jay, *Downcast Eyes: the Denigration of Vision in Twentieth-Century French Thought* (Berkeley: University of California Press, 1994).

Charles Jencks, *The Language of Post-modern Language* (New York: Rizzoli, 1977).
Alice Kaplan and Kristin Ross (eds), *Everyday Life* (New Haven: Yale French Studies no. 73, 1987).
Ian Katz, 'NBC's Schlock Tactics', *The Guardian*, 'Media' section (5 August 1996), p. 13.
Michael Keith and Steve Pile (eds), *Place and the Politics of Identity* (London: Routledge, 1993).
Stephen Kern, *The Culture of Time and Space, 1880–1918* (London: Weidenfeld and Nicolson, 1983).
Séan Kierkegaard, 'The XXX Files', *The Guardian*, Education Supplement (Tuesday 24 June 1997), p. iv.
Anthony D. King, *Global Cities* (London: Routledge, 1990).
Ken Knabb (ed.), *Situationist International Anthology* (Berkeley: Bureau of Public Secrets, 1981).
John Kremer, Karen Trew and Shaun Ogle (eds), *Young People's Involvement in Sport* (London: Routledge: 1997).
Henri Lefebvre, *Critique of Everyday Life. Volume 1: Introduction* (London: Verso, 1991).
Henri Lefebvre, *Éléments de rythmanalyse. Introduction à la connaissance des rythmes* (Paris: Syllepse-Périscope, 1992).
Henri Lefebvre, *Everyday Life in the Modern World* (London: Transaction Publishers, 1984).
Henri Lefebvre, *Introduction to Modernity: Twelve Preludes September 1959–May 1961* (London: Verso, 1995).
Henri Lefebvre, *La proclamation de la Commune* (Paris: Gallimard, 1965).
Henri Lefebvre, *La production de l'espace* (Paris: Anthropos, 1974).
Henri Lefebvre, *La somme et le reste* (Paris: Bélibaste, deuxième édition, 1973).
Henri Lefebvre, *Qu'est-ce que penser?* (Paris: Publisud, 1985).
Henri Lefebvre, 'Reflections on the Politics of Space', *Antipode*, vol. 8 no. 2 (May 1976), pp. 30–7.
Henri Lefebvre, 'Space: Social Product and Use Value', in J. Freiberg (ed.), *Critical Sociology: European Perspective* (New York, Irvington, 1979).
Henri Lefebvre, 'The Everyday and Everydayness', in Kaplan and Ross (eds), *Everyday Life*, pp. 7–11.
Henri Lefebvre, *The Explosion: Marxism and the French Revolution* (New York: Monthly Review, 1969).
Henri Lefebvre, *The Production of Space* (Oxford: Blackwell, 1991).
Henri Lefebvre, *The Sociology of Marx* (New York: Columbia University Press, 1982).
Henri Lefebvre, *The Survival of Capitalism: Reproduction of the Relations of Production* (New York: St. Martin's, 1976).

Henri Lefebvre, 'Toward a Leftist Cultural Politics: Remarks Occasioned by the Centenary of Marx's Death', in Nelson and Grossberg (eds), *Marxism and the Interpretation of Culture*, pp. 75–88.

Henri Lefebvre, *Writings on Cities* (Oxford: Blackwell, 1996), eds. Eleonore Kofman and Elizabeth Lebas.

Henri Lefebvre, with Gallia Burgel, Guy Burgel and M.G. Dezes, 'An Interview with Henri Lefebvre', *Environment and Planning D: Society and Space*, vol. 5 no. 1 (1987), pp. 27–38.

Henri Lefebvre, with Kristin Ross, 'Lefebvre on the Situationists: an Interview', *October*, no. 79 (Winter 1997), pp. 69–83.

Dean MacCannell, *The Tourist* (New York, Schocken, 1976/89).

Thomas F. McDonough, 'Situationist Space', *October*, no. 67 (Winter 1994), pp. 58–77.

Harry Francis Mallgrave and Eleftherios Ikonomou (eds), *Empathy, Form and Space: Problems in German Aesthetics, 1873–1893* (Santa Monica: Getty Center for the History of Art and the Humanities, 1994).

Mario Rui Martins, 'The Theory of Social Space in the Work of Henri Lefebvre', in Ray Forrest, Jeff Henderson and Peter Williams (eds.), Urban Political Economy and Social Theory: Critical Essays in Urban Studies, (Epping: Gower, 1983), pp. 160–85.

Karl Marx, *Capital: a Critique of Political Economy. Volume 1* (Harmondsworth: Penguin, 1976).

Karl Marx and Frederick Engels, *Selected Works* (New York: International Publishers, 1986).

Karl Marx, *Karl Marx, Selected Writings*, eds Tom Bottomore and M. Rubel (Harmondsworth: Penguin, 1956).

Doreen Massey, *Space, Place and Gender* (Cambridge: Polity, 1994).

J.A. May, *Kant's Concept of Geography and its Relation to Recent Geographical Thought* (Toronto: University of Toronto Press, Dept. of Geography Research Publications, 1970).

Maurice Merleau-Ponty, *Phenomenology of Perception* (London: Routledge & Kegan Paul, 1962).

Maurice Merleau-Ponty, *The Visible and the Invisible* (Evanston: Northwestern University Press, 1968).

Andrew Merrifield, 'Space and Place: a Lefebvrian Reconciliation', *Transactions of the Institute of British Geographers*, vol. 18 no. 4 (1993), pp. 516–31.

Chris Mihill, 'Sports "Myth" Scotched', *The Guardian* (12 December 1996), p. 9.

Malcolm Miles, Tim Hall and Iain Borden (eds), *The City Cultures Reader* (London: Routledge, 2000).

Michael Mitterauer, *A History of Youth* (Oxford: Blackwell, 1992).

David Moore, *The Lads in Action: Social Process in an Urban Youth Subculture* (Aldershot: Arena, 1994).

Cary Nelson and Lawrence Grossberg (eds), *Marxism and the Interpretation of Culture* (London: Macmillan, 1988).

Joan Ockman (ed.), *Architecture Culture 1943–1968* (New York: Rizzoli, 1993).

Joan Ockman, Deborah Berke and Mary McLeod (eds), *Architecture Criticism Ideology* (Princeton: Princeton University Press, 1985).

'Atlanta Chief Sees End of Free Enterprise Games Era', *Oman Daily Observer* (3 August 1996).

Imogen O'Rorke, 'This is Elk', *The Guardian*, 'Friday Review' section (28 June 1996), pp. 4–5.

Andreas Papadakis, Geoffrey Broadbent and Maggie Toy (eds), *Free Spirit in Architecture* (London: Academy Editions, 1992).

Steve Pile, *The Body and the City: Psychoanalysis, Space and Subjectivity* (London: Routledge, 1996).

Steve Pile and Nigel Thrift (eds), *Mapping the Subject: Geographies of Cultural Transformation* (London: Routledge, 1995).

Sadie Plant, *The Most Radical Gesture: the Situationist International in a Postmodern Age* (London: Routledge, 1992).

Martin Polley, *Sport and Society: a Contemporary History* (London: Routledge: 1997).

A. Pryke, 'An International City Going "Global": Spatial Change and Office Provision in the City of London', *Environment and Planning D: Society and Space*, vol. 9 (1991), pp. 197–222.

Paul Rabinow (ed.), *The Foucault Reader* (New York: Pantheon Books, 1984).

Jane Rendell, Barbara Penner and Iain Borden (eds), *Gender Space Architecture: an Interdisciplinary Introduction* (London: Routledge, 1999).

George Robertson, Melinda Mash, Lisa Tickner, Jon Bird, Barry Curtis and Tim Putnam (eds), *FutureNatural: Nature, Science, Culture* (London: Routledge, 1996).

George Robertson, Melinda Mash, Lisa Tickner, Jon Bird, Barry Curtis and Tim Putnam (eds), *Travellers' Tales: Narratives of Home and Displacement* (London: Routledge, 1994).

Paul Rodaway, *Sensuous Geographies: Body, Sense and Place* (London: Routledge, 1994).

Paul Rodgers, 'Winner Takes All', *The Independent on Sunday*, 'Business' section (4 August 1996).

Kristin Ross, *The Emergence of Social Space: Rimbaud and the Paris Commune* (London: Macmillan, 1988).

Katerina Rüedi, Sarah Wigglesworth and Duncan McCorquodale (eds), *Desiring Practices: Architecture, Gender and the Interdisciplinary* (London: Black Dog, 1996).

Robert Sack, *Conceptions of Space in Social thought: a Geographic Perspective* (London: Macmillan, 1980).

Simon Sadler, *The Situationist City* (Cambridge, Mass.: MIT, 1998).

Edward Said, 'Culture and Imperialism', *Design Book Review*, no. 29–30 (Summer/Fall 1993), pp. 6–13.
Leonie Sandercock (ed.), *Making the Invisible Visible: Insurgent Planning Histories* (Berkeley: University of California Press, 1998).
Leonie Sandercock, *Towards Cosmopolis: Planning for Multicultural Cities* (Chichester: New York, 1998).
Jean-Paul Sartre, *Being and Nothingness: an Essay on Phenomenological Ontology* (London: Routledge, 1989).
Mike Savage, 'Walter Benjamin's Urban Thought: a Critical Analysis', *Environment and Planning D: Society and Space*, vol. 13 no. 2 (April 1995), pp. 127–252.
Richard Sennett, *Flesh and Stone: the Body and the City in Western Civilization* (London: Faber & Faber, 1994).
Richard Sennett, *The Conscience of the Eye* (London: W.W. Norton, 1992).
Rob Shields, *An English Précis of Henri Lefebvre's 'La Production de l'Espace'* (University of Sussex: Urban and Regional Studies Working Paper no. 63, 1988).
Rob Shields, *Lefebvre, Love and Struggle: Spatial Dialectics* (London: Routledge, 1999).
Rob Shields, *Places on the Margin: Alternative Geographies of Modernity* (London: Routledge, 1991).
Chris Shilling, *The Body and Social Theory* (London: Sage, 1993).
Georg Simmel, 'Bridge and Door', *Theory, Culture and Society*, vol. 11 (1994), pp. 5–10.
Georg Simmel, 'The Metropolis and Mental Life', in P.K. Hatt and A.J. Reiss (eds), *Cities and Society: the Revised Reader in Urban Sociology* (New York: Free Press, 1951), pp. 635–46.
Georg Simmel, *The Philosophy of Money* (London: Routledge, 2nd edn, 1990).
Georg Simmel, 'The Sociology of Space', in Frisby and Featherstone (eds), *Simmel on Culture*.
Edward W. Soja, 'Henri Lefebvre 1901–1991', *Environment and Planning D: Society and Space*, vol. 9 (1991), pp. 257–9.
Edward W. Soja, 'Heterotopologies: a Remembrance of Other Spaces in the Citadel-LA', *Strategies*, 'Special Issue: In the City', no. 3 (1990), pp. 6–39, and in Watson and Gibson (eds), *Postmodern Cities and Spaces*, pp. 13–34.
Edward W. Soja, 'Inside Exopolis: Scenes from Orange County', in Sorkin (ed.), *Variations on a Theme Park*, pp. 94–122.
Edward W. Soja, 'On Spuistraat: the Contested Streetscape in Amsterdam', in Borden, Kerr, Rendell and Pivaro (eds), *The Unknown City*.
Edward W. Soja, *Postmodern Geographies: the Reassertion of Space in Critical Social Theory* (London: Verso, 1989).
Edward W. Soja, 'The Stimulus of a Little Confusion: On Spuistraat, Amsterdam', Borden, Kerr, Pivaro and Rendell (eds), *Strangely Familiar*, pp. 27–31.

Edward W. Soja, *Thirdspace: Journeys to Los Angeles and Other Real-and-Imagined Places* (Oxford: Basil Blackwell, 1996).
Michael Sorkin (ed.), *Variations on a Theme Park: the New American City and the End of Public Space* (New York: Noonsday, 1992).
Sport and Leisure (Sports Council) (May/June 1989).
Denis Staunton, 'Punks on Parade', *The Guardian* (29 July 1996), p. 16.
George Steiner, *Heidegger* (London: Fontana, 1992).
James Melvin Stewart, 'Henri Lefebvre and Marxist French Revisionism in France 1928–1968' (Ph.D. thesis, University of Colorado at Boulder, 1985. UMI Publication # AAC8522703).
Elizabeth Sussman (ed.), *On the Passage of a Few People Through a Rather Brief Moment in Time: the Situationist International 1957–1972* (Cambridge, Mass.: MIT, 1989).
Manfredo Tafuri, *Architecture and Utopia* (Cambridge, Mass.: MIT, 1976).
Sarah Thornton, *Club Cultures: Music, Media and Subcultural Capital* (Cambridge: Polity, 1995).
Alan Travis and Martin Wainwright, 'Labour "Under-10s Curfew" Plan Ignites Row', *The Guardian* (3 June 1996), p. 3.
Bernard Tschumi, *Architecture and Disjunction* (Cambridge, Mass.: MIT, 1996).
Bryan S. Turner, *The Body and Society* (London: Sage, 2nd edn, 1996).
John Urry, *Consuming Places* (London: Routledge, 1995).
John Urry, *The Tourist Gaze: Leisure and Travel in Contemporary Societies* (London: Sage, 1990).
Rudy Vanderlans, 'Design Will Eat Itself (Never Mind Paul Rand, Here's The Designers Republic!)', *Emigre*, no. 29 (Winter 1994), special issue 'The Designers Republic, New and Used', pp. 2–3.
Cornelis van de Ven, *Space in Architecture: the Evolution of a New Idea in the Theory and History of the Modern Movements* (Assen: van Gorcum, 1980).
John Vidal, 'Gone to Ground', *The Guardian*, 'Weekend' section (22 February 1997), pp. 30–1, 33, 35 and 37.
John Vidal and Alex Bellos, 'Protest Lobbies Unite to Guard Rights', *The Guardian* (27 August 1996), p. 5.
John Vidal and Alex Bellos, 'Trees Planted in Fast Land at Road Protestors' Party', *The Guardian* (15 July 1996), p. 7.
Anthony Vidler, 'Bodies in Space/Subjects in the City: Psychopathologies of Modern Urbanism', *Differences*, special issue 'The City', vol. 5 no. 3 (Fall 1993), pp. 31–51.
Sophie Watson and Katherine Gibson (eds), *Postmodern Cities and Spaces* (Oxford: Blackwell, 1995).
Hermann Weyl, *Symmetry* (Princeton: Princeton University Press, 1952).

Bruce Willems-Braun, 'Situating Cultural Politics: Fringe Festivals and the Production of Spaces of Intersubjectivity', *Environment and Planning D: Society and Space*, vol. 12 (1994), pp. 75–104.

Elliott Willensky and Norval White, *AIA Guide to New York* (New York: Harcourt Brace Jovanovich, 3rd edn, 1988).

Judith Williamson, *Consuming Passions: the Dynamics of Popular Culture* (London: Marion Boyers, 1988).

Paul Willis, *Common Culture: Symbolic Work at Play in the Everyday Cultures of the Young* (Milton Keynes: Open University Press, 1990).

Elizabeth Wilson, *The Sphinx in the City: Urban Life, the Control of Disorder, and Women* (London: Virago, 1991).

Dennis Woods, *The Power of Maps* (London: Routledge, 1993).

Patrick Wright, *A Journey Through Ruins: a Keyhole Portrait of British Post-war Life and Culture* (London: Flamingo, 1993).

SKATEBOARDING: ARTICLES AND BOOKS

American Academy of Pediatricians, *Skateboard Policy Statement* (1979).

Jan Andrejtschitsch, Raimund Kallée and Petra Schmidt, *Action Skateboarding* (New York: Sterling, 1992).

'Rolling Programme: a Skateboarder's Perspective on Architecture', *The Architects' Journal* (3 October 1996), p. 42.

Peter Arnold, *The Hamlyn Book of Skateboarding* (London: Hamlyn, 1977).

Adrian Ball, *How to Skateboard* (Barries and Jenkins).

Troy Bannon, *Power Grind* (New York: Dell, 1992).

Alexander Barrie and Rocky Barrie, *Skateboarding to Win* (London: Morris Vulcan, 1978).

'Hell On Wheels', *Bay Guardian* (San Francisco) (May 1994).

Becky Beal, 'Alternative Masculinity and Its Effects on Gender Relations in the Subculture of Skateboarding', *Journal of Sport Behaviour*, vol. 19 no. 3 (1996), pp. 204–21

Becky Beal, 'Disqualifying the Official: an Exploration of Social Resistance Through the Subculture of Skateboarding', *Sociology of Sport Journal*, vol. 12 no. 3 (1995), pp. 252–67.

Andy Blackford, *Advanced Skateboarding* (Feltham: Hamlyn, 1978).

Chris Blue, 'Board Stupid', *City Life* (c. August 2000), pp. 17–19.

Iain Borden, 'Another Pavement, Another Beach: Skateboarding and the Performative Critique of Architecture', in Borden, Kerr, Rendell with Pivaro (eds), *The Unknown City*.

Iain Borden, 'Beneath the Pavement, the Beach', *Xtreme*, no. 4 (September 1997), pp. 18–19.
Iain Borden, 'Beneath the Pavement, the Beach: Skateboarding, Architecture and the Urban Realm', in Borden, Kerr, Pivaro and Rendell (eds), *Strangely Familiar*, pp. 82–6.
Iain Borden, 'Body Architecture: Skateboarding and the Creation of Super-Architectural Space', in Hill (ed.), *Occupying Architecture*, pp. 195–216.
Iain Borden, 'Chariots of Ire', *Blueprint*, no. 174 (July 2000), pp. 38–42 and front cover.
Iain Borden, interview conducted by Saul Taylor for *Backside*, no. 9 (Spring 1999), n.p.
Iain Borden, 'Laws of Motion', *Adrenalin* (Autumn 1999).
Iain Borden, 'State of the Art', *Ergo Sum*, no. 2 (Summer 1997), n.p.
Iain Borden, 'Taking Over the City', interview with Mike Fordham, *Dazed and Confused*, no. 19 (April 1996), pp. 109–10.
Iain Borden, 'An Affirmation of Urban Life: Socio-Spatial Censorship in the Late Twentieth Century City', *Archis* (May 1998), pp. 46–51. Published on the internet at *www.archis.org/archis_art_e_1998/archis_art_9805_ENG.html* and also on *www.xbeam.org*.
Iain Borden, 'A Performative Critique of the City: the Urban Practice of Skateboarding, 1958–1998', *everything*, vol. 2 no. 4 (March 1999), pp. 38–43, and Taiwanese translation in *Intercity Networking* (National University of Taiwan), no. 7–8 (March 1999), pp. 25–44.
Iain Borden, 'Skateboarding', in Steve Pile and Nigel Thrift (eds), *City A–Z: Urban Fragments* (Routledge, 2000), pp. 226–8.
Iain Borden, 'Speaking the City: Skateboarding Subculture and Recompositions of the Urban Realm', in Ray Hutchison (ed.), *Constructions of Urban Space* (Stamford: JAI Press, 2000), pp. 135–154.
Iain Borden, 'Sprechende Architekur: Skateboarden auf der Stadt', *Bauwelt*, no. 30–1 (18 August 2000), pp. 54–7.
Sylvie Breguet, Isabelle Forestier and Pierre Hussenot, *Le skateboard: la planche à roulettes* (Paris: La Table Ronde, 1978).
Petronella Breinburg, *Sally-Ann's Skateboard* (1979).
British Medical Journal (24–31 December 1977), p. 1636.
Michael Brooke, *The Concrete Wave: the History of Skateboarding* (Toronto: Warwick, 1999).
Eve Bunting, *For Always* (Mankato: Creative Education, 1978).
Eve Bunting, *Skateboard Four* (Chicago: Whitman, 1976).
Glenn Bunting, *Skateboards: How to Make Them, How to Ride Them* (New York: Harvey House, 1977).
Patrick Burgoyne and Jeremy Leslie, *Bored: Surf/Skate/Snow Graphics* (London: Lawrence King and Creative Review, 1997).

Stephen Caitlin, *Skateboard Fun* (Mahwah: Troll Associates, 1988).
Nancy L. Carlson, *Arnie and the Skateboard Gang* (New York: Viking, 1995).
Albert Cassorla, *The Skateboarder's Bible: Technique, Equipment, Stunts, Terms, etc.* (Philadelphia: Running Press, 1976).
Albert Cassorla, *The Ultimate Skateboard Book* (Philadelphia: Running Press, 1988).
S.M. Christian and O. Khan, 'Skateboarding Injuries: a Current Appraisal', *British Journal of Sports Medicine* (August 1980).
Matt Christopher, *Skateboard Tough* (Boston: Little Brown, 1991).
Larry Clark (director) and Harmony Korine (writer), *Kids. A Film By Larry Clark* (New York: Grove, 1995).
'Board Stupid?', *Club International* (February 1995).
Jay Cocks, 'The Irresistible Air of Grabbing Air: Skateboarding, Once a Fad, is Now a National Turn-on', *Time*, vol. 131 (6 June 1988), pp. 90–1.
The Complete Skateboard Guide (London: Dewyaters, c. 1977).
Consumer Product Safety Commission, Directorate for Hazard Identification and Analysis, Division of Program Analysis, *Hazard Analysis Injuries Associated With Skateboards (Product Code 1333)* (Washington: The Directorate, 1978).
Jane Cox, *Sounds Plus: Fossils, the Middle Ages and Skateboarding* (Sunbury-on-Thames: Nelson, 1979).
Tom Cuthbertson, *Anybody's Skateboard Book* (Berkeley: Ten Speed, 1976).
Ben J. Davidson, *The Skateboard Book* (New York: Grosset & Dunlap, 1976, and London: Sphere, smaller format, 1978).
Damien Davis, *Skate Sports* (Oxford: Heinemann, 1990).
Diagram Group, *Enjoying Skating* (New York: Paddington, 1978).
Diagram Group, *The Sports Fan's Ultimate Book of Sports Comparisons* (New York: St. Martin's, 1982).
Lowell A. Dickmeyer, *Skateboarding is For Me* (Minneapolis: Lerner, 1978).
Peter L. Dixon, *The Complete Book of Surfing* (1965).
Pahl Dixon and Peter Dixon, *Your Complete Guide to Hot Skateboarding* (New York: Warner, 1977).
Michael Donner, *Bike, Skate, and Skateboard Games* (New York: Golden, 1977).
Barbara Douglass, *Skateboard Scramble* (Philadelphia: Westminster, 1979).
Jeremy Evans, *Skateboarding* (New York: Crestwood House, 1993).
Siân Liz Evans, 'Young, Gifted and Board Stupid', *The Big Issue* (London), no. 126 (17–23 April 1995), pp. 18–20.
Michael Foreman, *Trick a Tracker* (London: Gollancz, 1981).
Forskrift om Rullebrett (Oslo: Miljøverndepartementet, 3 May 1989).
Glen E. Friedman, *Fuck You Heroes: Glen E. Friedman Photographs, 1976–1991* (New York: Burning Flags, 1994).
Glen E. Friedman, *Fuck You Too: the Extras + More Scrapbook* (Los Angeles: 2.13.61 Publications and Burning Flags, 1996).

I.S. Fyfe and A.J. Guion, 'Accident Prevention in Skateboarding', *Journal of Sports Medicine and Physical Fitness* (September 1979).
Trip Gabriel, 'Rolling Thunder', *Rolling Stone* (16–30 July 1987), pp. 73–6.
Leah Garchik, 'The Urban Landscape', *San Francisco Chronicle* (late summer 1994).
Marilyn Gould, *Skateboarding* (Mankato: Capstone, 1991).
Marilyn Gould, *Skateboards, Scooterboards, & Seatboards You Can Make* (New York: Lothrop, Lee & Shepard, 1977).
Jack B. Grant, *Skateboarding: a Complete Guide to the Sport* (Millbrae: Celestial Arts, 1976).
Greater London Council, *Reports of the Chief Officer of Parks to the Open Spaces and Recreation Committee* (5 July 1977 and 28 November 1977).
Bill Green, *Freud and the Nazis Go Surfing* (1986).
Bill Green, *The Guide to Western Skateboard Parks* (La Jolla: Third Eye, 1978).
David Grogan and Carl Arrington, 'He's Not Lean But His Rap is Mean, So the Thrashers Relate to Skatemaster Tate', *People Weekly*, vol. 27 (8 June 1987), pp. 155–6.
'Age Barrier', *The Guardian*, 'Society' section (26 April 1995), p. 1.
Bill Gutman, *Skateboarding to the Extreme* (New York: Tom Doherty Associates, 1997).
Juanita Havill, *Embarcadero Upset* (New York: Lothrop, Lee & Shepard, 1994).
R.W. Hawkins and E.D. Lyne, 'Skateboarding Fractures', *The American Journal of Sports Medicine* (March/April 1981).
Neil Heayes, 'All Aboard for the Skateboard Take-Off', *Contract Journal* (19 January 1978), pp. 22–3.
Jeffrey A. Hess, *Skateboarding Skills* (Mankato: Creative Education, 1979).
Stan Hey, 'Wheelers and Dealers', *Time Out*, no. 381 (15–21 July 1977), pp. 12–13.
Gavin Hills, *Skateboarding* (Hove: Wayland, 1992, and Minneapolis: Lerner, 1993).
Kelvin Ho, 'Skateboarding: an Interpretation of Space in the Olympic City', *Architectural History and Theory*; (1999).
Tom Hodgkinson, 'Rad, Mad and Dangerous to Know?', *Midweek* (London) (18 January 1990), pp. 10–11.
Andy Holmes, 'Dysfunctional', lecture, Photographers' Gallery, London (14 August 1996).
Dean Hughes, *Lucky's Crash Landing* (Salt Lake City: Desert Book Co., 1990).
David Hunn, *Skateboarding* (London: Duckworth, 1977).
Intensity Skates (Maryland), mail order catalogue (1990).
'Stacy Peralta', *Interview*, no. 17 (July 1987), pp. 102–3.
Bob Italia, *Skateboarding* (Edina: Abdo & Daughters, 1991).
William Jaber, *Easy-to-Make Skateboards, Scooters, and Racers: 11 Inexpensive Projects* (New York: Dover, 1976/1987).

Jackson Jay, *Skateboarding Basics* (Mankato: Capstone, 1995).
Steve Kane, *Skateboard Workbook* (London: Duckworths, 1989).
Armen Keteyian, 'Chairman of the Board', *Sports Illustrated*, vol. 65 no. 23 (24 November 1986), pp. 46–50.
Ron King, *Rad Boards: Skateboarding, Snowboarding, Bodyboarding* (New York: Sports Illustrated for Kids, 1991).
Konsumentverket, *Rullbrador: risker och skadeforebyggande atgarder* (Vallingby: Konsumentverket, 1977).
Jane Mersky Leder, *Learning How: Skateboarding* (Marco: Bancroft-Sage, 1991).
Albert Ledu, *Skateboard: votre premier livre* (Paris: Les Editions Chiron-Sports, *c.* 1978).
Robert Levy, *Automatique, informatique, mesure, audio-visuel, planche à roulettes* (Québec: Gouvernement du Québec, Office de la langue francaise, 1980).
Christopher Makos and Ann Zemaitis, 'Road Warriors', *Interview*, no. 16 (July 1986), pp. 106–10.
Barbara Manning, 'Teenager Tony Hawk Soars Above Everybody in the Scary Sport of Skateboarding', *People Weekly*, vol. 27 (23 March 1987), pp. 48–9.
Jamie McCullough, *Meanwhile Gardens* (London: Calouste Gulbenkian Foundation, 1979).
Jean Pierre Marquant, *Le skateboard en 10 lecons* (Paris: Hachette, 1978).
Jeremy Millar, 'Larry Clark: Kids', *Great*, magazine of the Photographers' Gallery, London, no. 7 (July/August 1996), pp. 4–5.
G. Mirkin, 'Kid-Sulation: How to Protect Your Child From the Pitfalls of Roller-skating, Baseball and Other Rough and Tumble Sports', *Health* (November 1982).
Günter Mokulys, *Freestyle Skateboard Book* (*c.* 1989).
Günter Mokulys, *Miniramp Skateboard Book* (*c.* 1990).
Günter Mokulys, *Streetstyle Skateboard Book. Teil 1* (*c.* 1989).
Günter Mokulys, *Streetstyle Skateboard Book. Teil 2* (*c.* 1990).
Alain Morel and Gilles Ouaki, *Tout sur le skateboard* (Paris: Éditions Authier, 1978).
Anne Mountfield, *Skateboarding* (London: Harrap, 1979).
Jess Mowry, *Rats in the Trees* (London: Vintage, 1993).
Frederick Muir, 'On a Roll', *Los Angeles Times* (31 May 1989), pp. 1 and 8.
Paul Mulshine, 'Wild in the Streets', *Philadelphia Magazine*, vol. 78 no. 4 (April 1987), pp. 119–26.
Marty Nabham, *Skateboarding* (Vero Beach: Rourke, 1994).
National Playing Fields Association, *Information Sheet on Skateboarding* (14 October 1977).
National Safety Council, *Skateboarding* (Chicago: Bulletin, The Council, 1978).
Jane O'Hara, 'Trouble in Paradise', *Maclean's*, vol. 100 no. 14 (6 April 1987), p. 48.
Ross Robert Olney, *Better Skateboarding for Boys and Girls* (New York: Dodd and Mead, 1977).

John O'Malley and Jack Graham, *Skatepark Development* (La Jolla: Skatepark Publications, 1977).
'Venice Skaters Rolling to a Halt', *Outlook Mail* (Los Angeles), vol. 8 no. 7, p. 1.
Edward Packard, *Skateboard Champion* (New York: Bantam, 1991).
Elaine Paterson, 'Teenage Rampage', interview with Larry Clark, *Time Out*, London (24 April–1 May 1996), pp. 18–19.
Michael Pellowski, *Birthday Bear and the Runaway Skateboard* (Worthington: Willowisp, 1986).
Hazel Pennell, *Skateboarding* (London: GLC Intelligence Unit, London Topics no. 24, 1978).
Christopher Pick, *Safe Skateboarding* (London: Evans, 1978).
Anthony Pye-Jeary (ed.), *The Complete Skateboarding Guide* (Robert DeWynter, 1977).
Dan Radlauer, *Skateboard Mania* (Chicago: Children's Press, 1976).
Ed Radlauer, *Some Basics about Skateboards* (Chicago: Children's Press, 1978).
Giles Reed, *Supercool* (Windermere: Rourke Publications, 1981).
Howard Reiser, *Skateboarding* (New York: F. Watts, 1978).
Howard Reiser, *Skateboarding* (New York: F. Watts, rev. edn, 1989).
Enid Richemont, *The Magic Skateboard* (Cambridge, Mass.: Candlewick, 1992).
Jonathan Romney, 'Postcards from a Teenage Wasteland', *The Guardian*, 'Friday Review' section (9 August 1996), pp. 4–5.
Aaron Rose, *Dysfunctional* (London: Booth-Clibborn, 1999).
Cynthia Rose, *Design After Dark: the Story of Dancefloor Style* (London: Thames and Hudson, 1991).
Royal Society for the Prevention of Accidents (RoSPA), *Skatcats Quizbook* (London: RoSPA, 1978).
Royal Society for the Prevention of Accidents (RoSPA), *The Hidden Dangers* (London: RoSPA, December 1977).
Maggi Russell and Bruce Sawford, *The Complete Skateboard Book* (London: Fontana and Bunch, 1977).
G.W. Rutherford, J.I. Friedman, S.P. Beale and V.R. Brown, *Hazard Analysis Injuries Associated With Skateboards* (US Consumer Safety Product Commission, 1978).
John R. Sansevere and Erica Farber, *Over the Edge* (Racine: Western, 1993).
Bruce Sawford, *New Wave Roller Skating*, photographs by Tim Leighton-Boyce (London: Pan Books, 1980).
Allen Say, *Stranger in the Mirror* (Boston: Houghton Mifflin, 1995).
Dorothy Childers Schmitz, *Skateboarding* (Mankato: Crestwood House, 1978).
Martin Schultz, *Skateboard Manual* (Theorem, 1977).
Christian Seewaldt, *Alles über Skateboarding* (c. 1990).
Sally Shaw, 'Plasticity: a Questioning of Representational and Experiential Production of Space' (BA thesis, Chelsea College of Art and Design, 1998).

Joel Shoemaker, *Skateboarding Streetstyle* (Minneapolis: Capstone, 1995).

Richard Skinner, *Kate the Skate* (Torrance: Carson, 1979).

Anders Smith-Lindall, 'On Exhibit: the Hyde Park Center Picks Up Speed', *Reader*, vol. 29 no. 35 (2 June 2000).

David Snow, 'Skateboarders, Streets and Style', in R. White (ed.), *Australian Youth Subcultures: On the Margins and in the Mainstream* (Hobart: Australian Clearinghouse for Youth Studies, 1999), pp. 16–27.

The Sports Council, *Sports Development Bulletin*, no. 42 (Winter 1977/1978).

The Sports Council, *Technical Unit for Sport Data Sheet*, no. 19 (11 November 1977).

Elaine Stratford, 'Feral Skateboarding and the Field of Transport Planning: Some Observations on the Tasmanian Case', paper presented at 'Habitus 2000' conference, Perth (September 2000).

Robert Sullivan, 'Too Much Heat in Vancouver', *Sports Illustrated*, vol. 65 no. 9 (1 September 1986), p. 7.

Kevin J. Thatcher and Brian Brannon, *Thrasher: the Radical Skateboard Book* (New York: Random House, 1992).

Laura Torbet, *The Complete Book of Skateboarding* (New York: Funk and Wagnalls, 1976).

University of Westminster, BSc Architectural Engineering, *Architectural Engineering Yearbook 5* (London: University of Westminster, 1997).

Elizabeth Van Steenwyk, *Illustrated Skating Dictionary for Young People* (New York: Harvey House, 1979).

Marcia K. Vaughan, *Skateboard Bill* (Santa Rosa: SRA, School Group, 1994).

Katharine Viner, 'Which Girl is HIV Positive?', interview with Larry Clark, *The Sunday Times*, magazine supplement (21 April 1996), pp. 24–9.

La Vada Weir, *Advanced Skateboarding: a Complete Guide to Skatepark Riding and Other Tips for the Better Skateboarder* (New York: Julian Messner, 1979).

La Vada Weir, *Skateboards and Skateboarding: the Complete Beginner's Guide* (New York: Julian Messner, 1977).

Kevin Wilkins, *Skateboarding: the Ultimate Guide to Tricks, Ramps, Gear, Setting Up, and Letting Go!* (Philadelphia: Running Press, 1994).

Jamie Wilson, 'Skaters Face Ban From City Centres', *The Guardian* (6 December 1997), p. 6.

Phillip M. Wishon and Marcia L. Oreskovich, 'Bicycles, Roller Skates and Skateboards: Safety Promotion and Accident Prevention', *Children Today*, vol. 15 no. 3 (May/June 1986), pp. 11–15.

Tim Wood, *Skateboarding* (New York: F. Watts, 1989).

Nat Young with Craig McGregor and Rod Holmes, *The History of Surfing* (Angourie: Palm Beach Press, rev. edn, 1994).

SKATEBOARDING: INTERNET SITES

Acme internet site, URL http://www.sk8acme.com.
alt.skateboard Usenet group, URL news:alt.skate-board.
B-Grrrl internet site, URL http://netspace.net.au/~butta/butta1.htm.
DansWORLD internet site, URL http://web.cps.msu.edu/~dunhamda/dw/invent.html.
Downhill-longboard internet site, URL http://www.interlnk.net/longboard/.
Enternet internet site, URL http://www.enternet.com/skate/skate.html.
Faceshot internet site, URL http://www.faceshot.com/.
Flip internet site, URL http://www.skateboard.co.uk./flip/.
Foundation internet site, URL http://www.tumyeto.com/tydu/fsc/fsc.html.
Gullwing internet site, URL http://www.gullwingtrucks.com/opening/opening.html.
Heckler internet site, URL http://heckler.com.
Hupthur internet site, URL http://www.huphtur.nl.
Influx internet site, URL http://www.enternet.com/influx/.
Jibba internet site, URL http://www.io.org/~sassbro/jibba.ja.html.
Loudermild internet site, URL http://xx.acs.appstate.edu:80/hGET%20/%7Ejh13875/skate.html.
Knowhere internet site, URL http://www.state51.co.uk/state51/knowhere/skindex.html.
Kryptonics internet site, URL http://www.kryptonics.com/home.html.
Magic Rolling Board internet site, URL http://www.ecf.toronto.edu/~steve/sk8.html.
Makaha internet site, URL http://members.aol.com/makahask8/index.html.
Nicotine internet site, URL http://www.nicotine.com.
Nirvana internet site, URL http://www.geocities.com/Colosseum/Loge/8005/.
Ocean Bowl internet site, URL http://www.resortguide.com/oc/info/parks/skatebd.html.
Pig internet site, URL http://www.tumyeto.com/tydu/pig/pigteam.html.
Project internet site, URL http://www.skateboard.co.uk.
Sidewalk Surfer internet site, URL http://www.geocities.com/Colosseum/Field/2020.
Sk8punk Skateboarding internet site, URL http://www.geocities.com/Colosseum/2011.
Skate Geezer internet site, URL http://www.terraport.net/abrook/skategeezer.htm.
Skate.Net internet site, URL http://www.webtrax.com/skate/.
SkateTalk internet site, URL http://www.enternet.com/webchat/chat.html.
Skating in Finland internet site, URL http://www.jypoly.fi/~harpuupp/skate.htm.
Slam City Skates internet site, URL http://www.slamcity.com/.
Soul Doubt internet site, URL http://www.souldoubt.com/.
Toy Machine internet site, URL http://www.tumyeto.com/tydu/toy/toy.html.
Tum Yeto internet site, URL http://www.tumyeto.com/tydu/skatebrd/skate.htm.
World Industries internet site, URL http://www.worldind.com.
Zooyork internet site, URL http://www.zooyork.com.

SKATEBOARDING: MAGAZINES

Action Now (USA).
Alpine Sports Newsletter (UK).
Asylum (UK).
Australian Skateboarding (Australia).
Backside (UK).
Bicross and Skate (France).
Big Brother (USA).
Big Cheese (UK).
BMX Action Bike (UK).
Cake Fat (UK).
Check My Chops (UK).
Concrete Powder (Canada).
Cow Pat (UK).
Document (UK).
Duh (Belgium).
Ergo Sum (UK).
Euroskate 88 (Czechoslovakia).
Five 40 (Australia).
Mad Monks Magazines (UK).
Monster (Germany).
Noway (France).
Overall (Brazil).
Perfect Transition (Australia).
Poweredge (USA).
R.A.D. (UK).
Sidewalk Surfer (UK).
Sk8 Action (UK.
Skate (France).
Skateboard (Norway).
Skateboard! (UK).
Skateboard! (second series) (UK).
SkateBoarder (USA).
SkateBoarder Photo Annual (USA).
SkateBoarder's Action Now (USA).
Skateboard Magazine (France).
Skateboard News (UK).
Skateboard Scene (UK).
Skate France International (France).
Skatin' (Brazil).
Skatin' Life (Australia).
Skateline (UK).
Slam: Australian Skateboarding (Australia).
Slap (USA).
Speed Wheels (Australia).
Strength (USA).
Thrasher (USA).
TransWorld Skateboarding (USA).
Väggarna (Sweden).
Warp (USA).
xxx (Italy).

Index

CPSIA information can be obtained
at www.ICGtesting.com
Printed in the USA
LVHW110806221121
704097LV00004B/11